CONGRESS AND THE FIRST CIVIL
RIGHTS ERA, 1861–1918

Congress and the First Civil Rights Era, 1861–1918

JEFFERY A. JENKINS
AND JUSTIN PECK

The University of Chicago Press   Chicago & London

The University of Chicago Press, Chicago 60637
The University of Chicago Press, Ltd., London
© 2021 by The University of Chicago
Published 2021
Printed in the United States of America

30 29 28 27 26 25 24 23 22 21   1 2 3 4 5

ISBN-13: 978-0-226-75622-6 (cloth)
ISBN-13: 978-0-226-75636-3 (paper)
ISBN-13: 978-0-226-75653-0 (e-book)
DOI: https://doi.org/10.7208/chicago/9780226756530.001.0001

Library of Congress Cataloging-in-Publication Data

Names: Jenkins, Jeffery A., author. | Peck, Justin, author.
Title: Congress and the first civil rights era, 1861–1918 /
Jeffery A. Jenkins and Justin Peck.
Description: Chicago : University of Chicago Press, 2021. | Includes index.
Identifiers: LCCN 2020036674 | ISBN 9780226756226 (cloth) |
ISBN 9780226756363 (paperback) | ISBN 9780226756530 (ebook)
Subjects: LCSH: United States. Congress. | Civil rights movements—United
States—History. | African Americans—Civil rights—History.
Classification: LCC E185.61 .J46 2021 | DDC 323.1196/073—dc23
LC record available at https://lccn.loc.gov/2020036674

♾ This paper meets the requirements of ANSI/NISO Z39.48-1992
(Permanence of Paper).

Contents

Acknowledgments

This book tells the story of the rise and fall of the first civil rights era, viewed through the lens of action in the US Congress. The first civil rights era, as we define it, extends from 1861 through 1918, or from the Civil War through the First World War. During that time the formal status of African Americans shifted from slave to citizen and then to something in between. This distinctive path was largely determined by laws and, later, failed laws in Congress. Many books tell the story of African Americans during these years. Our book is explicitly about how the arc of civil rights was determined by Congress over these five decades and more. While there are some excellent accounts for particular periods, such as the Civil War or Reconstruction, we believe ours is the most systematic examination of congressional decision making on civil rights during this long and crucial period.

When we first sketched out an abstract for the book, we intended to cover the period from the Civil War to the present — about 150 years of civil rights lawmaking in Congress. But as we began writing the initial chapters we realized that for the kind of comprehensive account we intended, a single book would be too long and unwieldy. We also recognized early on that, when told from the congressional perspective, the story of black civil rights coheres into two distinct arcs, each deserving to be examined on its own. When we presented our idea for two books to Charles Myers of the University of Chicago Press, he supported the plan and helped us pursue it. We eventually obtained advance contracts for the two books, and this is the first.

Many people have given us generous help and support in writing this book. Along the way, we presented portions of our research at various conferences: the Congress and History meetings (2015), the Midwest Political Science Association meetings (2016), the Southern Political Science Association meetings (2016, 2017, 2018), and the American Political Science Association meetings (2016). We received useful feedback from several people, including Jeff Grynaviski, Kris Kanthak, Thad Kousser, Ellie Powell, Barbara Sinclair, Charles Stewart, Ryan Vander Wielen, and Ryan Williamson. Additionally, in March 2019 David Bateman (Cornell), Charles Finocchiaro (Oklahoma), and Steven White (Syracuse) met with us for a day at the University of Southern California to give the full manuscript a comprehensive review. They provided excellent comments that helped us make the book considerably better. Finally, while we were writing (and revising), Charles Myers was his usual patient, thoughtful, and supportive self, and Alicia Sparrow was incredibly hands-on in helping us navigate the various steps of publication.

Although this book is now complete, the overall project is not, and we are working on Congress and the second civil rights era. We hope the larger story's first arc will stoke readers' attention and satisfy their appetites until we can complete work on the second arc. It has been a long and fulfilling journey to this point, and we are pleased to have been able to provide a comprehensive account of a critical issue in premodern congressional history. We thank our families and friends for supporting us as we wrote this book and for their continuing encouragement during the second half of the project.

Abbreviations

These frequently cited congressional publications
and newspapers are abbreviated in the notes.

CG *Congressional Globe*
CT *Chicago Tribune*
CR *Congressional Record*
NYT *New York Times*
WP *Washington Post*

CHAPTER ONE

Introduction

Racial conflict is part of the bedrock of American politics. Although slavery is never explicitly mentioned in the Constitution itself, fights between those who opposed and supported it threatened to blow up the convention at which it was drafted. The framers (in)famously accommodated slaveholders' interests by stipulating that each of the enslaved would count as "three-fifths" of a person in determining representation in the House and the Electoral College. The Constitution also gave states the authority to determine that slaves were considered property before the law, including a fugitive slave provision obligating the federal government to aid in the return of escaped slaves, and prohibited, until 1808, any efforts to ban the international slave trade.[1] Slavery required policy intervention and state support even though the framers refused to record its name.[2]

From 1789 until the end of the 1850s, members of Congress protected slavery by carefully balancing free-state and slave-state preferences. After Abraham Lincoln's election in 1860, however, disagreements about slavery's potential expansion westward—which had reached fever pitch—caused

1. For more on the debate over slavery at the Constitutional Convention of 1787, see David Brian Robertson, *The Original Compromise: What the Constitution's Framers Were Really Thinking* (New York: Oxford University Press, 2013), 178–91; Andrew Delbanco, *The War before the War: Fugitive Slaves and the Struggle for America's Soul from the Revolution to the Civil War* (New York: Penguin, 2018), 43–85.

2. Joseph J. Ellis describes slavery's absence from the Constitution itself as "the silence." See Joseph J. Ellis, *Founding Brothers: The Revolutionary Generation* (New York: Vintage, 2000), 81–120.

the Union to fracture, and civil war followed. Once the Confederate army surrendered in 1865, elected officials at all levels of government faced the future with no plan for patching the country back together. The Republican Party ruled in Washington, DC, but save for the addition of the Thirteenth Amendment, the Constitution was unchanged. As a result, Republicans were governed by rules that did not acknowledge the outcome of the war. To make the Northern victory permanent, they needed to either amend the Constitution itself or work within prevailing conceptions of what the document allowed.

From the moment the war ended, the political and social status of African Americans consumed national attention. By 1865, after several years of internal struggle, Republicans agreed on abolition. But the substantive meaning of black freedom remained an open question. Also to be determined was how a Constitution that had protected slavery until 1865 could be altered to ensure the civil and political rights of former slaves. While the national debate over what freedom meant in postwar America played out in each of our primary political institutions and in the states, the rights and constitutional protections afforded to African Americans would be determined to a significant degree by Congress. Because the Constitution had for years made peace with human bondage, and because lawmakers were beholden to voters who themselves supported slavery, there was no guarantee that any legal changes would meaningfully incorporate and protect freedmen.

In this book we explore how Republicans in Congress, aided by the political activism of black citizens in the states, enacted laws to establish an inclusive, multiracial democracy in the United States. We also describe why their efforts could not survive a political onslaught by nineteenth-century white supremacists and their more "moderate" allies. More specifically, we explain how and why the "Grand Old Party" (GOP) created and enforced legal reforms extending freedom, citizenship, and voting rights to former slaves — and how former slaves, in turn, acted on those rights by voting, running for office, and demanding their fair share of government aid. But beginning in the 1870s, the GOP's political weakness throughout the South, as well as the shifting political preferences of Northern voters, allowed the white majority in the former Confederacy to degrade and ignore these reforms in ways specifically designed to deprive African Americans of their rights. Our analysis provides an explicitly "Congress-centered" perspective on this transformation by exploring the Republican Party's role in undermining the multiracial democracy it had helped to build.

We show that GOP infighting, a central feature of the party from its birth, was a major factor in its inability to sustain civil rights policies against a prolonged, multifront attack from white Democrats. Within the Republican Party, conflicts emerged over how much federal authority should be deployed to defend black civil rights and an inclusive democratic system. And through the years we analyze, factions representing these different perspectives vigorously competed for power and influence. The policies that Republicans passed when they controlled Congress, and the public response to these policies, bolstered the relative power of one of these factions. The GOP's retrenchment on civil rights is therefore one result of a particular sequence: policy enactments preceded a clear intraparty consensus on what the Constitution allowed, precipitating a fight among Republicans over the scope of federal authority that, over time, diminished official support for black civil rights.

Democrats exacerbated this tension. Once they returned to power, their nearly universal opposition to civil rights bolstered the position of those Republicans who were skeptical about deploying federal power on behalf of freedmen. Working together, by the later decades of the nineteenth century, Democrats and more "moderate" Republicans used state power to undermine much of the policy enacted in the immediate aftermath of the Civil War. Northern white attitudes also shifted to oppose a meaningful federal defense of black civil rights. And while some Republicans still made sporadic efforts to preserve and protect black civil rights, almost all their attempts failed. By the turn of the twentieth century, race politics in the country had hit their nadir.[3]

Focusing on party politics, we argue that policy enactments are a consequence of, and a window into, evolving public attitudes about civil rights. Without scientific polls, any assessment of public opinion will of course be an approximation. Yet for much of the period we analyze, voter turnout was dramatically higher than it is today.[4] And while the conditions promoting the "electoral connection" between representatives and their constituents were weaker in the late nineteenth and early twentieth centuries,

3. Rayford W. Logan, *The Negro in American Life and Thought: The Nadir* (New York: Dial Press, 1954).

4. Trends in voter turnout through the nineteenth century and into the twentieth are discussed in Michael E. McGerr, *The Decline of Popular Politics: The American North, 1865–1928* (New York: Oxford University Press, 1986); Richard L. McCormick, "The Party Period and Public Policy: An Exploratory Hypothesis," *Journal of American History* 66 (1979): 279–98; Walter Dean Burnham, *Voting in American Elections: The Shaping of the American Political Universe since 1788* (Palo Alto, CA: Academica Press, 2010).

they clearly were present.[5] Members of Congress had to take seriously their obligation to represent the preferences of voters back home. With Republicans pushing the civil rights agenda during these decades, policy decisions reflected the judgments of individual lawmakers about what their constituents would accept.

The electoral connection thus proved to be a double-edged sword for advocates of civil rights. When Republicans controlled Congress, and when a majority of them believed their political fortunes were contingent on the support of black voters, they passed civil rights initiatives. As Union troop levels in the occupied South dropped after 1868, however, white elites in the former Confederate states orchestrated a systematic campaign of violence and political terrorism against black voters.[6] The constant "drama" coming out of the South—often covered in lurid detail by partisan newspapers—amid a nationwide economic downturn ultimately turned the Northern white public against civil rights. As Northern opinion shifted, Republicans in Congress neglected and undermined those policies they had once advocated.[7] And though federal authorities fought Southern reactionaries for a time, violence and intimidation were ultimately successful in dampening black political participation and culminated in the "redemption" of Southern state governments by white Democrats.

Taken together, conflict within the Republican Party regarding the use of federal power to protect the black minority and electoral trends driven by shifting white attitudes explain the rise and fall of what we call the "first civil rights era." In the immediate aftermath of the war, the GOP served as a mechanism for advancing and defending black freedom. Yet the progressive disenfranchisement of black voters in the South, while the Northern public sought to refocus attention on economic issues that were central

5. See Jamie L. Carson and Jeffery A. Jenkins, "Examining the Electoral Connection across Time," *Annual Review of Political Science* 14 (2011): 25–46; Jamie L. Carson and Joel Sievert, *Electoral Incentives in Congress* (Ann Arbor: University of Michigan Press, 2018). For the classic treatment of Congress and the electoral connection, see David R. Mayhew, *Congress: The Electoral Connection* (1974; repr., New Haven, CT: Yale University Press, 2004).

6. For troop-level data by state, see Richard M. Valelly, *The Two Reconstructions: The Struggle for Black Enfranchisement* (Chicago: University of Chicago Press, 2004), 95. On violence and terror in the South during this time, see Allen W. Trelease, *White Terror: The Ku Klux Klan Conspiracy and Southern Reconstruction* (1971; repr., Baton Rouge: Louisiana State University Press, 1999); George Rable, *But There Was No Peace: The Role of Violence in the Politics of Reconstruction* (1984; repr., Athens: University of Georgia Press, 2007).

7. David Herbert Donald, Jean Harvey Baker, and Michael F. Holt, *The Civil War and Reconstruction* (New York: Norton, 2001), 626–28.

to their concerns, persuaded many congressional Republicans to withdraw their support for civil rights. As the electoral influence of black voters declined, the political power of those within the GOP who opposed expansive federal authority to protect black freedom grew. By the second decade of the twentieth century, the Republican Party had almost entirely abandoned its historic support for the protection and extension of black civil rights.

In the chapters to come, we provide a detailed analysis of what national lawmakers accomplished on freedom, citizenship, and civil rights for African Americans from the Civil War through World War I, what other options were possible, and how choices made immediately after the Civil War informed the decisions of elected leaders well into the twentieth century. Our analysis therefore highlights legislative paths not taken — "near misses" that could have significantly altered the course of political development in the postwar United States. By presenting the options available to lawmakers, we illustrate the role of choice in determining the direction of American political development in the decades after Confederate surrender. The Civil War radically expanded the range of choices available to lawmakers.[8] To many it looked as if the future would be dramatically different from the past. In a speech given just before he was murdered, President Lincoln described the situation this way: "So new and unprecedented is [Reconstruction] that no exclusive and inflexible plan can safely be prescribed as to details and collaterals."[9] Focusing on congressional action during the first civil rights era highlights a central feature of American democracy: how the same Constitution can be used as a mechanism to liberate oppressed minorities *and* to assert the power of the white majority against those same minority groups.

While we take seriously the influence of agency, choice, and contingency, we also draw out general political patterns enabling the shift from an inclusive, multiracial democracy to an exclusive democracy run by and for whites. Coming out of the Civil War, the Republican majority was divided on issues related to Reconstruction. Some believed the war justified a revolutionary change in the balance of federal and state power expressly to advance black civil rights. Others sought a return to the antebellum status quo, minus slavery. A third group tried to find some middle ground between these positions. Factionalism of this kind, we will show, consistently determined the

8. Giovanni Capoccia and R. Daniel Kelemen, "The Study of Critical Junctures: Theory, Narrative, and Counterfactuals in Historical Institutionalism," *World Politics* 59 (2007): 343.

9. Abraham Lincoln, "Speech on Reconstruction," in *Reconstruction: Voices from America's First Great Struggle for Racial Equality*, ed. Brooks D. Simpson (New York: Library of America, 2018), 18.

GOP's willingness and ability to advance black civil rights. These conflicts were exacerbated by the durability of geographic representation that forced African Americans into a party that was regionally weak.[10] Most black citizens lived in the South, but the GOP proved unable to secure a meaningful foothold there. Black rights were therefore contingent on support from external actors: Northern white lawmakers and voters. Tracking their attitudes toward civil rights policy is central to our analysis.

We also focus on Congress because it was the preeminent branch of the national government during the period in question and was formative in defining and enforcing civil rights protections.[11] Of course the constitutional questions at stake ensured a role for the executive and the judiciary. Actors from each—especially presidents—will emerge from time to time in our analytic narrative. But during the first civil rights era they were most often reacting to decisions made by Congress. To understand the behavior of a president or the Supreme Court, then, we must first understand *how* and *why* Congress enacted the policies it did.

The last reason for our rigorous attention to Congress is that it allows us to explore the "reciprocal links connecting politics to policy, the relationship of ideas and interests, the impact of sequencing and . . . the sources of preferences when situated historically."[12] We thus pay close attention to legislative debate over proposals dealing with black civil rights. This is not because we believe that "ideas" trump partisanship or the desire for personal political advancement. Instead, we argue that congressional debate clarifies how lawmakers thought about the relation between civil rights and the Constitution from the Civil War through the second decade of the twentieth century. The arguments they made were published in newspapers and otherwise communicated to constituents. They both reflect and influence public opinion. When written into policy, these ideas shaped subsequent politics concerning civil rights.

10. Valelly, *Two Reconstructions*; Boris Heersink and Jeffery A. Jenkins, *Republican Party Politics and the American South, 1865–1968* (New York: Cambridge University Press, 2020).

11. On "congressional preeminence" during this era, as compared with "presidential preeminence" during the late twentieth century, see Joseph Cooper, "From Congressional to Presidential Preeminence: Power and Politics in Late Nineteenth-Century America and Today," in *Congress Reconsidered*, ed. Lawrence C. Dodd and Bruce I. Oppenheimer, 9th ed. (Washington, DC: CQ Press, 2009), 361–91.

12. Ira Katznelson and John S. Lapinski, "At the Crossroads: Congress and American Political Development," *Perspectives on Politics* 4 (2006): 244.

Several prominent scholars have examined the development of black civil rights in the post–Civil War United States in great detail.[13] Our goal in this book is to add to their work by offering a policy history of all meaningful legislative proposals dealing with black civil rights from 1861 to 1918.[14] Before moving on to a more detailed substantive preview of the chapters to follow, we briefly describe the politics that preceded the Civil War to make it clear why the abolition of slavery and the extension of civil rights protections to African Americans proved such a monumental task. We also identify the partisan dynamics that gave rise to the Republican Party. The political tensions built into the party at the moment of its creation, as we demonstrate below, continued to manifest themselves through the later decades of the nineteenth century.

Slavery and the Rise of the Republican Party

Significant historical work has revealed that at least some of the framers recognized that slavery was at odds with the new nation's founding principles.[15]

13. See, for example, W. E. B. Du Bois, *Black Reconstruction in America, 1860–1880* (1935; repr., New York: Free Press, 1992); V. O. Key Jr., *Southern Politics in State and Nation* (1949; repr., Knoxville: University of Tennessee Press, 1984); C. Vann Woodward, *The Strange Career of Jim Crow* (1955; repr., New York: Oxford University Press, 2002); J. Morgan Kousser, *The Shaping of Southern Politics: Suffrage Restriction and the One-Party South, 1880–1910* (New Haven, CT: Yale University Press, 1974); Philip A. Klinkner, *The Unsteady March: The Rise and Decline of Inequality in America* (Chicago: University of Chicago Press, 1999); Valelly, *Two Reconstructions*; Kimberley Johnson, *Reforming Jim Crow: Southern Politics in the Age before Brown* (Oxford: Oxford University Press, 2010); Robert Mickey, *Paths out of Dixie: The Democratization of Authoritarian Enclaves in America's Deep South, 1944–1972* (Princeton, NJ: Princeton University Press, 2014); Megan Ming Francis, *Civil Rights and the Making of the Modern American State* (New York: Cambridge University Press, 2014); David A. Bateman, Ira Katznelson, and John S. Lapinski, *Southern Nation: Congress and White Supremacy after Reconstruction* (Princeton, NJ: Princeton University Press, 2018).

14. By "meaningful" legislative proposals, we refer to those bills that required floor action in Congress, where individual lawmakers would have to go on record — and thus stake out discernible positions that constituents back home could observe — on key issues with policy implications for the rights of African Americans.

15. See Edmund S. Morgan, *American Slavery, American Freedom* (New York: Norton, 1975); William W. Freehling, "The Founding Fathers and Slavery," *American Historical Review* 77 (1972): 81–93; Bernard Bailyn, *The Ideological Origins of the American Revolution* (Cambridge, MA: Harvard University Press, 1992), 235–46; Danielle Allen, *Our Declaration: A Reading of the Declaration of Independence in Defense of Equality* (New York: Liveright, 2014).

Regardless of their concerns, it quickly proved to be an immensely profitable enterprise. Roger Ransom shows that between ratification and 1860 "there was no prolonged period during which the value of slaves owned in the United States did not increase markedly."[16] While most Southern families never owned a slave, slave labor was integral to the Southern economy as a whole. Through the early decades of the nineteenth century, cotton was the world's most widely traded commodity; slavery allowed the South to become a dominant force in the global market.[17] One study estimates that by 1860 abolition would have produced a 23 percent reduction in income for *all* Southern whites.[18] In 1860, slaves as property were worth close to $3 billion. The capital invested in slaves "roughly equaled the total value of all farmland and farm buildings in the South."[19] As an asset, slaves were more valuable than the manufacturing, railroad, and other productive sectors of the country combined. By 1860, property in slaves made up nearly 20 percent of all national wealth.[20]

Slavery was also more than just an economic engine. It gave the Southern white elite a system for maintaining a particular social order. In his famous "Cornerstone Speech," vice president of the Confederacy Alexander H. Stephens described "American negro slavery" as the cornerstone Southern life was built on. "[T]he great truth [is] that the negro is not equal to the white man; that slavery — subordination to the superior race — is his natural and normal condition."[21] Building on Stephens, Ulrich Phillips argued that "the central theme in southern history is a common resolve indomitably maintained — that it shall be and remain a white man's country."[22] Slavery served as a system of racial adjustment and social order. Its power was just as much social as economic. Elizabeth Fox-Genovese and Eugene Genovese document this by making clear how the views on religion and history of the

16. Roger L. Ransom, "The Economics of the Civil War," accessed at http://eh.net /encyclopedia/the-economics-of-the-civil-war/.

17. Edward E. Baptist, *The Half Has Never Been Told: Slavery and the Making of American Capitalism* (New York: Basic Books, 2014), xxi; see also Sven Beckert, *Empire of Cotton: A Global History* (New York: Knopf, 2014).

18. Gerald Gunderson, "The Origin of the American Civil War," *Journal of Economic History* 34 (1974): 922.

19. Ransom, "Economics of the Civil War."

20. Baptist, *Half Has Never Been Told*, 246.

21. Henry Cleveland, *Alexander H. Stephens in Public and Private: With Letters and Speeches before, during, and since the War* (Philadelphia, 1866), 721.

22. Ulrich B. Phillips, "The Central Theme of Southern History," *American Historical Review* 34 (October 1928): 31.

"master class" were directly influenced by their commitment to racial hierarchy.[23]

By the time Confederate artillery opened fire on Fort Sumter in April 1861, slavery was deeply entrenched in Southern life. In 1860, four out of every ten people living in the South—nearly four million people—were enslaved.[24] The combination of an exploding slave population and the three-fifths compromise ensured that Southern whites would wield significant power in national political institutions. Eight of the first twelve presidents owned slaves.[25] In Congress, slave states consistently held 33 percent more seats than their free population warranted.[26] As William Lee Miller put it, "By 1860, the seven largest slave states, with a free population of 3,298,000, had 45 representatives in the House, while the state of New York, with a free population of 3,831,590, had only 31."[27] Guaranteed such disproportionate political influence at the national level, slavery's supporters used state power to defend it.[28]

For seventy years after the Constitution was ratified, conflicts over slavery proved impossible to disentangle from the country's westward expansion.[29] Congress, specifically, dealt with the policy questions associated with slavery and expansion in two ways. Members who feared that any national debate over the legality of slavery put the Union itself at risk took steps to keep Congress from debating the issue at all. To that end, the House of Representatives in 1836 voted to enact a "gag rule" stipulating that "all petitions,

23. Elizabeth Fox-Genovese and Eugene Genovese, *The Mind of the Master Class: History and Faith in the Southern Slaveholders' Worldview* (New York: Cambridge University Press, 2005).

24. Ransom, "Economics of the Civil War."

25. For more on the presidents who owned slaves, see Don E. Fehrenbacher, *The Slaveholding Republic: An Account of the United States Government's Relation to Slavery* (New York: Oxford University Press, 2002).

26. Leonard L. Richards, *The Slave Power: The Free North and Southern Domination, 1780–1860* (Baton Rouge: Louisiana State University Press, 2000), 56.

27. William Lee Miller, *Arguing about Slavery: John Quincy Adams and the Great Battle in the United States Congress* (New York: Vintage, 1995), 49.

28. For more on the ways the national state bolstered slave interests, see Desmond S. King and Rogers M. Smith, "Racial Orders in American Political Development," *American Political Science Review* 99 (2005): 75–92.

29. For more on the intersection of race and westward expansion, see Paul Frymer, *Building an American Empire: The Era of Territorial and Political Expansion* (Princeton, NJ: Princeton University Press, 2017); Aziz Rana, *The Two Faces of American Freedom* (Cambridge, MA: Harvard University Press, 2010).

memorials, resolutions, propositions, or papers, relating in any way, or to any extent whatever, to the subject of slavery, or the abolition of slavery, shall, without being either printed or referred, be laid upon the table, and that no further action whatever shall be had thereon."[30]

Thus one way Congress protected slavery was by keeping it off the national agenda entirely. And though the gag rule would not last long, the operation of the two-party system prevented slavery-based issues from rising to national prominence. Because both the Democrats and the Whigs were interregional coalitions—with members from both the North and the South—slavery was always an existential threat to their institutional success and ultimately their survival. Leaders in both parties thus actively worked to block consideration of any issues that threatened the status quo.[31]

When the prospect of territorial acquisition required that Congress address slavery, the Senate followed what Barry Weingast calls the "balance rule." Made explicit early in the nineteenth century, the balance rule held that North and South would always have equal representation. Slave states and free states would, in short, always be admitted in pairs.[32] This would allow slave-state lawmakers in the Senate to maintain an effective veto over any policy change bearing on slavery. Thus Congress also protected slavery by creating policy that perfectly balanced the interests of North and South.[33]

This approach mostly worked. From ratification until the repeated political crises of the 1850s, members of Congress enacted compromise measures allowing for territorial acquisition without upsetting the slave state/

30. For more on the enactment of the gag rule, see Robert P. Ludlum, "The Antislavery 'Gag-Rule': History and Argument," *Journal of Negro History* 26 (1941): 203–43.

31. See John H. Aldrich, *Why Parties?: The Origin and Transformation of Party Politics in America* (Chicago: University of Chicago Press, 1995), 126–36; Jeffery A. Jenkins and Charles Stewart III, *Fighting for the Speakership: The House and the Rise of Party Government* (Princeton, NJ: Princeton University Press, 2013).

32. Barry R. Weingast, "Political Stability and the Civil War: Institutions, Commitment, and American Democracy," in *Analytic Narratives*, ed. Robert H. Bates, Avner Greif, Margaret Levi, Jean-Laurent Rosenthal, and Barry R. Weingast (Princeton, NJ: Princeton University Press, 1998), 151. For a critique of the balance rule, see Gregory J. Wawro, "Peculiar Institutions: Slavery, Sectionalism, and Minority Obstruction in the Antebellum Senate," *Legislative Studies Quarterly* 30 (2005): 163–91.

33. Both parties also sought a second form of balance, by ensuring that their presidential and vice-presidential candidates were from different regions. This "balanced ticket" approach provided another layer of protection against unwanted change on the slavery issue. See Aldrich, *Why Parties?*, 130–32.

free state balance. Major legislation for this purpose included the Missouri Compromise, enacted in March 1820, which officially brought Maine (a free state) and Missouri (a slave state) into the Union. It also prohibited slavery's expansion north of the 36°30′ parallel.[34] Thirty years later, thanks to land acquired as a consequence of the Mexican-American War, the Compromise of 1850 brought California into the Union as a free state, banned the slave trade in the District of Columbia, implemented a tougher fugitive slave law, and opened new territory in the Southwest for (possible) settlement by pro-slavery advocates (under the doctrine of popular sovereignty).[35]

Despite its innocuous name, the Compromise of 1850 almost tore the nation apart.[36] The newly acquired western territory instigated a fight over whether and how slavery would be permitted to expand that broke through Congress's traditional defenses against serious debate. Four major land annexations brought more than one million square miles under the control of the federal government, and much of this new land was below the Missouri Compromise line dividing free and slave states.[37] Additionally, the 1860 census reported that more than half of the existing slave population was held in states brought into the Union in the years after the Constitution was ratified. Slavery was pushing westward, and decisions about its status in the territories would need to be made.

In the 1850s, according to Arthur Bestor, slavery's defenders came to believe that "the power to decide the question of slavery for the territories was the power to determine the future of slavery itself."[38] They worried that a cordon of free states surrounding the South would, over time, destroy slavery. For them, expansion became the only way to ensure that slavery would survive. The Kansas-Nebraska Act of 1854—which repealed the Missouri

34. See Robert Pierce Forbes, *The Missouri Compromise and Its Aftermath: Slavery and the Meaning of America* (Chapel Hill: University of North Carolina Press, 2007).

35. Popular sovereignty was premised on self-determination. Advocates like Sen. Stephen Douglas (D-IL) and Sen. Lewis Cass (D-MI) held that the people of the territories should decide for themselves whether slavery would exist there. See Michael A. Morrison, *Slavery and the American West: The Eclipse of Manifest Destiny and the Coming of the Civil War* (Chapel Hill: University of North Carolina Press, 1997); Christopher Childers, "Interpreting Popular Sovereignty: A Historiographical Essay," *Civil War History* 57 (2011): 48–70.

36. See Fergus M. Bordewich, *America's Great Debate: Henry Clay, Stephen A. Douglas, and the Compromise That Preserved the Union* (New York: Simon and Schuster, 2012).

37. Arthur Bestor, "The American Civil War as a Constitutional Crisis," *American Historical Review* 69 (1964): 335.

38. Bestor, "American Civil War as a Constitutional Crisis," 345.

Compromise, raising the prospect of slavery's expanding into the former Louisiana Purchase land where it had been prohibited — was the policy intervention they believed would guarantee slavery's future.[39] Far from protecting slavery, however, the Kansas-Nebraska Act led to a political crisis that gave rise to the very forces that would end it for good.[40]

The Republican Party has its origins in the political environment created by the Kansas-Nebraska Act. One faction of the soon-to-be party comprised Northern Whigs who fled the party after 1854. Under the leadership of Henry Clay, the Whigs had avoided sectional controversy by grudgingly accepting slavery's movement west while telling themselves that the physical environment would prevent it from taking root. The Kansas-Nebraska Act outraged Northern Whigs, who feared that slave labor in Kansas would undermine the economic prospects of independent white farmers, split the party, and eventually destroy it. Southern Whigs took on temporary labels — Americans, Opposition, and Constitutional Unionists — before eventually migrating to the Democratic Party, while Northern Whigs found themselves looking for a new political home.[41]

A second faction comprised Free Soilers. Since the 1840s, the Free Soil Party had sought to enact policy that would prevent slavery's migration out of the states where it already existed. From their perspective, slavery was a state institution rather than a national one. The federal government could not change existing state law, but it could outlaw slavery in states not yet incorporated into the Union. The party's 1848 platform stipulated that slavery depended "on State laws alone, which cannot be repealed or modified by the Federal Government."[42] The argument that slavery's only legal support came from state laws justified the Free Soil Party's unrelenting opposition

39. On the Kansas-Nebraska Act and its aftermath, see Nicole Etcheson, *Bleeding Kansas: Contested Liberty in the Civil War Era* (Lawrence: University Press of Kansas, 2004).

40. For more on the political debates around slavery in the western territories, see Michael F. Holt, *The Political Crisis of the 1850s* (New York: Wiley, 1978); William W. Freehling, *The Road to Disunion*, vol. 2, *Secessionists Triumphant, 1854–1861* (New York: Oxford University Press, 2007); James M. McPherson, *Battle Cry of Freedom: The Civil War Era* (New York: Ballantine Books, 1988), 47–170.

41. Holt, *Political Crisis of the 1850s*, 139–82; Kenneth C. Martis, *The Historical Atlas of Political Parties in the United States Congress, 1789–1989* (New York: Macmillan, 1989), 41–43, 108–13; William E. Gienapp, *The Origins of the Republican Party, 1852–1856* (New York: Oxford University Press, 1987), 167–88.

42. Platform quoted in James Oakes, *Freedom National: The Destruction of Slavery in the United States, 1861–1865* (New York: Norton, 2013), 4.

to slavery's extension into the western territories. If they prevented slavery's expansion, Free Soil leaders believed, it would gradually die on its own.[43]

As a direct descendant of the Free Soil movement, the Republican Party exploded onto the political scene as a defense against the "nationalization" of slavery. From the perspective of Republican politicians, the Constitution "*restricted* slavery to the states while committing the federal government to policies that would expand freedom everywhere it could."[44] Lincoln spoke to this position in his first inaugural address when, in an attempt to calm nervous Southerners, he made it clear that he had "no purpose, directly or indirectly, to interfere with the institution of slavery in the States where it exists." This echoed his private communication with trusted aides. In a letter to William H. Seward, for example, Lincoln wrote, "I say now as I have all the while said, that on the territorial question—that is, the question of extending slavery under the national auspices—I am inflexible. I am for no compromise which *assists* or *permits* the extension of the institution on soil owned by the nation."[45]

The Republican Party thus served as an umbrella coalition for abolitionists, Northern Whigs, and Free Soilers—groups that were all opposed to the Democrats.[46] During the war, factions within the party continued to disagree about whether slavery could be legally abolished. Once abolition became the consensus position, new factions within the party disagreed over what the future would look like for freed slaves. Lincoln himself admitted "embarrassment that we, the loyal people, differ among ourselves as to the mode, manner, and means of Reconstruction."[47] Firmly in control of government at war's end, the GOP had no set plan for reintegrating Southern

43. For more on this point see James Oakes, *The Scorpion's Sting: Anti-slavery and the Coming of the Civil War* (New York: Norton, 2014); Sean Wilentz, "Jeffersonian Democracy and the Origins of Political Antislavery in the United States: The Missouri Crisis Revisited," *Journal of the Historical Society* 4 (2004): 375–401.

44. Oakes, *Freedom National*, 43.

45. Lincoln quoted in Bestor, "American Civil War as a Constitutional Crisis," 337.

46. Many abolitionists were members of the Liberty Party, which formed in 1840. Later in the decade, many Liberty Party members supported fusion with the (new) Free Soil Party. Some devoted abolitionists resisted the move, however, and a much weaker Liberty Party remained in existence. Eventually, most Liberty Party holdouts joined the Republican Party in 1854. For more on the Liberty Party, see Reinhard O. Johnson, *The Liberty Party, 1840–1848: Antislavery Third-Party Politics in the United States* (Baton Rouge: Louisiana State University Press, 2009).

47. Brooks D. Simpson, ed., *Reconstruction: Voices from America's First Great Struggle for Racial Equality* (New York: Library of America, 2018), 14.

states or for dealing with the fate of former slaves who rightly saw themselves as entitled to all the privileges and immunities of citizens.

Congress, the Republican Party, and the First Civil Rights Era

The Civil War (1861–65) has been rightly described as America's second revolution.[48] It would prove unimaginably destructive. More than 700,000 soldiers died, and much of the South was left in ruins.[49] Yet neither Lincoln nor many Republicans went into the conflict intending to abolish slavery. As we described above, antislavery advocates generally believed slavery was constitutionally protected in those states where it existed before the first shot was fired. Even after the Emancipation Proclamation and ratification of the Thirteenth Amendment, no consensus existed at the federal level about what would happen to the millions of African Americans living in the South. In 1865 lawmakers thus found themselves forced to create out of whole cloth a process for readmitting Southern states to the Union and to construct a system for guaranteeing that African Americans would be able to live freely.

From 1866 to 1872, Republicans in Congress passed a series of laws that created the concept of civil rights and established the ways the federal government would ensure that these rights were protected. They also legislated federal policies to help former slaves and their descendants support themselves. Yet without a consensus on what the postwar policy would look like or who would be responsible for implementing it, the stage was set for the continuation of intraparty conflict. Once the South was readmitted and Democrats reclaimed power in Congress, disagreement within the GOP led to a national-level retrenchment from civil rights.

Beginning in the Forty-Second Congress (1871–73), many within the Republican Party turned away from, and even against, black civil rights. In 1872 Congress granted amnesty to many former Confederates who were still legally barred from holding political office, but a GOP majority defeated an effort to link the reestablishment of political rights for Southern traitors with an expansion of federally protected civil rights. Three years later, a majority of Republicans worked to weaken what became the Civil Rights

48. Charles A. Beard and Mary R. Beard, *The Rise of American Civilization: The Industrial Era* (New York: Macmillan, 1927); James M. McPherson, *Abraham Lincoln and the Second American Revolution* (New York: Oxford University Press, 1990).

49. Drew Gilpin Faust, *This Republic of Suffering: Death and the American Civil War* (New York: Vintage, 2008).

Act of 1875 so much that one contemporaneous analysis declared it "struck at the principle of the whole Republican policy of reconstruction."[50] After 1875, *all* legislation—with the exception of the Second Morrill Act in 1890— that would have advanced civil rights for African Americans failed. Furthermore, those bills dealing with civil rights that did pass directly undermined the gains made in the immediate postwar years. By the second decade of the twentieth century, civil rights had nearly disappeared from the congressional agenda. It appeared at this time that Jim Crow would reign unchallenged into the future.

We characterize 1861 to 1918 as the first civil rights era. Central to our argument is the claim that these fifty-eight years should be thought of as a distinct period in American political development, and our data provide an empirical basis for this view. Using the congressional proceedings and roll-call voting record, we can identify all legislative proposals dealing specifically with African American rights introduced and voted on from the Thirty-Seventh though the Sixty-Fifth Congress (see table 1.1). The record makes it clear that by 1918 Congress had all but given up on promoting black civil rights. It was not until the early 1920s, after the first Great Migration, that the national legislature once again asserted itself in promoting black civil rights—when Congress debated and voted on federal antilynching legislation introduced by Rep. Leonidas Dyer (R-MO).[51] This book therefore describes a dynamic central to race politics in America: a period of progress followed by a period of backlash and reversal, followed in turn by a new period of advance.

We also set out to explain why civil rights policymaking fits this pattern. In what follows we argue that congressional behavior was driven to a significant degree by public opinion in Northern states. Republicans held a majority in the US Senate for twenty-four of the twenty-nine legislative terms covered in this book.[52] In the House, they were in the majority for seventeen of twenty-nine terms. After the South was "redeemed" by the Democratic

---

50. "The Civil Rights Bill," *Harper's Weekly*, March 20, 1875, 231.

51. Jeffery A. Jenkins, Justin Peck, and Vesla M. Weaver, "Between Reconstructions: Congressional Action on Civil Rights, 1891–1940," *Studies in American Political Development* 24 (2010): 57–89. This is not to say that civil rights advocacy outside the federal government also went dormant. For more on early twentieth-century civil rights organizing, see Megan Ming Francis, *Civil Rights and the Making of the Modern American State* (New York: Cambridge University Press, 2014).

52. We will often refer to a two-year legislative term as "a Congress." And each Congress often comes with a number prefix. To identify the opening year of a given Congress, the equa-

TABLE 1.1. The First Civil Rights Era

Congress	Civil Rights Policies Considered
37th–38th (1861–65)	Confiscation Acts
	Thirteenth Amendment
	Freedmen's Bureau
	Failed Wade-Davis bill
39th–41st (1865–71)	Voting rights in Washington, DC
	Freedmen's Bureau extension
	Civil Rights Act of 1866
	First Reconstruction Act
	Fourteenth Amendment
	Fifteenth Amendment
	First, Second, and Third Enforcement Acts
42nd–44th (1871–77)	Fourth and Fifth Enforcement Acts
	General amnesty
	Civil Rights Act of 1875
	Failed enforcement bill of 1875
45th–51st (1877–91)	*Failed* Enforcement Acts repeal
	Failed equal accommodations amendment
	Failed federal education bill
	Second Morrill Act
	Failed federal elections bill
52nd–65th (1891–1918)	Enforcement Acts *repeal*
	Failed segregated streetcars in the District of Columbia
	Discharge of black troops in Brownsville, TX
	Failed section 2 enforcement
	Failed antimiscegenation bills
	Failed repeal of federal supervision of Senate elections
	Failed separate but equal educational appropriations

Party, Republican lawmakers took political cues from voters living in northern, and increasingly in western, states. During these years, voter turnout was high and party competition intense. Without the insights into public opinion provided by polls, members of Congress relied on local newspapers, frequently run by party organizations, and off-cycle elections to offer some

tion is 1787 + 2 × (Congress number). So, for example, the Thirty-Seventh Congress, which was the first Civil War Congress, first convened in 1861.

insight into what regional and home-state constituencies were thinking.[53] They also argued among themselves about what the public would accept and what their positions in Congress required. The choices lawmakers made should be seen, we argue, as insights into what they guessed would best promote their reelection. The Republican Party's turn against civil rights reflects the party's collective assessment that its political future was, over time, less dependent on the support and enthusiasm of black voters.

As pivotal as we think the electoral connection is to congressional behavior, we do not argue that lawmakers simply reflected prevailing public sentiment: their arguments and decisions also shaped public attitudes. As Bestor puts it, "The arguments of the period were public ones, addressed to contemporaries, and designed to influence their actions."[54] Factions within the GOP were constantly seeking enough influence to determine the party's position on black civil rights. These factions prevented the party from acting as a unit, simply legislating an agreed-upon set of principles. Instead, policy choices reflect the relative political influence of "conservatives," "moderates," and "radicals," all considering themselves Republicans. While historians often disagree about which members were in what faction — since the factions were informal and often fluid — Hans Trefousse provides useful descriptions of each:

[Radicals consisted] largely of former Free-Soilers and other determined anti-slavery politicians [who] before the war . . . believed in taking an uncompromising stand against the advocates of slavery by asserting the fundamental wrong of the institution and refusing to recede in any way from their insistence that it be kept from spreading. After the start of the conflict, they advocated complete emancipation and vigorous prosecution

53. During much of the nineteenth century, states could hold elections at their discretion. In 1872 Congress institutionalized the first Tuesday after the first Monday in November as the date for all federal elections. See 17 *Stat.* 28. It took until about 1880 for all states to fall in line. Until then, in some election cycles, states would elect their members of Congress as much as eighteen months apart. For example, in the congressional midterms during the Civil War, Oregon held its election in June 1862 while Maryland held its election in November 1863. On the "public opinion value" of off-cycle elections in the nineteenth century, see Scott C. James, "Timing and Sequence in Congressional Elections: Interstate Contagion and America's Nineteenth-Century Scheduling Regime," *Studies in American Political Development* 21 (2): 181-202.

54. Bestor, "American Civil War as a Constitutional Crisis," 331.

of the war, and during Reconstruction, no restoration of the South until the freedmen had been granted full civil rights. The conservatives, on the other hand, in the 1850's attempted to compromise with slaveholders; in the early sixties, procrastinated about emancipation; and in the late sixties, were willing to maintain the Negro in an inferior position. The moderates, generally sympathizing with many radical objectives but objecting to extreme methods, stood somewhere in between.[55]

Members of each faction framed proposals and assessed the public response to what Congress passed. In the chapters that follow we show how the radical position progressively weakened over time. Legislative enactments, in other words, created new politics that empowered more conservative members of the party. This weakening also helps to explain why civil rights disappeared from the legislative agenda.

Outline of the Book

This book is a policy history of all legislation dealing with black civil rights from 1861 to 1918. We move chronologically through these decades, recounting the debates in Congress, elucidating what issues were on the national agenda, and identifying the final outcome for all relevant policy proposals. Each chapter uses a variety of data and evidentiary sources including bill introductions and text, legislative proceedings and debate, roll-call votes, and media (newspaper) coverage. We give special attention to those issues that elicited roll calls on the floor, since they were able to effect meaningful change. Focusing on the roll-call record lets us highlight the intra-Republican conflicts that had such an influence on civil rights policy through these years. When analyzing votes, we use standard descriptive techniques (like reporting the yeas and nays by party and region) as well as statistical measures and techniques (like NOMINATE scores and regression analysis) to discern more specific patterns based on factors like member ideology and district/state characteristics.[56] To make the book accessible to the

---

55. Hans L. Trefousse, *The Radical Republicans: Lincoln's Vanguard for Racial Justice* (New York: Knopf, 1968), 4–5.

56. NOMINATE scores represent a measure of ideology (or "central tendencies") for members of Congress that is now ubiquitous in the literature. See Keith T. Poole and Howard Rosenthal, *Congress: A Political-Economic History of Roll Call Voting* (New York: Oxford University Press, 1997). For a useful introduction to NOMINATE, see Phil Everson, Rick Valelly,

widest possible audience, we have placed most of the statistical results (and their discussion) in footnotes or appendixes.

Chapter 2 begins by examining congressional action during the Civil War years (1861–65). Here we detail Congress's first real legislative efforts to confront black civil rights, by tracing how the Republican Party's position on slavery evolved over the course of the war, from acceptance where it existed in 1861 to abolition in 1865. We detail congressional debates over the First and Second Confiscation Acts, and their influence on the slavery debate, as well as the Freedmen's Bureau, a new federal entity created to assist millions of former slaves in their transition to freedom and independence. We also examine the political wrangling over what would become the Thirteenth Amendment once the GOP had made abolition its goal. Finally, we discuss the disagreement between President Lincoln and Republicans in Congress over how the South would in fact be "reconstructed" after the war's end.

Chapter 3 covers the early Reconstruction years (1865–71). The two years after the Civil War, which broadly overlap with the Thirty-Ninth Congress (1865–67), were a defining period in postwar civil rights policy. These years saw President Andrew Johnson attempt to set the conditions by which the South would be integrated back into the Union. Johnson's policy, implemented during a congressional recess, afforded white elites in the South an opportunity to reestablish power by forcing freedmen back into subservience. Once Congress was back in session, Republicans fought Johnson, and after several veto battles they successfully took control of Reconstruction and enacted a series of landmark laws: the Civil Rights Act of 1866, which gave former slaves citizenship and equal protection of the laws; a new Freedmen's Bureau Act, which extended the institution's life; the Fourteenth Amendment, which broadened the rights provided under the 1866 act and stipulated a reduction in congressional representation for any state found denying black citizens the right to vote; and the First Reconstruction Act, which created five military zones in the former Confederacy to govern readmission and allowed freedmen to vote in the establishment of new state constitutional conventions. Finally, the four years that comprised the Fortieth and Forty-First Congresses (1867–71) represent the high-water mark of Reconstruction. During these years the Republicans completed their vision of Southern Reconstruction, enacting the Fifteenth Amendment, which eliminated race, color, or previous condition of servitude as restrictions on

Arjun Vishwanath, and Jim Wiseman, "NOMINATE and American Political Development: A Primer," *Studies in American Political Development* 30 (2016): 97–115.

voting, and the first three Enforcement Acts, which empowered the federal courts to oversee elections, preserve order at polling places, and enforce voting rights.

Chapter 4 examines the demise of Reconstruction (1871–77). Across these years, Congress backslid in its efforts to create an inclusive, multiracial democracy. The period began optimistically enough, with the passage of a new (fourth) Enforcement Act, which empowered the president to use the military and suspend habeas corpus to eliminate violent conspiracies in the South and ensure that civil and voting rights were protected. President Ulysses Grant used this power when he sent the army into the South to break the Ku Klux Klan and protect voters going to the polls. As a result the GOP did very well in Southern elections in 1872. After this success, however, the outlook darkened. Republican divisions surfaced in a public way during debate on a fifth Enforcement Act, which sought to provide further protections at polling stations. The legislation was enacted, but only after it was stripped of real enforcement power. And the GOP was unable to extend a key provision of the Fourth Enforcement Act to continue federal efforts against the Klan. Amid this institutional turmoil, the Panic of 1873 and the subsequent economic downturn cost the GOP majority control of the House in 1874 as Northern public opinion turned against Reconstruction and protecting black rights. As a result, efforts to pass an ambitious new civil rights bills stalled until the "emasculated" Civil Rights Act of 1875 was finally enacted. Finally, before the 1876 elections, the Republicans were unable to pass a new enforcement bill to protect voting rights in the South. And the 1876 elections would not be kind to the GOP: a complete Democratic takeover of the South occurred, and Republicans lost both chambers of Congress.

Chapter 5 explores congressional action during the "Redemption" years (1877–91). By 1877, with the entire South now in Democratic hands, black citizenship and voting rights came under assault. Republicans nevertheless continued to work to maintain a Southern wing of the party and protect African Americans. For example, when Southern Democrats, after winning majorities in both chambers of Congress, moved to repeal the various Enforcement Acts, Republican President Rutherford Hayes issued a series of vetoes to stop them. Pro-civil rights Republicans then tried—but ultimately failed—to use an interstate commerce bill as a way to guarantee equal accommodations in interstate travel. The GOP also worked to build a cross-partisan coalition to enact the first federal education program. Led by Sen. Henry Blair (R-NH), the legislation (after multiple attempts) ultimately came up short. Finally, Republicans pushed unsuccessfully for a new federal elections bill to protect voting rights in the South. Sponsored by Rep. Henry Cabot Lodge (R-MA), this legislation passed in the House in 1890 but stalled in the Senate when several western Republicans joined with the Democrats to defeat it. Civil rights advocates could cheer the Second Morrill Act, which provided federal aid to public land-grant colleges and ultimately led to the creation of a number of "traditionally black colleges" in the South. But even this success came with a caveat: the legislation could be passed only because it included a "separate but equal" provision that allowed Southern states to segregate by race.

Chapter 6 covers the "wilderness years" (1891–1918). During these three decades, black political participation was limited by small population numbers in the North and widespread disenfranchisement in the South. As a result, congressional Republicans were largely uninterested in advancing meaningful civil rights legislation. A few GOP members tried to enforce section 2 of the Fourteenth Amendment, reducing Southern representation as a punishment for disenfranchising black voters, but these efforts came to naught. Congressional Democrats, meanwhile, sought to actively undermine Reconstruction era civil rights reforms. Their most notable achievement was repealing the Enforcement Acts. Yet they lacked the political support to ban interracial marriage, segregate streetcars in Washington, DC, or erase federal supervision of senators, who after the Seventeenth Amendment would be directly elected. On the whole, this was a period of stalemate. Although the Republicans did not promote new civil rights legislation, they did seek to keep the Democrats from using the federal government as a tool to advance white supremacy. Stalemate was of course terrible for black citizens living under Jim Crow, but the conditions were not yet in place for the irrevocable split between black voters and the GOP that would culminate in the "second Reconstruction." The events we cover here laid the groundwork for this significant political realignment.

Finally, in chapter 7 we step back and consider the first civil rights era as a whole. In doing so, we reflect on key moments and review the more than half-century of events as a coherent period in American political development. We show how, by the turn of the twentieth century, a broad consensus had emerged both in Congress and in the nation that Southern state governments should be allowed to exist essentially as a separate nation within the United States. And while the nadir of the first civil rights era was very low, we also note that an exclusive focus on the era's end obscures the significant achievements that were made in the early postwar period. That is, for a time, African Americans' lives in the South improved greatly, the Republican Party operated as a true interregional coalition, and a normal (though fragile) period of two-party politics in the South seemed to have begun.

The first civil rights era is bookended by two wars: the Civil War and World War I. Over the nearly six decades covered in this book, civil rights politics went from being a central preoccupation for members of Congress to almost entirely disappearing from the agenda. By the second decade of the twentieth century both political parties wholly abandoned black civil rights in the name of national reconciliation and political opportunism. Our detailed analysis of civil rights bills provides a granular look at the way the Republican Party slowly withdrew its support for a meaningful civil rights agenda. We also look at how Democrats and Republicans, at various points, worked together to keep civil rights off the legislative docket. Even as an epidemic of lynching gripped the nation, for example, legislators chose to mostly ignore the plight of black citizens. It was only after the first Great Migration was under way and at the conclusion of World War I — a conflict in which black Americans suffering under Jim Crow fought and died — that civil rights again gained national attention and demanded recognition by members of Congress.

In sum, we posit the first civil rights era as a coherent epoch in the larger story of American political development. With civil rights on the national agenda in the early years of our study, the lives and fortunes of black Americans improved. As both parties converged on an uneasy truce, mostly by agreeing to allow Southern whites to govern their region unimpeded, black Americans found themselves subjected to new forms of rights restrictions and arbitrary state power. Viewed this way, we argue, the years after World War I mark the beginning of yet another civil rights era, culminating in the landmark civil rights laws of the 1960s. In the aftermath of these reforms, with civil rights politics once again forced off the national agenda, black Americans found themselves yet again confronting hostile state power. We therefore intend for this book to contribute more broadly to scholarship in American political development, demonstrating the central role that race plays in state formation in this country.

CHAPTER TWO

The Civil War Years, 1861–1865

In the years that spanned the American Civil War, the societal standing of African Americans — especially those in the slave states — changed dramatically. When President Abraham Lincoln took office in early March 1861, a last-ditch effort was under way to keep the Union together by enticing the seven slave states of the Deep South that had seceded to reconsider their decision. Congress had passed a new constitutional amendment — the Thirteenth — in the waning days of the previous (Thirty-Sixth) Congress that would have protected slavery where it existed, and it had the shared support of congressional Republicans and the incoming president. By early 1865, however, a different Thirteenth Amendment was passed, and later that year it was ratified. This version abolished slavery for all time.

The political path from guaranteeing slavery to providing freedom for African Americans is the subject of this chapter. The process of change was not linear or planned — often it was influenced by outcomes on the battlefield. Freedom was pushed first by Republicans in Congress, to the dismay (and often opposition) of President Lincoln, who preferred a more guarded approach aimed at keeping the remaining slave states in the Union.[1] Eventually Lincoln's thinking evolved, and preservation of the antebellum status quo gave way to a higher moral purpose: the eradication of slavery. And

1. For Lincoln's position on the border states, and their role in the sectional conflict, see William C. Harris, *Lincoln and the Border States: Preserving the Union* (Lawrence: University Press of Kansas, 2011).

though Lincoln responded accordingly through his Emancipation Proclamation, there was only so much he could do as president; congressional action—through a constitutional amendment—was ultimately needed to put an end to slavery once and for all.

The Civil War years also saw the first discussions of how the rebel states would be reintegrated into the Union at war's end. Lincoln and congressional Republicans had very different views on how "Reconstruction" should be handled. Lincoln preferred a quick and relatively painless reconciliation, while some congressional Republicans advocated a more punitive approach. These different perspectives promised very different outcomes for Southern whites and blacks on issues like the return to power of the white governing authority, the abolition of slavery, and the civil rights (and potentially voting rights) of African Americans. Ultimately these disagreements between Lincoln and Republicans in Congress would foreshadow similar battles during Andrew Johnson's administration.

Over these years, the congressional GOP increasingly found its voice and institutional footing. When the war began the Republican Party was barely six years old. It had risen to power as an antislavery party, built specifically on opposition to slavery's *extension* into the western territories. While some Republicans were abolitionists, most were not. Many simply opposed the unfair economic and political advantages enjoyed by Southern slaveholders (whom they often referred to as the "Slave Power").[2] Over the course of the Civil War, congressional Republicans divided over slavery's continuation, the course and manner of abolition, and how Southern society should be reconstructed (if at all) after the war. Different perspectives would emerge— both moderate and radical—with each holding sway at different times. This intraparty conflict laid the groundwork for battles that would occupy Congress through Reconstruction and beyond.

Our focus in this chapter will be the politics of black civil rights during the Thirty-Seventh (1861–63) and Thirty-Eighth (1863–65) Congresses. To guide the analysis, we break the rest of the chapter into six sections, each dealing with a particular issue, bill, or constitutional amendment: Republican policy on slavery in 1861, the first year of the war; the passage of the two Confiscation Acts; the move to abolish slavery in the District of Columbia and federal territories; the passage of the Thirteenth Amendment; the en-

---

2. See Leonard L. Richards, *The Slave Power: The Free North and Southern Domination, 1780–1860* (Baton Rouge: Louisiana State University Press, 2000).

actment of the Freedmen's Bureau; and the back-and-forth between Lincoln and Congress over early Reconstruction policy.

Republicans and Slavery: Positions before and Early in the War

On November 6, 1860, Republican Abraham Lincoln of Illinois was elected president of the United States. His election followed a divisive presidential campaign where the Democrats were split by region, old-line Whigs asserted themselves in the border states, and Republicans enjoyed support almost exclusively in the North. Lincoln's victory in the four-way contest — against Democrats Stephen Douglas (IL) and John C. Breckenridge (KY) and Constitutional Unionist John Bell (TN) — was seemingly the last straw in a decades-long battle between slavery advocates and abolitionists. Specifically, the GOP had emerged as an organized response to the continued extension of slavery into the western territories. Over the preceding decades, those who defended slavery had won a series of important political battles on the Missouri Compromise, the War with Mexico, the Compromise of 1850, and the Kansas-Nebraska Act of 1854. But in the years directly preceding the outbreak of war, antislavery advocates began pushing back successfully. For example, they elected an antislavery advocate as Speaker of the House (Nathaniel Banks in 1856) and defeated slavery's extension into Kansas. As a consequence, slaveholding leaders from various Southern states had threatened to separate from the Union.[3]

Lincoln's election turned threats into action. He was on record only for opposing slavery's extension, not for its abolition. Southern "fire eaters," however, viewed a Republican president as a natural enemy of their "peculiar institution" — one who would inevitably seek slavery's total demise. Secession movements (and conventions) quickly followed. South Carolina was the first state to secede (on December 20, 1860), with Mississippi (January 9, 1861), Florida (January 10, 1861), Alabama (January 11, 1861), Georgia (January 19, 1861), Louisiana (January 26, 1861), and Texas (February 1, 1861) following soon thereafter. On February 4, 1861, these seven states convened in Montgomery, Alabama, to form the Confederate States of America.[4]

---

3. This history is covered nicely by David M. Potter, *The Impending Crisis: America before the Civil War, 1848–1861* (New York: Harper and Row, 1976).

4. See William C. Davis, *"A Government of Our Own": The Making of the Confederacy* (Baton Rouge: Louisiana State University Press, 1994).

Watching the Union dissolve before their eyes, some federal legislators used the waning days of the lame-duck session of the Thirty-Sixth Congress to seek a compromise that might put the Union back together as it was.[5] In the Senate, John J. Crittenden (A-KY) offered an elaborate proposal built on six constitutional amendments and four congressional resolutions that would (among other things) prohibit Congress from legislating on slavery, including in the District of Columbia; strengthen fugitive slave laws; and extend the Missouri Compromise 36°30′ line all the way to the Pacific Ocean, thereby allowing slavery's extension into any future territories south of the line.[6] The "Crittenden Compromise," as it became known, also stipulated that, once adopted, it could not be repealed or amended. Senate Republicans rejected the plan as too extreme, especially on the issue of extending slavery.[7]

In the House, Thomas Corwin (R-OH) offered a single constitutional amendment that he believed would satisfy the concerns of both Republicans and his slave-state colleagues. Proposed as a joint resolution (H.J. Res. 80), it read: "No amendment shall ever be made to the Constitution which will authorize or give to Congress the power to abolish or interfere, within any State, with the domestic institutions thereof, including that of persons held to labor or service by the laws of said State."[8]

Corwin's amendment was considered on February 27, 1861, but failed to

5. These various compromise efforts are described in detail in David M. Potter, *Lincoln and His Party in the Secession Crisis* (New Haven, CT: Yale University Press, 1942); Roy Franklin Nichols, *The Disruption of American Democracy* (New York: Macmillan, 1948); Kenneth M. Stampp, *And the War Came: The North and the Secession Crisis, 1860–61* (Baton Rouge: Louisiana State University Press, 1950); Daniel W. Crofts, *Lincoln and the Politics of Slavery: The Other Thirteenth Amendment and the Struggle to Save the Union* (Chapel Hill: University of North Carolina Press, 2016).

6. Crittenden was a longtime Whig senator who migrated to the American (Know Nothing) Party after the Whig Party collapsed. In the Thirty-Seventh Congress, he would become a member of the Unionist Party.

7. Crittenden's proposals would be repackaged at the Peace Conference of 1861, which met in Washington, DC, in February 1861. The Peace Conference was led by former president John Tyler of Virginia and included more than 130 Northern and Southern politicians. The Peace Conference's ultimate proposal differed little from the Crittenden Compromise and was rejected 28-7 in the Senate on March 4, 1861. For a detailed description of the Peace Conference, see Mark Tooley, *The Peace That Almost Was: The Forgotten Story of the 1861 Washington Peace Conference and the Final Attempt to Avert the Civil War* (Nashville, TN: Nelson Books, 2015).

8. *CG*, 36-2, 2/26/1861, 1236.

achieve the necessary two-thirds majority, 120-71.[9] The House reconsidered the vote the following day, and this time it garnered the necessary two-thirds, 133-65.[10] While a majority of Republicans voted against H.J. Res. 80 on February 28, a minority (46 of 109) voted with nearly every other House member to achieve the necessary vote total. Passage occurred largely because enough Republicans had been persuaded overnight either to vote in favor, after not participating on the earlier roll call, or to change their vote from nay to yea (since only 38 of 108 Republicans had voted yea on the initial roll call).[11]

The joint resolution then went to the Senate, where Stephen Douglas (D-IL) served as floor manager. There was no time to lose. The lame-duck session was soon to expire, and GOP senators like Charles Sumner (R-MA) sought to run out the clock. Eventually, after a short and fierce debate, a vote was taken on March 2, 1861, and Corwin's amendment garnered exactly the two-thirds necessary to pass, 24-12.[12] Just as in the House, a majority of Republicans voted against the joint resolution, but a large enough minority (eight of twenty) voted with pro-slavery members to achieve its passage.

President James Buchanan was delighted with the result and affixed his signature, even though it was not constitutionally necessary. President-Elect Lincoln also supported the Corwin amendment and advised members of Congress from his home state of Illinois to support it.[13] Lincoln would validate the joint resolution's content in his inaugural address, saying he believed he and his party had no "lawful right" or "inclination" to "interfere with the institution of slavery in the States where it exists."[14] Thus "the man who would later be known as the Great Emancipator," argues Daniel Crofts,

9. *CG*, 36-2, 2/27/1861, 1264.

10. *CG*, 36-2, 2/28/1861, 1285.

11. Of the eight additional GOP votes cast in favor of the Corwin amendment on February 28, four came from Republicans who did not vote on February 27, while four others came from Republicans who initially voted nay. Four additional votes in favor came from Democrats (two from the North and two from the South). On Republican attempts to ensure the passage of the Corwin amendment on February 28, see R. Alton Lee, "The Corwin Amendment in the Secession Crisis," *Ohio Historical Quarterly* 70 (1961): 1–26.

12. *CG*, 36-2, 3/2/1861, 1403.

13. Leonard L. Richards, *Who Freed the Slaves?: The Fight over the Thirteenth Amendment* (Chicago: University of Chicago Press, 2015), 23. Daniel Crofts also contends there is substantial circumstantial evidence that Lincoln "worked behind the scenes to get the amendment passed." Crofts, *Lincoln and the Politics of Slavery*, 231.

14. For the full text of Lincoln's first inaugural address, see http://avalon.law.yale.edu /19th_century/lincoln1.asp.

"first came to power having just accepted a constitutional amendment designed to prevent any attack on slavery" where it was already entrenched.[15] Regardless, the Corwin amendment was not ratified by the requisite number of states to become law. Only Kentucky voted to approve the amendment (on April 4, 1861) before hostilities started between North and South. Thereafter, only five states pursued some form of ratification.[16]

Why did a significant portion of congressional Republicans support the Corwin amendment? Some felt that its narrowly written text was consistent with general GOP ideology, which was predicated on eliminating slavery's spread but not on its abolition. Others backed the amendment to support Southern Unionists and stop secession movements in the remaining slave states.[17] Eight such states—Virginia, North Carolina, Tennessee, Arkansas, Kentucky, Maryland, Missouri, and Delaware—were still firmly in the Union, and support for the amendment was meant to reassure their leaders that their property in slaves would not be threatened.[18]

Confederate forces fired on Fort Sumter on April 12, 1861, escalating the North-South conflict and hastening the move toward war. Lincoln immediately called for 75,000 volunteers to support the federal cause. And over the next two months, four more Southern states seceded and joined the Confederacy: Virginia, Arkansas, North Carolina, and Tennessee.[19]

In response, in July 1861 Lincoln called an emergency session of Congress. Without members from the states that had seceded, the Thirty-Seventh Congress was small and dominated by Republicans. Despite the violence, the party's position on slavery did not immediately change. Keeping the remaining slave states—Kentucky, Missouri, Maryland, and Dela-

15. Crofts, *Lincoln and the Politics of Slavery*, 236.

16. These five were Ohio on May 13, 1861 (ratification would be rescinded on March 31, 1864); Rhode Island on May 31, 1861; Maryland on January 10, 1862; the "Restored Government of Virginia" (much of which would become the state of West Virginia) on February 13, 1862; and Illinois on February 14, 1862 (although there were conflicting decisions between the convention—which ratified the amendment—and a popular referendum that did not and possibly invalidated the convention decision). See Crofts, *Lincoln and the Politics of Slavery*, 243–54.

17. A roll-call analysis (logistic regression) of Republican votes finds that first (negative) and second (positive) NOMINATE dimensions are statistically significant, with Republican members nearest to the Democrats on both dimensions being more likely to support the Corwin amendment.

18. Crofts, *Lincoln and the Politics of Slavery*, 215, 226–27.

19. Dates of secession were April 17 (Virginia), May 6 (Arkansas), May 20 (North Carolina), and June 8 (Tennessee).

ware — in the Union and their male inhabitants out of the Confederate army continued to drive GOP thinking.[20]

As a result, despite their small numbers, Unionist members from the four remaining slave states wielded considerable power. This became clear after the First Battle of Bull Run, on July 21, 1861, when the Confederate army routed the Union forces and forced them back to Washington, DC. After Bull Run the Republicans were, according to Herman Belz, "chastened by defeat and aware more than ever of the necessity of holding the border states in the Union."[21] This led two border-state members — Unionist John Crittenden (KY) in the House and War Democrat Andrew Johnson (TN) in the Senate — to offer separate, but very similar, resolutions in their respective chambers. Together these resolutions specified the "war aims" of the Union.

The texts of the Crittenden (first) and Johnson (second) Resolutions were as follows:

[Clause 1] *Resolved by the House of Representatives of the Congress of the United States*, That the present deplorable civil war has been forced upon the country by disunionists of the southern States now in revolt against the constitutional Government, and in arms around the capital.

[Clause 2] That in this national emergency Congress, banishing all feeling of mere passion or resentment, will recollect only its duty to the whole country; this war is not waged upon our part in any spirit of oppression, or for any purpose of conquest or subjugation, or purpose of overthrowing or interfering with the rights or established institutions of those States, but to defend and maintain the supremacy of the Constitution and to preserve the Union with all the dignity, equality, and rights of the several States unimpaired; and that as soon as these objects are accomplished the war ought to cease.[22]

Resolved, That the present deplorable civil war has been forced upon the country by the disunionists of the southern States now in revolt against the constitutional Government and in arms around the capital; that in this national emergency Congress, banishing all feeling of mere passion or resentment will recollect all of its duty to the whole country; that this war is not prosecuted upon our part in any spirit of oppression, nor for any purpose of conquest or subjugation, nor for the purpose of overthrowing

20. See Harris, *Lincoln and the Border States.*

21. Herman Belz, *Reconstructing the Union: Theory and Policy during the Civil War* (Ithaca, NY: Cornell University Press, 1969), 24.

22. *CG*, 37-1, 7/22/1861, 223.

or interfering with the rights or established institutions of those States, but to defend and maintain the supremacy of the Constitution and all laws made in pursuance thereof, and to preserve the Union, with all the dignity, equality, and rights of the several States unimpaired, that as soon as these objects are accomplished the war ought to cease.[23]

Both resolutions blamed the Southern states for the war, while specifying the Union's prime goal as suppressing the "disunionist" insurrection, preserving the Constitution, and maintaining the rights and institutions of the states as they were before hostilities began. More to the point, as Belz notes, the resolutions were "supposed to convey that slavery was not, under any circumstances, to be interfered with, nor the rebellious states divested of any of their power or privileges."[24]

President Lincoln, fully aware of the importance of keeping the border states in the Union, strongly supported both resolutions.[25] As a result, when voting commenced, congressional Republicans fell in line. On July 22, in the House, both parts of the Crittenden Resolution passed by near-unanimous margins, with no dissenting GOP votes on the first clause and only two on the second.[26] The same was true of the Johnson Resolution three days later: it passed easily, with only one of twenty-five Republican senators defecting.[27] Even amid the pressure to maintain a united front and support their commander-in-chief, however, two dozen Republicans across the two chambers abstained on the resolution votes.[28]

A Shift on Slavery: The Confiscation Acts

Through July 1861, congressional Republicans had largely worked to protect slavery where it existed. But that was about to change. The exigencies of war forced the slavery issue into the political sphere in new and different ways, providing strategic politicians with the ability to erode the traditional

23. *CG*, 37-1, 7/25/1861, 257.

24. Belz, *Reconstructing the Union*, 25.

25. Richards, *Who Freed the Slaves?*, 28–29; Harris, *Lincoln and the Border States*, 80–81.

26. *CG*, 37-1, 7/22/1861, 223. The votes were 121-2 and 117-2, respectively.

27. *CG*, 37-1, 7/25/1861, 265. The vote was 30-5. Lyman Trumbull (IL) was the only GOP defection.

28. Many of these members would go on to adopt extreme (punitive) positions on postwar Reconstruction policy. See Belz, *Reconstructing the Union*, 27; Richards, *Who Freed the Slaves?*, 29.

view of maintaining slavery rights at all costs. As the war progressed, the notion that the Union could squelch a rebellion by eleven Southern states while assuming that the legalities governing slavery had not changed became increasingly untenable. While Crittenden, Johnson, and Lincoln preferred to keep slavery "in a box" and somehow fight and conclude a civil war that would return the country to its prewar institutions, events around them would shatter these naive hopes. Sympathy for complete abolition was growing among Republican lawmakers. Two Confiscation Acts demonstrate their shifting preferences.[29]

As the Union army crept into Confederate territory, advance forces began to encounter slaves, many of them "fugitives." A key moment came on the evening of May 24, 1861, when three slaves attached to the 115th Virginia Militia at Hampton Roads decided to escape. They paddled across the James River and approached Union-controlled Fortress Monroe at the mouth of the Chesapeake Bay. Benjamin Butler, in command at the fort, interviewed the escapees and discovered they were helping reinforce rebel batteries nearby. Butler responded by treating the slaves as "contraband of war." When approached by a Confederate emissary, under flag of truce, who sought the slaves' return under the Fugitive Slave Act of 1850, Butler replied that the law could be invoked only by US citizens.[30] This was a radical position at the time; most Union commanders were turning away fugitive slaves or returning them to their owners.

Butler's decision, although it distressed President Lincoln, found considerable support within the GOP. Secretary of War Simon Cameron, for example, publicly backed Butler. The decision had far-reaching consequences, as word spread and slaves began "freeing themselves" by leaving their plantations, walking north, and seeking refuge at Fortress Monroe and other points behind Union lines.[31] Thus slaves' pursuit of freedom, and their daily

29. Foundational works on the Confiscation Acts include Leonard P. Curry, *Blueprint for Modern America: Nonmilitary Legislation of the First Civil War Congress* (Nashville, TN: Vanderbilt University Press, 1968), 75–100; Silvana R. Siddali, *From Property to Person: Slavery and the Confiscation Acts, 1861–1862* (Baton Rouge: Louisiana State University Press, 2005); John Syrett, *The Civil War Confiscation Acts: Failing to Reconstruct the South* (New York: Fordham University Press, 2005); Daniel W. Hamilton, *The Limits of Sovereignty: Property Confiscation in the Union and the Confederacy during the Civil War* (Chicago: University of Chicago Press, 2007).

30. More specifically, Butler stated that the Fugitive Slave Act "did not affect a foreign country, which Virginia claimed to be." James Oakes, *Freedom National: The Destruction of Slavery in the United States, 1861–1865* (New York: Norton, 2012), 95–96.

31. Richards, *Who Freed the Slaves?*, 28–29.

appearance in Union camps, made slavery much more than a sterile public policy issue.

The second event was the First Battle of Bull Run. In the aftermath of the humiliating Union defeat, several congressional Republicans wanted to know what went wrong. Through interviews with Union troops involved in the battle, they learned that slaves supported Confederate forces in various ways—by building and maintaining fortifications, resupplying ammunition, tending the injured, maintaining draft animals, and cooking and dispensing food—freeing white Southerners to kill Union troops.[32]

This information gathering helped many Republicans reenvision the slavery issue in more pragmatic terms. Slavery was no longer just an "institution" that was established in the Constitution and under the purview of the individual states. It was now a major factor contributing to the overall effectiveness of Southern military forces—and perhaps influencing the eventual outcome of the war. As a result, Republicans began asking themselves some hard questions. As Leonard Richards writes, "[Republicans] had voted for the Crittenden and Johnson Resolutions. They had agreed that Congress had no right to legislate against slavery in a state. But what about individuals who allowed their slaves to be used against the United States? Couldn't such traitors be punished? Didn't the laws of war authorize the seizure of any property, including slave property, used to aid the war effort directly?"[33]

In answering yes to these questions, congressional Republicans had reached a turning point. They were increasingly ready to question slavery's future in a postwar union. The result was the First Confiscation Act. Drafted by Sen. Lyman Trumbull (R-IL), chairman of the Judiciary Committee, the underlying bill (S. 25) sought to confiscate property used for insurrectionary purposes. Specifically, section 4 of the eventual law eliminated any claims of individuals on persons (slaves) who were employed directly or indirectly in hostile services against the United States. Thus, individuals in the South, rather than states, were the targets of the confiscatory language.

While radical Republicans saw the First Confiscation Act as a step toward their preferred outcome—general emancipation for slaves—the provisions of the law were narrow.[34] Thanks to amending activity in the House, the

32. Siddali, *From Property to Person*, 76–77; Syrett, *Civil War Confiscation Acts*, 4; Richards, *Who Freed the Slaves?*, 30.

33. Richards, *Who Freed the Slaves?*, 31.

34. Although historians often note Republican factions during and after the Civil War, explicit caucuses of radicals, moderates, and conservatives did not exist. And quantitative historical scholars have long sought to use roll-call votes as a means of identifying these

FIGURE 1. Sen. Lyman Trumbull (R-IL). Library of Congress, Prints & Photographs Division, LC-DIG-cwpbh-00478.

legislation applied only to slaves used in support of the rebellion. And as John Syrett notes, these slaves "did not go free under the act; those claiming their services — the owners — simply forfeited their claim to them. The only liberty granted to [confiscated slaves] was not to remain slaves of rebels."[35]

While border-state Unionists and Democrats argued against the measure — on constitutional grounds and as a strategic prelude to emancipa-

---

implicit factions, without reaching a clear consensus. For a summary of these efforts, see Allan G. Bogue, *The Congressman's Civil War* (New York: Cambridge University Press, 1989), 132–37. Nevertheless, the description by Hans Trefousse quoted in chapter 1 provides a useful shorthand.

35. Syrett, *Civil War Confiscation Acts*, 6.

tion—it passed easily: 61-48 in the House on August 3, 1861, and 24-11 in the Senate two days later.[36] Near-uniform Democratic and Unionist opposition was trumped by overwhelming GOP support, as fifty-seven of sixty-four Republicans in the House and twenty-three of twenty-four in the Senate voted yea. Lincoln signed the bill, but he thought congressional Republicans were moving too quickly. He was concerned that the measure lacked bipartisan support and could be struck down by the pro-slavery Supreme Court led by Chief Justice Roger Taney.[37] And while Lincoln felt compelled to back his fellow partisans, he also did not pressure his attorney general, Edward Bates, to enforce the law. (And Bates, a conservative, had little interest in doing so.) As a result, the First Confiscation Act was mostly symbolic, since Union generals were allowed to follow it or not. Some might behave as Butler did and confiscate, while others, like George McClellan, Don Carlos Buell, and Henry Halleck, all with Democratic leanings, were free to honor the Fugitive Slave Act and continue returning slaves to their Confederate masters.[38]

External pressure for emancipation continued, however, and it was initially linked to the border state of Missouri, which was undergoing its own civil war. Support for the rebellion was strong in Missouri, as pro-Confederate guerrillas fought pro-Union forces for control in various parts of the state.[39] Throughout July and August 1861, Major General John C. Frémont, Union commander in the West, struggled to turn the tide and eventually resorted to force to restore order, declaring martial law throughout the state and stipulating that any individuals aiding the rebellion would have all real and personal property confiscated for public use and their slaves set free.

Frémont's proclamation—with its "emancipation clause"—shocked Northerners. While radical Republicans approved of his boldness, President Lincoln was not pleased. He asked Frémont to amend his order so that it

---

36. *CG*, 37-1, 8/3/1861, 431; 8/5/1861, 434.

37. In addition, according to William Harris, "[Lincoln] believed that it would create more harm than good in that it would cause the rebels to fight harder and would hurt the Union cause in the border states." See William C. Harris, *Lincoln and Congress* (Carbondale: Southern Illinois University Press, 2017), 23.

38. Siddali, *From Property to Person*, 91; Richards, *Who Freed the Slaves?*, 31–32.

39. See Michael Fellman, *Inside War: The Guerrilla Conflict in Missouri during the American Civil War* (New York: Oxford University Press, 1989). Pro-Confederate support was so strong in Missouri—as well as Kentucky—that the Confederate Congress recognized rump governments organized in these states and provided them with representation. See Kenneth C. Martis, *The Historical Atlas of the Congress of the Confederate States of America: 1861–1865* (New York: Simon and Schuster, 1994).

complied with the First Confiscation Act, which allowed the seizure of only those slaves who were involved in military operations against the United States and made no mention of "freedom" for them on confiscation. Lincoln's response was again driven by concerns about losing the border states, as he received scores of letters from Unionists in Kentucky and Missouri condemning Frémont's action. Frémont, however, refused to comply with Lincoln's request. As a result, in September Lincoln revoked Frémont's order, and six weeks later he relieved him of his command and installed Henry Halleck, an opponent of slave confiscation, in his place.

Lincoln had effectively squelched Frémont's emancipatory initiative and lowered the temperature in the border states, but not without consequences. Support for emancipation was growing in the North, and radical Republicans were becoming frustrated with their president and increasingly eager for positive action.[40] Lincoln was blindsided yet again in December 1861 as the second session of the Thirty-Seventh Congress opened, when Secretary of War Cameron issued his annual report. In it Cameron strongly supported property confiscation (including slaves). He went further, calling for slaves to be armed and used in battle against the Confederates. Once again, Lincoln had to defuse the situation. He directed Cameron to collect all existing copies of his report and excise the offending text before reissuing it. A month later he removed Cameron from his position and sent him to Russia as an American diplomat.[41]

Radical Republicans in Congress had seen enough and were now willing to push back against Lincoln's hesitant approach on emancipation.[42] Their first effort occurred in the House and was largely symbolic, but important. William Holman (D-IN) sought to have the House renew the Crittenden Resolution — maintaining the Constitution and the rights of the states and thus preserving slavery where it existed. Much had changed between July and December 1861, however. Thaddeus Stevens (R-PA), chairman of

40. The Frémont episode in Missouri, Lincoln's response, and their various repercussions are discussed in Siddali, *From Property to Person*, 95–109; Syrett, *Civil War Confiscation Acts*, 7–12; Richards, *Who Freed the Slaves?*, 32–37; and Harris, *Lincoln and Border States*, 98–106.

41. Siddali, *From Property to Person*, 117–19; Richards, *Who Freed the Slaves?*, 40–41. Richards notes that Lincoln's decision to remove Cameron was not exclusively due to his overreach on arming slaves, but also likely involved other matters like "mismanagement, corruption, and abuse of patronage."

42. Robert Harris notes that, after Lincoln's rejection of Frémont's initiative, radical Republican leaders were ready "to make emancipation an objective in the war when Congress assembled in December." See Harris, *Lincoln and Congress*, 26.

the Ways and Means Committee, moved to table Holman's motion, which passed 71-65, with seventy of eighty-eight Republicans voting in favor.[43] This was a seismic shift as Republicans who had almost uniformly supported the Crittenden Resolution in July were now on record as opposing the prewar status quo. Slavery — not just extension of slavery or slavery utilized in military operations against the Union — had thus become a viable target.

The second effort began in the Senate and involved a new confiscation bill. Republicans had grown frustrated with the narrowness of the First Confiscation Act and the lack of enforcement by many Union commanders. To make their wishes clear to generals who were actively turning away fugitive slaves, they sought a tougher law.[44] In early December Lyman Trumbull introduced a bill (S. 151) that would go far beyond the measure he had ushered through to enactment earlier in the year.[45] S. 151 sought to confiscate *all* real and personal property of those supporting the rebellion, for all time (beyond the life of the person judged guilty). The Union military would assist with confiscation in areas where the US courts could not operate. Slaves confiscated would be declared free and, should they choose, could pursue colonization in "some tropical country" arranged by the president. (This was a concession to GOP moderates, like President Lincoln, who favored colonization.) Other property seized would be sold, and the proceeds would fund the war and compensate loyal citizens for property damage related to the rebellion.

Trumbull and his supporters soon realized that their preferences on confiscation would not carry the day. Conservatives — Democrats and Unionists, by and large, but also some Republicans like Orville Browning (IL) and Jacob Collamer (VT) — attacked the bill's constitutionality, especially its disregard for private property rights. For conservatives, property could be seized only after an individual was tried for treason — and only for life. They blasted Trumbull for his willingness to confiscate in a blanket way through legislative edict and to entirely disavow the role of the judiciary. Overall,

43. *CG*, 37-2, 12/4/1861, 15. A roll-call analysis (logistic regression) of Republican votes finds that the first (positive) and second (negative) NOMINATE dimensions are statistically significant, with Republican members furthest from the Democrats on both dimensions being more likely to support tabling the Holman motion.

44. The politics of the Second Confiscation Act are discussed in Curry, *Blueprint for Modern America*, 75–100; Syrett, *Civil War Confiscation Acts*, 20–72; Siddali, *From Property to Person*, 120–250; and Hamilton, *Limits of Sovereignty*, 20–81.

45. *CG*, 37-2, 12/4/1861, 18–19.

as Daniel Hamilton notes, conservatives presented a "cohesive ideological counterattack that successfully drove a wedge between moderate and radical Republicans."[46]

John Sherman (OH), Henry Wilson (MA), and Daniel Clark (NH) would lead the moderate Republican opposition by fashioning a substitute that limited property confiscation to civil and military leaders in the Confederacy, thus excluding "ordinary" Southerners who, moderates believed, were largely coerced by elites to participate in the rebellion. Their substitute also proposed a formal role for the judiciary and stipulated that while property could be seized and immediately put to use, transfer of title could occur only after individual judicial rulings. Slaves, however, would be set free on confiscation; whether subsequent judicial rulings would also be required to "validate" their freedom was not stated (and thus open to legal interpretation).

Conservatives pushed their own substitute bill, written by Jacob Collamer, which required that the judiciary—rather the legislature—handle confiscation and that individual treason trials accompany each case of property seizure. On conviction of the party in question, property could be confiscated only for life—not permanently.

Eventually all sides agreed to the creation of a select committee, with Daniel Clark as chair, to draft a new bill that might garner majority support.[47] The committee used Collamer's conservative bill as a starting point and added elements that would appeal mostly to moderates: all property of those aiding the rebellion would be forfeited upon a conviction (but only for life); property of civil and military leaders could be seized and held upon completion of judicial proceedings; slaves of rebels could be set free if, sixty days after the president issued a warning proclamation to swear allegiance to the Union, it was ignored; freed slaves could pursue voluntary colonization; and slaves could be enlisted in the US military. The bill (S. 310) was reported on May 14, 1862.[48]

Save for the provision to arm escaped slaves, radicals were largely unhappy with Clark's bill. After a week of debate, they successfully moved for a

46. Hamilton, *Limits of Sovereignty*, 48.

47. The vote to create the committee, on May 6, was 24-14, with Republicans voting 15-13. Members of the committee included Clark, Jacob Collamer (R-VT), James Sherman (R-OH), Henry Wilson (R-MA), Edgar Cowan (R-PA), Ira Harris (R-NY), John Brooks Henderson (D-MO), and Waitman Willey (U-VA). Trumbull refused to serve on the committee, believing it would accomplish little. See Syrett, *Civil War Confiscation Acts*, 48.

48. *CG*, 37-2, 5/14/1862, 2112, 2165.

postponement.[49] The Senate then moved on to other business and the House took center stage.

The House had shuffled along on confiscation since March, with little to show for its efforts. Finally, on May 14 Thomas Eliot (R-MA), chairman of the select committee charged with developing legislation, reported two bills, one dealing with confiscation (H.R. 471) and the other with emancipation (H.R. 472).[50] Both measures tended toward radicalism. The confiscation measure allowed for the immediate seizure of all property of civil and military leaders of the Confederacy, authorized the president to issue a proclamation of allegiance and give rebels sixty days to comply or else all of their property would be seized, and subjected all property to limited judicial proceedings (but did not require trials of property owners). The emancipation measure freed all slaves of owners who aided the rebellion and did not require judicial action.

The following week was set aside for debate, and thirty-seven speeches were made in a series of marathon sessions.[51] Finally, on May 26 the House passed the confiscation bill (H.R. 471) 82-68, with Republicans voting 79-8.[52] Later that day, after defeating four amendments, the Republicans sought to pass the emancipation bill (H.R. 472). To their dismay, the measure was defeated 74-78.[53] Fifteen Republicans voted in opposition, seven more than on the confiscation bill.[54] The perception in the chamber was that the bill was too sweeping for some (conservative) Republicans, who feared their constituents might view its provisions as too radical.[55]

On June 23, 1862, the Senate took up the House confiscation bill (H.R. 471), and Clark immediately moved his Senate bill (S. 310) as a substitute. Four days of debate followed, with radicals complaining that Clark's substitute was ineffective as a confiscation measure. Clark responded that he

---

49. *CG*, 37-2, 5/21/1862, 2253-54.

50. *CG*, 37-2, 5/14/1862, 2128.

51. Curry, *Blueprint for Modern America*, 89.

52. *CG*, 37-2, 5/26/1862, 2361.

53. *CG*, 37-2, 5/26/1862, 2363.

54. A roll-call analysis (logistic regression) of Republican votes on the emancipation bill finds that the first (positive) and second (negative) NOMINATE dimensions are statistically significant. This suggests that Republicans who were nearest ideologically to the Democrats on both dimensions voted nay. These were members who could be labeled conservative Republicans.

55. Curry, *Blueprint for Modern America*, 89-90; Heather Cox Richardson, *The Greatest Nation of the Earth: Republican Economic Policies during the Civil War* (Cambridge, MA: Harvard University Press, 1997), 224.

would not support the House bill and insisted that only his substitute could be enacted. Finally, on June 28, the Senate passed Clark's substitute 21-17; Republicans were split (15-15), with half favoring the more radical elements in the House confiscation bill, which left the Democrats and Unionists to decide the matter.[56] The Senate then passed the amended H.R. 471 bill (encapsulating the text of the S. 310 substitute) 28-13; most Republicans (twenty-seven of thirty) voted yea, with most of the dissenters from the previous roll call "coming home" (albeit grudgingly).[57]

There was action still to come, however. On July 3 the House received the amended H.R. 471 from the Senate and voted overwhelmingly (8-123) not to concur.[58] Five days later the Senate voted 28-10 to insist on its amendment and asked for a conference committee to sort out the chambers' difficulties. House members agreed to the request.[59]

The conference committee got to work and reported back a bill on July 11.[60] The revised measure was clearly a compromise designed to avoid deadlock.[61] Sections 1–4 and 10–14 of the amended H.R. 417 — which provided for punishments and fines for those committing treason or involved in insurrection; forbade the return of fugitive slaves; allowed the president to colonize former slaves abroad (should they wish) and to employ them in putting down the rebellion; granted the president the ability to pardon rebels; and placed enforcement in the hands of the federal courts — were left largely intact. Sections 5–8 were taken from the original H.R. 417. They allowed the president to seize the property of six classes of civilian and military leaders of the Confederacy as well as other rebels (conditional on a proclamation giving them sixty days to declare allegiance to the United States). Confiscated property could be used immediately but would ultimately require judicial proceedings before title was permanently transferred. Section 9 was the most controversial, holding that all slaves of rebels who were captured or escaped, or were behind Union military lines in former rebel areas, were considered "forever free."

56. *CG*, 37-2, 6/28/1862, 2996.

57. *CG*, 37-2, 6/28/1862, 3006.

58. *CG*, 37-2, 7/3/1862, 3107.

59. *CG*, 37-2, 7/8/1862, 3166, 3178, 3187–88.

60. *CG*, 37-2, 7/8/1862, 3166, 3178; 7/11/1862, 3187–88. The Senate conferees included Clark, Ira Harris (R-NY), and Joseph Wright (U-IN), while the House conferees were Eliot, James Wilson (R-IA), and Erastus Corning (D-NY).

61. Five of the six conferees signed the conference report. Only Corning withheld his signature. See *CG*, 37-2, 7/11/1862, 3188.

Conservatives in the House, led by Robert Mallory (U-KY) and Samuel S. Cox (D-OH), complained that the conference committee went beyond its mandate and created (in sections 5–9) what amounted to new legislation. But their complaints were in vain as the House proceeded to pass the conference report 82-42, with seventy-eight of seventy-nine Republicans voting in favor.[62] The following day, July 12, the Senate considered the conference report, and the result was the same: it passed 28-13, with twenty-seven of twenty-nine Republicans voting yea.[63]

One hurdle remained: President Lincoln had reservations about the measure and was contemplating a veto. His chief concern was over the bill's treatment of private property. Lincoln believed that property seizure should not extend beyond the life of the offender, and GOP leaders acted quickly to address his concern. The solution was first implemented in the Senate when Clark moved an amendment to a joint resolution (H.J. Res. 110) introduced by Horace Maynard (U-TN). The Maynard resolution was meant to be a straightforward clarification of the confiscation legislation—that it was to be prospective rather than retrospective (a noncontroversial interpretation)—to which Clark offered the following amendment: "Nor shall any punishment or proceedings under said act be so construed as to work a forfeiture of the real estate of the offender beyond his natural life."[64]

Clark explained that his amendment was intended to prevent a possible Lincoln veto. Nevertheless Lyman Trumbull, Henry Lane (R-IN), Preston King (R-NY), and Benjamin Wade (R-OH) strongly objected to the amendment's weakening of the bill.[65] Yet the Senate proceeded to pass the Clark amendment 25-15 as twenty-two of thirty Republicans voted yea.[66] Maynard's joint resolution then passed without a roll call, and the measure moved to the House. There the amendment was concurred in 83-21, with seventy-four of seventy-nine Republicans voting in favor.[67]

62. *CG*, 37-2, 7/11/1862, 3266–67. The only Republican to oppose the conference report was Bradley Granger (MI).

63. *CG*, 37-2, 7/12/1862, 3276. The two Republicans who opposed the conference report were Orville Browning (IL) and Edgar Cowan (PA). Note that the initial vote tally was 27-12. Two others—Timothy Howe (R-WI) and Benjamin Stark (D-OR)—were recorded later (as yea and nay votes, respectively). See *CG*, 37-2, 7/12/1862, 3276, 3287.

64. *CG*, 37-2, 7/16/1862, 3374.

65. *CG*, 37-2, 7/16/1862, 3374–77.

66. *CG*, 37-2, 7/16/1862, 3383.

67. *CG*, 37-2, 7/16/1862, 3400.

With the "explanatory resolution" now in place, Lincoln signed the conference bill, making the Second Confiscation Act law.[68] From the radicals' perspective it was a disappointment. They saw aggressive and punitive property confiscation, led by Congress, as a means to spur true social and economic reform in the South. By the end of the process, however, their hopes had been dashed. As Daniel Hamilton writes, "The moderates had . . . won the crucial battle over whether confiscation would be legislative or judicial. Now [with the explanatory resolution adopted], not only would confiscation take place one trial at a time, but even after conviction all the government could seize was cumbersome life estate in the offender's land."[69] To the radicals, this method of property confiscation was unworkable and unenforceable. Ensuring that decisions about property would be made by the courts rather than Congress would, as we show, prove to be a reliable strategy for moderates and conservatives.

Regardless of radical complaints, Section 9 was clearly bold in declaring that rebel-owned slaves who were captured, escaped, or in rebel areas occupied by Union forces were to be "forever free." On its face this was a clear departure for congressional Republicans, who only one year earlier had supported the Crittenden and Johnson Resolutions. But the actual force of the Second Confiscation Act regarding emancipation was more limited. John Syrett notes,

> If the prospect of confiscation encouraged hopes of emancipation, the law itself made it difficult to free slaves. Under the act, slaves of rebels were free only when they came within the military's control. The assumption was that emancipation would advance along with the army. However, slaves could be freed individually or in groups only when a federal court found their owners to be rebels; the military had no power to adjudicate the matter themselves. Doubts even arose about whether the military had the power to transfer slaves to federal courts for such proceedings. The second act would have required hundreds of thousands of trials of individual masters. Furthermore, it did not affect slaves owned by non-rebels who could prove they had given no aid to the rebellion or by those who swore allegiance to the North, even minutes before the act became law.

68. He also passed along the draft of his would-be veto message to Congress, laying out his views and arguments. Curry, *Blueprint for America*, 98.

69. Hamilton, *Limits of Sovereignty*, 76.

It also omitted a method for resolving the issue if slaves claimed freedom under the act while their masters insisted on their loyalty to the Union, a conflict that seemed likely to arise.[70]

A more fundamental question also remained unanswered: Could Congress legally legislate on slavery, which the Supreme Court ruled in *Dred Scott* to be constitutionally protected?[71]

The Second Confiscation Act was mostly symbolic. It underscored that the old status quo — allowing slavery where it existed — was gone forever. Returning to the Union "as it was" would be impossible. Lincoln was slow to accept this perspective early in the war — he fretted about keeping the border states in the Union — but he was increasingly persuaded as the war progressed. Emancipation, he came to believe, would require more than a simple act of Congress. Instead, according to Syrett, "a more effective and constitutional means to that end, for instance by executive proclamation, had to be found."[72]

Lincoln, Congress, and Emancipation

Lincoln's singular goal at the outset of the sectional conflict was to preserve the Union.[73] While he abhorred slavery, Lincoln believed that respecting established constitutional norms, thereby quelling the fears of those who owned slaves, was right legally and politically. As we have already noted, Lincoln supported the Corwin amendment, backed the Crittenden and Johnson Resolutions, and was on record as willing to accept slavery where it existed if it meant keeping the Union intact.

Thanks to the exigencies of war — fugitive slaves entering Union military camps; Union forces capturing rebel territory and coming in contact with slaves; and commanders and cabinet officials issuing unilateral directives — and congressional action (the First Confiscation Act), Lincoln's views would evolve. He came to believe the emancipation of slaves in loyal areas should be gradual and compensated, not unlike the way many North-

70. Syrett, *Civil War Confiscation Acts*, 57. Similar points are made in Hamilton, *Limits of Sovereignty*, 74, and Siddali, *From Property to Person*, 233–34.

71. On *Dred Scott*, see Potter, *Impending Crisis*, 267–96.

72. Syrett, *Civil War Confiscation Acts*, 58.

73. For Lincoln's evolving views on emancipation over time, see Edna Greene Medford, *Lincoln and Emancipation* (Carbondale: Southern Illinois University Press, 2015).

ern states had handled emancipation in the nation's early years. In addition, he held that colonization outside the United States, in a country like Liberia or Haiti, should accompany such emancipation. Like many of his generation, Lincoln thought blacks and whites could not live together and remain at peace. He believed that conflict between the races would naturally arise and that only racial intermixing or complete dominance by one race would result. Neither of these outcomes was desirable, so colonization seemed the best alternative.[74]

In October 1861 Lincoln proposed emancipating slaves over thirty years with compensation funded by a US bond issue. He pitched this plan to officials in Delaware, the border state with the fewest slaves. While it generated some support, compensated emancipation ran afoul of pro-slavery interests in the state legislature. Lincoln then took his case to the Congress, and on two occasions (December 3, 1861, in his annual message, and March 6, 1862, in a special message) asked for federal money to be set aside for states that pursued a policy of gradual emancipation with voluntary colonization. As Leonard Richards notes, "For Lincoln . . . [t]his was not simply a humanitarian gesture. . . . It was a means for shortening the war, for if the border states abolished slavery it would reduce the lure that the Confederacy had for them, and that in turn would cause the rebellion to collapse."[75]

Lincoln then organized a private meeting at the White House in which he tried to persuade border-state representatives to support his plan. In the end Lincoln found himself with few enthusiastic supporters.[76] Nonetheless, he did make inroads with some fellow partisans. Congressional Republicans were slowly endorsing forms of emancipation—the confiscation laws were being developed at the same time, and on March 13, 1862, the GOP passed a law preventing US military commanders from returning fugitive slaves to their masters. They were also open to the president's plan on compensated emancipation, even if many lacked enthusiasm for it.[77]

---

74. On Lincoln's beliefs regarding colonization, along with those of his contemporaries, see Phillip W. Magness and Sebastian N. Page, *Colonization after Emancipation: Lincoln and the Movement for Black Resettlement* (Columbia: University of Missouri Press, 2011).

75. Richards, *Who Freed the Slaves?*, 55.

76. Harris, *Lincoln and the Border States*, 166–69; Eric Foner, *The Fiery Trial: Abraham Lincoln and American Slavery* (New York: Norton, 2010), 197–98.

77. The fugitive-slave law (12 *Stat.* 354) was based on H.R. 299, which passed 95-51 in the House (with Republicans voting 91-0) and 29-0 in the Senate (with Republicans voting 27-0). See *CG*, 37-2, 2/25/1862, 955; 3/10/1862, 1143.

H.J. Res. 48, introduced by Roscoe Conkling (R-NY) on March 10, 1862, proposed to implement compensated, gradual emancipation in line with the president's special message to Congress. It stated:

> *Resolved by the Senate and House of Representatives of the United States in Congress assembled,* That the United States ought to cooperate with any State which may adopt gradual abolishment of slavery, giving to such State pecuniary aid, to be sued by such State in its discretion, to compensate for the inconveniences, public and private, produced by such change of system.[78]

Conkling was able to secure the two-thirds majority necessary to suspend the rules, and after two days of debate and the defeat of several dilatory motions, the House passed the resolution 97-35, with Republicans voting as a unified bloc (85-0).[79] The Senate spent several days debating the measure, and on April 2 it passed 32-10, with all Republicans voting in favor.[80] Congressional Republicans were now on record as endorsing compensated emancipation.

Almost simultaneously, Congress debated a more targeted compensated emancipation bill, directed at the District of Columbia. Introduced in the Senate by Lot Morrill (R-ME) on March 12, 1862, the bill (S. 108) sought to abolish slavery in the District, compensate loyal slaveholders up to $300 for each slave freed, establish penalties for those who attempted to reenslave those freed, and create a three-man board of commissioners to rule on all claims up to a total outlay of $1,000,000.[81] The $300 payment per slave was suggested by Lincoln and Salmon Chase, secretary of the treasury; Lincoln also wanted emancipation to be gradual, but congressional leaders balked at this request.[82]

Border-state representatives opposed the measure, continuing their opposition to compensated emancipation, and raised the (now familiar) concern regarding conflict between the races should blacks be allowed to live freely among whites. Conservative GOP senators, reflecting public opinion, shared this concern.[83] In response, Garrett Davis (U-KY) offered an amend-

78. *CG*, 37-2, 3/10/1862, 1149.
79. *CG*, 37-2, 3/11/1862, 1179.
80. *CG*, 37-2, 4/2/1862, 1496.
81. *CG*, 37-2, 3/12/1862, 1191.
82. Richards, *Who Freed the Slaves?*, 58.
83. As William Harris notes: "Senators on both sides of the aisle, especially those from the

ment to require that freed slaves be colonized outside the United States and
that $100,000 be allocated out of the Treasury for the purpose.[84] After an ad-
journment, the debate was picked up again on March 18, when James Doolittle (R-WI) sought to amend Davis's amendment by making colonization
voluntary; he later agreed to modify his amendment such that the colonization expenditure was not to exceed $100 per person.[85]

On March 24 voting commenced. The Doolittle amendment passed 23-16,
with Republicans voting 19-9 against a majority of Democrats and Unionists.[86] However, the amended Davis bill—now effectively the Doolittle
amendment as a substitute—went down to defeat when a 19-19 tie was broken by the nay vote of Vice President Hannibal Hamlin.[87] A slim majority of
Republicans (fifteen of twenty-eight), most of whom were radicals, had in
fact opposed the Doolittle substitute. The breakdown on the two roll calls
indicated that many GOP senators preferred voluntary colonization to com-
pulsory colonization, but also no colonization to voluntary colonization.[88]

Debate continued as Doolittle tried again to push his amendment
through. This time it passed 27-10, with a majority of Republicans (eighteen of twenty-eight) now in favor.[89] Six Republicans, including Benjamin
Wade (OH) and Henry Wilson (MA), two prominent radicals, changed their
votes to support Doolittle.[90] As Leonard Curry notes: "It was apparent that

---

West (today's Midwest), had received reports from their constituents of the bitter opposition
to the prospect of freed black people flooding their communities and causing racial conflict."
See Harris, *Lincoln and Congress*, 36.

84. *CG*, 37-2, 3/12/1862, 1191.

85. *CG*, 37-2, 3/18/1862, 1266; 3/24/1862, 1333.

86. *CG*, 37-2, 3/24/1862, 1333.

87. *CG*, 37-2, 3/24/1862, 1333.

88. A roll-call analysis (logistic regression) of Republican votes on the Doolittle amendment to the Davis bill finds that neither NOMINATE dimension is statistically significant.
A roll-call analysis (logistic regression) of Republican votes on the Doolittle substitute (the
amended Davis bill) finds that only the first (negative) NOMINATE dimension is statistically significant. The latter suggests that more radical Republican senators were more likely
to oppose the Doolittle substitute and to prefer no colonization to voluntary colonization.

89. *CG*, 37-2, 4/3/1862, 1522.

90. In addition to Wade and Wilson, James Dixon (CT), Solomon Foot (VT), Preston
King (NY), and David Wilmot (PA) also switched their votes and supported the amendment.
Foot was considered a moderate, with Dixon, King, and Wilmot more conservative. A roll-
call analysis (logistic regression) of Republican votes on the second Doolittle amendment
finds that only the first (negative) NOMINATE dimension is statistically significant. This

a number of the Republican opponents of colonization had come to doubt their ability to push through an unamended emancipation bill."[91] With the Doolittle amendment now attached, S. 108 passed 29-14 on a pure party-line vote.[92]

The bill then moved to the House, where voting commenced on March 11. After several amendments were defeated, the House passed S. 108 92-38, with Republicans fully unified in support.[93] Once the vote was concluded and the outcome announced, House Republicans rose to celebrate "the first real break in the southern slave system."[94] There was some concern that President Lincoln would veto the bill—he was disappointed that emancipation would be immediate rather than gradual—but he agreed that it embodied his primary policy aims: compensation and colonization. He therefore signed it into law.[95] Over the next nine months nearly three thousand men, women, and children in the District were set free, and over nine hundred petitions for compensation were granted.[96]

Border-state representatives were not happy with the DC bill, viewing it as the first attack on slavery in the Union "where it existed." Lincoln warned them that the politics of slavery and emancipation were ever changing, especially as they related to the evolution of the war itself, and another incident with a Union military commander underscored this point. In early May 1862 Major General David Hunter, who was in charge of Union-controlled areas in Florida, Georgia, and South Carolina, declared all slaves under his purview to be "forever free." He then proceeded to enlist all able-bodied freedmen into the military. Lincoln was furious with Hunter, telling Treasury Secretary Chase that "no commanding general shall do such a thing upon my responsibility without consulting me," and rescinded his orders.[97]

In May 1862 radicals tried yet a different approach to emancipation. On

---

suggests that Republican senators who voted yea were nearest ideologically to the Democrats; again, more radical Republican senators were most likely to vote nay.

91. Curry, *Blueprint for Modern America*, 40–41.

92. *CG*, 37-2, 4/3/1862, 1526.

93. *CG*, 37-2, 4/11/1862, 1648.

94. Curry, *Blueprint for Modern America*, 42.

95. 12 *Stat.* 376–78.

96. Richards, *Who Freed the Slaves?*, 59.

97. Foner, *Fiery Trial*, 206–8; Harris, *Lincoln and the Border States*, 174–76. Since March, Hunter had been taking smaller steps toward this larger action and gained notice only in May with his "bombshell" orders. See Richards, *Who Freed the Slaves?*, 59–61.

May 8 Owen Lovejoy reported a measure (H.R. 374) targeting areas of exclusive federal jurisdiction—the territories, along with forts, dockyards, arsenals, armories, vessels on the high seas, and national highways, among others—for immediate, uncompensated emancipation.[98] The House debated the bill for two days, and Lovejoy eventually narrowed its scope to cover all current and future territories only (many members felt the bill's original coverage was too broad). On March 12 the House passed the bill 85-50, with Republicans unanimous in their support.[99] On June 9, the Senate passed a slightly modified version of the bill 28-10, with Republicans voting as a bloc.[100] Soon thereafter the House adopted the amended bill 72-38, with all Republicans again voting yea.[101] Despite H.R. 374's not allowing for gradual or compensated emancipation, President Lincoln—staying true to the party's Free Soil tenets—affixed his signature two days later and it became law.[102]

With the territories bill, Congress had taken the initiative. Radicals were pushing for general emancipation, and moderate Republicans were increasingly open to that position. Lincoln continued to hold out hope for a gradual, compensated emancipation plan for the loyal slave states and called another meeting of border-state representatives. On July 12 he made his case, citing recent events—like Hunter's unilateral move and congressional Republicans' desire for general emancipation—as a warning that unless they agreed to his plan, they might in the end find themselves with nothing. Two days later, twenty of the twenty-nine border-state representatives rejected Lincoln's plan: they were loyal to the Union, but they felt that emancipation in any form would appear too radical to their constituents.[103] Lincoln still plunged ahead, sending to Congress on July 14 a bill draft that would have provided federal compensation through an authorized 6 percent bond issue to any states that pursued emancipation, either immediate or gradual. Through the early months of 1863, Congress made various attempts to legislate on the president's plan but largely failed.[104]

---

98. *CG*, 37-2, 5/8/1862, 2030. See also Curry, *Blueprint for Modern America*, 55; Foner, *Fiery Trial*, 203–4.

99. *CG*, 37-2, 5/12/1862, 2068.

100. *CG*, 37-2, 6/9/1862, 2618.

101. *CG*, 37-2, 6/17/1862, 2769.

102. 12 *Stat.* 432.

103. Richards, *Who Freed the Slaves?*, 64–66.

104. On these various efforts, see Curry, *Blueprint for Modern America*, 46–55.

Although his efforts to appeal to the border states continued, Lincoln also grew to appreciate how much slavery was wrapped up in the preservation of the Union. As Union forces drove deeper into rebel territory, it became clear how important the slave population was to the military and economic condition of the Confederacy. Union officers discovered that confiscating and employing slaves was a win-win proposition: an extra laborer to help the Union cause and one fewer to keep the Confederacy afloat. In addition, captured slaves provided valuable intelligence about the makeup of Confederate forces, the nature and effectiveness of supply lines, and the location of roads, rivers, and other landmarks. In short, Lincoln increasingly recognized that slaves were vital to the Union war effort. Accordingly, on July 17, 1862, he signed the Militia Act, authorizing escaped slaves to enlist as laborers and soldiers.[105] Congress had thus continued to take the lead on formulating aggressive emancipation policy.

Lincoln, however, had been pondering an ambitious move of his own. On July 13 he met with Secretary of State William Seward and Secretary of the Navy Gideon Welles and informed them that, in his estimation, a presidential proclamation of emancipation was "absolutely essential for the salvation of the Union."[106] He then convened his full cabinet on July 22 and shared his plans to issue a proclamation that would free rebels' slaves.[107] Lincoln planned his emancipation proclamation as a military order and thus based it on his presidential war powers. In this way he hoped to avoid reversal by the Supreme Court based on the Fifth Amendment's "taking clause," which limits the federal government's ability to take private property for public use ("eminent domain") without just compensation. As Leonard Richards notes, "That the Taney Court would strike down emancipation if given the chance was beyond question. In fact, the chief justice had already written a preliminary opinion declaring emancipation unconstitutional."[108] Lincoln

---

105. 12 *Stat.* 597. The Senate passed the measure on July 15 on a 28-9 vote, with Republicans voting 26-0. The House passed the measure on July 16 without a roll call. See *CG*, 37-2, 7/15/1862, 3351; 7/16/1862, 3398.

106. Taken from David Herbert Donald, Jean Harvey Baker, and Michael F. Holt, *Civil War and Reconstruction* (New York: Norton, 2001), 332. Seward may have been consulted on the proclamation idea even earlier; he indicated to Sen. Charles Sumner (R-MA) on May 28 that such a proclamation of emancipation would be delivered in July. See Curry, *Blueprint for America*, 71.

107. Harris, *Lincoln and Congress*, 43–44.

108. Richards, *Who Freed the Slaves?*, 72.

also believed a proclamation would sidestep some of the legal hurdles in the section 9 design of the Second Confiscation Act and thus be a more efficient emancipation solution.[109] Lincoln's cabinet approved of his decision,[110] but Seward believed it would be better delivered after a Union victory. So Lincoln agreed to set it aside until then.

That moment arrived in September 1862, after a nominal Union victory at Antietam. On September 22 Lincoln issued the preliminary proclamation.[111] Among other things, the proclamation reinforced his goals of restoring the Union and working with the loyal states on a system of compensated emancipation.[112] It then made it clear to the Confederate states that they had until January 1, 1863 — effectively one hundred days — to end their rebellion, at which time their slaves would be "then, thenceforth, and forever free."[113]

None of the Confederate states responded positively to the preliminary proclamation, and on January 1 Lincoln issued a final proclamation — making good on his September promise.[114] As David Donald, Jean Harvey Baker, and Michael Holt state, "For Lincoln, by 1863 emancipation was a military necessity, an act of justice, and an end to his placating approach to the slave border states. For although the proclamation did not interfere with

109. See earlier section on the Confiscation Acts. In short, there was ambiguity in the Second Confiscation Act. The general belief was that permanent freedom could not be granted by the military, but only by the federal courts. In effect, a slaveholder would have to be found guilty of being a rebel (or have aided the rebellion). That, per Silvana Siddali, would have required judicial proceedings "on a case by case basis, [which] would have hopelessly snarled the courts for years to come. This would have presented insurmountable obstacles for persons freed by the confiscation law, if one assumed slaves were to be treated like all other property under the law." See Siddali, *From Property to Person*, 141.

110. The one exception was Postmaster General Montgomery Blair (of Maryland), who worried about how the proclamation would be perceived in the border states.

111. A number of works examine the Emancipation Proclamation and its consequences. See, for example, Foner, *Fiery Trial*, 206–89; Allen C. Guelzo, *Lincoln's Emancipation Proclamation: The End of Slavery in America* (New York: Simon and Schuster, 2004); Louis Masur, *Lincoln's Hundred Days: The Emancipation Proclamation and the War for the Union* (Cambridge, MA: Harvard University Press, 2012).

112. The transcript of the Preliminary Emancipation Proclamation can be found at https://www.archives.gov/exhibits/american_originals_iv/sections/transcript_preliminary_emancipation.html.

113. Timothy Huebner, *Liberty and Union: The Civil War Era and American Constitutionalism* (Lawrence: University Press of Kansas, 2016), 231–32.

114. The transcript of the Emancipation Proclamation can be found at https://www.archives.gov/exhibits/featured-documents/emancipation-proclamation/transcript.html.

what he considered the domestic institutions of Maryland, Delaware, Kentucky, and Missouri, slavery, now surrounded everywhere by freedom, was in fact fatally compromised."[115]

The proclamation's provisions extended to the states (or portions thereof) still in rebellion and thus excluded loyal states and rebel areas that were Union occupied. Over three million men, women, and children were granted their freedom. A provision also authorized the enrollment of black soldiers in the US military (following up on the Militia Act of 1862).

The proclamation was, of course, symbolic, as the president had no way to execute the freedom provisions. Yet it yielded immediate diplomatic benefits by eliminating the possibility that European nations would recognize the Confederacy.[116] Moreover, as Timothy Huebner notes, "The Proclamation in practice transformed the war effort into a moral crusade."[117] It established the eradication of slavery as a new — and critical — Northern war objective. Union and emancipation would now go hand in hand.

The Thirteenth Amendment

Despite framing the Emancipation Proclamation as a military necessity and invoking his constitutional war powers to fashion it, Lincoln worried that it would not stand up to Supreme Court scrutiny. He thus began to envision a new way to abolish slavery that would have greater staying power. Congress was working toward a similar end through different means. Lincoln sought to tie emancipation to a broader scheme of restoring rebellious states to the Union. Such a plan would require state-by-state action and thus state-by-state decisions on emancipation. Congressional Republicans, on the other hand, sought a more definitive solution: a constitutional amendment to permanently abolish slavery.

Lincoln's plan sought to bring the rebel states back into the Union as quickly and painlessly as possible. If 10 percent of a state's white voting base from 1860 took an oath of loyalty and agreed to abide by the Emancipation Proclamation and any other slavery-related legislation enacted by Congress, the state would be entitled to federal representation once again (subject to the decision of each chamber of Congress). Lincoln thus "recognized the traditional power of the states to determine the civil and politi-

---

115. Donald, Baker, and Holt, *Civil War and Reconstruction*, 332.

116. Donald, Baker, and Holt, *Civil War and Reconstruction*, 334.

117. Huebner, *Liberty and Union*, 235.

cal rights of their inhabitants."[118] Congressional Republicans—led by the radicals—sought something more punitive against the secessionists. They also hoped to raise the stature of blacks in the civil and political order of the South rather than to allow their former masters to regain power. (Lincoln's plan, and Congress's response, will be covered in considerably more detail later in this chapter.)

Thus, as the Thirty-Eighth Congress opened in December 1863, Lincoln and congressional Republicans were on different paths. Lincoln announced his ten percent plan in his annual message,[119] while individual members of Congress began introducing abolition amendments.[120] The Senate was the first chamber to act, on February 10, 1864, as Lyman Trumbull reported a bill (S.J. Res. 16) from the Judiciary Committee.[121] S.J. Res. 16 was succinct, containing only two sections, and was built on the language of the Northwest Ordinance:

> *Section 1.* Neither slavery nor involuntary servitude, except as a punishment for crime whereof the party shall have been duly convicted, shall exist within the United States, or any place subject to their jurisdiction.
>
> *Section 2.* Congress shall have power to enforce this article by appropriate legislation.

Section 1 of Trumbull's bill indicated that Congress intended not only to abolish slavery where it currently existed, but also to ensure that it applied to "all territory over which the flag of the Union should fly in sovereign power." Section 2 made it clear that Congress now retained the authority to impose this restriction on the states.[122]

Debate in the Senate extended from mid-March through early April. Democrats raised a host of objections, many involving raw racist appeals as well as claims that the amendment was unconstitutional. They also argued that the framers, who had established a compromise around slavery, would

118. Foner, *Fiery Trial*, 272.

119. See http://www.freedmen.umd.edu/procamn.htm.

120. In the House, bills were proposed by James Ashley (R-OH) and James Wilson (R-IA); in the Senate, bills were proposed by John B. Henderson (U-MO) and Charles Sumner (R-MA). See Michael Vorenberg, *Final Freedom: The Civil War, the Abolition of Slavery, and the Thirteenth Amendment* (Cambridge: Cambridge University Press, 2001), 48–53.

121. *CG*, 38-1, 2/10/1864, 553. For the politics of the drafting process, see Vorenberg, *Final Freedom*, 53–60.

122. John W. Burgess, *Reconstruction and the Constitution, 1866–1876* (New York: Charles Scribner's Sons, 1902), 27–28.

never have approved such a change.[123] Republicans supported the amendment and believed success was inevitable. Efforts to derail the bill—such as denying blacks citizenship or the right to hold office, or requiring that slaveholders be compensated before emancipation could take effect—were easily defeated.[124] The Senate then came to a final vote on S.J. Res. 16, and it passed 38-6 (with the required two-thirds majority).[125] Republicans were unanimous in support.

The scene now shifted to the House, where the partisan dynamics were very different. GOP seat share had dropped considerably after the midterm elections of 1862-63. Unlike their fellow partisans in the Senate, Republicans in the House would need support from Democrats and Unionists to achieve the required two-thirds.[126] Debate began on May 31. That day a splinter party—calling itself the "Radical Democracy"—met in Cleveland, nominated John Frémont for president, and endorsed an antislavery constitutional amendment.[127] Advocates of this new party felt Lincoln was moving too slowly on slavery, and they hoped to cleave off some traditional Republicans and War Democrats. Recognizing the threat Frémont posed, Lincoln endorsed the congressional GOP's proposed amendment in his June 9 speech accepting the Republican presidential nomination.[128] As Michael Vorenberg notes, "By grafting an antislavery amendment onto Republican policy and claiming the plank as his own, Lincoln derailed the efforts of his rivals to use the amendment to rebuke his administration."[129]

Thus the House debate—and ultimate vote—on S.J. Res. 16 occurred at a time when presidential politics ramped up public attention to the emancipa-

123. See Vorenberg, *Final Freedom*, 99–112.

124. *CG*, 38-1, 3/31/1864, 1370; 4/5/1864, 1424-25.

125. *CG*, 38-1, 4/8/1864, 1490.

126. Whereas the Republicans maintained a supermajority (66 percent) of Senate seats in the Thirty-Eighth Congress, they possessed only a plurality (47 percent) of House seats. Between the end of the Thirty-Sixth Congress and the beginning of the Thirty-Seventh, the GOP's share of House seats had dropped by twenty-one. See Kenneth C. Martis, *The Historical Atlas of Political Parties in the United States Congress* (New York: Macmillan, 1989).

127. See Harold M. Hyman, "Election of 1864," in *History of American Presidential Elections, 1841–1868*, vol. 3, ed. Arthur M. Schlesinger Jr. (New York: Chelsea House, 1985), 1155–78; Vorenberg, *Final Freedom*, 116-21. The Radical Democracy's constitutional amendment most resembled the one introduced by Sen. Charles Sumner, which included language guaranteeing "to all men absolute equality before the law."

128. Lincoln's endorsement came one day after the Republicans' "Union" convention in Baltimore (June 7-8). See Vorenberg, *Final Freedom*, 123-25.

129. Vorenberg, *Final Freedom*, 126.

tion amendment. Remarks were similar to those of the Senate debate. Opponents relied on racist invective and raised constitutional arguments, while supporters stressed egalitarianism and downplayed constitutional concerns. The emancipation amendment had also become a plank in the GOP's convention platform. This made the job of James Ashley (R-OH), the Republican floor manager on the bill, that much harder, since he needed to secure the votes of some Northern Democrats before a closely contested national election.

When a final vote on S.J. Res. 16 occurred, on June 15, 1864, Ashley was not able to win the two-thirds majority necessary to enact it. Although a majority backed the amendment (94-64), it was eleven votes short of the required number. Republicans voted as a unified bloc, along with most Unionists, but only four of sixty-two Northern Democrats provided their support. The final vote became 93-65, as Ashley — facing defeat — changed his vote from yea to nay before the House clerk's final tally so that he could offer a motion to reconsider at a later date.[130]

When such a motion might be tried, however, was unclear. During the summer of 1864, Union forces were bogged down in multiple areas throughout the South, and casualties were mounting. "The result," according to Eric Foner, "was a crisis of morale and a growing clamor for peace."[131] Lincoln was despondent, fearing he would lose the presidential election in November, jeopardizing the Union and the course of emancipation. Finally, a major victory occurred in early September when General William Tecumseh Sherman captured Atlanta. Sherman's victory turned the tide of the war, boosted Northern morale, and lifted Lincoln's flagging spirits.[132] Congressional Republicans, many of whom had been critical of Lincoln's management of the war and his support for aggressive emancipation policy, rallied around their commander-in-chief, and the party was united going into the election.[133]

In November 1864 Lincoln faced former general George McClellan, nominated by the Democrats on a peace plank, and beat him handily —

---

130. *CG*, 38-1, 6/15/1864, 2995. See also Richards, *Who Freed the Slaves?*, 8–9.

131. Foner, *Fiery Trial*, 303.

132. Harold M. Dudley, "The Election of 1864," *Mississippi Valley Historical Review* 18 (1932): 500–518.

133. Lincoln helped boost this copartisan support by removing Montgomery Blair from his cabinet position, much to the pleasure of congressional radicals who had grown tired of Blair's conservative opinions on race and emancipation. John Frémont dropped out of the race at this point as well, and some speculated that Blair's removal was part of quid pro quo agreement in this regard. See Vorenberg, *Final Freedom*, 155; Foner, *Fiery Trial*, 308.

FIGURE 2. Rep. James Ashley (R-OH). Library of Congress, Prints & Photographs Division, LC-DIG-cwpbh-03557.

winning 212 of 233 electoral votes.[134] The GOP also won supermajorities in the next (Thirty-Ninth) Congress.[135] Thus the pieces appeared to be in place

134. Lincoln won 55 percent of the popular vote and carried all states except Delaware, Kentucky, and New Jersey.

135. Martis, *Historical Atlas of Political Parties in the United States Congress*.

for a reconsideration of S.J. Res. 16 in the House once the Thirty-Ninth Congress convened. But the Republicans were not interested in waiting. Many in the GOP — including Lincoln — interpreted the election results as a mandate to abolish slavery. And Lincoln hoped to act on that mandate immediately, once the lame-duck session of the Thirty-Eighth Congress convened in December 1864. He made this clear in his annual message, with his vocal support of the (would-be) Thirteenth Amendment.[136]

James Ashley got to work. He knew he needed to add about a dozen votes, assuming he could hold together his initial coalition from June.[137] To get a sense of whom in the border states might be persuaded to back the amendment — and whose initial support needed to be shored up — Ashley consulted with Unionists Frank Blair (MO) and Henry Winter Davis (MD). To identify a set of Northern Democrats to target, Ashley sought out Republicans Reuben Fenton (NY) and Augustus Frank (NY) for their advice. Ashley came away from these meetings with thirty-five names, eighteen border-state Unionists and seventeen Northern Democrats.[138]

136. Foner, *Fiery Trial*, 311–12. Why was Lincoln insistent on getting the amendment passed immediately rather than waiting for more favorable partisan conditions in the next Congress? Michael Vorenberg makes the following case: "If Congress quickly adopted the amendment and submitted it to the states, Lincoln could say that slavery was out of his hands. No longer could his opponents spread the false word that only his demands for emancipation stood in the way of peace. Also, the adoption of the amendment sooner rather than later might heal divisions among Republicans for reconstruction . . . and narrow the breach between Republicans and Democrats. [But] of all Lincoln's reasons for wanting a speedy adoption of the amendment, by far the most influential was the public's demand for the measure. Although the amendment was generally neglected during the campaign of 1864, people proclaimed the election results an endorsement of abolition." See Vorenberg, *Final Freedom*, 177–78.

137. More than twenty-five years later, Ashley documented his efforts in getting the Thirteenth Amendment passed in the House. See James M. Ashley, "The Passage of the Thirteenth Amendment to the Constitution," *Magazine of Western History* 13 (1891): 663–79. For recent accounts of Ashley's efforts, and the general twists and turns of acquiring enough votes to pass S.J. Res. 16 in the House, see Richards, *Who Freed the Slaves?*, 118–217, and Vorenberg, *Final Freedom*, 176–210.

138. For a list, see Ashley, "Passage of the Thirteenth Amendment to the Constitution," 674–75. Note that Ashley lists nineteen members from the border states. The problem is that one of the names was Frank Blair, who was unseated (in a contested election case) by Samuel Knox. And Knox was seated on June 10, 1864, five days before the first House vote on the Thirteenth Amendment. Given that Ashley shared his personal history of the amendment's passage more than twenty-five years after the fact, his memory could have been slightly hazy. (Especially troublesome is that Ashley claimed the names of the Missouri members came

TABLE 2.1. House Members Targeted for Amendment-Vote Lobbying, 38th Congress

Northern Democrats

Member (State-District)	Lame Duck	Vote 1 (6/15/1864)	Vote 2 (1/31/1865)
Augustus C. Baldwin (MI-5)	Yes	Nay	Yea
Alexander H. Coffroth (PA-16)	No	Nay	Yea
Samuel S. Cox (OH-7)	Yes	Nay	Nay
James E. Edwards (CT-2)	Yes	Nay	Yea
James Ganson (NY-30)	Yes	Nay	Yea
John A. Griswold (NY-15)	No	Yea	Yea
Anson Herrick (NY-9)	Yes	Nay	Yea
Wells A. Hutchins (OH-11)	Yes	Nay	Yea
Francis C. Le Blond (OH-5)	No	Nay	—
Archibald McAllister (PA-17)	Yes	Nay	Yea
John F. McKinney (OH-4)	Yes	Nay	—
Homer A. Nelson (NY-12)	Yes	—	Yea
Warren P. Noble (OH-9)	Yes	Nay	Nay
Moses F. Odell (NY-3)	Yes	Yea	Yea
William Radford (NY-10)	No	Nay	Yea
John B. Steele (NY-13)	Yes	Nay	Yea
Charles H. Winfield (NY-11)	No	—	Nay

A feature common to the members on Ashley's list was their electoral condition. As table 2.1 indicates, most were lame ducks who either ran for reelection and lost or did not seek reelection. Overall, twelve of the seventeen Northern Democrats and eleven of the eighteen Unionists were lame ducks. These members were no longer linked to their constituents through an electoral connection and thus were more open to persuasion.[139] Thirteen of the seventeen Northern Democrats and two of the eighteen Unionists had

---

from Blair himself, who certainly would not have listed himself after being unseated.) Regardless, in referencing Ashley's list, we have chosen to note eighteen names instead of nineteen.

139. An electoral connection, in the modern sense, did not exist in the nineteenth-century Congress. But while members were not congressional careerists, most did pursue a political career more generally. Such careers usually occurred within the party. See Jamie L. Carson and Jeffery A. Jenkins, "Examining the Electoral Connection across Time," *Annual Review of Political Science* 14 (2011): 25–46. Nonetheless, the larger point holds: members without an electoral tie (and without a political position in the short term, once the Congress ended) should have been more receptive to lobbying efforts, all else equal.

TABLE 2.1. Continued

		Unionists	
Member (State-District)	Lame Duck	Vote 1 (6/15/1864)	Vote 2 (1/31/1865)
Lucien Anderson (KY-1)	Yes	Yea	Yea
Jacob B. Blair (WV-1)	Yes	Yea	Yea
Henry T. Blow (MO-2)	No	Yea	Yea
Sempronius H. Boyd (MO-4)	Yes	Yea	Yea
William G. Brown (WV-2)	Yes	—	Yea
Brutus J. Clay (KY-7)	Yes	—	Nay
John A. J. Creswell (MD-1)	Yes	Yea	Yea
Henry Winter Davis (MD-3)	Yes	—	Yea
Austin A. King (MO-6)	Yes	Nay	Yea
Benjamin F. Loan (MO-7)	No	Yea	Yea
Joseph W. McClurg (MO-5)	No	Yea	Yea
James S. Rollins (MO-9)	Yes	Nay	Yea
Green Clay Smith (KY-6)	No	Yea	Yea
Nathaniel B. Smithers (DE-AL)	Yes	Yea	Yea
Francis Thomas (MD-4)	No	Yea	Yea
Edwin H. Webster (MD-2)	No	Yea	Yea
Kellian V. R. Whaley (WV-3)	No	Yea	Yea
George H. Yeaman (KY-2)	Yes	—	Yea

Note: Dash indicates not voting.

cast nay votes on the first amendment roll call, and six others (two Northern Democrats and four Unionists) had abstained. Thus, if those Northern Democrats and Unionists who had voted for the amendment were maintained—fourteen in total—then Ashley had the names of twenty-one others who could potentially be "flipped."

In December 1864 Ashley announced that debate on the amendment would begin the following month.[140] The lobbying began right away. According to Ashley, "Every honorable effort was made by the Administration to secure the passage of the amendment."[141] Lincoln was active in rounding up votes, working through various congressmen and other Republican operatives.[142] Secretary of State Seward also played a significant role in lobbying

140. *CG*, 38-2, 12/15/1864, 53–54.
141. Ashley, "Passage of the Thirteenth Amendment to the Constitution," 675.
142. Harris, *Lincoln and Congress*, 121–23.

"persuadable" House members, and he employed four lieutenants to handle the face-to-face negotiations.[143]

Debate on S.J. Res. 16 began on January 5, 1865, and extended over the next week. Republican lobbying was met by similar Democratic efforts, and by January 13 Ashley estimated he was several votes short of the necessary two-thirds. In response, he postponed the final vote until the end of the month.[144] At that point Lincoln and Seward ramped up their lobbying, with the president intimating that rewards would follow for those who showed the courage to back the amendment.[145] While little systematic evidence for vote buying exists, anecdotal accounts suggest that over the next two weeks patronage and outright bribery were used to persuade holdouts.[146]

On January 31, 1865, after supporters and opponents were allowed some final comments, the House proceeded to a roll call. After all votes were tabulated, the amendment achieved the necessary two-thirds majority and passed 119-56.[147] Every Republican who voted (eighty-six in all) supported the amendment; they were joined by fourteen Northern Democrats and nineteen Unionists. Overall, Ashley was able to add fifteen new yea votes from the list of "persuadables" he had compiled — ten Northern Democrats and five Unionists — all but two of them lame ducks.[148]

Once the clerk announced the final tally, the House erupted in jubilation. Opponents of slavery had finally won. The Speaker tried to call the membership — and the gallery — to order, but there was no quieting the celebration. The reporter for the *Congressional Globe* described the scene this way:

> The announcement was received by the House and by the spectators with an outburst of enthusiasm. The members on the Republican side of the House instantly sprang to their feet, and, regardless of parliamentary rules, applauded with cheers and clapping of hands. The example was followed by the male spectators in the galleries, which were crowded to excess, who waved their hats and cheered loud and long, while the ladies,

143. For a detailed analysis of the "Seward Lobby," see LaWanda Cox and John H. Cox, *Politics, Principle, and Prejudice, 1865–66: Dilemma of Reconstruction America* (New York: Free Press, 1963), 1–30.

144. *CG*, 38-2, 1/13/1865, 257.

145. Vorenberg, *Final Freedom*, 198–99.

146. Vorenberg, *Final Freedom*, 199–203.

147. *CG*, 38-2, 1/31/1865, 531.

148. Two other Unionists *not* on Ashley's list — Samuel Knox (MO) and William H. Randall (KY) — voted for the amendment after not voting on the earlier (June 15) roll call.

hundreds of whom were present, rose in their seats and waved their hand-kerchiefs, participating in and adding to the general excitement and intense interest of the scene. This lasted for several minutes.[149]

Outside Congress, friends of emancipation welcomed the good news. Chief among them, perhaps, was President Lincoln, who declared that the amendment, once ratified, would eclipse his own effort in ridding the nation of slavery. Lincoln also wanted to affix his name to the effort, and thus he signed the joint resolution even though it was not a constitutional requirement.[150] Lincoln would not see the amendment become a formal part of the Constitution, however; he was assassinated on April 15, 1865, when only twenty-one states had ratified it. The necessary three-quarters majority (twenty-seven states) was not achieved until December 6, 1865.[151]

Enactment of the Thirteenth Amendment ended debate over slavery's future. Legal abolition was a clear milestone in the history of the nation. Yet the legal prohibition on slavery gave rise to a new and divisive subject: What would freedom mean, and how would freed slaves be treated by the federal government and the states? We now take up Congress's first effort to address this topic.

Creating the Freedmen's Bureau

As the war progressed, a significant problem began to confront policy-makers and the military elite: What was to be done with the lives and property taken by Union forces? How would the millions of former slaves be integrated into society as free men and women? Military victory and Lincoln's Emancipation Proclamation generated huge numbers of "internally displaced persons" without homes or political status. While the Confiscation Acts made possible the taking of Confederate property, it was not clear

149. *CG*, 38-2, 1/31/1865, 531.

150. *CG*, 38-2, 2/4/1865, 588. Michael Vorenberg suggests another reason for Lincoln's signature: "He may also have wanted to redress the wrong done by his predecessor, James Buchanan, who signed the 'first' Thirteenth Amendment of 1861, the one that would have given slavery eternal life." See Vorenberg, *Final Freedom*, 210.

151. The twenty-seventh state to ratify was Georgia. Eight of the twenty-seven were Confederate states, which had not yet been approved for federal representation in Congress. For the politics of ratification, and the arguments for and against including the eleven Confederate states in the denominator count (i.e., group of thirty-six), see Richards, *Who Freed the Slaves?*, 218–51, and Vorenberg, *Final Freedom*, 211–50.

how slaves would be dealt with at war's end. It would take members of Congress until spring 1865 to provide clearly articulated policy addressing the issue.

ORGANIZING FREEDMEN WITHOUT CONGRESSIONAL MANDATE

Without a clear policy to guide the treatment of escaped slaves, Union military leaders retained broad discretion. As a result, commanders in the South had implemented a variety of policies. General Benjamin Butler, as we discussed, ordered his troops in Virginia to put "contraband" former slaves to work building military fortifications. As their numbers continued to grow, however, Butler empowered Horace James, a military chaplain, to serve as his "superintendent of Negro affairs." In this role James oversaw the construction of homes for freedmen, grouping these homes into small villages and developing schools there.[152]

Butler's replacement, General John Wool, expanded on his work by regulating the number of hours each day freedmen were to work, the ration allotment owed those employed at various tasks, and the wage paid to male workers—$8 a month. While policy implemented by Butler and Wool proved effective, a commission of three officers sent to study its operations in early 1862 found that it was "incapable of expansion because of the expense involved and because the increase in the demand for labor in military departments could not keep pace with the increased demand for charity."[153]

Even as Butler and Wool were feeding and housing freedmen in Virginia, General Thomas W. Sherman and Commodore Samuel F. Dupont were implementing a different policy in South Carolina. Having taken control of Port Royal, the Sea Islands, and Beaufort in November 1861, Sherman and Dupont found a large population of abandoned slaves and requested direction and material support from Washington. They were ordered to put the former slaves to work harvesting cotton and building military installations. The War Department promised to pay these workers out of the proceeds from cotton sales so that no additional appropriations from Congress would be necessary.

In addition, Edward Pierce, whose article in the *Atlantic Monthly* describ-

---

152. Paul Skeels Pierce, *The Freedmen's Bureau: A Chapter in the History of Reconstruction* (Iowa City: University of Iowa Press, 1904), 6–7.

153. Pierce, *Freedmen's Bureau*, 7.

ing Butler's efforts in Virginia had earned him a job in the Treasury Department, was sent to South Carolina to determine what could be done to aid the former slaves.[154] By the time he arrived, Union forces were responsible for nearly two hundred plantations housing upward of 12,000 freedmen and producing 2,500,000 pounds of cotton.[155] Pierce recommended the appointment of three "superintendents" — one for administration, one for agriculture, and one for education — and organized Port Royal's black population into camps under their direction. He also provided families in these camps with plots of land for cultivation, clothing from captured confederate soldiers, and abandoned homes as well as the promise of schooling.[156]

Despite the effectiveness of Pierce's plan, officials from the War Department frequently obstructed his efforts. Pierce saw his primary task as social uplift. He viewed South Carolina's black population as persons in need of education and training. He therefore directed subordinates to "instruct those anxious to learn and read, and in every possible manner prepare them to become self-supporting citizens."[157] Military officials in Port Royal, on the other hand, focused on getting cotton harvested and shipped north where it could be sold to aid the war effort.[158] This conflict between the War and Treasury Departments over the goals of aid programs would emerge repeatedly throughout the early 1860s.

When Lincoln issued the Emancipation Proclamation, the federal government took on yet more responsibility for the freedmen. Lincoln had pledged to recognize and maintain the freedom of former slaves and recommended "that in all cases when allowed, they labor faithfully for reasonable wages." He also promised to protect them from the "natural prejudice of southerners and the inordinate greed of northerners."[159] Yet no clear and uniform policy existed to guide military or civilian officials in practice. In September 1863 the Treasury Department took steps to provide a coherent policy when it divided the South into five "special agencies." Each agency was to be administered by a superintendent, who would be responsible for distributing land parcels, overseeing the treatment of freedmen, and en-

154. Edward L. Pierce, "The Contrabands at Fortress Monroe," *Atlantic Monthly* 8 (November 1861): 632–36.

155. Pierce, *Freedmen's Bureau*, 21.

156. Pierce, *Freedmen's Bureau*, 21.

157. Pierce quoted in George R. Bentley, *A History of the Freedmen's Bureau* (Philadelphia: University of Pennsylvania Press, 1955), 10.

158. Bentley, *History of the Freedmen's Bureau*, 10.

159. Pierce, *Freedmen's Bureau*, 10.

suring that agricultural production did not cease. "It was this small beginning," argues J. W. Schuckers, "which resulted afterward in the creation of the Freedmen's Bureau."[160]

CONGRESS STEPS IN

The programs implemented throughout the South in the early years of the war provided legislators with a guide for policymaking. They also took cues from the War Department's American Freedmen's Inquiry Commission (AFIC), created in 1863 to study "those measures which may best contribute to the protection and improvement of the recently emancipated," as well as whether a system of provisional or permanent guardianship would be necessary for "self-defense and self support." The AFIC warned that there is "as much danger in doing too much [for freedmen] as in doing too little," for "under the guise of guardianship, slavery, in a modified form, may be practically restored." Further, it noted that while "refugees from slavery" were in need of aid, their needs were not more significant than those of "indigent southern whites fleeing from secessionism."[161]

Where the War Department counseled caution, freedmen's aid societies sought decisive action. In a letter to President Lincoln, society members in Boston, Philadelphia, New York, and Cincinnati called for the immediate creation of a bureau of emancipation to provide the centralized leadership necessary to ensure that the freedmen would receive financial appropriations commensurate with the challenges they would soon face. Moreover, these reformers sought just the kind of guardianship warned against by the War Department: "Has the government any moral right to free the slave without seeing to it that, with every chain it breaks, the best within its power is done to keep the freedman from hankering after his master and his bondage?"[162] These dueling perspectives from the War Department and private aid societies would shape the congressional debate over the freedmen from 1863 to 1865.

Congressional action began in the House. In January 1863 Thomas Eliot

160. J. W. Schuckers, *The Life and Public Services of Salmon Portland Chase* (New York: Appleton, 1874), 327–28.

161. The final report of the American Freedmen's Inquiry Commission can be read at http://www.civilwarhome.com/commissionreport.htm. For more on the AFIC see James M. McPherson, *The Struggle for Equality* (Princeton, NJ: Princeton University Press, 1964), 182–86.

162. Quoted in Bentley, *History of the Freedmen's Bureau*, 30.

(R-MA) introduced the first legislative proposal to create a freedmen's bureau.[163] It was immediately referred to the House Select Committee on Emancipation, where it sat untouched until the end of the Thirty-Seventh Congress. When members reconvened in December 1863 for the Thirty-Eighth Congress, Eliot immediately reintroduced his bill as H.R. 51.[164]

As written, Eliot's bill would set up a bureau of freedmen's affairs within the War Department. The commissioner of this bureau would be empowered to create individual "departments of freedmen" within Southern states, which would be populated by assistant commissioners who would "adjust and determine all questions touching the general superintendence, disposition, and direction" of freedmen. The commissioner would be further charged with making "suitable regulations for the economical and judicious treatment" of freedmen so that "their rights and those of the government may be duly determined and maintained." H.R. 51 also stipulated that freedmen would be allowed to occupy, cultivate, and improve abandoned Southern land, or land to which the Union government had acquired title.[165]

In February 1864, H.R. 51 came to the floor for debate, and Eliot stressed the obligations owed to the freedmen once Lincoln issued his Emancipation Proclamation. "The shackles have been loosened for the slave," he argued, "but defeated armies would leave the conquerors free to weld them on again with bolts that could not be stricken off." He was not confident that black freedom would be assured even if the North won the war. Echoing the argument the aid societies made to President Lincoln, Eliot warned that without legislation to protect them, freedmen could just as easily be reenslaved. Further, he argued that only through legislative protection could freedmen be assured of fair pay for their work.[166] Responding to those who might question Congress's power to provide these protections, Eliot cited the bureau's location within the War Department. If the government retained the power to free slaves, he contended, then it certainly had the power to guarantee that such freedom would last.[167]

Republican supporters of H.R. 51 generally noted its practical advantages rather than any moral obligations to the freedmen. Cornelius Cole (R-CA),

163. *CG*, 37-3, 1/12/1863, 282.

164. *CG*, 38-1, 12/14/1863, 19.

165. The text of H.R. 51 can be found at http://memory.loc.gov/cgi-bin/ampage?collId=llhb&fileName=038/llhb038.db&recNum=202.

166. For more on this point, see Herman Belz, *A New Birth of Freedom: The Republican Party and Freedmen's Rights, 1861–1866* (Westport, CT: Greenwood Press, 1976), 77–78.

167. *CG*, 38-1, 2/10/1864, 567–71.

for example, claimed that the bill "proposes, in effect, to shorten the war." By protecting the families of freedmen and ensuring their livelihoods and education, Cole claimed, the Union government would encourage black enlistment. "Every slave added to the Union army is, in effect, also taking a soldier from the ranks of the rebels," he concluded.[168] William Kelley (R-PA) argued that freedmen "must not be permitted to contract habits of idleness, indolence, and vagrancy." H.R. 51, he contended, counteracts these vices by providing "legal, constitutional, and inexpensive means" by which the federal government could ensure continued cultivation of millions of acres of land.[169]

House Democrats vehemently opposed Eliot's proposal. Claiming that it made the government a "grand plantation speculator and overseer, and the Treasury a fund for the helpless Negro," Samuel S. Cox (D-OH) condemned the bill as a revolutionary break with constitutional federalism. He then went on to argue that the bureau would open a "vast opportunity for greed, tyranny, corruption, and abuse." Concluding, Cox portrayed the entire Civil War as an "irrepressible conflict . . . not between freedom and slavery, but between black and white." Radical reformers like Eliot, he argued, intended not just to end slavery, but to promote "miscegenation" and "amalgamation."[170] Through the final two weeks of February, House Democrats expanded on each aspect of Cox's argument.[171]

On March 1 Eliot's proposal came to a vote. After a motion to table failed, H.R. 51 passed narrowly, 69-67.[172] All Democrats opposed the measure while all but four Republicans voted in favor.[173] Those Republicans voting yea were joined by six of nineteen Unionists from border states. Having passed the House, Eliot's proposal now moved to the Senate.

Once in the Senate, H.R. 51 went first to the Select Committee on Slavery and Freedmen, chaired by Charles Sumner (R-MA). Sumner was dissatisfied with President Lincoln's cautious approach to abolition. His political preferences overlapped more with those of Treasury Secretary Chase.[174] Sumner

168. *CG*, 38-1, 2/18/1864, 741.

169. *CG*, 38-1, 2/23/1864, 773.

170. *CG*, 38-1, 2/17/1864, 709.

171. For speeches on each of these points, see *CG*, 38-1, 2/17/1864, 709–711; 2/19/1864, 761; 2/24/1864, 804–5; and 3/1/1864, appendix 54.

172. *CG*, 38-1, 3/1/1864, 895.

173. These four Republicans were John McBride (OR), Thomas Williams (PA), Henry Tracy (PA), and James Hale (PA).

174. Leonard L. Richards, *Who Freed the Slaves?*, 134–37.

thus led the committee to revise H.R. 51 by placing the Bureau of Emancipation in the Treasury Department. His committee also broadened the language of Eliot's proposal to ensure that it covered all slaves, not simply those emancipated by Lincoln's proclamation. Republicans warned Sumner that his changes might jeopardize enactment of the measure, but he was undeterred.[175]

When considering the disposition of property, Sumner's bill stipulated that the Bureau of Emancipation would retain authority to lease confiscated or abandoned land to freedmen "on such terms . . . and under such regulations as the commissioner may determine."[176] Bureau commissioners were to act as "advisory guardians" for freedmen to ensure that labor contracts were fair and all their obligations satisfied. Sumner envisioned a system wherein freedmen would serve as contract laborers on government-leased plantations.[177] As agents contracting with the federal government through the Bureau of Emancipation rather than leasing or purchasing land from private owners, he believed, the freedmen would be better protected. Indeed, Sumner believed the House bill provided "no protection to the freedmen so as to keep them from being made serfs or apprentices."[178]

When Sumner's version of the Bureau bill came to the floor of the Senate in spring 1864, Republicans immediately attacked the guardianship provisions. Presaging a dynamic of intraparty conflict that would occur throughout the Reconstruction era, Sumner's radicalism met its match in the form of moderate antislavery Republicans from western states. James Grimes (R-IA), for example, opposed the provision empowering commissioners to "take care that the freedmen do not suffer from ill treatment or any failure of contract on the part of others, and that on their part they perform their duty." He asked, "Why do you confer upon these commissioners . . . the unlimited power to see to it that these colored men perform what . . . may be their duty? How are you going to enforce it? By stripes and lashes?" From Grimes's perspective, freedmen must be left alone to "stand as free men."[179]

Echoing Grimes was Timothy Howe (R-WI), who asserted that the bill would "give to commissioners, the right to control the action and the efforts

---

175. McPherson, *Struggle for Equality*, 190.

176. Sumner's bill can be found at https://memory.loc.gov/cgi-bin/ampage?collId=llsb &fileName=038/llsb038.db&recNum=1115.

177. Belz, *New Birth of Freedom*, 80.

178. Sumner (echoing comments made by Unionist senator R. Gratz Brown of Missouri) quoted in Belz, *New Birth of Freedom*, 80.

179. *CG*, 38-1, 6/15/1864, 2972.

of all these freedmen."[180] Here Howe repeated an argument Frederick Douglass had made in 1862. When asked what should be done with freedmen after the war, Douglass replied, "do nothing with them . . . your *doing* with them is their greatest misfortune."[181] Recognizing that his bill would fail without the support of Republicans who did not share his faith in "guardianship," Sumner agreed to change the bill's language so as to reaffirm that "every freedman be treated in every respect as a free man, with all proper remedies in courts of justice."[182]

Unionist Waitman Willey (WV) proposed to grant Bureau commissioners the power to resettle freedmen in northern and western states when it was not possible to find them work or land in the South.[183] Sumner opposed Willey, arguing that his language went too far.[184] In reality, Sumner likely believed that Willey's amendment would sink the bill, since antislavery Northerners and Westerners were "acutely sensitive to the issue of Negro migration." Many of the Senate's most reliable abolitionists recognized that black migration outside the South would incite opposition from voters in their home states.[185] Despite Sumner's opposition, Willey's amendment passed 19-15, with Republicans split (11-12).[186]

To salvage his bill, Sumner offered an amendment stripping Willey's language, which failed in a 14-14 tie vote.[187] Instead, through voice vote, the Senate adopted language encouraging bureau commissioners to correspond with governors regarding the resettlement of freedmen.[188] Then, before moving to a final vote, senators considered an effort to relocate the Bureau of Emancipation in the War Department, as originally intended. This amendment, drafted by Unionist Reverdy Johnson (MD), failed 15-20.[189] The

---

180. *CG*, 38-1, 6/28/1864, 3331.

181. Herman Belz, "The Freedmen's Bureau Act of 1865 and the Principle of No Discrimination according to Color," *Civil War History* 21 (1975): 207.

182. *CG*, 38-1, 6/27/1864, 3299.

183. *CG*, 38-1, 6/28/1864, 3239.

184. *CG*, 38-1, 6/28/1864, 3239-40.

185. As Herman Belz notes, "The purpose [of Willey's amendment] was to embarrass the bill and put its radical supporters in the position of opposing a measure that could be construed as aiding blacks." Belz, *New Birth of Freedom*, 84. See also V. Jacque Voegeli, *Free but Not Equal: The Midwest and the Negro during the Civil War* (Chicago: University of Chicago Press, 1967), 58-61.

186. *CG*, 38-1, 6/28/1864, 3330.

187. *CG*, 38-1, 6/28/1864, 3337. Republicans voted 12-6 for the Sumner amendment.

188. *CG*, 38-1, 6/28/1864, 3341.

189. *CG*, 38-1, 6/28/1864, 3337. Republicans voted 8-16 for the Johnson amendment.

Senate then passed Sumner's bill 21-9, with all but one of the Republicans voting for it and all Democrats voting against.[190]

Sumner's bill — H.R. 51 as amended — now moved back to the House. On July 2, 1864, the House's Select Committee on Emancipation refused to concur with the Senate changes to Eliot's proposal. House members then chose to delay further consideration of the bill until the following session. When Congress reconvened in December 1864, the House quickly moved to a vote on whether to concur in the Senate amendments made to H.R. 51, which failed 52-71, with sixty-two of sixty-three Republicans voting nay.[191] After this failed vote, the House and Senate organized a conference committee to forge a compromise.[192]

On February 2, 1865, Eliot unveiled the conference committee's H.R. 51 substitute on the House floor. The revised bill proposed creating an independent Bureau of Freedmen's Affairs, unconnected with any existing executive department. Like the Department of Agriculture, it would "communicate directly with the president" instead of working through the head of an existing agency.[193] Eliot and Sumner thus tried to sidestep the conflict between those who believed the bureau should be under military control and those who wanted it to be a permanent civilian-led agency. Those pushing for civilian control worried that the military cared little for the lives of former slaves, that military officers were amenable to freedmen's working as de facto serfs, and that support for the bureau would dissolve when hostilities ended if it was located within the War Department. Those pushing for military control saw it as the only way to protect freedmen from racist white Southerners and economically rapacious Northerners. They also believed that the wage system proposed by some of the bill's advocates would generate its own system of serfdom by constructing "a scheme of controlled labor . . . as the former slaves were incapable of supporting themselves."[194]

After detailing this important modification, Eliot went on to explain that the bill empowered the commissioner of freedmen's affairs — appointed by

---

190. *CG*, 38-1, 6/28/1864, 3350. The lone GOP nay vote was cast by Edgar Cowan (PA).

191. *CG*, 38-2, 12/20/1864, 80.

192. House members on the committee included Eliot, Warren P. Noble (D-OH), and William D. Kelley (R-PA). Senators on the committee included Sumner, Jacob Howard (R-MI), and Charles R. Buckalew (D-PA). An account of the conference committee's work and subsequent floor action in the Senate appears in Allan G. Bogue, *The Earnest Men: Republicans in the Civil War Senate* (Ithaca, NY: Cornell University Press, 1981), 213–16.

193. *CG*, 38-2, 2/2/1865, 562–66.

194. Belz, *New Birth of Freedom*, 97.

the president and confirmed by the Senate — to create not more than two "freedmen's districts" in each state, which would be "brought under the military power of the United States" and in turn be "governed by assistant commissioners whose primary responsibility was "general supervision of freedmen."[195] These "advisory guardians" would determine the wages paid to freedmen, arbitrate any disputes they were party to, ensure that they received fair trials when charged with a crime, and guarantee that labor contracts were upheld.

The bill also stipulated that assistant commissioners were to provide freedmen with leases "not to continue beyond one year." During that year, freedmen were encouraged to develop and cultivate their land so they could renew the lease in the following year. Freedmen would be responsible for negotiating the terms of these leases with their districts' advisory guardians. The conference committee report demonstrated that members of Congress never envisioned a land reform plan that would grant *permanent* ownership rights to former slaves.[196] The bill's final section proposed a system for punishing, under military law, any commissioner charged with criminal acts while employed by the bureau.

In both chambers the terms of the debate echoed those outlined in 1864. Radicals defended the guardianship system because, in Eliot's words, freedmen were "unused to self-reliance and dependent for a season somewhat upon our sympathy and aid."[197] Once again, western Republicans objected. In the words of Rep. James Wilson (R-IA), "the better course for us . . . is to let [freedmen] have the responsibility upon themselves of disposing of their own services in such a way as they may deem proper."[198] New to this iteration of the debate, however, were arguments from some members who wanted to see additional support for Southern whites. Sen. Henry Lane (R-IN), for example, proclaimed that he supported "temporary relief and temporary support to colored persons and equally to the white refugees."[199] More than one Republican agreed with Lane. Their skepticism portended trouble for the bill.

In the House, the conference committee's version of H.R. 51 came up for a vote on February 9, 1865. It passed 64-62 despite the opposition of all

195. *CG*, 38-2, 2/2/1865, 564.
196. Belz, *New Birth of Freedom*, 95.
197. *CG*, 38-2, 2/2/1865, 564.
198. *CG*, 38-2, 2/10/1865, 689.
199. *CG*, 38-2, 2/22/1865, 984–85.

Democrats and a large majority of Unionists, thanks to the support of sixty out of sixty-four Republicans.[200] The bill then moved to the Senate, where Sumner brought it up for debate on February 13. Nine days later, senators overwhelmingly rejected the compromise measure, 14-24, with six western and five eastern Republicans voting nay.[201]

In a last-ditch effort to salvage the bill, the House and Senate formed a second conference committee composed of members who did *not* sit on the Senate/House committees on Emancipation/Freedmen. The bill crafted by this new conference committee would largely be based on a measure introduced earlier in February by Rep. Robert Schenck (R-OH). Despite his own opposition to slavery, Schenck had voted against the earlier conference committee's version of H.R. 51. Like many western Republicans, he opposed the guardianship principle pushed by the radicals. Schenck also made it clear that he believed H.R. 51 failed to adequately support loyal Southern whites. Accordingly, on February 9 — the same day the House voted on the first conference committee's version of H.R. 51 — Schenck introduced his own freedmen's bureau bill (H.R. 698).[202]

Schenck's bill included just two substantive provisions. First, it created a "Bureau for the Relief of Freedmen and Refugees" within the War Department, which would operate throughout the South only "during the present war of rebellion." Bureau agents were empowered to "supervise, manage, and control" all matters affecting "refugees and freedmen from the rebel states." Second, it granted the president power to distribute aid and to authorize the "temporary" transfer of abandoned land to both freedmen and white refugees. Schenck stressed that the bureau would serve as a solution to "one of the incidents of war — temporary in its character . . . to be disposed of as the war progresses, and to be ended about the time when the war ends." He then noted that his bill "makes no discrimination on account of color . . . [and] proposes to take care of all refugees, as well as all freedmen, who may need the help of the federal government."[203]

Schenck's bill passed in the House by voice vote on February 18, 1865.[204] When the Senate took up debate on the first conference committee's version

---

200. *CG*, 38-2, 2/9/1865, 694. The four Republicans were Thomas Davis (NY), Elihu Washburne (IL), Robert Schenck (OH), and Henry Tracy (PA).

201. *CG*, 38-2, 2/22/1865, 989-90.

202. *CG*, 38-2, 2/9/1865, 691.

203. *CG*, 38-2, 2/9/1865, 691.

204. *CG*, 38-2, 2/18/1865, 908.

of H.R. 51, it had this bill as a potential alternative. Once the conference bill failed in the Senate, the second conference committee drafted a measure that was "substantially in accord with the Schenck bill."[205] Introduced in the Senate on February 28, 1865, this third revision of H.R. 51 created a Bureau for the Relief of Freedmen and Refugees within the War Department "to continue during the present war of rebellion and for one year thereafter."[206] The bureau would be led by a presidentially appointed commissioner and supported by Senate-confirmed assistants, who would be appointed to each rebel state. The bureau would manage all subjects relating to refugees and freedmen, would give temporary aid to those made destitute by the war, and would be authorized to set aside forty acres for each male citizen — white or black — to cultivate for up to three years. After three years these tracts of land would be rented at a rate not exceeding 6 percent of their value. The new H.R. 51, unlike its two predecessors, largely abandoned the guardianship principle and, despite the stipulation of forty acres, allowed for only "temporary use of rebel estates, with the rather remote possibility of subsequent ownership."[207]

On the final day of the Thirty-Eighth Congress, the Senate concurred with this new conference committee bill after almost no debate and without a roll-call vote.[208] In the House, it passed with no debate and no roll call.[209] Congress had finally created a Freedmen's Bureau — one quite different from the initial version stipulated by the radicals. Yet, as we document in the next chapter, their creation would not survive long.

Wrangling over Reconstruction

During the war, Lincoln and the Republicans in Congress found themselves debating not only how to emerge victorious, but also how to put the nation back together once hostilities ended. On July 4, 1861, in his message to Congress, Lincoln offered an early perspective on what reunion might look like. He alluded to the "understanding of the powers and duties of the federal government relative to the rights of the states" expressed in his first inaugural address, when he asserted that the federal government had no authority

---

205. Belz, *More Perfect Union*, 103.
206. *CG*, 38-2, 2/28/1865, 1182.
207. Belz, *More Perfect Union*, 105.
208. *CG*, 38-2, 3/3/1865, 1348.
209. *CG*, 38-2, 3/3/1865, 1402.

to "interfere with the institution of slavery in the states where it exists."[210] He also reaffirmed his commitment to the "maintenance inviolate of . . . the right of each state to order and control its own domestic institutions." Lincoln thus characterized the war as a military effort designed to reestablish the antebellum status quo. On this point he spoke for many conservative Republicans and Unionists.[211]

Radical Republicans in Congress did not share Lincoln's view. Led by Sen. Charles Sumner (R-MA), they sought to ensure that rebel states would not be readmitted to the Union, and their representatives seated in Congress again, without significant reform. Accordingly, in February 1862 Sumner introduced a resolution explicating the radical vision of the postwar world:

> *Resolved*, That any vote of secession or other act by which any State may undertake to put an end to the supremacy of the Constitution within its territory is inoperative and void against the Constitution, and when sustained by force it becomes a practical *abdication* by the State of all rights under the Constitution, while the treason which it involves still further works an instant *forfeiture* of all those functions and powers essential to the continued existence of the State as a body-politic, so that from that time forward the territory falls under the exclusive jurisdiction of Congress as other territory, and the State being, according to the language of the law, *felo-de-se*, ceases to exist.[212]

In what was dubbed the "state suicide" theory, Sumner argued that seceded states should be downgraded to territories and run by Congress. State suicide, or more technically, "territorialization," would never be implemented. Yet the back-and-forth between Lincoln and congressional radicals over the terms of reunion would occupy Congress for the next two years.

210. Lincoln's message to Congress can be read at http://www.presidency.ucsb.edu/ws/?pid=69802.

211. Lincoln's views on Reconstruction, along with congressional Republicans' reactions to them, are covered in William B. Hesseltine, *Lincoln's Plan of Reconstruction* (Gloucester, MA: Peter Smith, 1963); Herman Belz, *Reconstructing the Union: Theory and Policy during the Civil War* (Ithaca, NY: Cornell University Press, 1969); Michael Les Benedict, *A Compromise of Principle: Congressional Republicans and Reconstruction, 1863–1869* (New York: Norton, 1974); William C. Harris, *With Charity for All: Lincoln and the Restoration of the Union* (Lexington: University Press of Kentucky, 1997); Paul D. Escott, *Lincoln's Dilemma: Blair, Sumner, and the Republican Struggle over Racism and Equality in the Civil War Era* (Charlottesville: University of Virginia Press, 2014); and Louis P. Masur, *Lincoln's Last Speech: Wartime Reconstruction and the Crisis of Reunion* (New York: Oxford University Press, 2015).

212. *CG*, 37-2, 2/11/1862, 737.

This debate would play out in two distinct phases. In the first, members debated whether to impose territorialization on the rebellious states.[213] In the second, members fought among themselves, and with the president, over whether the terms to be met before a state would be readmitted should be set by the legislature or the executive branch.

PERIOD ONE: TERRITORIALIZATION

The period between Lincoln's July 4 message and mid-1862 was dominated by one basic question: What did secession "do" to the rebel states relative to the federal government? From Lincoln's perspective, the rebellion implied nothing about the status of Confederate states. He did not believe any state had the legal authority to remove itself from the Union. "Having never been states either in substantive or in name outside of the Union," Lincoln argued in his July 4 message, "Whence this magical omnipotence of 'state rights' asserting a claim of power to lawfully destroy the Union itself? . . . The states have their status in the Union, and they have no other status." Lincoln's view of secession as unlawful led him to posit the rebellion as a criminal act perpetrated by disloyal residents of the eleven Confederate states. Reconstruction, then, "consisted simply in placing the loyal elements in a 'state' in possession of the government of 'the state.'"[214] Before the Emancipation Proclamation, one's position on slavery was largely irrelevant to one's status as a "loyal" citizen. For this reason, Lincoln's early position on readmission could be seen as envisioning a postwar world in which slavery persisted within readmitted southern states.

Even before delivering his July 4 message, Lincoln was taking steps to act on his vision of Reconstruction. In April 1861 he provided federal military protection to loyal Virginians seeking readmission to the Union. With aid from Washington, a small group of loyalists elected Francis Pierpont governor of the "restored government of Virginia," along with three Unionist congressmen. The reconstituted state legislature then elected John Carlile and Waitman Willey to the Senate.[215] Believing a similar outcome might be possible in North Carolina, Lincoln claimed in his December 1861 annual message to Congress that "the cause of the Union is advancing steadily and

---

213. The concept of territorialization, and plans for it, are covered extensively in Belz, *Reconstructing the Union*, 40–99.

214. Burgess, *Reconstruction and the Constitution*, 9.

215. Donald, Baker, and Holt, *Civil War and Reconstruction*, 509.

certainly southward."[216] Yet when elections were held, Unionist representative Charles H. Foster was the only candidate and received a total of 268 votes. The House Committee on Elections, recognizing that Foster was in no way a "representative" of North Carolina, refused to admit him.[217] By rejecting Foster, House members served notice that they intended to weigh in on state-restoration policy. And with the new year came a prolonged debate over the status of the rebel states.

James M. Ashley (R-OH) would emerge as Lincoln's primary radical antagonist in the House.[218] In March 1862 Ashley — then chairman of the Committee on Territories — drafted H.R. 356, which would authorize President Lincoln to "establish temporary civil government possessing full legislative power over the seceded states." Ashley intended this legislative power to cover "all rightful subjects of legislative power, not inconsistent with the Constitution and laws of the United States."[219] It thus would have allowed provisional governments to amend or repeal all state laws protecting slavery. Once created, these provisional governments would exist "until such time as the loyal people residing therein shall form new state governments, Republican in form, as prescribed by the Constitution of the United States, and obtain admission into the Union as states."[220]

The Ashley and Sumner plans met with opposition from Democrats and Republicans alike. Democrats invoked the Constitution as they railed against radical proposals. "There is no power in this Congress to declare that the people of a state of this Union shall not govern themselves in all matters touching their local and domestic affairs," complained Sen. Lazarus Powell (D-KY).[221] Republicans, meanwhile, claimed that territorialization acknowledged the validity of secession. Sen. John Sherman (R-OH) even likened Sumner's "state suicide" resolution to the decisions made by the Confederate president. "[Sumner] puts the states in the condition of abject territories, to be governed by Congress," Sherman claimed, "[while] Jefferson Davis puts it in the power of the states to govern themselves. As

216. Lincoln's message can be read at http://www.presidency.ucsb.edu/ws/?pid=29502.

217. William C. Harris, "Lincoln and Wartime Reconstruction in North Carolina," *North Carolina Historical Review* 53 (April 1986): 149–68; Harris, *With Charity for All*, 33.

218. Belz, *Reconstructing the Union*, 53.

219. In *Reconstructing the Union*, Belz reports details of Ashley's bill. It was never formally introduced into Congress, so it exists in his papers but is not publicly available. All quotations from the bill come from Belz's book.

220. Belz, *Reconstructing the Union*, 53–63.

221. *CG*, 37-2, 7/7/1862, 3141.

to which is the most dangerous or obnoxious doctrine, I leave every man to determine."[222]

The resolute opposition by Democrats, Unionists, and some Republicans prevented the House from even debating Ashley's bill. When he attempted to bring it to the floor in March 1862, it was immediately attacked by George Pendleton (D-OH). "This bill ought to be entitled 'A bill to dissolve the Union and abolish the Constitution,'" he proclaimed. Pendleton then moved to table H.R. 356, and the House voted 65-56 to do just that.[223] The pivotal votes came from eighteen Republicans with more conservative proclivities who broke party ranks to vote with the Democrats and Unionists.[224]

In the Senate, a more moderate approach to reconstruction, introduced by Ira Harris (R-NY), met a similar fate. Harris's bill (S. 200) also proposed to establish provisional governments in rebel states, but it included a provision stipulating that provisional governments had no power to interfere "with the laws and institutions existing in such state at the time it seceded."[225] The provisional governments would thus not be empowered to repeal state laws protecting slavery. According to Harris, his proposal was simply intended to "govern these states *ad interim* during the interval that shall elapse between the time when the rebellion is subdued . . . and when [the states] shall be willing to reorganize themselves and come back and govern themselves in the Union."[226] Despite the bill's moderate approach, Harris could not persuade the Senate to take it up before the end of the Thirty-Seventh Congress.

With Congress unable to develop a policy to guide the readmission of seceded states, President Lincoln pursued his own approach. Lincoln's strategy centered on appointing military governors to take charge of Southern states controlled by Union military forces.[227] These military governors were to organize each state's population of loyal citizens and then hold elections to reconstitute state governments and send representatives to Washington. To preempt any legislative efforts to contest his readmission policy,

222. *CG*, 37-2, 4/2/1862, 1493.

223. *CG*, 37-2, 3/12/1862, 1193.

224. A roll-call analysis (logistic regression) of Republican votes finds that first (negative) and second (positive) NOMINATE dimensions are statistically significant, with Republican members nearest to the Democrats on both dimensions being more likely to support tabling Ashley's territorialization bill.

225. S. 200 can be read at https://memory.loc.gov/cgi-bin/ampage?collId=llsb&fileName=037/llsb037.db&recNum=707, section 3.

226. *CG*, 37-2, 7/7/1862, 3141.

227. Donald, Baker, and Holt, *Civil War and Reconstruction*, 510.

Lincoln appeased congressional radicals by taking stronger steps toward abolishing slavery. The Emancipation Proclamation should thus be seen as one consequence of this tacit agreement with the radical wing of his party.[228] Indeed, despite one more unsuccessful attempt by Ira Harris in early 1863 to get a provisional government bill enacted, the course of Reconstruction was now largely in Lincoln's hands.[229]

PERIOD TWO: CONGRESS VERSUS THE PRESIDENT

To formalize his Reconstruction policy, Lincoln issued a "Proclamation of Amnesty and Reconstruction" in December 1863.[230] The proclamation set forth terms that each rebel state would need to satisfy before readmission. It offered a full pardon to all who participated in the rebellion — except political and military elites — contingent on their swearing an oath to "faithfully support, protect, and defend the Constitution" as well as all acts of Congress and executive proclamations issued since 1861. It then specified that for a given state's government to be reconstituted, 10 percent of the number of voters who participated in the 1860 election would need to sign the loyalty oath. Once this threshold was met, elections could be organized and new state governments formed.

Finally, and most crucially, Lincoln's proclamation left it up to readmitted state governments to set their own policies regarding the future treatment of freedmen. To be readmitted, states would need to swear to abide by the Emancipation Proclamation, but that was the only condition imposed on them regarding former slaves. In particular, the proclamation stated, "Any provision which may be adopted by such state government in relation to the freed people of such state . . . will not be objected to by the national executive." Explaining this language in his annual message to Congress, Lincoln said he hoped that the people of readmitted states would be more likely to permanently abolish slavery, and deal favorably with freedmen, "to the extent that this vital matter be left to themselves."[231] Radicals read this statement as a signal that Lincoln had endorsed abolition. Combined with the oath requiring all reconstituted state governments to abide by the Eman-

228. Belz, *Reconstructing the Union*, 101.

229. For more on Harris's second failed proposal see Belz, *Reconstructing the Union*, 200.

230. Lincoln's proclamation can be read at http://www.freedmen.umd.edu/procamn .htm.

231. Lincoln's 1863 annual message can be read at http://millercenter.org/president /speeches/speech-3738.

cipation Proclamation, Lincoln appeared to indicate that "emancipation would be a condition of reconstruction."[232]

Lincoln's ten percent plan relied almost entirely on the powers wielded by military governors, however, and congressional Republicans spent a good part of 1862 and 1863 raising concerns about the incompatibility of martial law and republican governance.[233] Nevertheless, through December 1863, Union military victories, combined with Lincoln's growing popularity, prevented Republicans in Congress from countermanding the president's approach.[234]

This would change in early 1864, when Lincoln's military governor in Louisiana—General Nathaniel Banks—made a series of decisions that enraged radicals. Banks tried to reorganize Louisiana's government without first amending the state constitution to outlaw slavery. Instead, he simply made use of his military authority to nullify those aspects of the state charter protecting it. Louisiana's abolitionists warned that Banks's approach would allow the election of conservatives who might recognize slavery.[235] And, indeed, the House candidates who were victorious in the 1864 elections—which were organized by Banks—came from Louisiana's conservative planter class.[236] When they arrived in Washington to take their seats, the House Committee on Elections rejected their credentials.

Shortly after the Louisiana election controversy—amid military stalemate in Virginia and Georgia—Henry Winter Davis (R-MD) introduced legislation in the House setting out a Reconstruction policy designed to challenge Lincoln's authority.[237] H.R. 244, introduced on February 15, 1864, sought to ensure that legislative statute—not executive proclamation—would determine the conditions under which states would be readmitted.[238] Davis's bill thus represents the opening of the second phase of Reconstruction—a phase that would outlast Lincoln—in which Congress and the

232. Belz, *Reconstructing the Union*, 162.

233. Belz, *Reconstructing the Union*, 168–97.

234. Donald, Baker, and Holt, *Civil War and Reconstruction*, 511–12.

235. Belz, *Reconstructing the Union*, 191.

236. Donald, Baker, and Holt, *Civil War and Reconstruction*, 514.

237. The best account of what would become known as the "Wade-Davis bill" is Belz, *Reconstructing the Union*, 198–243. See also see Allan Nevins, *The War for the Union*, vol. 4, *The Organized War to Victory, 1864–1865* (New York: Scribner's, 1971), 83–88; Benedict, *Compromise of Principle*, 70–83.

238. Benedict, *Compromise of Principle*, 75–77.

president engaged in protracted conflict over the constitutionally legitimate source of Reconstruction policy.

More generally, H.R. 244 stipulated that before elections could be held to reorganize rebel state governments, there must be constitutional conventions to rewrite state charters for the purpose of abolishing slavery.[239] Davis thus sought to ensure that formal abolition *preceded* readmission — a requirement Lincoln was unwilling to impose. In the period between enactment and readmission, H.R. 244 would establish provisional governments led by civilian governors who would be appointed by the president and confirmed by the Senate. They would also be called on to enforce all of a given state's laws *except* those protecting slavery because, as H.R. 244 made clear, all "persons held to involuntary servitude or labor in the states . . . are hereby emancipated."[240]

Over the course of six weeks, supporters of H.R. 244 worked to defend its constitutionality. Davis built his argument on the idea that article 4, section 4 of the Constitution "imposes upon Congress the duty of guarantying [*sic*] to every state in this Union a republican form of government."[241] Slavery was not coincident with republicanism, he claimed. On this point, Davis had to invoke a crafty argument. From the day the Constitution was ratified until the outbreak of war, slave states were considered sufficiently "republican" to govern themselves. Davis was thus left to argue that slavery induced rebel-

239. H.R. 244 can be read at https://memory.loc.gov/cgi-bin/ampage?collId=llhb&fileName=038/llhb038.db&recNum=1091.

240. H.R. 244 also included a number of important provisions not directly related to race. The bill stipulated that Reconstruction would not officially begin until military resistance within a given state had been reduced to the point that the provisional governor could judge that the populace had "sufficiently returned to their obedience to the Constitution and the laws of the United States." Having reached that point, all white male citizens could register to vote by taking an "iron clad" oath swearing that they had never participated in the rebellion. Once 50 percent of those who voted in 1860 had taken the oath, provisional governors would organize elections to choose convention delegates. These delegates would then meet to redraft state charters. Once these new charters were approved, statewide elections could be held. Finally, the bill stripped citizenship and future voting rights from the Confederate political and military elite, set state residency requirements determining those eligible to vote in state elections, and made no mention of restoring property to those dispossessed by the war. Some of these provisions were amendments to the original bill (more below). For a summary of the bill, see Belz, *Reconstructing the Union*, 200–205; Donald, Baker, and Holt, *Civil War and Reconstruction*, 514–15; and Hesseltine, *Lincoln's Plan of Reconstruction*, 111–13.

241. *CG*, 38-1, 3/22/1864, appendix 82.

lion; and once rebellion was under way, republican governments perished. According to Davis and his allies, no state governments in the Confederacy were, in 1864, affording their citizens republican institutions. As a result, slavery made permanent republican government impossible.[242]

H.R. 244 generated opposition from both radicals and conservatives. Thaddeus Stevens (R-PA) charged that it "takes for granted that the president may partially interfere in [the states'] civil administration."[243] He also opposed the bill because it failed to be explicit about the federal government's power to confiscate Confederate property and keep it for public use. From his perspective, the bill was not radical enough. Similarly, William Kelley (R-PA) continued to insist on "state suicide."[244] Democrats, meanwhile, held that defeated Southern states were entitled to readmission with their powers unchanged. "When the rebellion is suppressed," argued Aaron Harding (D-KY), any state readmitted is "thereby restored to all its rights and privileges."[245]

To appease the bill's GOP critics, Davis won approval for two substantive amendments—both of which were added without roll-call votes. The first increased the percentage of voters required to take the loyalty oath before elections could begin from 10 (Lincoln's policy) to 50. Davis's original proposal also proposed to strip citizenship and voting rights from all state officers who participated in the Confederate government. By voice vote, however, the House approved a change disqualifying only "civil officers of ministerial rank and military officers with at least the rank of colonel."[246] Davis also agreed to allow Republican critics of the bill to draft language that could be used for the bill's preamble. Thaddeus Stevens offered the following:

> Whereas the Confederate States are a public enemy, waging an unjust war, whose injustice is so glaring that they have no right to claim the mitigation of the extreme rights of war which are accorded by modern usage to an enemy who has a right to consider the war a just act; and whereas none of the States which, by a regularly recorded majority of its citizens, have joined the southern confederacy can be considered and treated as

242. *CG*, 38-1, 3/22/1864, appendix 85.
243. *CG*, 38-1, 4/19/1864, 1741.
244. *CG*, 38-1, 3/3/1864, 2080.
245. *CG*, 38-1, 5/2/1864, 2029.
246. *CG*, 38-1, 5/4/1864, 2107.

entitled to be represented by Congress, or to take any part in the political government of the Union.

On May 4, 1864, voting in the House commenced, and Stevens's preamble was rejected 57-75, with fifteen Republicans voting nay.[247] GOP attrition on this vote, according to Herman Belz, was because "Stevens' proposition was substantially more radical than the bill itself on the constitutional status of the states."[248] Immediately thereafter, the House passed H.R. 244 by a vote of 74-66, with all Republicans unified in support.[249]

H.R. 244 then moved to the Senate. The Committee on Territories, chaired by Benjamin Wade (R-OH), reported the bill in May 1864, but the Senate took no action on it until July. When H R. 244 was finally considered, senators immediately rejected an amendment protecting voting rights for all male citizens without distinction to color. Wade explained his own nay vote — despite supporting the amendment in committee — by declaring that "this amendment, if adopted, will probably jeopardize the bill."[250] B. Gratz Brown (R-MO) then offered an amendment to disallow those living within Confederate states from casting any electoral votes, or from voting for members of the House or Senate, until the president issued a proclamation declaring that the rebellion had come to an end. Recognizing that his amendment would undermine Davis's original proposal, Brown acknowledged that he wanted to "leave the matter of reconstruction to a later day when events shall have perhaps altered some of the relations in which these districts now stand to us." Wade opposed the amendment based on electoral politics: "The question will be asked of every man who goes out to canvass during the coming election what do you propose to do with these seceded States in regard to their coming back? . . . and we must be prepared to give an answer to it."[251] Despite Wade's opposition, the Senate passed the Brown amend-

247. *CG*, 38-1, 5/4/1864, 2107.

248. Belz, *Reconstructing the Union*, 212. A roll-call analysis (logistic regression) of Republican votes on the Stevens preamble finds that the first (positive) NOMINATE dimension is statistically significant. This suggests that more radical Republican senators were more likely to vote in favor, thus supporting Belz's take on the Stevens preamble. It also suggests that Republican senators who voted nay were nearest ideologically to the Democrats on the first dimension. These were Republicans who were more moderate or conservative in ideology.

249. *CG*, 38-1, 5/4/1864, 2108.

250. *CG*, 38-1, 7/1/1864, 3449. The vote on the amendment was 5-24, with Republicans voting 4-14.

251. *CG*, 38-1, 7/1/1864, 3449.

ment 17-16. Only five of twenty-one Republicans voted for the amendment, but those five votes were pivotal for its success.[252]

When the amended version of H.R. 244 moved back to the House, Davis called on members to refuse to concur in the Senate amendments. And they did just that, 42-63, as Republicans voted nay as a bloc.[253] Thus it appeared that nothing would be enacted on Reconstruction before adjournment. However, a "startling development took place" in the Senate.[254] Wade, on learning of the House action, moved that the Senate once again take up the Reconstruction bill — but this time vote to recede from the Brown amendment and agree to the original (House) version of H.R. 244. Democrats cried foul and sought a recess in order to round up opposition to Wade's motion. But Wade, with the help of Sumner and James Henry Lane (R-KS), organized GOP senators to narrowly defeat the motion to recess. Then, on an 18-14 vote, the Senate receded from the Brown amendment and adopted Davis's original H.R. 244 bill, with eighteen of twenty-two Republicans voting in support.[255] As a result, H.R. 244 — henceforth known as the "Wade-Davis bill" — was now passed by both chambers of Congress.

What explains the Senate's reversal on H.R. 244 across the two days? The reversal was a mix of some abstentions on July 2 and some new votes on July 2 (members who did not vote on July 1). For example, of the five GOP senators who supported the Brown substitute on July 1, only three voted on July 2 (and voted against receding). There were also five Republican senators on July 2 who did not vote on July 1 — and they broke 4-1 in favor of receding. And of the six Unionists who voted for the Brown substitute on July 1, only four voted on July 2 (and voted against receding). Finally, while six Democrats voted for the Brown substitute on July 1 and six Democrats voted against receding on July 2, the mix of individuals was a bit different — one senator who voted on July 1 did not vote on July 2, while one senator who voted on July 2 did not vote on July 1.

Belz argues that "much credit for the passage [of H.R. 244, shorn of the Brown amendment] must go to Wade," although any details on how he

---

252. *CG*, 38-1, 7/1/1864, 3460. The five Republicans who voted for the Brown amendment were Edgar Cowan (PA), James Doolittle (WI), James Grimes (IA), Henry Lane (IN), and Lyman Trumbull (IL). These five were among the eight most conservative Republicans (i.e., closest to the Democrats) on the first NOMINATE dimension in the Thirty-Eighth Senate. Democrats voted 6-0 and Unionists voted 6-0.

253. *CG*, 38-1, 7/2/1864, 3518. A roll call was not taken; the vote was by teller.

254. Belz, *Reconstructing the Union*, 221.

255. *CG*, 38-1, 7/2/1864, 3491.

managed it are lost.[256] However, it seems likely that with the House's insistence on its version of H.R. 244, and with time running out in the congressional session, enough senators preferred some bill (the unamended H.R. 244) to no bill — and behaved accordingly, through votes or strategic abstentions.

These speculations aside, the Senate vote to recede from the Brown amendment was not the last surprise for advocates of the Wade-Davis bill. Noah Brooks, a Washington newspaper correspondent during the Civil War and Reconstruction, spoke for most observers when he recalled years later that "nobody seemed to think that this extraordinary scheme [the Wade-Davis bill] would be disapproved by the president."[257] Yet Lincoln did "disapprove" via pocket veto.[258] On July 8, less than a week after Congress adjourned, Lincoln issued a proclamation explaining his opposition to the measure. "I am . . . unprepared by a formal approval of this bill, to be inflexibly committed to any single plan of restoration," Lincoln argued.[259] Continuing, he explained his unwillingness to "declare that the free state constitutions and governments, already adopted and installed in Arkansas and Louisiana, shall be set aside and held for naught." At the same time, and rather confusingly, Lincoln declared himself "fully satisfied with the system for restoration contained in the bill, as one very proper plan for the loyal people of any state choosing to adopt it."

If passage of the bill and Lincoln's pocket veto were surprising, the reaction from Wade and Davis was anything but: they were furious. Their response came one month later in the form of a *New-York Tribune* article vehemently condemning Lincoln. This "manifesto" refuted every point Lincoln had made in his July proclamation. Previewing future battles between the legislative and executive over the terms of sectional reconciliation, they concluded by stating,

256. For example, Belz notes that "No evidence has turned up to explain why five senators, who by maintaining their earlier opposition could have defeated the Wade-Davis Bill, were absent, or what pressures were exerted on those who had previously been absent but were there to vote for the bill on July 2. The final disposition of the measure went almost unnoticed as the newspapers gave full attention to the resignation of Salmon P. Chase as Secretary of the Treasury and to Confederate raids near Washington." Belz, *Reconstructing the Union*, 222.

257. Noah Brooks, *Washington in Lincoln's Time* (New York: Century, 1896), 164.

258. With fewer than ten days remaining before Congress was to adjourn, Lincoln did not have to issue a formal veto.

259. Lincoln's proclamation can be read at http://quod.lib.umich.edu/l/lincoln/lincoln7/1:955?rgn=div1;view=fulltext.

Our support is of a cause, and not of a man: that the authority of Congress is paramount, and must be respected; that the whole body of the Union men of Congress will not submit to be impeached by him of rash and un-constitutional legislation; and if he wishes our support he must confine himself to his executive duties — to obey and execute, not make the laws; to suppress by arms armed rebellion, and leave political reorganization to Congress.[260]

Their attack on Lincoln's authority failed to have the desired effect. And most Republicans in Congress, angry as they might be, set their feelings aside to rally around Lincoln before the November elections.[261] Yet the posi-tion Wade and Davis set out would soon be taken up by Republicans who found a new enemy — President Andrew Johnson.

Conclusion

The American Civil War upended the country's social, economic, and po-litical status quo. Before the outbreak of war, one out of every three people living south of the Mason-Dixon line was enslaved. Slavery was so impor-tant to the Southern economy that many believed the slave system to be, in the words of Frederick Douglass, "impregnable."[262] Even after Lincoln's election, Congress passed a constitutional amendment that would have pro-tected slavery where it existed.

Once the war came, Lincoln and his Republican allies in Congress were responsible for crafting the military and political strategies to defeat the South and then reconstitute the Union. As we have documented, Repub-licans groped their way through the crisis. This new party — like the citi-zenry — was divided. Some members were committed abolitionists; some were sympathetic to abolition but skeptical about the constitutionality of federal emancipation; and some were simply Free Soilers. As a consequence, the policies crafted in 1861–65 reflected the ongoing intraparty struggle be-tween radicals, moderates, and conservatives. Each policy we have dis-cussed represented a hard-fought compromise by Republicans with differ-ent ideological viewpoints.

This political dynamic previews the coming battles over Reconstruc-

260. "To the Supporters of the Government," *New-York Tribune*, August 5, 1864, 5.

261. Donald, Baker, and Holt, *Civil War and Reconstruction*, 516.

262. John Stauffer and Henry Louis Gates Jr., eds., *The Portable Frederick Douglass* (New York: Penguin Books, 2016), 250.

tion policy. In short, both radicals and conservatives were consistently incapable of putting together the majorities needed to enact their most preferred policies. As we will show, the importance of intraparty compromise to all legislation involving the fate of freed slaves is reinforced again and again. Furthermore, aside from a period when Andrew Johnson controlled the presidency, the political moderation of many within the GOP would only grow more pronounced once Ulysses Grant ascended to the White House. As a result, Republican moderates would effectively limit the impact of what might otherwise have been revolutionary changes to the American political system. They would also prevent the party's more conservative faction from simply declaring victory and moving on after ratification of the Thirteenth Amendment. The Civil War, in other words, led to the abolition of slavery but not to destruction of those political impulses that had protected slavery for so long.

CHAPTER THREE

The Early Reconstruction Era, 1865–1871

In April 1865, less than a week after Confederate general Robert E. Lee surrendered at Appomattox, Abraham Lincoln was murdered by John Wilkes Booth. Lincoln's death brought to power Vice President Andrew Johnson, a War Democrat from Tennessee, dissolving the Republican Party's unified control of government. Yet the GOP maintained overwhelming majorities in both chambers of Congress as the Confederate states, from which the Democratic Party drew its strength, were denied representation.

Southern Reconstruction would last from 1865 to 1877. President Johnson immediately took the initiative by unilaterally creating provisional Southern governments and setting the terms for readmission of the rebellious states. Yet Johnson's political miscalculations, and widespread dissatisfaction with the leniency he exhibited toward Southern "traitors," soon inspired a backlash. Beginning in 1866, congressional Republicans challenged Johnson's political authority, and in 1868 they nearly removed him from office through impeachment. More important, they took charge of Reconstruction by repeatedly passing legislation over Johnson's vetoes. Republicans in Congress are thus rightly seen as responsible for the Fourteenth and Fifteenth Amendments, landmark enactments guaranteeing equal protection of the law and voting rights for black men. They are also responsible for a number of supplementary statutes to protect freedmen from the recrudescence of the Slave Power.

But these legislative victories should not mask deep tensions within the majority party. At war's end, Republicans had not yet developed a plan for determining the political status of millions of former slaves or a process for readmitting the former Confederate states. Complicating efforts to deal with these issues were significant ideological disagreements within the party. Radicals sought the immediate guarantee of full civil and political rights for freedmen and advocated federal intervention into the states to provide them with aid and education. In addition, they sought to punish the South by prohibiting former Confederates from participating in the political process. Moderate and conservative Republicans were more reluctant to bolster federal authority. Like the radicals, they believed the lives and property of blacks and loyal whites must be protected. Yet they did not believe the federal government held the authority to provide substantive equality within the states, nor did they believe the former slaves were prepared to enter the polity as full voting citizens. They also prioritized readmission of Southern states, and a quick return to the "normal" functioning of the constitutional system, over punishing Southerners for their rebellion.

Once Congress took control of Reconstruction from Johnson, policymaking became a contest of strength between these factions. While no single faction controlled the congressional majority, the preponderance of Republican moderates meant their political preferences were usually written into successful policy enactments. Yet radicals got their way when Johnson's decisions alienated moderates. Radicals also held enough power to block any bill they believed was too conservative, and they sometimes joined with Democrats in hopes of embarrassing the moderates. The radicals' willingness to side with Democrats frequently forced Republican leaders to cobble together majorities on the fly. Successful policy enactments were often written to generate compromise at the expense of clarity. These compromises set the stage for later fights over implementation and enforcement.

Civil rights policymaking during the early Reconstruction years was thus "developmental." Legislating involved day-by-day (sometimes hour-by-hour) negotiations that progressively narrowed the range of policy options. Often members needed to revisit issues confronted in successful policy enactments because their purposes were not fully achieved or because of unanticipated reactions by citizens.

Our analysis focuses on the three Congresses from 1865 to 1871: the Thirty-Ninth (1865–67), Fortieth (1867–69), and Forty-First (1869–71). During these six years, congressional Republicans instigated revolutionary changes to the political and social structure of the country. Legislation introduced by Sen. Lyman Trumbull (R-IL) in January 1866 to extend the life of the Freedmen's Bureau defined for the first time those civil rights guaranteed to all citizens by the federal government and initiated a sequence of policymaking that included the Civil Rights Act of 1866 and voting rights in Washington, DC, and culminated in the Fourteenth and Fifteenth Amendments and the Enforcement Acts. By examining these in turn, we observe the political dynamics at work in the early Reconstruction years. Before doing so, we set the stage by describing what congressional Republicans were up against as President Johnson made the first move in initiating sectional reconciliation.

Presidential Reconstruction

Once Andrew Johnson ascended to the presidency,[1] he envisioned a plan for sectional reconciliation that was more in line with Lincoln's than with that of congressional Republicans.[2] Johnson also took advantage of Congress's adjournment — the Thirty-Ninth Congress (1865–67) would not convene until December 1865, and he had no intention of calling them into special session beforehand — to take control of Reconstruction and dictate its direction via proclamation.

Johnson sought a swift sectional reconciliation whereby white-led states voluntarily arranged to rejoin the Union under certain conditions. To that end, he appointed a provisional civilian governor for each state to organize whites-only constitutional conventions. Although to receive amnesty white Southerners had to take a basic oath of allegiance requiring them to accept emancipation, Johnson specified exceptions to help prevent the antebellum planter elite from returning to power.[3] Through his efforts, Johnson be-

1. In 1864 Lincoln chose Johnson to replace Republican Hannibal Hamlin (ME) as vice president to broaden his electoral coalition before what he perceived would be a difficult election. In 1862 Lincoln had made Johnson military governor of Tennessee after much of the state was under the Union army's control.

2. For Johnson's views on Reconstruction, along with congressional Republicans' reactions to them, see Eric L. McKitrick, *Andrew Johnson and Reconstruction* (Chicago: University of Chicago Press, 1960); Michael Les Benedict, *A Compromise of Principle: Congressional Republicans and Reconstruction, 1863–1869* (New York: Norton, 1974), chap. 5; Hans L. Trefousse, *Andrew Johnson: A Biography* (New York: Norton, 1997).

3. Proclamation 134, Granting Amnesty to Participants in the Rebellion, with Certain Exceptions (May 29, 1865), can be read at https://www.presidency.ucsb.edu/node/203492. The chief amnesty exception related to "all persons who have voluntarily participated in said rebellion and the estimated value of whose taxable property is over $20,000."

lieved he might initiate a political realignment by which extreme elements on both the left and the right would be marginalized and a new party of the center would emerge that would elect him president in 1868. Key to this plan was a moderate South, chastened in defeat, that would rejoin the Union and provide him with a base of electoral support for his broader "National Union Party."[4]

By the end of 1865 Johnson's plan had fallen apart. Although state conventions in Alabama, Florida, Georgia, Mississippi, North Carolina, South Carolina, and Texas all adopted new constitutions and organized new state governments that elected new members of Congress,[5] the white Southerners who formed these institutions departed from Johnson's wishes in a variety of ways. For example, they rejected the Thirteenth Amendment, failed to nullify earlier secession ordinances and repudiate the Confederate debt, and elected some prominent Confederates who were not granted amnesty.[6]

White-dominated state governments also recreated an antebellum social order while acknowledging the reality of the Thirteenth Amendment. Wealthy planters, whom Johnson eventually pardoned,[7] worked to keep black labor subjugated, first through threats and violence and then through legal maneuvers. Specifically, "Black Codes," which restricted the rights of blacks and pushed them to return to plantation work through draconian vagrancy laws, were passed in most Southern states in 1865–66.[8] While many of these provisions were vetoed by Union military commanders associated with the Freedmen's Bureau, their adoption signaled that the white South was defiant even after military defeat.

The Northern public was horrified by these developments, and congres-

4. See LaWanda Cox and John H. Cox, *Politics, Principle, and Prejudice, 1865–1866: Dilemma of Reconstruction* (Glencoe, IL: Free Press, 1963).

5. These states thus joined Arkansas, Louisiana, Tennessee, and Virginia from the Lincoln era.

6. See Michael Perman, *Reunion without Compromise: The South and Reconstruction, 1865–1868* (New York: Cambridge University Press, 1973); Dan T. Carter, *When the War Was Over: The Failure of Self-Reconstruction in the South, 1865–1867* (Baton Rouge: Louisiana State University Press, 1985). Several convention delegates were also among those not granted amnesty.

7. By fall 1865 Johnson had issued scores of individual pardons. See McKitrick, *Andrew Johnson and Reconstruction*, 146; Jonathan Truman Dorris, *Pardon and Amnesty under Lincoln and Johnson: The Restoration of the Confederates to Their Rights and Privileges, 1861–1898* (Chapel Hill: University of North Carolina Press, 1953), 316.

8. On the Black Codes, see Theodor B. Wilson, *The Black Codes of the South* (University: University of Alabama Press, 1965).

sional Republicans were emboldened to strike back. Arguing that Southern governments were trying to nullify the Union victory and thereby dishonor the memory of the Northern troops who had sacrificed their lives to win the war, GOP lawmakers sought to prevent Johnson's Reconstruction policy from taking effect. They made their move at the opening of the Thirty-Ninth Congress in December 1865. At the direction of Thaddeus Stevens (R-PA), Edward McPherson, clerk of the US House, passed over the names of Southern representatives when calling the roll of members-elect.[9] This invalidated their election credentials, allowing Congress to take charge of Reconstruction.[10] Shortly thereafter, a Joint Committee of Fifteen—six members from the Senate and nine from the House—was appointed to investigate conditions in the former Confederacy and advise on the issue of Southern representation in Congress.[11]

In early 1866 the Joint Committee of Fifteen began collecting testimony from witnesses regarding civil atrocities that had recently occurred in the South.[12] At the same time, Senate Republicans took the lead in offering a congressional response to Johnson that would guarantee rights and protections for blacks in the hostile Southern environment. Two bills were drawn up in the Senate Judiciary Committee: a measure that extended the life of the Freedmen's Bureau and expanded its authority and activities and a civil rights bill that provided national citizenship to all persons born in the United States (except Indians) without regard to race; enumerated specific rights such citizens enjoyed; and provided federal protection of those rights.

Extending the Freedmen's Bureau

As we noted in chapter 2, Congress first established the Freedmen's Bureau in March 1865 and tasked it with providing former slaves with food, estab-

9. McPherson was considered a protégé of Stevens. He had been a Republican member of the US House in the Thirty-Sixth and Thirty-Seventh Congresses but was defeated for re-election to the Thirty-Eighth. He would go on to be elected House clerk eight times.

10. Trefousse, *Andrew Johnson*, 174–76; Jeffery A. Jenkins and Charles Stewart III, *Fighting for the Speakership: The House and the Rise of Party Government* (Princeton, NJ: Princeton University Press, 2013), 252.

11. The Joint Committee of Fifteen was Stevens's creation. He unveiled it in the Republican caucus before the convening of the Thirty-Ninth Congress, and it was adopted unanimously. See "From Washington," *Baltimore Sun*, December 4, 1865, 1. The committee included twelve Republicans and three Democrats.

12. Eric Foner, *Reconstruction: America's Unfinished Revolution, 1863–1877* (New York: Harper and Row, 1988), 239, 246–47.

lishing schools and hospitals throughout the South, and monitoring labor contracts between freedmen and landowners. Agents of the Freedmen's Bureau, working with Union soldiers, were also responsible for settling the freedmen on Southern land that had been abandoned or confiscated during the war. Supporters depicted it as purely a war measure, however, so the legislation stipulated that the bureau would operate for just one year after the war's end.

On January 12, 1866, Lyman Trumbull, chair of the Senate Judiciary Committee, introduced a new proposal (S. 60) that aimed to "enlarge the powers of the Freedmen's Bureau."[13] The bill called on the president to divide the South into districts and appoint agents who would distribute aid and buy property for building schools and asylums. The bill also empowered the president, for three years, to rent out to loyal refugees and freedmen parcels of public land, not exceeding forty acres, in Florida, Mississippi, and Arkansas. The bill made it clear that it would be the "duty of the President of the United States, through the commissioner [of a district branch of the bureau], to extend military protection and jurisdiction" to *anybody* denied the right to "make and enforce contracts, to sue, to be parties, and give evidence, to inherit, purchase, lease, sell, hold and convey real and personal property, and to have full and equal benefit of all laws . . . on account of race, color, or previous condition of servitude." In cases of potential discrimination, victims could pursue remedies in military courts administered by bureau agents. Those judged guilty could be fined, sent to prison, or both. Finally, S. 60 stipulated that the Freedmen's Bureau would remain in place until otherwise provided by law.

Although Trumbull's bill provided aid and guaranteed rights to freedmen and others, he once again tied these proposals to the military occupation. The civil rights provisions, for example, could be enforced only in those states where court systems were not functioning owing to military occupation. Once the occupation ended, the bill's provisions would terminate. Defending his decision to make protection of rights contingent on military occupation, Trumbull argued that the "military power governs and controls where no courts can exist."[14] He stated that laws barring freedmen from purchasing real estate, serving on juries, or intermarrying with whites would not be annulled in "loyal and patriotic" states with governments not "usurped or overthrown by traitors."[15] Once Southern states were re-

13. *CG*, 39-1, 1/12/1866, 209.
14. *CG*, 39-1, 1/25/1866, 420.
15. *CG*, 39-1, 1/19/1866, 320.

admitted to the Union, they would presumably be free to enact all manner of discriminatory laws, and all federal authorities created by S. 60 would disappear. This caveat allowed Trumbull and Senate moderates to provide some protection to freedmen without sacrificing their commitment to constitutional federalism.

From January 22 to January 25, the Senate rejected a series of amendments designed to further constrain the bureau. The first, offered by Edgar Cowan (R-PA), would have legally barred the government from establishing branches of the Freedmen's Bureau in states outside the former Confederacy. Cowan, a conservative, gave voice to fears that policy enforced in the South might one day be enforced nationwide. According to Cowan, the Freedmen's Bureau should be "circumscribed . . . to the states lately in rebellion, as those are the only states over whom we can have a shadow of a pretense for exercising this right, which must be a belligerent right, if it is any right at all." The Senate defeated Cowan's amendment 33-11, with all Democrats and Cowan voting against all remaining Republicans.[16]

Garrett Davis (U-KY) then offered seven amendments, each seeking to weaken the bureau.[17] Each failed on a party-line vote. Davis also forced the Senate to consider an amendment that would have made public land outside the South available to freedmen. If Republicans backed his amendment, they would be signaling to Northern voters that the federal government might one day distribute land outside the South to freedmen. If they opposed it, they would be signaling that civil rights protections applied only in the South. Republicans defeated Davis's amendment by voice vote.[18]

Two days later the Senate passed Trumbull's bill 37-10 in a pure party-line vote.[19] Despite the bill's limitations, it won praise from the *Chicago Tribune*, a newspaper associated with congressional radicals. "Though, perhaps, not perfect," the editors argued, the bill "would confer the greatest attainable benefit upon the freed people, and at the same time be so framed as to insure its passage through the Senate, and its final approbation by the President."[20]

In the House, Democrats attacked S. 60 as an unconstitutional effort to legislate equality in the states.[21] Some Republicans, however, thought it did

16. *CG*, 39-1, 1/22/1866, 347.

17. Davis was a member of the Unionist Party until 1867, when he declared himself a Democrat.

18. *CG*, 39-1, 1/23/1866, 372.

19. *CG*, 39-1, 1/25/1866, 421.

20. "From Washington: Senator Trumbull's Freedmen's Bill," *CT*, January 26, 1866, 2.

21. For example, see the comments of John Dawson (D-PA), *CG*, 39-1, 1/31/1866, 538-41,

not go far enough. Thaddeus Stevens led the GOP effort to enhance S. 60 when he introduced amendments that would have set the maximum rental price for land made available to freedmen at ten cents an acre per year; set the maximum purchase value at two dollars an acre; removed a provision stipulating that the rental and purchase prices hold for only three years; and stipulated that bureau commissioners would be empowered to provide free schooling to all freedmen and refugees.[22] Stevens also sought to prevent the president from pardoning former rebels and then returning to them land that had been seized during the war. According to Stevens, such authority would allow President Johnson to evict loyal freedmen in order to make room for "reeking rebels."[23]

On February 6 the House voted on a substitute bill written to include Stevens's amendments, and it lost 37–127.[24] Most Republicans recognized that Stevens's substitute would never pass in the Senate and sought to plow ahead. Through voice votes, however, the House did amend S. 60 in ways that would require further Senate action.[25] For example, the bill was altered to allow the president to divide into districts those places where, as of February 1, 1866, habeas corpus was suspended. This change ensured that the Freedmen's Bureau could operate in Kentucky. In addition, the House added language to stipulate that S. 60 could not be enforced in Maryland, Delaware, Missouri, or any Northern state. Members then voted to pass S. 60, as amended, 137–34, with all but one Republican opposing all Democrats.[26] On February 8, the Senate concurred with the House amendments.[27]

Attention now turned to President Johnson. During Senate debate over the Freedmen's Bureau extension, Republicans frequently mentioned the importance of retaining Johnson's support as a defense of the bill's limited aims, especially compared with Stevens's alternative. William Fessenden

---

and of Michael Kerr (D-IN), Samuel Marshall (D-IL), and Lovell Rousseau (D-KY), *CG*, 39-1, 2/2/1866, 618–29.

22. *CG*, 39-1, 2/5/1866, 655.

23. *CG*, 39-1, 2/5/1866, 658.

24. *CG*, 39-1, 2/6/1866, 688. Republicans voted 37–85. A roll-call analysis (logistic regression) of Republican votes finds that the first (positive) and second (negative) NOMINATE dimensions are statistically significant, with Republican members furthest from the Democrats being more likely to support the Stevens substitute. These were the radicals.

25. *CG*, 39-1, 2/8/1866, 742–47.

26. *CG*, 39-1, 2/6/1866, 688. Thomas E. Noell (MO) was the lone Republican to vote against the bill. He would switch to the Democratic Party in his election to the Fortieth Congress.

27. *CG*, 39-1, 2/8/1866, 747.

(R-ME), a senator whose opinion was respected by both radicals and moderates, took to the floor to put to rest all rumors of an impending split between the president and congressional Republicans.[28] Fessenden believed "the President desires, and means, to stand by those who elected him" and stated that he was "resolved to keep him there, if it can be done consistently with the best interests of the country."[29] Newspapers also wrote of Johnson's "repeated assurances that he entirely approves the bill in its present comprehensive form."[30] In short, many moderate Republicans in Congress thought that, because of their efforts to beat back radical opposition, Johnson would sign the Freedmen's Bureau extension.[31]

Yet on February 19, 1866, Johnson vetoed the bill, thus signaling his opposition to even "moderate" civil rights protections. Moreover, the tenor of his veto message cast further doubt on his willingness to work with congressional Republicans. Congress had no right to "shut out, in time of peace, any state from the representation to which it is entitled by the Constitution," Johnson contended. In so doing he suggested that Congress lacked the authority to pass legislation of any kind until the former Confederate states were readmitted.[32] Johnson also condemned the provisions offering federal aid to freedmen. "The idea on which the slaves were assisted to freedom," he argued, "was that on becoming free they would be a self sustaining population. Any legislation that shall imply that they are not . . . must have a tendency injurious alike to their character and their prospects."[33]

The following day, Trumbull expressed his "surprise and regret" at the veto message and restated the moderate position on civil rights protections. He portrayed federal jurisdiction over legal proceedings in the former Confederacy as a "wartime" measure to be lifted as each Southern state was "restored to [its] constitutional relations and when the courts . . . are not inter-

28. *CG*, 39-1, 1/23/1866, 364–67.

29. McKitrick, *Andrew Johnson and Reconstruction*, 284. See also Robert J. Cook, *Civil War Senator: William Pitt Fessenden and the Fight to Save the American Republic* (Baton Rouge: Louisiana State University Press, 2011), 200.

30. "The Freedmen," *CT*, February 3, 1866, 2.

31. McKitrick, *Andrew Johnson and Reconstruction*, 284; Benedict, *Compromise of Principle*, 155.

32. For a general analysis of Johnson's veto message see McKitrick, *Andrew Johnson and Reconstruction*, 288–90; Benedict, *Compromise of Principle*, 155–156; and John H. Cox and LaWanda Cox, "Andrew Johnson and His Ghost Writers: An Analysis of the Freedmen's Bureau and Civil Rights Veto Messages," *Mississippi Valley Historical Review* 48 (December 1961): 460–79.

33. Johnson's veto message is printed in *CG*, 39-1, 2/19/1866, 915–17.

rupted or interfered with in the peaceable course of justice." Trumbull then argued that the federal aid provided by the bureau was a temporary solution, necessary because freedmen

> do not know where to go; they have no means to pay for subsistence by the way; they do not know whither the railroads lead; the railroads would not carry them if they did, and were able to pay. . . . They cannot read the finger-boards by the wayside; and where are they to go, and what is to be done with them? They are to go to the same place . . . they are to be taken and reduced to slavery again or they are to perish and die for want of subsistence, or somebody must temporarily look after and provide for them.[34]

Trumbull's claim that S. 60 proposed no permanent change to federal-state relations did not persuade two-thirds of the Senate to override Johnson's veto. With seven conservative Republicans voting against an override, the attempt failed 30-18.[35] Five of these seven Republicans voted both for the bill and to sustain Johnson's veto. None of them took to the floor to explain why. Yet two senators, Edgar Cowan (PA) and Waitman Willey (WV), who voted nay but abstained on the initial passage vote, did seek to defend themselves. In both cases they attacked aspects of the bill they considered unconstitutional.[36]

Johnson's successful veto of S. 60 did not permanently defeat efforts to extend the life of the Freedmen's Bureau. In May 1866 the House debated H.R. 613, a bill specifically designed to overcome Johnson's objections. As explained by sponsor Thomas Eliot (R-MA), H.R. 613 extended the life of the Freedmen's Bureau for two years. Aid to freedmen would be considered only if it would "enable them as speedily as practicable to become self-supporting citizens of the United States." His bill also jettisoned the provision allowing the president to divide former Confederate states into districts to be overseen by bureau agents. Instead, the small number of officials already working for the bureau would be sent wherever the president deter-

34. *CG*, 39-1, 2/20/1866, 939.

35. *CG*, 39-1, 2/20/1866, 943. Republicans voting to sustain the veto included Edgar Cowan (PA), James Dixon (CT), James Doolittle (WI), Edwin Morgan (NY), Daniel Norton (MN), William Stewart (NV), and Waitman Willey (WV). A roll-call analysis (logistic regression) of Republican votes finds that the first (positive) NOMINATE dimension is statistically significant, with Republican members furthest from the Democrats (i.e., the radicals) being more likely to support overriding Johnson's veto.

36. *CG*, 39-1, 2/20/1866, 942–43.

mined their services could "best be employed." Eliot's bill also made it clear that freedmen would not be entitled to property abandoned or confiscated during the war. Instead, white landowners would be allowed to petition the government to reclaim what was once theirs. When such petitions were approved, bureau agents would then work to resettle freedmen occupying reclaimed land. Finally, the bureau could help to identify buildings that might be used as schools, but the federal government would not take any role in educating the nation's children.[37]

Thaddeus Stevens was furious about H.R. 613's land provision, arguing that it would ensure that "the moment these former owners apply, the land is to be restored."[38] Accordingly, he introduced an amendment stipulating that the land taken by William T. Sherman at Sea Islands, Georgia, specifically, would never be returned to its previous owners. Stevens's amendment passed 79-46, though it drew opposition from seventeen Republicans who feared it would doom the bill.[39] Finally, on May 29 the House passed the amended H.R. 613 by a vote of 96-32, with ninety-one of ninety-seven Republicans voting yea.[40]

A month later the Senate considered H.R. 613 and passed an amended version by voice vote.[41] The one substantive change was to strip Stevens's amendment and replace it with language allowing freedmen on the Sea Islands to purchase twenty-acre plots at a price determined by federal tax commissioners in the event the land they occupied was reclaimed. The House approved the Senate-amended bill by voice vote soon thereafter.[42] Johnson was not convinced by this effort, and on July 16 he once again issued a veto. This time, however, both the House and Senate — that same day — successfully voted to override.[43] Only four Republicans in the House and two in the Senate defected.

The Freedmen's Bureau would provide a variety of valuable services to former slaves over the next couple of years. Beginning in July 1868, the bureau began winding down as rebel states were brought back into the Union.

37. *CG*, 39-1, 5/23/1866, 2772–73.
38. *CG*, 39-1, 5/24/1866, 2808.
39. *CG*, 39-1, 5/24/1866, 2808. Republicans voted 78-17.
40. *CG*, 39-1, 5/29/1866, 2878.
41. *CG*, 39-1, 6/26/1866, 3413.
42. *CG*, 39-1, 7/3/1866, 3562.
43. *CG*, 39-1, 7/16/1866, 3842, 3850. The votes were 33-12 in the House and 97-4 in the Senate.

As Marc Summers states, "Congress ordered the commissioner to bring most bureau activities to an end at the start of the new year and relinquish its duties before then in states fully reconstructed."[44] Bureau courts soon closed, and supervision over labor contracts ended. Finally, in June 1872 Congress shuttered the Freedmen's Bureau for good.

The Civil Rights Act of 1866

On the day he introduced S. 60, Lyman Trumbull also introduced S. 61, a civil rights bill. This was Congress's first effort to define in real terms the meaning of "practical freedom." S. 61 prohibited "discrimination in civil rights or immunities" and explicitly granted citizenship to native-born black Americans. It defined civil rights as the power to "make and enforce contracts, to sue, to be parties and give evidence, to inherit, purchase, lease, sell, hold, and convey real and personal property, and to full and equal benefit of all laws and proceedings for the security of person and property." S. 61 also established a punishment for those found guilty of depriving "any inhabitant of any state or territory . . . [of] any right secured or protected by this act," as well as a process for moving cases from state to federal court in order to avoid discriminatory laws.[45]

Trumbull portrayed the bill as a necessary response to the enactment of the Black Codes throughout the South. In November 1865, for example, Mississippi passed a law intended to "regulate the relation of Master and Apprentice to Freedmen, Free Negroes, and Mulattoes," which among other things empowered masters to "inflict such moderate corporeal chastisement" on their apprentices "as a father or guardian is allowed to inflict on his or her child or ward."[46] Elsewhere, Georgia amended its penal code so as to make it lawful for black residents to be imprisoned or sentenced to manual labor for the crime of "strolling about in idleness" or "leading an idle, immoral or profligate life."[47] As Black Codes "impose upon [freedmen] the very restrictions which were imposed upon them in consequence of the

44. Marc Wahlgren Summers, *The Ordeal of the Reunion: A New History of Reconstruction* (Chapel Hill: University of North Carolina Press, 2014), 140.

45. *CG*, 39-1, 1/12/1866, 211–12.

46. Edward McPherson, *The Political History of the United States of America during the Period of Reconstruction* (Washington, DC: James J. Chapman, 1880), 29.

47. McPherson, *Political History of the United States of America during Reconstruction*, 33.

existence of slavery and before it was abolished," Trumbull stated, "the purpose of the bill is to destroy these discriminations."[48]

Moderate Republicans joined with radicals in support of S. 61. Both factions believed that guaranteeing equal rights was necessary to safeguard freedmen's lives. To allow the South to effectively create a racial caste system would surrender the fruits of victory and invalidate the moral basis of the war. On this, moderate Republicans believed they were on safe footing with their constituents.[49]

Critics quickly emerged, especially those who were skeptical of applying federal power to decisions traditionally made at the state level. Trumbull sought to allay such concerns. For example, when James McDougall (D-CA) asked if his bill "involved the question of political rights [voting rights]," Trumbull confirmed that it had "nothing to do with the political rights" of citizens. In addition, he stated that citizens would be allowed to take their cases from state courts to federal courts only if they could prove that state laws did not provide equal protection. According to Trumbull, the law would "have no operation in any state where all persons have the same civil rights without regard to color or race." His aim was to offer freedmen as much protection as possible with as little federal coercion as necessary.[50]

Willard Saulsbury (D-DE) kept up the pressure, portraying S. 61 as a disguised attempt to grant freedmen voting rights. "What are civil rights?" he asked. "Here you use a generic term which in its most comprehensive signification includes every species of right that man can enjoy."[51] Saulsbury then introduced an amendment declaring that freedmen had no voting rights. It

48. *CG*, 39-1, 1/29/1866, 474. According to historian Eric McKitrick, by December 1865 "public awareness of this legislative trend in the South had become general . . . and unusually hostile." Northern citizens feared that Southern legislatures were reviving slavery under a different name, and public opinion moved in the direction of federal action to protect freedmen. McKitrick, *Andrew Johnson and Reconstruction*, 277.

49. On the thinking and beliefs of moderate Republicans, see Foner, *Reconstruction*, 241–43. On the degree to which Reconstruction policy was shaped by moderates with an eye toward their Northern constituencies, see William Gillette, *Retreat from Reconstruction, 1869–1879* (Baton Rouge: Louisiana State University Press, 1979). On the moderates' relationship with the radicals in the GOP, see Benedict, *Compromise of Principle*.

50. Quotations by McDougall and Trumbull appear in *CG*, 39-1, 1/29/1866, 476. For a longer analysis of the "conservative" aspects of the civil rights bill, see Michael Les Benedict, "Preserving the Constitution: The Conservative Basis of Radical Reconstruction," *Journal of American History* 61 (1974): 80–82.

51. *CG*, 39-1, 1/29/1866, 476–77.

failed 7–39, with all but one Republican voting against all but three Democrats.[52] With a similar lack of subtlety, Thomas Hendricks (D-IN) portrayed the bill's enforcement provision, which allowed presidentially appointed commissioners to pursue those convicted of discrimination, as analogous to the Fugitive Slave Act. Hendricks then forced the Senate to vote on an amendment that would have excised all mechanisms for enforcing S. 61. It failed 12–34, with near unanimous Republican opposition.[53]

Trumbull himself offered the only successful amendment to S. 61. It declared that "all persons born in the United States, and not subject to any foreign Power, excluding Indians not taxed, are hereby declared to be citizens of the United States, without distinction of color." Here Trumbull sought to make it clear that all blacks born in the United States were citizens of the country. While such language seemed obvious enough not to need formal statutory language, Trumbull explained why he felt it must be included: "I think that the declaration that 'all men are created equal,' applied as much to the black as to the white man; but the Senator from Kentucky [Mr. Davis] will not admit that. I think it is best, therefore, when we are enacting a statute on this subject declaratory of what the law is . . . to put it beyond question."[54]

On February 1 Trumbull's amendment passed 31–10, with Republicans in near unanimous support.[55] One day later the Senate passed the entire bill 33–12, with only two GOP defections.[56]

The House did not begin debate on the civil rights bill until the beginning of March, *after* President Johnson had vetoed the Freedmen's Bureau extension. James Wilson (R-IA), a member of the Judiciary Committee, managed the bill and emphasized that it did not involve voting rights. This bill "provides for the equality of citizens of the United States in the enjoyment of civil rights and immunities," he claimed. "What do these terms mean? Do they mean that in all things civil, social, political, all citizens without distinction

52. *CG*, 39-1, 2/2/1866, 606. The one Republican was Edgar Cowan (PA), who had argued earlier that Trumbull's goals were legitimate only if pursued through a constitutional amendment. *CG*, 39-1, 1/30/1866, 500.

53. *CG*, 39-1, 2/2/1866, 606. Republicans voted 2–34. The two GOP yea votes were Edgar Cowan (PA) and Daniel Norton (MN), the Republicans who were closest to the Democratic side on the first NOMINATE dimension. They anchored the conservative wing of the GOP.

54. *CG*, 39-1, 2/1/1866, 569, 573–74.

55. *CG*, 39-1, 2/1/1866, 575. Cowan was the only defector.

56. *CG*, 39-1, 2/2/1866, 607. Cowan and Norton were the two Republican nay votes.

of race or color, shall be equal? By no means can they be so construed. Do they mean that all citizens shall vote in the several states? No."[57]

House Democrats followed the lead of their Senate counterparts. Anthony Thornton (IL), for example, condemned the proposal for its "loose and liberal mode" of defining civil rights.[58] From his perspective, civil rights might one day be construed to mean voting rights. He and other Democrats pushed Wilson to make it clear that S. 61 would not give black citizens the right to vote. Whereas Trumbull and Senate Republicans fought this provision when it was introduced, Wilson folded. During the floor debate, he moved to amend the bill to include a new section stipulating that "nothing in this act shall be so construed as to affect the laws of any state concerning the right of suffrage." The House added this provision through voice vote.[59] Wilson's motion was intended to calm the nerves of House Republicans who were less supportive of the bill than their fellow partisans in the Senate.

Indeed, John Bingham (R-OH), a member of the Joint Committee of Fifteen, proved to be a significant obstacle in the House. He believed that, if enacted, S. 61 would "strike down by congressional enactment every state constitution which makes a discrimination on account of race or color." From his perspective, any governor who obeyed a discriminatory state law would be subject to criminal prosecution. Such federal intervention into state authority, Bingham argued, was clearly unconstitutional.[60] To address this concern, he moved to recommit the bill to the Judiciary Committee with instructions to excise the language forbidding state-level legal discrimination. While Bingham's effort failed 37-113, thirty-two of the yea votes came from Republicans.[61] As a result, Wilson and GOP leaders feared that without some change the bill would not pass. This left them contemplating a fall election campaign with little to offer voters.[62]

Wilson thus worked diligently to win support from conservative Republicans. On March 13, 1866, the House considered an amended version

57. *CG*, 39-1, 3/1/1866, 1117–18.

58. *CG*, 39-1, 3/2/1866, 1157.

59. *CG*, 39-1, 3/3/1866, 1162.

60. *CG*, 39-1, 3/9/1866, 1291.

61. *CG*, 39-1, 3/9/1866, 1296. A roll-call analysis (logistic regression) of Republican votes finds that the first (negative) and second (positive) NOMINATE dimensions are statistically significant, with Republican members closer to the Democrats being more likely to support Bingham's motion.

62. Benedict, *Compromise of Principle*, 162.

of S. 61. Among other things, it eliminated the language proclaiming that "there shall be no discrimination in civil rights or immunities among the citizens of the United States in any State or territory of the United States on account of race, color, or previous condition of servitude." This change constrained the power of black citizens to challenge discriminatory laws in the states. Cutting it ultimately persuaded conservative Republicans to back the bill. Without any additional debate, the House immediately moved to a vote, and the bill passed 111-38.[63] All Republicans except Bingham voted in support. Two days later the Senate concurred with the House amendments and passed the amended bill.[64]

Many congressional Republicans believed Johnson would sign the civil rights bill in order to assuage those angry about his veto of the Freedmen's Bureau bill. On March 17, for example, Sen. John Sherman (R-OH) told a gathering of Ohio Republicans that he anticipated the president's support. Echoing Sherman, James Bennett, editor of the pro-Johnson *New York Herald*, published an article arguing that because "we can find nothing in [S. 61] conflicting with the constitution as it now stands, and nothing in conflict with the declared opinions and policy of President Johnson, we have no doubt that he will approve the measure."[65] Nonetheless, on March 27 Johnson issued a veto.

Long and "dyspeptic," Johnson's veto message signaled to Republicans once and for all that they could not trust him to lead the Reconstruction effort.[66] Johnson condemned Congress for attempting to "fix by federal law" a "perfect equality of the white and colored races." Then he accused Republicans of seeking to establish "for the colored race safeguards which go infinitely beyond any . . . ever provided for the white race." He then concluded with an argument nearly identical to the position taken by Democratic opponents of the bill: "It is another step, or rather stride, towards centralization, and the concentration of all legislative powers in the national government. The tendency of the bill must be to resuscitate the spirit of re-

63. *CG*, 39-1, 3/13/1866, 1366-67.

64. Only one of the changes the House made to S. 61 received a roll-call vote in the Senate (it involved providing protection to civil and military officers). It passed 30-7 on a pure party-line vote. See *CG*, 39-1, 3/15/1866, 1413.

65. Both Sherman and Bennett are quoted in McKitrick, *Andrew Johnson and Reconstruction*, 163, 306.

66. David Herbert Donald, Jean Harvey Baker, and Michael F. Holt, *Civil War and Reconstruction* (New York: Norton, 2001), 533.

bellion, and to arrest the progress of those influences which are more closely drawing around the states the bonds of union and peace."[67]

By accusing Republicans of rebellious tendencies and by casting doubt on any federal effort to protect the rights of freedmen, Johnson declared war on the GOP.

Most important, Johnson's veto precipitated an irreconcilable break between him and moderate Republicans. To that point moderates had been wary of radical initiatives — fearing electoral reprisals back home — and sought to avoid a public break with Johnson. This veto convinced them they must cut the president out of their deliberations.[68] One week after Congress received the president's veto, Trumbull channeled the frustration of the president's onetime Republican allies. First noting that the veto was "calculated to alienate [Johnson] from those who elevated him to power," Trumbull then undertook a point-by-point refutation of the president's veto message. He characterized Johnson's position as illogical and hypocritical and questioned the president's integrity by charging that he would "approve no measure" designed to protect freedmen. He also impugned Johnson's loyalty to the Constitution by condemning him for yet again vetoing a bill that had won large majorities in both chambers.[69]

On April 9, 1866, with moderate Republicans on his side, Trumbull successfully orchestrated a veto override, which passed 33-15; the House followed suit later that day in a lopsided 122-41 vote.[70] The first major civil rights victory of the Reconstruction era had been achieved.

The Fourteenth Amendment

The Fourteenth Amendment is one of the most significant laws Congress has passed. With this single proposal, congressional Republicans attempted for the first time to comprehensively answer the most significant outstanding political questions generated by the end of the war: How and to what extent should the federal government intervene in the states in order to guarantee civil rights to former slaves? How should the rules governing ap-

---

67. McPherson, *Political History of the United States of America during Reconstruction,* 74–78.

68. See Gillette, *Retreat from Reconstruction.*

69. *CG,* 39-1, 4/4/1866, 1755–60.

70. *CG,* 39-1, 4/9/1866, 1809, 1861. There were four GOP defections in the Senate — Edgar Cowan (PA), James Doolittle (WI), James Lane (KS), and Daniel Norton (MN) — and two in the House — Thomas Noell (MO) and Henry Raymond (NY).

portionment and representation change so that Southern political influence would not increase now that the Three-Fifths Compromise was no longer in effect? Should former Confederates be banned from voting and holding office? Should the federal government grant freedmen the right to vote? and What should be done about the financial debts incurred by the war?[71] Answers to these questions cut across ideological and geographical divisions within the GOP. Any proposal would need to win the support of the party's contending factions. The result was an ambiguous bill that pleased no one, was largely open to interpretation, and set the stage for future conflict.

The process by which the Fourteenth Amendment came to be reflects that by early 1866 the Republican Party had not settled on a plan for managing Reconstruction.[72] No single committee took the lead in crafting a comprehensive proposal addressing these questions. Instead, sections of what would become the Fourteenth Amendment appeared as stand-alone bills and constitutional amendments beginning as early as December 1865. Members in both chambers debated a number of potential amendments, and many approaches were possible.[73]

On December 5, 1865, the second day of the Thirty-Ninth Congress, Thaddeus Stevens introduced in the House a measure stipulating that seat shares would in the future be based on the number of "legal voters" living within a given state and that Congress would "provide for ascertaining the number of said voters."[74] In short, Stevens's proposal would leave it up to the states to determine voting requirements while "indirectly promoting black suffrage."[75] One consequence of this resolution would be to reduce New England's representation in Congress. As James Blaine (R-ME) noted in a floor speech on January 8, 1866, the westward migration of many northeastern males, combined with a larger population of immigrants, meant that this provision would (unfairly in his mind) diminish the political power of

71. Because this analysis focuses on civil rights, we limit our attention to those aspects of the Fourteenth Amendment that apply to black citizens.

72. For a narrative account of the politicking behind the Fourteenth Amendment, see Garrett Epps, *Democracy Reborn: The Fourteenth Amendment and the Fight for Equal Rights in Post–Civil War America* (New York: Henry Holt, 2006).

73. Much of the debate over what would become the Fourteenth Amendment occurred within the Joint Committee of Fifteen. While our analysis will focus primarily on floor debates, the decisions of the committee are important in their own right. They are reported in Benjamin B. Kendrick, "The Journal of the Joint Committee of Fifteen on Reconstruction, 89th Congress, 1865–1867" (PhD diss., Columbia University, 1914).

74. *CG*, 39-1, 12/5/1865, 10.

75. Foner, *Reconstruction*, 252.

FIGURE 3. Rep. Thaddeus Stevens (R-MA). Library of Congress, Prints & Photographs Division, LC-DIG-cwpbh-00460.

his region. Blaine's opposition and the threat of a northeastern revolt convinced Stevens and his supporters they should forgo further consideration of the bill.[76] The debate between Stevens and Blaine illustrated the GOP's geographical fault lines.

Roscoe Conkling (R-NY) argued that there were only two straightforward methods for dealing with the problem of apportionment: basing it on the representation of the total population of a state or basing it on the population of "legal voters" living in the state.[77] Since neither option would please Republicans from every region, the Joint Committee of Fifteen worked toward a compromise. On January 22, 1866, Sen. William Fessenden (R-ME) and Stevens introduced H.J. Res. 51, a stand-alone apportionment amendment, in their respective chambers. The amendment stated that

> Representatives and direct taxes shall be apportioned among the various states which may be included within this Union, according to their respective numbers, counting the whole number of persons in each state, excluding Indians not taxed; provided that whenever the elective franchise shall be denied or abridged in any state on account of race or color, all persons of such race or color shall be excluded from the basis of representation.[78]

Here the committee made it possible for New England states to continue to set voting restrictions without penalty while preventing the South from benefiting from the disenfranchisement of black residents.

The House debated H.J. Res. 51 for a week after its introduction. In the end a small textual change — excising the words "direct taxes" from the first line — was made before the House passed it 120-46 on January 31.[79] The support of all but six Republicans helped H.J. Res. 51 achieve the necessary two-thirds.

In the Senate, H.J. Res. 51 met insurmountable opposition in the person of Charles Sumner (R-MA), who claimed that any explicit reference to race or color would do an injustice to the Constitution. He then moved an amendment that would have granted equal "civil and political rights" to every-

76. Benjamin B. Kendrick, *The Journal of the Joint Committee of Fifteen on Reconstruction* (New York: Columbia University Press, 1914), 41–42; McKitrick, *Andrew Johnson and Reconstruction*, 337.

77. Conkling's position is summarized in Kendrick, *Journal of the Joint Committee*, 199.

78. *CG*, 39-1, 1/22/1866, 337, 351.

79. *CG*, 39-1, 1/31/1866, 538.

one in the United States "regardless of race or color."[80] William Fessenden opposed Sumner's amendment because it simply could not pass. "My constituents did not send me here to philosophize," Fessenden stated, "they sent me here to act . . . and they are not so short-sighted as to resolve that if they cannot do what they would, therefore they will do nothing."[81] Fessenden spoke for those Republicans who believed that any effort to grant full equality nationwide would prove politically ruinous. Sumner's amendment failed 8-39, with twenty-seven Republicans opposing it.[82] However, Sumner and eleven other Republicans were not persuaded by Fessenden's appeal, and they went on to vote against H.J. Res. 51. While it won a majority, 25-22, it did not achieve the required two-thirds support.[83]

Meanwhile the Joint Committee of Fifteen continued to work toward an alternative solution. On February 3, 1866, the committee voted to endorse a resolution endowing the federal government with the authority to guarantee civil rights protections to all citizens. It read, "The Congress shall have power to make all laws which shall be necessary and proper to secure to the citizens of each state all privileges and immunities of citizens in the several states [article 4, section 2]; and to all persons in the several states equal protection in the rights of life, liberty and property."[84]

On February 13, John Bingham introduced the committee proposal in the House as a stand-alone constitutional amendment.[85] Debate opened on February 26, and Republicans opposed the measure because they "considered it poor political ammunition, and feared it would have an adverse effect on the Connecticut election which was then held in early April."[86] And in an overwhelming vote, 110-37, the House set aside Bingham's proposal until after

---

80. *CG*, 39-1, 2/5/1866, 673–87; 3/7/1866, 1124–32.

81. *CG*, 39-1, 2/7/1866, 705.

82. *CG*, 39-1, 3/9/1866, 1287. Seven Republican senators joined Sumner in voting yea. They were Benjamin Brown (MO), John Brooks Henderson (MO), Timothy Howe (WI), Luke Poland (VT), Samuel Pomeroy (KS), Benjamin Wade (OH), and Richard Yates (IL). A roll-call analysis (logistic regression) of Republican votes finds that the second (positive) NOMINATE dimension is statistically significant, with Republican senators furthest from the Democrats (the radicals) being more likely to support Sumner's amendment.

83. *CG*, 39-1, 3/9/1866, 1289.

84. Kendrick, *Journal of the Joint Committee*, 214.

85. *CG*, 39-1, 2/13/1866, 813.

86. Kendrick, *Journal of the Joint Committee*, 215. On the nonsnychronous character of elections during this era (both within and across states) and its effect both on subsequent elections and on elite decision making, see Scott C. James, "Timing and Sequence in Con-

the Connecticut election.[87] Congress would not consider its language again until it appeared as section 1 of the Fourteenth Amendment.

At the end of March 1866, congressional Republicans were losing on all fronts. They had passed an extension of the Freedmen's Bureau but failed to override President Johnson's veto. Johnson had also vetoed the civil rights bill, and many were worried that Congress lacked the votes to override. By this time the party had also failed to shepherd two constitutional amendments, backed by the Joint Committee of Fifteen, through both chambers of Congress. It seemed that internal party politics would undermine public support for the GOP right before the midterm elections. Giving voice to this concern, the *Nation* published an editorial warning that "the more people reflect, the better satisfied they are that Congress . . . is the branch which has and ought to have most to do with such a work of reorganization as is now before us. . . . But then it was assumed that Congress would have a policy. It has now, however, sat for nearly four months, and has nothing of the kind."[88]

Members of the Joint Committee recognized the political and policy dilemma now facing the GOP and committed themselves to a new approach: a comprehensive constitutional amendment that would allow Republicans to distance themselves from an increasingly unpopular Andrew Johnson.

The foundation for such a plan came from Robert Dale Owen, a Republican activist who had worked for the Freedmen's Bureau. In April 1866 he met with Stevens and proposed an amendment that protected civil rights but delayed suffrage for ten years.[89] According to an article written by Owen himself and published in an 1875 issue of the *Atlantic Monthly*, all Republicans on the Joint Committee viewed his proposal favorably save for one key feature. They chose to remove language outlawing all voting discrimination based on "race, color, or previous servitude." According to Owen, Stevens reported that members from northeastern and midwestern states met to consider "whether equality of suffrage, present or prospective, ought to form a part of the Republican programme for the coming canvass," and they were

gressional Elections: Interstate Contagion and America's Nineteenth-Century Scheduling Regime," *Studies in American Political Development* 21 (2007): 181–202.

87. *CG*, 39-1, 2/28/1866, 1095.

88. Article quoted in McKitrick, *Andrew Johnson and Reconstruction*, 344.

89. All information relevant to Owen and his proposal can be found in Kendrick, *Journal of the Joint Committee*, 296–303.

afraid that voting rights for black citizens would be used against them as an "electioneering handle."[90]

On April 30, 1866, Fessenden and Stevens introduced H.J. Res. 127, the Joint Committee's draft amendment.[91] Section 1 provided for "equal protection of laws." Section 2 developed a formula for apportioning representatives based on the total population of a state, but if a state denied voting rights to any adult males it would have its "representation reduced in the proportion which the number of such male citizens shall bear to the whole number of male citizens." More straightforwardly, section 2 stipulated that "if two-fifths of a state's potential voters were African Americans and if that state refused to enfranchise them, it would lose two-fifths of the members it would have been allotted in the House of Representatives and suffer a proportionate reduction in its electoral vote for president."[92]

Section 3 prohibited former Confederates from voting until July 4, 1870. Section 4 prohibited paying Confederate war debt and compensating slaveholders. Finally, section 5 granted Congress the power to "enforce by appropriate legislation the provisions of this article."

Debate on the proposed amendment began on May 8, when Stevens explained his support for the measure. While the bill fell short of his wishes, he believed it was all that could be achieved in the current state of public opinion.[93] Opponents of the bill took aim at the language proscribing suffrage for former Confederates (section 3). William Finck (D-OH) characterized it as a "scheme to deny representation to eleven states; to prevent indefinitely a complete restoration of the Union and perpetuate the power of a sectional party."[94] Some Republicans, too, were skeptical of section 3 based on concerns about banning political participation and fears that the provision could not be enforced.[95] Stevens offered a vehement response. "Give us the third section or give us nothing," he proclaimed. "Do not balk us with the pretense of an amendment which throws the union into the hands of the

---

90. After March 1866, from the perspective of moderate Republicans on the Joint Committee, "The crucial argument for settling a clash on everything would tend more and more to come down to this question: *'Will it win or lose us votes in November?'*" McKitrick, *Andrew Johnson and Reconstruction*, 336 (emphasis in original).

91. *CG*, 39-1, 4/30/1866, 2265, 2286–87.

92. Donald, Baker, and Holt, *Civil War and Reconstruction*, 547.

93. *CG*, 39-1, 5/8/1866, 2459.

94. *CG*, 39-1, 5/8/1866, 2462.

95. For a summary of these arguments, see Kendrick, *Journal of the Joint Committee*, 307.

enemy before it becomes consolidated." [96] In the end, the House voted 127-37 to pass the measure, with all but one Republican voting yea. [97]

On May 23, 1866, the Senate took up H.J. Res. 127. Jacob Howard (R-MI) served as floor manager. Like Stevens in the House, Howard framed his advocacy as a concession to political circumstances. On the issue of black voting, Howard claimed, "If I could have my own way, if my preferences could be carried out, I certainly should secure suffrage to the colored race." But, he argued, "the committee were of opinion that the States are not yet prepared to sanction so fundamental a change as would be the concession of the right of suffrage to the colored race." Howard also made explicit his opposition to section 3 of the bill. "I do not believe if adopted, [section 3] will be of any practical benefit to the country," he argued. "Rather than this I should prefer a clause prohibiting all persons who have participated in the rebellion, and who were over twenty-five years of age at the breaking out of the rebellion" from holding elective office. [98] Howard thus signaled to Senate Republicans that this provision would need to change for the bill to be passed.

Over the next six days, Senate Republicans convened a series of caucuses to agree on a final draft. They decided to rewrite section 3 along the lines suggested by Howard: former Confederates who had broken their oath to defend the Constitution were barred from holding national or state elective office. On June 8 this amendment passed 42-1. [99] Soon thereafter the Senate passed the amended H.J. Res. 127 by a vote of 33-11, with only three Republicans defecting. [100] Five days later the House concurred in the Senate amendments 137-37, with Republicans voting as a bloc, including Stevens, who accepted the need to compromise. [101] The Fourteenth Amendment then went to the states. On July 9, 1868, it achieved the three-quarters majority (twenty-eight states) necessary for ratification.

The Republicans correctly predicted that the fall 1866 elections would serve as a referendum on the Fourteenth Amendment. Not long before voters went to the polls, the *New York Times* declared that the campaign was

---

96. *CG*, 39-1, 5/10/1866, 2533, 2545.

97. *CG*, 39-1, 5/10/1866, 2545. The only GOP defector was Edward Rollins (NH).

98. *CG*, 39-1, 5/23/1866, 2766, 2768.

99. *CG*, 39-1, 6/8/1866, 3041. The one nay vote was cast by Reverdy Johnson (D-MD).

100. *CG*, 39-1, 6/8/1866, 3042. The three GOP defectors were Edgar Cowan (PA), James Doolittle (WI), and Peter Van Winkle (WV).

101. *CG*, 39-1, 6/13/1866, 3149. Hans L. Trefousse, *Thaddeus Stevens: Nineteenth-Century Egalitarian* (Chapel Hill: University of North Carolina Press, 1997), 185–86.

in "exclusive reference" to the amendment.[102] Congressional Republicans now openly contested Johnson, who was left to argue that the GOP was standing in the way of a speedy sectional reconciliation and pursuing policies that favored freedmen at the expense of the white majority. Republicans countered that their actions were intended to protect the country's hard-won achievements in the Civil War and ensure that the freedmen were afforded their basic rights as US citizens.

Johnson's campaign efforts against the GOP were disastrous. His hope of creating a centrist National Union Party fizzled, and his behavior before the election was erratic.[103] He actively campaigned against Republican congressional candidates in a ten-city, three-week tour known as the "swing around the circle."[104] On several occasions he made embarrassing (and widely reported) verbal gaffes that demeaned both him and the presidency in the eyes of the Northern public. In addition, events in the South made it clear that the region was unrepentant about the war and unwilling to protect the rights of the freedmen. Racial violence broke out in two former Confederate cities — Memphis in May and New Orleans in July — leaving dozens of blacks dead, countless more injured, and many homes, schools, churches, and businesses destroyed. Even more troubling, local law enforcement appeared to participate in the violence.[105] Racial terrorism of this kind suggested that Johnson and his Democratic supporters intended white supremacists to "win the peace."

Republicans won the fall 1866 elections in a landslide — sweeping every state save Delaware, Kentucky, and Maryland — and expanded their veto-proof majorities in Congress.[106] The victory guaranteed that they would be

102. "The People's Verdict," *NYT*, October 11, 1866, 4.

103. Johnson called for a National Union convention to meet in August 1866 in Philadelphia, hoping to use it to build his broad centrist coalition. But aligning the different partisan types proved harder than he had anticipated, and eventually the convention narrowed to a set of Democrats and Democratic-leaning Unionists. Moreover, extreme Democrats actively participated, negating Johnson's former goal of a centrist-only party. In short, Johnson's hoped-for partisan realignment did not occur. These events are told best by Cox and Cox, *Politics, Principle, and Prejudice*. See also Benedict, *Compromise of Principle*, 191-96.

104. The tour included Philadelphia, New York, Albany, Buffalo, Cleveland, Chicago, Indianapolis, Louisville, Cincinnati, and Pittsburgh. For a description of events during the tour, see McKitrick, *Andrew Johnson and Reconstruction*, 429-30, and Brooks D. Simpson, *The Reconstruction Presidents* (Lawrence: University Press of Kansas, 1998), 107-9.

105. Donald, Baker, and Holt, *Civil War and Reconstruction*, 551-53.

106. Donald, Baker, and Holt, *Civil War and Reconstruction*, 555. Congressional election

able to set Reconstruction policy. What the election did not do, however, was persuade Johnson to reconcile with congressional Republicans or to accept the Fourteenth Amendment. Instead, he and his advisers encouraged Southern states not to ratify the amendment. They believed that refusal would lead radicals to overreact and try to force through legislation that would split the party.[107] When the second session of the Thirty-Ninth Congress convened in December 1866, confrontations would occur within the Republican caucus and between Johnson and Congress. The result would be military-led Reconstruction and African American suffrage in the South.

The Military Reconstruction Acts

Southerners did not wait long to quash hopes for a quick ratification of the Fourteenth Amendment.[108] Between October 1866 and February 1867, the legislature in every former Confederate state (save Tennessee) voted to reject the amendment.[109] The summer riots in Memphis and New Orleans, with claims that police murdered white loyalists and freedmen, made matters worse. As Hans Trefousse notes, "The feeling that something more was needed to guarantee security for the nation and safety for the Negroes became more widespread, not merely among radicals, but among moderates as well."[110]

To that end, on January 3, 1867, Thaddeus Stevens introduced H.R. 543, which aimed to dissolve the provisional governments of Southern states by declaring them "illegally formed in the midst of marshal law." He called for new elections in May 1867 for delegates to state constitutional conventions

---

results taken from Michael J. Dubin, *United States Congressional Elections, 1788–1997* (Boston: McFarland, 1998).

107. Benedict, *Compromise of Principle*, 212; McKitrick, *Andrew Johnson and Reconstruction*, 462.

108. According to Benedict and McKitrick, most Republican moderates believed ratification was the only precondition for readmission to the Union. Kendrick argues, however, that no formal guarantees were in place at this point. Tennessee successfully ratified in July 1866 and was promptly readmitted. See Benedict, *Compromise of Principle*, 211–12; McKitrick, *Andrew Johnson and Reconstruction*, 452–55; Kendrick, *Journal of the Joint Committee*, 327.

109. Joseph P. James, "Southern Reaction to the Proposal of the Fourteenth Amendment," *Journal of Southern History* 22 (1956): 477–97.

110. Hans L. Trefousse, *The Radical Republicans: Lincoln's Vanguard for Racial Justice* (New York: Knopf, 1968), 352.

where founding charters would be rewritten.[111] All male citizens twenty-one and over living in each state for at least one year would be allowed to participate, except those who broke their oath to the Constitution after Lincoln's victory. Finally, the bill provided that until these obligations were met, and until Congress decided to readmit each state, the military would remain in charge.

Stevens implored Congress to protect freedmen from "the barbarians who are now daily murdering them . . . who are daily putting into secret graves not only hundreds but thousands of the colored people of that country." He also argued that ratifying the Fourteenth Amendment was insufficient for readmission. Instead, the rebel states should be "placed under the guardianship of loyal men."[112] In response, John Bingham characterized H.R. 543 as an attempt to "patch up a restoration by the usurpation of powers which do not belong to the Congress" and claimed the bill would "subject the future of this republic to all those dread calamities which have darkened its recent past."[113] Sensing he had the chamber on his side, Bingham moved to recommit Stevens's proposal to the Joint Committee of Fifteen where, he believed, it would be buried. Bingham's motion passed 88-65, with forty-nine Republicans voting in support.[114] The radicals lacked the votes needed to push Stevens's proposal forward, even though a majority of the GOP caucus supported him (by opposing the recommittal motion).

Once the House voted to recommit his bill, Stevens threw his support behind H.R. 1143, a proposal developed by George Julian (R-IN), which protected military rule and delayed any decision about readmission criteria until the Fortieth Congress—with its larger share of radical members—convened.[115] H.R. 1143 was introduced on February 6, but debate stalled a week later owing to an amendment proposed by James Blaine (R-ME), which stipulated that former Confederate states would be welcomed back

111. *CG*, 39-2, 1/3/1867, 250.

112. *CG*, 39-2, 1/3/1867, 251.

113. *CG*, 39-2, 1/16/1867, 500-501.

114. *CG*, 39-2, 1/28/1867, 817. Republicans voted 49-61, Democrats 30-1, and Unionists 9-3. A roll-call analysis (logistic regression) of Republican votes finds that the first (negative) and second (positive) NOMINATE dimension are statistically significant, with Republican members closest to the Democrats being more likely to support Bingham's recommittal motion. Republicans in the lower right of the choice space (furthest from the Democrats) were the most likely to support Stevens by opposing Bingham's motion.

115. Trefousse, *Radical Republicans*, 359.

once they ratified the Fourteenth Amendment and guaranteed black residents equal voting rights. Blaine then sought to have H.R. 1143 recommitted to the Judiciary Committee with his amendment attached, and with instructions for it to be immediately reported back to the floor for a final vote.[116]

At this point, Stevens gave a "masterpiece" of a speech in opposition to Blaine's proposal.[117] Calling the measure "universal amnesty and universal Andy Johnsonism," Stevens urged Republicans to oppose it. They did. Blaine's recommittal motion was defeated 69-94, with a majority of the GOP voting nay.[118] The House then voted 109-55 to pass Julian's original bill unchanged, with all but ten Republicans lending their support.[119] The Democrats had thought moderate Republicans would join them in opposing Julian's bill, making it more likely the session would end without Congress's enacting any Reconstruction-related policy. According to McKitrick, they misjudged the moderates' willingness to "take a military bill rather than allow the opposition to achieve a stalemate."[120]

Even before they passed Julian's bill, House Republicans adopted a more radical proposal offered by Thomas Eliot (R-MA) and Samuel Shellabarger (R-OH). Having led an inquiry into the New Orleans riot from the previous summer, they proposed a bill (H.R. 1162) for establishing a new government in Louisiana.[121] H.R. 1162 directed President Johnson to appoint a governor and a city council, subject to congressional approval, composed of Louisiana residents who had "never indicated approval of secession or support for the rebellion."[122] The bill then mandated an election in which all adult males twenty-one and over would be allowed to participate except those determined to have been loyal to the Confederacy. Victors would then participate in a constitutional convention responsible for writing a new state charter explicitly outlawing legal discrimination. All these steps were to be overseen by a military commander. The bill passed 113-47, with Republicans voting 107-6. Radicals came to believe this proposal could serve as a model for the nine other former Confederate states.[123]

116. *CG*, 39-2, 2/13/1867, 1213.

117. McKitrick, *Andrew Johnson and Reconstruction*, 480.

118. *CG*, 39-2, 2/13/1867, 1215. Republicans voted 46-69.

119. *CG*, 39-2, 2/13/1867, 1215.

120. McKitrick, *Andrew Johnson and Reconstruction*, 481.

121. Foner, *Reconstruction*, 274.

122. Benedict, *Compromise of Principle*, 228.

123. *CG*, 39-2, 2/12/1867, 1175.

Decisions made in the House left the Senate with three options to consider: Julian's unamended military government bill; Julian's bill amended to include provisions regarding equal suffrage and ratification of the Fourteenth Amendment; and the Eliot-Shellabarger plan. Of these three, conservative and moderate Republicans found the second option most appealing because the readmission conditions it set, even with voting protections for freedmen included, were very lenient. Radicals preferred the Eliot-Shellabarger proposal, but they would settle for a basic military reconstruction bill as long as it did not include the conditions for readmission proposed by Blaine.

On February 14, 1867, the Senate began consideration of the proposals. William Fessenden, speaking on behalf of the conservative-moderate faction, was skeptical of the Eliot-Shellabarger plan. The bill is "narrow in its application," he argued, and "it is a matter of serious doubt whether if passed it should go beyond the state of Louisiana." The military government bill, on the other hand, "is as reasonable and perfect as any bill of this kind can be made." Fessenden then suggested that the Senate add an amendment like Blaine's to make the bill "as complete a system . . . as could possibly be offered now."[124] However, Sumner, speaking on behalf of the radicals, praised H.R. 1162 and H.R. 1143, characterizing "one [as] the beginning of a true reconstruction" and the other as "the beginning of a true protection." "Both must be had," he declared.[125]

Debate held the following day quickly spun out of control. Senators were asked to limit the number of amendments they offered so that passage could be expedited. That request was promptly ignored as conservative opponents of military reconstruction sought to change the bill in ways unpalatable to radicals.[126] After many hours of discussion, Republicans met as a caucus and decided to form a seven-member committee to put together a compromise proposal. The committee produced a bill that incorporated aspects of each of the three plans under consideration.[127] To appease the radicals, the bill mandated constitutional conventions with delegates chosen through voting open to all adult males. For moderates and conservatives, it stipulated that former Confederate states would be readmitted, with congressional approval, as long as the new constitutions incorporated the Fourteenth Amendment. Finally, in keeping with the spirit of "military" government,

124. *CG*, 39-2, 2/14/1867, 1304.
125. *CG*, 39-2, 2/14/1867, 1303.
126. *CG*, 39-2, 2/15/167, 1364-98.
127. Cook, *Civil War Senator*, 216-17.

the bill divided former Confederate states into military districts and empowered the army to protect people and property within those districts and
to try all accused criminals in military courts. Once states were readmitted, however, the military provisions of the bill would no longer apply.[128]
Radicals were largely displeased by the compromise, but they persuaded
the caucus to require state constitutions in reconstructed states to guarantee
"universal suffrage."[129] Sumner was so disappointed by the bill that he "left
the Senate in a rage and refused to vote."[130] H.R. 1143 came up for a vote on
February 16, 1867. It passed 29-10, with twenty-seven of thirty Republicans
voting in support.[131] It then moved back to the House, where an incensed
Thaddeus Stevens lay in wait.

The Senate had almost completely undermined Stevens's efforts to prevent "unreconstructed" states from reentering the Union and former Confederates from participating in the process of reconstruction. He planned to
fight these changes by defeating the motion to concur in the Senate amendments and to insist on a conference committee so that House radicals could
try to improve the bill. Stevens's allies spent most of February 18 characterizing the bill as "fraught with great and permanent danger to the country,"
which allowed "disloyal men" to play a direct role in the reconstruction of
former Confederate states.[132]

Supporters of the compromise once again based their support on "pragmatism." Future president James Garfield (R-OH) denounced Stevens's
allies for characterizing any incremental effort to improve the lives of freedmen in the South as "poor and mean and a surrender of liberty."[133] Despite
the moderates' best efforts, however, a coalition of Stevens's allies and
Democrats, who once again hoped to block all congressional action, defeated the motion to concur 73-98.[134] The House then immediately agreed
to Stevens's motion to convene a conference committee. By this time, however, both Democratic and Republican senators believed that a conference

128. For a summary of the compromise bill see Benedict, *Compromise of Principle*, 235.

129. Cook, *Civil War Senator*, 217. The caucus voted 17-15 to add this provision.

130. Benedict, *Compromise of Principle*, 236.

131. *CG*, 39-2, 2/16/1867, 1469. The three Republicans who voted against were Edgar
Cowan (MO), James Doolittle (WI), and Daniel Norton (MN)—all conservatives. They were
the Republicans in the Senate nearest to the Democrats on the first NOMINATE dimension.

132. *CG*, 39-2, 2/18/1867, 1316.

133. *CG*, 39-2, 2/18/1867, 1320.

134. *CG*, 39-2, 2/18/1867, 1340. Republicans voted 65-55, Democrats 0-35, and Unionists
8-8.

committee would not guarantee them a better deal. Radicals in particular believed that a bill crafted by the incoming Fortieth Congress would prove stronger than any compromise.[135] On February 19, without a roll-call vote, the Senate rejected the House request for a conference and insisted on its amendments.[136] House Republicans now faced a dilemma: either concur in the Senate amendments or end the session without enacting anything.

In desperation, James Wilson (R-IN) offered a compromise. His proposal disenfranchised those residents of the former Confederate states whom the Fourteenth Amendment barred from holding office. When combined with an additional amendment from Stevens and Shellabarger declaring current state governments "provisional and subject to the authority of Congress," the bill now had radical support.[137] On February 20 the House-amended version of H.R. 1143 passed 127-46, with only three Republicans voting nay.[138] Later that day the Senate concurred in the House amendments 35-7.[139] Johnson promptly vetoed the bill, but both chambers of Congress overrode his veto on March 2, 1867.[140]

Viewed as a whole, the First Reconstruction Act was a compromise between GOP factions. It divided the former Confederate states (except for Tennessee) into five military districts and put army commanders in charge of protecting lives and property. It also stipulated the conditions under which Congress would readmit each state: hold elections in which all men of voting age could participate regardless of race, color, or previous condition of servitude; select delegates to attend new constitutional conventions; charge these conventions with rewriting state charters that guaranteed universal manhood suffrage in all future elections; put these new state charters up for approval by a majority of eligible voters; and ratify the Fourteenth Amend-

135. Benedict, *Compromise of Principle*, 238.

136. *CG*, 39-2, 2/19/1867, 1570.

137. For a summary of the compromise, see Benedict, *Compromise of Principle*, 238.

138. *CG*, 39-2, 2/20/1867, 1400. The three Republicans were James Hubbell (OH), Thomas Noell (MO), and Andrew Jackson Kuykendall (IL).

139. *CG*, 39-2, 2/20/1867, 1645. Only one Republican — Edgar Cowan (PA) — voted nay.

140. *CG*, 39-2, 3/2/1867, 1733, 1976. The votes were 135-48 in the House and 38-10 in the Senate. Four conservative Republicans in the House voted against the veto override: Thomas Noell (MO), Thomas Stilwell (IN), Andrew Jackson Kuykendall (IL), and Robert Hale (NY). These four were among the eight Republicans in the House nearest to the Democrats on the first NOMINATE dimension. Four conservative Republicans in the Senate voted against the veto override: Edgar Cowan (MO), James Doolittle (WI), Daniel Norton (MN), and James Dixon (CT). These four were the Republicans nearest to the Democrats in the Senate on the first NOMINATE dimension.

ment. In addition, it barred any participation by white southerners who were prohibited from holding office by the Fourteenth Amendment.[141] The only way Southern states would concede to ratification of the Fourteenth Amendment, or to allowing black voting rights, was if such terms were imposed by the federal government and enforced by military power.

Over the next year Congress passed three supplementary Reconstruction Acts, each designed to ensure that the goals set out in the first act would be achieved. Since none of these bills significantly altered the agenda set out by the first act, we will forgo detailed discussion of them here.[142] In short, by March 1867 Republicans in Congress had decided on a course of action that blended the radicals' idealism with the moderates' pragmatism. As Boris Heersink and Jeffery A. Jenkins state:

> [By 1867], moderates had come around to an idea pushed in recent years by the Radicals: black suffrage. And this signaled a profound shift in how they viewed the South in the post-war Union. Less than a year earlier, moderate Republicans had focused on limiting Democratic representation (the second section of the Fourteenth Amendment) in the event that Southerners proved unwilling to protect the rights of the freedmen. Now, faced with Southern intransigence and buoyed by the Northern electorate's rejection of Johnson and the Democrats, they saw an opportunity for *Republican* representation in the South.[143]

141. Foner, *Reconstruction*, 276–77; Donald, Baker, and Holt, *Civil War and Reconstruction*, 559.

142. The remaining three Reconstruction Acts would be adopted during the Fortieth Congress, which convened in March 1867, immediately after the Thirty-Ninth Congress adjourned. The second and third Reconstruction Acts were also vetoed by Johnson and overridden by Congress, and the fourth became law without his signature. The Second Reconstruction Act (enacted March 27, 1867) required army commanders to register all males twenty-one and over to vote for delegates to state conventions and to set dates for holding delegate elections. It also stipulated that registered voters would have the right to vote on the constitution produced by the state delegation and that a constitution approved by the voters would be submitted to Congress before the state would be considered for representation. The Third Reconstruction Act (enacted July 19, 1867) gave army commanders the authority to remove civil or military officials from office and to determine voter eligibility. The Fourth Reconstruction Act (enacted March 11, 1868) required that a majority of votes cast would determine whether a proposed constitution was accepted or rejected, rather than a majority of registered voters (as stipulated in the Second Reconstruction Act).

143. Boris Heersink and Jeffery A. Jenkins, *Republican Party Politics and the American South, 1865–1968* (New York: Cambridge University Press, 2020), 77. On the change in the

The primary benefit for former slaves was guaranteed voting rights. Yet by the time Congress provided for black suffrage, even that appeared as a moderate alternative to prolonged federal intervention. Ballot access provided freedmen with an opportunity, as Eric Foner put it, to "defend themselves against abuse, while relieving the nation of that responsibility."[144]

Voting Rights in Washington, DC

About the time Republicans were considering the First Reconstruction Act and moving toward an agreement that ensured universal manhood voting in the South, Congress passed a law guaranteeing voting rights to the black residents of Washington, DC. This battle for "impartial" voting rights in the District of Columbia started early in 1866 — as Congress was debating the Fourteenth Amendment — but would not culminate until more than a year later. Legislation enacted in the interim demonstrates that a majority of congressional Republicans distinguished civil rights from political rights. Before successfully pushing the Fifteenth Amendment through Congress, the GOP's position on whether federal power could be used to guarantee voting rights remained unclear. Indeed, during his discussion of one version of the bill, Sen. Lot Morrill (R-ME) noted that whatever Congress decided in reference to the District of Columbia would inaugurate a policy for the country at large.[145] Through the debate over voting rights in Washington, DC, members previewed arguments that would reemerge when national voting rights again made it onto the agenda.

When the Thirty-Ninth Congress convened in December 1865, radicals sought to overcome the defeat of the Wade-Davis bill by immediately taking the initiative on black voting rights. At the time, Republican opinion on the subject was divided. Radicals insisted on immediate and unqualified voting rights for all freedmen. Moderates had no clear position.[146] President Johnson, meanwhile, believed that universal suffrage "would breed a war of the races."[147] In January 1866 radicals orchestrated a fight over suffrage rights in the District of Columbia that put moderates on the spot and threatened to

---

thinking of moderate Republicans between 1866 and 1867, also see Donald, Baker, and Holt, *Civil War and Reconstruction*, 547, 563.

144. Foner, *Reconstruction*, 278.

145. *CG*, 39-2, 12/10/1866, 38.

146. Benedict, *Compromise of Principle*, 145.

147. McPherson, *Political History of the United States of America during the Period of Reconstruction*, 49.

upend any potential alliance between congressional Republicans and President Johnson.

On January 10, 1866, the House began debate on H.R. 1, a bill that would strike the word "white" from the laws governing voting rights in Washington, DC, and stipulate that "from and after passage of this act, no person shall be disqualified from voting at any election held in the said District on account of color."[148] H.R. 1 followed a referendum in DC asking voters to weigh in on whether black citizens should be guaranteed voting rights. That referendum lost, 7,268 to 36.[149] Opponents of the bill thus argued against extending the franchise.[150] House Republicans recognized that conservatives within their own caucus were skeptical about the measure. To craft a compromise that could win majority support, a special committee was appointed to draft a new bill that would appease all sides.[151] But the committee failed to work out a deal.

On January 18, 1866, H.R. 1, was debated, even though the GOP had no clear position on it. Large majorities voted against postponing consideration of the bill and recommitting it to the Judiciary Committee with instructions to add a literacy test for all "new voters" who had not served in the Union army.[152] The coalition against delay included both Democrats and Republicans. Democrats believed they would gain political advantage by helping to force a final vote on the bill, and they worked with radical Republicans to do just that. They miscalculated. Angry moderates ended up voting with the radicals to pass the bill, 116-54.[153] When the bill moved to the Senate, Republican moderates buried it in the Committee on the District of Columbia, where it languished until the end of the year. As William Gillette notes, "The more conservative Senate never voted on [H.R. 1] because Republicans wanted to avoid the controversial Negro suffrage issue, and there was a fear that even if the bill passed the Senate it could not override a presidential veto there."[154]

After the fall 1866 elections, where GOP handling of Reconstruction was

148. *CG*, 39-1, 1/10/1866, 162.

149. *CG*, 39-1, 1/10/1866, 175.

150. *CG*, 39-1, 1/10/1866, 176–83.

151. Benedict, *Compromise of Principle*, 146.

152. *CG*, 39-1, 1/18/1866, 310–11. The votes were 34-135 and 53-117, with Republicans voting 27-95 and 52-71.

153. *CG*, 39-1, 1/18/1866, 311. Republicans voted 114-10.

154. William Gillette, *The Right to Vote: Politics and the Passage of the Fifteenth Amendment* (Baltimore: Johns Hopkins University Press, 1965), 29.

vindicated in a face-off with President Johnson and the Democrats, congressional Republicans were emboldened to act on black suffrage in the District of Columbia. In December 1866 the Senate moved first. Benjamin Wade (R-OH) introduced S. 1, which would guarantee voting rights for all males twenty-one and older except those convicted of crimes or those who had lived in the District less than six months before the election. S. 1 also set out punishment for anyone deemed guilty of preventing a qualified voter from exercising the franchise. Almost immediately Lot Morrill successfully substituted a new version (S. 9) that had won support from members of the Committee on the District of Columbia. Morrill's version simply added language clarifying that it would be the duty of officials in the District to put together lists of qualified voters.[155] S. 1 (as amended) set off yet another long discussion of whether the federal government had the constitutional authority to guarantee voting rights and whether black citizens should be granted suffrage. Imposing new conditions for ballot access took center stage as Republicans went back and forth over whether freedmen were "prepared" to vote. In the process, the Senate voted down a series of amendments sponsored by Democrats opposed to the bill.[156]

In the end, on December 13, 1866, the Senate passed a slightly amended version of S. 1 32-13, with all but five Republicans voting yea.[157] The House took up the bill the following day and passed it 127-46, with all but three Republicans voting in support.[158] On January 7, 1867, Johnson vetoed the bill. In his veto message, Johnson made frequent reference to the referendum proposing black suffrage in Washington, DC, that had been rejected by residents. In doing so Johnson portrayed himself as simply obeying "the wishes of the people of District of Columbia."[159] He also made clear his view that black citizens were not prepared to exercise the franchise. Republicans

155. *CG*, 39-2, 12/10/1866, 38.

156. The first proposed to limit voting to those who could read and write and paid taxes. It failed 1-41. See *CG*, 39-2, 12/10/1866, 45. Senators then voted 9-37 against an amendment guaranteeing universal female suffrage within the District of Columbia. See *CG*, 39-2, 12/12/1866, 84. Finally, the Senate voted 11-34 against a proposal limiting suffrage to those who had voted previously and could read and write. See *CG*, 39-2, 12/13/1866, 98.

157. The Senate agreed, through voice vote, to extend the residency requirement from six months to one year. *CG*, 39-2, 12/13/1866, 108-9. The five Republican nay votes were Edgar Cowan (PA), James Dixon (CT), James Doolittle (WI), Lafayette Foster (CT), and Peter Van Winkle (WV).

158. *CG*, 39-2, 12/14/1866, 138. The three Republican nay votes were Andrew Jackson Kuykendall (IL), Thomas Noell (MO), and Thomas Stilwell (IN).

159. *CG*, 39-2, 1/7/1867, 303.

quickly voted to override the veto.[160] Two days later, on January 10, 1867, both chambers of Congress extended black voting rights to the federal territories.[161] President Johnson, "apparently in a state of resignation," did not veto the measure, and it became law without his signature.[162] These GOP victories on black suffrage set the stage for the adoption of the fifth section of the First Reconstruction Act on March 2, 1867.

The Fifteenth Amendment

The 1868 elections were a mixed bag for the Republicans. Ulysses S. Grant was elected president with a resounding Electoral College victory, and the Republicans retained control of both chambers of Congress. Yet Grant's popular vote margin over Democratic challenger Horatio Seymour (NY) was slim. Grant won California, Connecticut, Indiana, Nevada, and Pennsylvania narrowly while losing New Jersey, New York, and Oregon. On the congressional side, Republicans maintained overwhelming majorities in both chambers of Congress, but the Democrats picked up twenty additional seats in the House. In short, continued unified control of government obscured political trends suggesting that the GOP's political standing was more tenuous.

The Republicans, in fact, had been struggling electorally since the fall elections of 1867, when the GOP's Reconstruction efforts came up against Northern public opinion. Electoral defeats in Ohio, New York, and Pennsylvania, where the Democrats took the state legislature in the first two and the entire state government in the third, signaled to many that the party's agenda had perhaps outpaced Northern support. Some Republicans believed they had overreached by impeaching Andrew Johnson, confiscating rebel land in the South, and promoting black suffrage.[163] On voting rights in

160. The votes were 29-10 in the Senate and 113-38 in the House; *CG*, 39-2, 1/7/1867, 314; 1/8/1867, 344. In the Senate, the same five Republicans voted nay as on S. 1. In the House, Andrew Jackson Kuykendall (IL) and Thomas Noell (MO) voted nay, while Thomas Stilwell (IN) did not vote.

161. *CG*, 39-2, 1/10/1867, 382, 399. The Senate voted 24-8, with Republicans voting 22-1. The House voted 104-38, with Republicans voting 99-1. The GOP dissenters were Peter Van Winkle (WV) in the Senate and Thomas Noell (MO) in the House.

162. Gillette, *Right to Vote*, 30.

163. On February 24, 1868, the House voted 126-47 to impeach Johnson, but on March 15 and 26 the Senate voted 35-19, one vote short of the two-thirds majority needed for conviction. Thus Johnson was acquitted. For an account, see Michael Les Benedict, *The Impeachment and Trial of Andrew Johnson* (New York: Norton, 1973).

particular, while the GOP enacted policy that provided suffrage for blacks in the former Confederate states (by the First Reconstruction Act), the District of Columbia, and the federal territories, they were stopped in their attempts to extend black suffrage into the North. Ballot initiatives in Connecticut, Wisconsin, Kansas, Minnesota (twice), Ohio, and the Colorado Territory all went down to defeat.[164]

Even as Republicans feared pursuing black political rights beyond where the public was willing to go, they also understood that their electoral performance in 1868 would be affected by the return of former Confederate states to the Union. After the passage of the Reconstruction Acts, the army and the Freedmen's Bureau successfully registered a high proportion of black voters,[165] and roughly 80 percent of those registered went to the polls.[166] Their support was crucial to the state conventions' being approved, since many whites boycotted them. This raised some concerns, however, as national GOP leaders believed that for a Southern wing of the party to be viable, it needed to comprise more than just the region's newly enfranchised black citizens.[167] Nonetheless, high black turnout meant that conventions in all ten states — which convened at various times from late 1867 through mid-1868 — were approved.[168]

Republican leaders actively worked to steer the conventions away from adopting punitive policies that would divide the races and hamper the GOP's viability and growth.[169] They were mostly successful, thanks to white delegates' controlling all key convention committees. Most important, no constitutions allowed for confiscation and redistribution of former Confederate property, while all provided for universal manhood suffrage, equal protection of the law, and public education. Republicans were also successful in getting the new Southern state constitutions adopted, GOP state governments elected, and conditions for returning to the Union (ratification of the

164. Gillette, *Right to Vote*, 25–26.

165. See Valelly, *Two Reconstructions*, 32–34.

166. Richard H. Abbott, *The Republican Party and the South, 1855–1877: The First Southern Strategy* (Chapel Hill: University of North Carolina Press, 1986), 137.

167. Martin E. Mantell, *Johnson, Grant, and the Politics of Reconstruction* (New York: Columbia University Press, 1973), 47–49; Abbott, *Republican Party and the South*, 137–38.

168. For coverage of the politics of the Southern constitutional conventions, see Richard L. Hume and Jerry B. Gough, *Blacks, Carpetbaggers, and Scalawags: The Constitutional Conventions of Radical Reconstruction* (Baton Rouge: Louisiana State University Press, 2008); Foner, *Reconstruction*, 316–33; Abbott, *Republican Party and the South*, 139–49.

169. For examples of such efforts, see Abbott, *Republican Party and the South*, 139–49.

Fourteenth Amendment) satisfied. By the end of June 1868, seven of the ten reconstructed states—Arkansas, Florida, North Carolina, Louisiana, South Carolina, Alabama, and Georgia—had adopted new constitutions, elected unified Republican governments (except Georgia),[170] and were readying for readmission.[171] By the end of July, all seven would once again have representation in Congress, which would add twenty-eight House seats and twelve Senate seats to the GOP column against only four Democratic/Conservative House seats.[172] And, finally, all seven—along with Tennessee—would participate in the 1868 presidential election in November.

Grant benefited from the high turnout of freedmen (and the temporary disenfranchisement of some whites). But the broad biracial coalition some Republicans hoped to build in the South did not immediately materialize. Grant carried Alabama, Arkansas, Florida, North Carolina, South Carolina, and Tennessee, but Georgia and Louisiana went for Seymour. The Democratic victories in Georgia and Louisiana—and partial electoral recoveries down the ticket in Florida, South Carolina, and Tennessee—were in part the result of increased white turnout, but also of strategic black demobilization efforts by the Ku Klux Klan and other domestic terrorist organizations. Klan-related violence and intimidation reduced black turnout considerably in select areas of the South.[173] Political activities in Georgia were even more troubling: two months before the presidential election some white GOP state legislators, under intense social pressure, joined with Democrats to oust twenty-eight black legislators on the grounds that the new Georgia constitution gave blacks only the right to vote, *not* the right to hold office.[174]

170. Partisan control of the Georgia House was disputed; the best account identified eighty-eight Democrats, eighty-four Republicans, and three members of unknown partisanship.

171. The seven states would be readmitted in two separate acts in June (one act for Arkansas specifically, and one omnibus act for the other six states).

172. Georgia would have members seated only in the House; one of its House seats and both of its Senate seats remained vacant through the rest of the Fortieth Congress.

173. On the use of violence and intimidation in Southern elections, along with the rise of the Klan, see Allen W. Trelease, *White Terror: The Ku Klux Klan Conspiracy and Southern Reconstruction* (Baton Rouge: Louisiana State University Press, 1971), 3–188; George C. Rable, *But There Was No Peace: The Role of Violence in the Politics of Reconstruction* (Athens: University of Georgia Press, 1984), 74–79.

174. See Alan Conway, *The Reconstruction of Georgia* (Minneapolis: University of Minnesota Press, 1967), 162–81. Twenty-five of these black legislators were from the lower house, and three were from the upper house. The situation grew so dire that in December 1869 Congress denied the state further representation and returned it to military rule. Georgia would

The difficulties in Louisiana and Georgia were extreme cases of a more general pattern throughout the South. While the Republicans were technically successful in the 1868 elections, there were clear undercurrents of white conservatism throughout the former Confederacy as well as indications of black electoral vulnerability that threatened future GOP success in the region. Moreover, the Democratic gains throughout the North suggested that Republican strength there was also eroding. In the aftermath of the 1868 elections, Republican leaders believed that the party was under attack on two fronts and that a new strategy was needed to maintain their hold on the federal levers of power. They decided that a new initiative to enfranchise African Americans was their best bet for further promoting black rights and for the GOP's continued political success. This initiative would take the form of a new amendment to the Constitution—the Fifteenth.

Republican leaders contended that a constitutional amendment would protect black voting rights for all time. The Fifteenth Amendment would serve as a legislative response to the Democrats' recent electoral reemergence in the South. In addition, a constitutional amendment would extend black voting rights *outside* the South, into Northern areas that had resisted black suffrage.[175] Republican leaders believed that additional black votes would help preserve the narrow Northern victories the party enjoyed in 1868, add votes in other Northern areas that were lost (like New Jersey and New York), and perhaps even make the border states (like Kentucky, Maryland, Missouri, and Delaware) viable for GOP electoral success. An amendment would effectively circumvent state electorates in the North that had refused to support voting rights for black citizens.[176]

The Republicans officially began their legislative pursuit of the Fifteenth Amendment during the lame-duck session of the Fortieth Congress.[177] On

---

rejoin the Union in July 1870, after the black legislators were reinstated and all the white legislators with Confederate backgrounds were removed.

175. On black voting rights in the North during the antebellum era, see Christopher Malone, *Between Freedom and Bondage: Race, Party, and Voting Rights in the Antebellum North* (New York: Routledge, 2008).

176. Amid the GOP's somewhat disappointing electoral performance in 1868, black-enfranchisement referenda were successful in Iowa and Minnesota. See Gillette, *Right to Vote*, 26.

177. Histories of the legislative proceedings on the Fifteenth Amendment include A. Caperton Braxton, *The Fifteenth Amendment: An Account of Its Enactment* (Lynchburg, VA: J. P. Bell, 1903); John Mabry Mathews, *Legislative and Judicial History of the Fifteenth Amendment* (Baltimore: Johns Hopkins Press, 1909); Gillette, *Right to Vote*; Benedict, *Compromise of*

January 11, 1869, George Boutwell (R-MA), acting on behalf of the House Judiciary Committee, introduced H.J. Res. 402, which had two sections:

> Section 1. The right of any citizen of the United States to vote shall not be denied or abridged by the United States or any State by reason of the race, color, or previous condition of slavery of any citizen or class of citizens of the United States.
>
> Section 2. The Congress shall have the power to enforce by proper legislation the provisions of this article.[178]

Boutwell's joint resolution faced two amendments offered by Samuel Shellabarger (R-OH) and John Bingham (R-OH), both seeking to substitute different criteria for section 1. Shellabarger argued that Boutwell's provision for "impartial suffrage" did not go far enough in protecting black voting rights. He stated, rightly, that race-neutral tests based on education or property could be adopted to effectively produce race-based disenfranchisement. Shellabarger advocated instead for "universal suffrage" excepting rebels. The text of his substitute for section 1 read:

> No State shall make or enforce any law which shall deny or abridge to any male citizen of the United States of the age of twenty-one years or over, and who is of sound mind, an equal vote at all elections in the State in which he shall have his actual residence, such right to vote to be under such regulations as shall be prescribed by law, except to such as have engaged, or may hereafter engage, in insurrection or rebellion against the United States, and to such as shall be duly convicted of infamous crime.[179]

Bingham also proposed a form of universal suffrage, with a short-term residency requirement, an allowance for state registration laws, and proscriptions only for those who might engage in *future* acts of rebellion or insurrection. The text of his substitute for section 1 read:

> No State shall make or enforce any law which shall abridge or deny to any male citizen of the United States of sound mind and twenty-one years of age or upward the equal exercise, subject to such registration laws as the State may establish, of the elective franchise at all elections in the State

Principle, 327–35; Earl M. Maltz, *Civil Rights, the Constitution, and Congress, 1863–1869* (Lawrence: University Press of Kansas, 1990), 142–56.

178. See *CG*, 40-3, 1/11/1869, 285–86.

179. *CG*, 40-3, 1/29/1869, 728.

wherein he shall have actually resided for a period of time of one year next preceding such election, except such of said citizens as shall engage in rebellion or insurrection, or who may have been, or shall be, duly convicted of treason or other infamous crime.[180]

The Shellabarger amendment was the most radical option, since it would have eliminated any state-level voting restrictions implemented through literacy tests, poll taxes, or other registration requirements. It also banned former Confederates and active insurgents. The Bingham amendment was more conservative. It proposed to eliminate various state restrictions—like requirements concerning education, religion, or property—while allowing states to adopt particular registration laws and enfranchise former Confederates.[181]

Boutwell's bill aimed to steer a moderate course by facilitating black suffrage *outside the South* for those who were currently denied the vote because of their race. Boutwell sympathized with some of Shellabarger's and Bingham's arguments, especially the potential application of (ostensibly) race-neutral conditions in pursuit of racial disenfranchisement. But he believed that proscriptions of various state-level restrictions could not realistically be achieved and might put the whole enterprise at risk. "If we should attempt to grasp at too much we shall lose the whole," Boutwell argued. "I believe that if we adhere to the proposition to protect the people of this country against distinction on account of race, color, or previous condition of slavery we undertake all that is probably safe for us to undertake now."[182]

On January 30, 1869, voting on H.J. Res. 402 commenced.[183] According to Gillette, "[The voting] showed the moderates were in control."[184] The Shellabarger amendment was considered first, and it failed 62-125. All Democrats voted against it, chafing at the restrictions on former Confederates, along with most Republicans (with only the most radical members voting in favor).[185] The Bingham amendment was then considered, and it failed by

180. *CG*, 40-3, 1/29/1869, 728.

181. Earl Maltz refers to Bingham's amendment as evoking "universal suffrage and universal amnesty." Maltz, *Civil Rights, the Constitution, and Congress*, 148.

182. *CG*, 40-3, 1/29/1869, 727.

183. The relevant roll calls can be found in the *CG*, 40-3, 1/30/1869, 744–45.

184. Gillette, *Right to Vote*, 54.

185. *CG*, 40-3, 1/30/1869, 744. Republicans voted 62-83. A roll-call analysis (logistic regression) of Republican votes finds that the first (positive) NOMINATE dimension is statisti-

an even larger margin, 24-160. Some Democrats supported the legislation, thanks to its Confederate amnesty provision, but nearly all Republicans opposed it.[186] Finally the underlying Boutwell proposal was voted on, and it passed 150-42, with all but four Republicans voting in favor.[187] Having won the support of two-thirds of voting members of the House, H.J. Res. 402 now moved on to the Senate.

As the House was considering the Boutwell proposal, the Senate was pursuing its own constitutional amendment. Led by William Stewart (R-NV), the Senate proposal went further than Boutwell's by making it clear that black citizens had the right to vote and to hold office. This provision came in response to the purge of black legislators in Georgia.[188] Yet Democratic obstruction prevented the Stewart bill from coming to a vote by the time H.J. Res. 402 passed. Stewart then shelved his measure and threw his support behind the House-passed Boutwell proposal.

After nearly a week of debate, Stewart sought a vote on Boutwell's bill. A host of amendments would be tried on February 8 and 9, some of them offered by Democrats with little chance of success. The larger concern was the heterogeneity within the Republican ranks. Gillette lays out the factions and interests at stake:

> Moderate Republicans, especially from the Northeast and from the West, wanted Negro voting but also wished to retain freedom of state action either in conferring suffrage and setting voting qualifications, especially the literacy test, or in restricting Irish or Chinese by the nativity test. In short, moderates were not at all agreed on the price worth paying for Negro suffrage. Radical Republicans from the North championed Negro suffrage and wanted firm guarantees that it would be permanent and effective, but they were not in agreement on the form required or on the scope of reform desired. Those from the South, with varying gradations of radicalism, were primarily interested in keeping and protecting south-

cally significant, with Republican members furthest from the Democrats (the radicals) being more likely to support the Shellabarger amendment.

186. *CG*, 40-3, 1/30/1869, 744. Republicans voted 10-134.

187. *CG*, 40-3, 1/30/1869, 745. Republicans voted 147-4. The four GOP dissidents were Jehu Baker (IL), John Bingham (OH), Isaac Hawkins (TN), and Daniel Polsley (WV). As William Gillette notes, "Reportedly furious over the defeat of his pet measure, John Bingham led the lonely group of Republican opponents." Gillette, *Right to Vote*, 54n37.

188. *CG*, 40-3, 1/28/1869, 668.

FIGURE 4. Sen. William Stewart (R-NV). Library of Congress, Prints & Photographs Division, LC-DIG-cwpbh-00571.

ern Negro voting, but there was less cohesion on the means to secure it, and still less on guaranteeing Negro officeholding and the means to be undertaken to achieve it.[189]

Although Boutwell encountered different GOP perspectives in the House, he was able to persuade Republicans that an amendment based on impartial suffrage would yield a partisan benefit (enfranchising blacks in the North, while also better protecting black voters in the South) and could be

189. Gillette, *Right to Vote*, 56–57.

ratified by three-quarters of the states. Stewart would find such pragmatic arguments a more difficult sell in the Senate.

Stewart achieved an initial victory when the Senate voted down an amendment offered by Jacob Howard (R-MI) proposing that "citizens of the United States of African descent shall have the same right to vote and hold office in States and Territories as other citizen electors of the most numerous branch of their respective Legislature." While Howard's amendment drew support from radicals as well as some moderate Republicans who sought to limit Chinese and Irish voting power, it was easily defeated, 16-35.[190] But a more daunting challenge lay ahead.

As in the House, various GOP senators raised concerns that the Boutwell amendment's focus on impartial suffrage would not prevent (ostensibly) race-neutral criteria from being used to disenfranchise black voters. In this vein Henry Wilson (R-MA) proposed a comprehensive suffrage amendment: "There shall be no discrimination in any State among the citizens of the United States in the exercise of the elective franchise in any election therein, or in the qualifications for office in any State, on account of race, color, nativity, property, education, or religious belief."

The Wilson amendment drew some support, but it went down to defeat, 19-24.[191] Republicans were almost evenly split on allowing states the discretion to restrict voting in nonracial ways, and thus Democrats were pivotal in defeating the measure.

Several hours later Wilson offered a "modification" of his earlier amendment, one he considered "more comprehensive": "No discrimination shall be made in any State among the citizens of the United States in the exercise of the elective franchise or in the right to hold office in any State on account of race, color, nativity, property, education, or religious creed."[192]

This modified Wilson amendment "guaranteed the right to hold office but did not, as in the preceding version, bar states from setting qualifications for holding office."[193] Wilson's modified amendment passed 31-27, as six senators from the GOP's Southern wing joined the yea side (four had previously voted nay and two had abstained).[194] Gillette argues that this

190. Gillette, *Right to Vote*, 58; *CG*, 40-3, 2/8/1869, 1012. Republicans voted 16-27.

191. *CG*, 40-3, 2/9/1869, 1029. Republicans voted 19-20.

192. *CG*, 40-3, 2/9/1869, 1035.

193. Gillette, *Right to Vote*, 60.

194. *CG*, 40-3, 2/9/1869, 1040. Republicans voted 30-21. William Gillette mistakenly characterizes this swing of six Republicans to the yea column as coming from three nay voters and three nonvoters on the original bill. See Gillette, *Right to Vote*, 60.

swing between the two Wilson amendments "showed that [Southern Republicans] seemed to care more about Negro voters electing whites to public office than about Negro voters electing Negro officials."[195] In all, ten of the thirteen Republican senators from the former Confederate states supported the modified Wilson amendment (with one voting nay and two not voting).[196]

While Stewart and moderate senators were dismayed by the radical turn in the voting, they saw little alternative to supporting the amended bill. A positive (two-thirds) vote would keep the constitutional amendment alive and allow the House to potentially reverse the changes Wilson and his supporters fought to incorporate. Thus the Republicans came together and produced a 40-16 win, with forty of forty-eight Republicans supporting H.J. Res. 402 with the modified Wilson amendment attached.[197] The action would now shift to the House.

The House did not take long to act. On February 15, at Boutwell's urging, the House failed to concur in the Senate amendments to H.J. Res. 402 by an overwhelming margin, 37-133.[198] A conference committee would be needed to reconcile the two approaches, but before that could happen, on February 17 the Senate voted 33-24 to recede from its former amendments.[199] More than two-thirds of GOP senators supported receding; only a few radicals and several Southern Republicans fought the move. Wilson's universal suffrage addition had thus been excised.

Now the Senate once again considered the original Boutwell measure (H.J. Res. 402, unamended), passed by the House on January 30. The 31-27 vote, however, was well below the two-thirds requirement.[200] A coalition of eighteen Republicans and nine Democrats formed to prevent Boutwell's plan for "impartial suffrage" from winning the day. Shortly before the vote,

195. Gillette, *Right to Vote*, 61.

196. The nay voter was George Spencer (AL). The two nonvoters were William Kellogg (LA) and Joseph Fowler (TN).

197. *CG*, 40-3, 2/10/1869, 1044. The eight Republican nay votes were Henry Anthony (RI), Henry Corbett (OR), James Dixon (CT), George Edmunds (VT), James Doolittle (WI), Joseph Fowler (TN), James Grimes (IA), and William Sprague (RI).

198. *CG*, 40-3, 2/15/1869, 1226. Republicans voted 36-95. A roll-call analysis (logistic regression) of Republican votes finds that the first (negative) and second (negative) NOMINATE dimensions are statistically significant, with Republican members closest to the Democrats being more likely to support concurring in the Senate amendments. Thus the more radical the member, the less likely that he would support concurring.

199. *CG*, 40-3, 2/17/1869, 1295. Republicans voted 33-15.

200. *CG*, 40-3, 2/17, 1869, 1300.

Frederick Sawyer (R-SC) summarized the Republican dissidents' feelings on the matter:

> I am not obliged here, I do not feel bound here, to vote for an amendment to the Constitution which accomplishes nothing and under which any State may pass a law which shall disenfranchise four fifths of the colored population without mentioning the word "color"; and I do not hold myself ready to answer to the appeal which has been made by the distinguished senator from Nevada [Stewart] to vote for this or we shall have nothing. I had rather have nothing than to have this; and when I go back to my constituents they will say to me that I voted right.[201]

It seemed that the Boutwell amendment was dead.

With the defeat of H.J. Res. 402, the Senate immediately resumed consideration of Stewart's *original* constitutional amendment (S.J. Res. 8), which Stewart had set aside after the House passed the initial Boutwell proposal. Stewart's amendment read:

> The right of citizens of the United States to vote and hold office shall not be denied or abridged by the United States or by any State on account of race, color, or previous condition of servitude.
>
> The Congress shall have the power to enforce this article by appropriate legislation.[202]

The debate over Stewart's language took twelve hours, and a series of amendments were defeated along the way. Finally, S.J. Res. 8 passed 35-11, with only two GOP defections.[203] As Gillette notes, "This measure was just enough more radical than Boutwell's because of the mild officeholding provision to win twelve additional votes."[204] Many of these votes came from Southern Republicans, consistent with their support for the modified Wilson amendment. S.J. Res. 8 now made its way to the House, as the Senate asked for concurrence rather than a conference.[205]

Boutwell did his best to move things forward despite disagreement within the GOP. First up was an amendment offered by John Logan (R-IL)

201. *CG*, 40-3, 2/17, 1869, 1300; portions also cited in Benedict, *Compromise of Principle*, 333.

202. *CG*, 40-3, 2/17, 1869, 1300.

203. *CG*, 40-3, 2/17/1869, 1318. The Republicans voted 35-2. The two GOP nay voters were Daniel Norton (MN) and Joseph Fowler (TN).

204. Gillette, *Right to Vote*, 67.

205. *CG*, 40-3, 2/18/1869, 1329.

to strike the officeholding right. Logan argued that decisions about who could hold office were not the province of the federal government. Earl Maltz suggests that deeper race-based concerns were behind Logan's offering: "To allow blacks to vote was one thing, to be ruled by them was another."[206] Although Logan's amendment garnered some support—as thirty-six Republicans broke ranks and joined with all the Democrats—it ultimately failed 70-95.[207]

Next came an amendment from John Bingham proposing to add "nativity, property, and creed" as additional criteria that could not be used to restrict voting and officeholding rights. Bingham did not specify education as a fourth criterion, however, suggesting that literacy tests were fair game. This "omission" was critical, since it allowed the amendment to pass 92-71.[208] The Republicans were split 68-64 as radicals and some moderates voted in favor while Southern Republicans and some moderates voted against.[209] This level of support was enough to guarantee success, however, since nearly all Democrats—pleased by the literacy-test omission—also voted for the amendment.[210]

While moderates like Boutwell and even some radicals like Benjamin Butler (R-MA) believed Bingham was making the amendment more extreme in an attempt to kill it, he in fact stopped short of pushing for "true" universal suffrage as he did earlier in the session. As Maltz argues, "[Bingham's] language was something of a compromise, allowing states to continue to disenfranchise citizens on the basis of educational qualifications. The change from the Wilson language was deliberately calculated to win approval not only in Congress but also in the ratification process."[211] Disappointed or not, Boutwell and his compatriots closed ranks and voted for S.J.

---

206. Maltz, *Civil Rights, the Constitution, and Congress*, 151. William Gillette agrees with Maltz, viewing Logan's measure as "no doubt accurately reflecting the will of his constituency, where opinion against Negro officeholding ran strong, as it did in Indiana, Ohio, West Virginia, Pennsylvania, and Connecticut." Gillette, *Right to Vote*, 68.

207. *CG*, 40-3, 2/20/1869, 1428. Republicans voted 36-95.

208. *CG*, 40-3, 2/20/1869, 1428.

209. A roll-call analysis (logistic regression) of Republican votes finds that the second (negative) NOMINATE dimension is statistically significant, with Republican members furthest from the Democrats on that dimension being more likely to support the Bingham amendment.

210. As William Gillette notes, "The Democrats—with the sweetener that education tests, which would bar southern Negroes, would not be banned—joined the radical Republicans to effect a radical result." Gillette, *Right to Vote*, 69.

211. Maltz, *Civil Rights, the Constitution, and Congress*, 151.

Res. 8 as amended by Bingham. It easily achieved the necessary two-thirds majority, 139-37.[212]

By this point both the House and Senate had tired of interbranch conflict. Members chose to delegate further legislative action to a conference committee.[213] Six members were appointed to the conference, three from each chamber: Bingham, Boutwell, and Logan from the House, and Stewart, Roscoe Conkling (R-NY), and George Edmunds (R-VT) from the Senate. On its face, the committee was constructed to produce a moderate outcome: no Southern Republicans and no die-hard radicals were chosen, and Bingham was the only advocate of universal suffrage. While some believed conferees would be obliged to report a less than moderate bill to the floor—given the right of officeholding included in both House and Senate bills and the prohibition of additional voting/officeholding qualifications (beyond race, color, or previous condition of servitude) included in the Senate bill—no such norm would be followed.

On February 24 the conference committee met and, after some internal disagreement and politicking, reported an amendment that was similar in many ways to the *initial* Boutwell and Stewart amendments.[214] The text of the amendment read:

Section 1. The right of citizens of the United States to vote shall not be denied or abridged by the United States or by any State an account of race, color, or previous condition of servitude.

Section 2. The Congress shall have the power to enforce this article by appropriate legislation.[215]

212. *CG*, 40-3, 2/20/1869, 1428. Republicans voted 137-2. The only nay votes were Isaac Hawkins (TN) and Thomas Jenckes (RI).

213. On February 23 the Senate voted 32-17 to disagree with the House's amendment and request a conference, with Republicans voting 32-11. See *CG*, 40-3, 2/23/1869, 1481. Most of the GOP nay voters were from the South, perhaps fearing that the officeholding right might be eliminated in conference. On this point, see Maltz, *Civil Rights, the Constitution, and Congress*, 154. That same day, the House agreed 117-37 to accept the Senate's request for a conference, with only two Republicans dissenting. See *CG*, 40-3, 2/23/1869, 1470.

214. Bingham and Logan opposed a right to hold office and brought along Stewart and Conkling (who thought a right to hold office was assumed by a right to vote). All four also agreed to delete the additional qualifications (nativity, property, and creed). Edmunds objected, but he was outnumbered. In disgust, Edmunds refused to sign the report. See Gillette, *Right to Vote*, 71; Benedict, *Compromise of Principle*, 334; and Maltz, *Civil Rights, the Constitution, and Congress*, 154.

215. See *CG*, 40-3, 2/26/1869, 1623.

The House considered the conference report first, and it was adopted 143-44 without debate, thereby achieving the necessary two-thirds majority, with only three of 144 Republicans defecting.[216] In the Senate, debate turned ugly as various Republicans voiced their displeasure about the removal of the officeholding right. Stewart continued to argue for what was achievable with the time left in the lame-duck session, even as he insisted that the right to vote guaranteed the right to hold office. Stewart's pragmatic appeal found support in statements made by Jacob Howard, Henry Wilson, and Oliver Morton (R-IN), who all expressed their displeasure with the conference report but also their intent to vote for the amendment as the best that could practically be achieved.[217] Finally a vote was taken, and the Senate agreed 39-13 to concur in the conference report, thus achieving the two-thirds requirement, with only five of forty-four Republicans voting nay.[218]

In adopting the conference report, the GOP endorsed "impartial suffrage." Voting could be restricted, but not based on race, color, or previous condition of servitude. This version of the amendment fit with the policy aims of those who worried about coming out too strongly on behalf of guaranteed voting rights. At the same time, the policy also achieved the political aims sought by the congressional GOP: to enfranchise blacks in areas where they were not allowed to vote; to protect black suffrage in areas like the South, where opponents (should they come to power) would seek to eliminate such rights with a simple statute; and to leave open the possibility that additional qualifications (beyond race) could be employed to limit the right to vote generally. The last point was important in order to make the amendment palatable to Northern and Western states — where Republicans worked to limit Irish and Chinese suffrage — in the ratification process.[219]

The party's gambit was successful, as the conference report on S.J. Res. 8 won the approval of twenty-eight states (three-quarters of the thirty-seven) a little less than a year later,[220] and Secretary of State Hamilton Fish certi-

---

216. CG, 40-3, 2/25/1869, 1563–64. The three Republicans were Isaac Hawkins (TN), William Loughridge (IA), and Rufus Mallory (OR).

217. For the Senate debate, including remarks by Stewart, Howard, Wilson, and Morton, see CG, 40-3, 2/26/1869, 1623–33, 1638–41.

218. CG, 40-3, 2/26/1869, 1641. The five Republicans were James Dixon (CT), James Doolittle (WI), Joseph Fowler (TN), Daniel Norton (MN), and John Pool (NC).

219. Gillette, Right to Vote, 151–58.

220. On February 3, 1870, Iowa became the twenty-eighth state to ratify the amendment. Nevada was the first, on March 1, 1869.

fied the Fifteenth Amendment at the end of March 1870. Ratification was a struggle in some states, and Republicans used their influence where it counted. For example, President Grant strongly endorsed the amendment, while Congress made its ratification a condition for the four former Confederate states (Virginia, Mississippi, Texas, and Georgia) still seeking to rejoin the Union.

Radicals' fears regarding the use of race-neutral qualifications to disenfranchise black votes would be realized two decades later. But during the still-early part of Reconstruction, the Republicans had their victory and black citizens seemed to have their guarantee. The enforcement provision of the Fifteenth Amendment (as well as the Fourteenth Amendment) would soon be put to the test, however, as Congress would have to address the constant acts of "white terror" in the South.

The Enforcement Acts

Many celebrated the enactment of the Fifteenth Amendment. Black citizens and longtime opponents of slavery reveled in its success and looked hopefully to the future. The Northern public also cheered the amendment, not just for what it protected but also as a signal that Reconstruction policymaking might be at an end. Within Congress many Republicans were satisfied, believing they had protected black voting rights while ensuring their party a bloc of reliable electoral support. That they had stopped short of adopting universal suffrage did not dampen the mood. Moderates believed that active Reconstruction was at an end because black citizens now had everything they needed to be successful and to protect what was theirs. Radicals remained concerned about loopholes that could be used at some future point to disenfranchise black voters; yet they also acknowledged the substantive and symbolic importance of the amendment.[221]

Such optimism did not last long in the face of increasing violence against the freedmen. Republicans were already aware of paramilitary groups like the Ku Klux Klan, based on their successful efforts at depressing GOP vote totals in Georgia and Louisiana in 1868. But now the Klan and similar groups stepped up their tactics in nearly every Southern state. Republican govern-

221. For a summary of reactions to the Fifteenth Amendment, see Xi Wang, *The Trial of Democracy: Black Suffrage and Northern Republicans, 1860–1910* (Athens: University of Georgia Press, 1997), 50–53.

ments in the South struggled to respond effectively to the Klan's actions and petitioned the federal government for help.[222]

As the GOP convened in the Forty-First Congress (1869–71), reports out of the South convinced them that something needed to be done. To counteract the growing Southern white insurgency, Republicans came to believe that the Civil Rights Act of 1866 and the Fourteenth and Fifteenth Amendments would need to be actively implemented throughout the South. They could not rely on local officials to abide by the provisions of these laws. From 1870 to 1872 the Republican-led Congress would pass five Enforcement Acts, each designed to protect both Southern and Northern voting rights and to prevent abuses in the electoral process.[223] (The first three were enacted in the Forty-First Congress and are the subject of this chapter, while the remaining two were enacted in the Forty-Second Congress and will be covered in chapter 4.) However, major differences of opinion existed within the GOP over how enforcement should be structured, what provisions should be included, and how far to extend federal power in the pursuit of noble and shared goals.

THE FIRST ENFORCEMENT ACT

Congressional debate over what would become the First Enforcement Act began in both chambers in May 1870. The substance of the bills discussed, and the tenor of the debate, varied considerably between the House and the Senate. The bill managers in both chambers were familiar: Rep. John Bingham (R-OH) and Sen. William Stewart (R-NV). Bingham's bill (H.R. 1293) aimed to "enforce the right of citizens of the United States to vote in the several States of this Union who have hitherto been denied that right on account of race, color, or previous condition of servitude." It was national in scope and sought to respond to abuses in both North and South.[224] Bingham introduced the bill on May 16 after seeking to suspend the rules so as to prevent any debate or amendments. In doing so he was taking advantage of the large GOP majority. His ploy was successful, as the Republicans easily defeated

222. For descriptions of Klan violence in the South during this time, see Trelease, *White Terror*, 191–273, and Foner, *Reconstruction*, 425–30.

223. For a short summary of the five Enforcement Acts, see Gillette, *Retreat from Reconstruction*, 25–26.

224. Indeed, when reporting the bill, Bingham spoke to rights "definitely denied in his own State [of Ohio] as well as in others." See *CG*, 41-2, 5/16/1870, 3503.

FIGURE 5. Rep. John Bingham (R-OH). Library of Congress, Prints & Photographs Division, LC-DIG-cwpbh-00525.

a Democratic motion to adjourn and then voted 131-44 to suspend the rules and pass H.R. 1293.[225]

Bingham's bill sought primarily to punish state and federal officials who failed to protect black voters.[226] But it also contained provisions to punish individuals who prevented black voting through violence. Its provisions ex-

225. *CG*, 41-2, 5/16/1870, 3504. The Republicans voted 128-1, with only Isaac Hawkins (TN) defecting.

226. See *CG*, 41-2, 5/16/1870, 3503-4.

tended to federal, state, and municipal elections. To ensure enforcement, the bill vested all power in federal circuit and district courts. Thus charges and cases would need to be brought, and no additional enforcement infrastructure was created in the bill to ensure that this was accomplished.

Following enactment, H.R. 1293 was sent to the Senate. After consulting with Charles Sumner (R-MA) and John Sherman (R-OH), William Stewart decided to amend the House bill by striking everything after the enacting clause and substituting his own bill (S. 810).[227] S. 810, which contained seventeen sections, was far more expansive than Bingham's bill.[228] It interpreted voting rights broadly, extending them to the act of registering as well, and sanctioned state and federal officials if prerequisites for voting were infringed because of race. The Senate bill also moved beyond punishing individuals who used violence and intimidation to prevent black citizens from voting by incorporating language to punish conspiracies to achieve these ends. Stewart's bill gave federal officials the ability to use the law against the Klan and other paramilitary groups. S. 810 also allowed judges to appoint election supervisors and deputies to oversee registration and voting and make arrests if necessary, and it granted the president discretion to use military force to pursue violations of the law. Finally, S. 810 enforced elements of both the Fourteenth Amendment and the 1866 Civil Rights Act by continuing to disenfranchise rebels and remove them from office and to punish the Klan for actions outside polling places.[229]

Before voting on Stewart's substitute, the Senate worked to perfect it through a host of amendments. Several were successful, the most important being one offered by John Sherman, who gained the floor and took the proceedings on enforcement in a different direction: "There is one other grievance that I feel ought to be dealt with at this very moment, as we have this bill before us; a grievance that has become of greater magnitude even than the denial of the right to vote to the colored people; and that is the open, glaring, admitted frauds by wholesale in the great cities of this country, by which our Government is about to be subverted."[230]

Sherman went on to speak of the scope of fraud he believed was committed in New York City during the 1868 presidential election. "There were thousands and tens of thousands of illegal votes," he proclaimed, "liberty

227. *CG*, 41-2, 5/17/1870, 3518; 5/18/1870, 3560–63.
228. *CG*, 41-2, 5/18/1870, 3561–62.
229. These points are covered in Wang, *Trial of Democracy*, 59.
230. *CG*, 41-2, 5/20/1870, 3663.

and law were subverted."[231] According to Sherman, Horatio Seymour won the state only because of voter fraud.

Sherman's proposed amendment listed a variety of fraudulent activities and behaviors in elections and stipulated that the punishment upon conviction would involve a fine up to $500, three years in jail, or both.[232] Democrats cried foul, but they did not have the numbers or arguments to stop him. On May 20 the Senate approved Sherman's amendment 31-12, with only four Republicans defecting.[233] In terms of impact, Xi Wang argues, "Sherman's sections on election fraud actually opened up a new vista for enforcement, which would become a major issue in the debates over the next two enforcement laws and for the next two decades."[234] Later that day, after additional provisions were added to the bill, Stewart sought to move things forward by calling on the Senate to substitute the new bill for Bingham's initial proposal. The Senate voted 40-9 to do just that.[235] The amended bill then went back to the House for its concurrence.

Rather than accept the new language, House Republicans sought a conference with the Senate.[236] Conferees were chosen in each chamber,[237] and a conference report was quickly produced. The report was completed and sent back to the chambers the next day (May 24).[238] Changes were minimal. Conferees simply added specificity about evidentiary standards in cases involving suspected vote fraud or irregularities.[239] The revised bill easily achieved the two-thirds necessary in both chambers on near party-

231. *CG*, 41-2, 5/20/1870, 3664.

232. Sherman's initial proposal covered all representatives and delegates to Congress as well as presidential and vice-presidential electors. Over the course of the debate, he agreed to restrict the amendment exclusively to the former.

233. *CG*, 41-2, 5/20/1870, 3678. Republicans voted 31-4. The four Republicans voting nay were Joseph Fowler (TN), John Pool (NC), Edmund Ross (KS), and Waitman Willey (WV).

234. Wang, *Trial of Democracy*, 65.

235. *CG*, 41-2, 5/20/1870, 3687. Republicans voted 40-1, with Joseph Fowler (TN) voting nay.

236. *CG*, 41-2, 5/23/1870, 3726.

237. Bingham, Noah Davis (R-NY), and Michael Kerr (D-IN) represented the House, while Stewart, George Edmunds (R-VT), and John Stockton (D-NJ) represented the Senate. See *CG*, 41-2, 5/23/1870, 3726, 3734.

238. The conference report was read in its entirety before the vote in each chamber. See *CG*, 41-2, 5/24/1870, 3752; 5/26/1870, 3853.

239. Stewart carefully discussed the changes in the Senate before the conference vote. See *CG*, 41-2, 5/24/1870, 3753-54.

line votes.[240] On May 30, 1870, H.R. 1293 became law (the First Enforcement Act) with President Grant's signature.

THE SECOND ENFORCEMENT ACT

Roughly two weeks later, Congress began work on the Second Enforcement Act (otherwise known as the Naturalization Act). This bill followed from John Sherman's charges of voter fraud in Northern cities. Republicans, as Sherman noted, were still enraged by the party's loss in New York in 1868, which they believed was due to widespread Democratic fraud in the electoral process. They were determined to do something about it, and they did not believe Sherman's amendment to the First Enforcement Act went far enough. As Xi Wang notes, "With the elections of 1870 coming, the elimination of fraud in Northern elections became an urgent issue for the Republicans. The Republicans in Congress proposed to make the process of naturalization a federal matter and to eliminate such corruption in elections."[241]

Naturalization was the process by which a noncitizen (or "alien") might acquire citizenship. Although the first federal naturalization law was adopted in 1790, the process of naturalization was typically left to the states. The way naturalization was applied to aliens, and the extent to which aliens—naturalized or having declared the intention to be naturalized—could vote often varied considerably by state.[242] Thus if one party controlled the process of naturalization in places that saw a significant influx of immigrants, the system could be rigged to expedite suffrage rights, permit wholesale fraud, or both. In seeking to establish a national system for naturalizing aliens and setting severe penalties for fraud in the naturalization process, the GOP hoped to dampen the Democrats' urban electoral advantage.

On June 13, 1870, the Republicans' naturalization campaign began when Noah Davis (R-NY) introduced a measure (H.R. 2201) to determine penalties for fraud in the form of forged or bogus naturalization certificates. Davis suggested one to five years of jail time and fines up to $1,000. His bill also made it clear that federal courts would handle cases alleging such fraudu-

240. The Senate and House votes were 48-11 and 133-58, respectively. Republicans voted 48-1 and 132-1. The two Republican defections were, once again, the Tennesseans Fowler and Hawkins. See *CG*, 41-2, 5/25/1870, 3809; 5/27/1870, 3884.

241. Xi Wang, "The Making of Federal Enforcement Laws, 1870–1872," *Chicago-Kent Law Review* 70 (1995): 1035.

242. See Wang, *Making of Federal Enforcement Laws*, 1035n86.

lent actions, thereby taking this authority away from the states.[243] To pass the bill without debate or amendment, Davis called for suspending the rules that required a two-thirds majority. He was successful, and the House voted 130-49, with Republicans voting as a bloc.[244]

H.R. 2201 now moved to the Senate, where Roscoe Conkling (R-NY), representing the Judiciary Committee, offered a substitute amendment that was considerably more elaborate than Davis's House bill.[245] Eleven of the bill's thirteen sections dealt with procedures and qualifications for naturalization and citizenship, as well as penalties for fraud in the naturalization process and the domain of authority in hearing cases. The final two sections dealt strictly with enforcement issues regarding congressional elections. In cities with more than 20,000 inhabitants, federal judges could designate two citizens (one from each party) as deputies at the polls, to watch registration, voting, and the counting of votes. These deputies would be empowered to challenge the legitimacy of a vote at any stage. In addition, US marshals in those same cities were granted the power to appoint as many special deputies as necessary to keep the peace at the polls and preserve order in the voting. In short, Conkling proposed federal oversight of state elections.

While Conkling's bill was structured to federalize citizenship and voting, the last two sections were specifically designed to address the problems the GOP faced in urban centers — mostly in the North — controlled by the Democrats.[246] These sections gave the Republicans a set of mechanisms to challenge nonnaturalized voters and to prevent fraud at polling places. While Democrats recognized these two sections as a raw partisan ploy, they did not have the numbers to raise a serious challenge. Conkling would face problems within his own party, however, as western Republicans whose states benefited from immigration were reluctant to federalize naturalization procedures and qualifications. These senators preferred to keep decision making on naturalization matters at the state level.

Debate on Conkling's amendment was drawing to a close when Charles Sumner offered an amendment that would put the entire naturalization bill at risk. Sumner's amendment read: "*And be it further enacted*, That all acts of Congress relating to naturalization be, and the same are hereby, amended

---

243. For the full text of Davis's bill, see *CG*, 41-2, 6/13/1870, 4366–67.

244. *CG*, 41-2, 6/13/1870, 4368.

245. For the full text of Conkling's substitute, see *CG*, 41-2, 6/25/1870, 4834–36.

246. Of the nation's sixty-eight cities with populations of 20,000 or more, sixty-three were outside the former Confederacy; Donald, Baker, and Holt, *Civil War and Reconstruction*, 613.

by striking out the word 'white' wherever it occurs, so that in naturalization there shall be no distinction of race or color."[247]

Several Republicans quickly rose to oppose Sumner. Their concern related to Chinese immigrants, who were contract laborers on the West Coast. Several Republicans worried that Sumner's amendment, if passed, would encourage Chinese immigrants to seek citizenship and subsequently the right to vote. Their concerns were also influenced by the Fifteenth Amendment's guarantee of voting rights to "citizens," not simply to "persons" or "residents." Cultural and religious fear motivated Republican opposition, along with labor concerns, but practical politics were also very much in play. As Andrew Gyory writes, "Unlike black suffrage, Chinese naturalization promised scant electoral benefits. With most of the Chinese congregated in the small states of California, Oregon, and Nevada, Republicans had little incentive to push for Chinese citizenship. Without this pressure, many of the egalitarian principles that had inspired Radical Reconstruction began to wane."[248]

After much (angry) debate, Sumner's amendment failed by a single vote, 22-23.[249] Republicans were divided, but a majority voted to defend equal rights and racial justice. The amendment lost, however, as fifteen Republicans joined the Democrats, who voted as a bloc.

With Sumner's amendment out of the way, the Senate turned back to Conkling's original proposal. Conkling knew that some Republicans opposed his bill's federalizing the naturalization process, so he tried to persuade them to vote for the bill as written and then take their concerns to the conference committee. He failed when a majority of Republicans voted against him, defeating his substitute 17-33.[250] Conkling responded by seeking to attach two enforcement sections of his substitute to Davis's original proposal. This strategy was successful: the Senate voted 37-9 to add his sections to H.R. 2201.[251] Only one of thirty-eight Republicans opposed the amendment, since greater election enforcement in Northern cities was a winning issue for the party.[252]

247. *CG*, 41-2, 7/2/1870, 5121.

248. Andrew Gyory, *Closing the Gate: Race, Politics, and the Chinese Exclusion Act* (Chapel Hill: University of North Carolina Press, 1998), 52.

249. *CG*, 41-2, 7/2/1870, 5123. Republicans voted 22-15.

250. *CG*, 41-2, 7/2/1870, 5123. Republicans voted 17-25.

251. *CG*, 41-2, 7/2/1870, 5123.

252. The one defector was Arthur Boreman (R-WV).

Before Conkling could celebrate, however, Sumner was recognized and again moved his antidiscrimination amendment. And this time he was victorious as the Senate voted 27-22.[253] Sumner picked up five additional Republican votes, which proved decisive.[254] Consternation gripped several members, most notably William Stewart (R-NV), who argued passionately (with a kind of racist paternalism) that as a result of this vote the Chinese "will be persecuted—persecuted to an extent that will make humanity blush. I know what the result will be. The fact that we are trying to do an unreasonable thing; the fact that we are trying to make American citizens out of pagans, who are bound by obligations such as no other race are—obligations which will make them sacrifice themselves and their families—will only result in their oppression and slaughter."[255]

Stewart was a bit overheated, of course, since no law had yet been passed and the Senate had not even approved the amended bill.

On July 4 the Senate spent an entire morning session discussing naturalization. During this debate western Republicans once again resorted to fearmongering about the threat posed by Chinese immigrants. Stewart made lengthy arguments about the dangers of naturalizing the Chinese. George H. Williams (R-OR) argued that Chinese naturalization threated American free-labor ideology. Carl Schurz (R-MO) claimed that perhaps the time was not right for such a dramatic change to naturalization procedures.[256]

In the evening, after a short debate, voting commenced. Taken up first was a motion from Conkling to reconsider the vote on the Sumner amendment from two days earlier, which passed 27-14.[257] Sumner's amendment was then voted down 14-30.[258]

How did the Sumner amendment go from success (27-22) to defeat (14-30) in two days? Eight Democrats voted against Sumner's amendment on

253. *CG*, 41-2, 7/2/1870, 5124.

254. Only two Republicans switched their votes, however. Abijah Gilbert (FL) and Timothy Howe (WI) voted nay on Sumner's initial amendment and then voted yea on the follow-up amendment. Twenty-one Republican senators voted "yea-yea" and thirteen voted "nay-nay." Four other Republican votes came from senators who had abstained on the first roll call: Conkling, Reuben Fenton (NY), James Patterson (NH), and John Thayer (NE). Hiram Revels (MS) voted yea on the first roll call and abstained on the second.

255. *CG*, 41-2, 7/2/1870, 5125.

256. For the entire debate, see *CG*, 41-2, 7/4/1870, 5148-67.

257. *CG*, 41-2, 7/4/1870, 5173.

258. *CG*, 41-2, 7/4/1870, 5176.

each day, so Republicans were ultimately the pivotal actors. Six Republican senators who had voted yea on June 2 switched to nay on June 4, while seven other Republicans who voted yea on June 2 did not cast a vote on June 4. Thus a combination of vote switching and strategic abstention ultimately doomed the Sumner amendment.[259] In the end, party leaders — led by Conkling — convinced enough Republican senators that Sumner's amendment would threaten to sink the entire bill, and opponents coordinated to first reconsider the amendment and then defeat it.[260]

As a face-saving measure, while Republicans fought Sumner's efforts to strike "white" from the naturalization laws, Willard Warner (R-AL) offered the following amendment: "*And be it further enacted*, That the naturalization laws are hereby extended to aliens of African nativity and to persons of African descent."[261]

Warner's amendment passed by the slimmest of margins, 21-20.[262] And while its language, in time, would prove important for the immigration of blacks to the United States, Republicans passed it only because they did not anticipate inflows on a par with the Chinese.[263] As Xi Wang asserts, "[This] section served largely as a political gesture to accord with what Warner called 'a ripened public opinion' on black rights rather than a sincere policy to attract Africans to America."[264]

With this amendment added, Senate proceedings approached a conclusion. The body first moved from the Committee of the Whole back to the Senate and concurred in all amendments.[265] At that point Sumner tried his amendment one last time. Before the vote, Lyman Trumbull made a passionate plea for Chinese naturalization, asking his fellow senators whether they truly wanted "to deny the right of naturalization to the Chinaman, who is infinitely above the African in intelligence, in manhood, and in every

259. A roll-call analysis (logistic regression) of Republican defection from the initial Sumner amendment, wherein each of these thirteen Republicans is coded 1 and all other Republicans are coded 0, finds that neither NOMINATE dimension is statistically significant. The GOP defections from the Sumner bill — either by vote switching or by strategically abstaining — do not appear to have an ideological basis.

260. *New-York Tribune*, July 5, 1870, 5; *San Francisco Chronicle*, July 6, 1870, 2.

261. *CG*, 41-2, 7/4/1870, 5176.

262. *CG*, 41-2, 7/4/1870, 5176. Republicans voted 21-12.

263. On Republicans' beliefs about African immigration, see the comments made by Oliver Morton (R-IN) during the debate. *CG*, 41-2, 7/4/1870, 5177.

264. Wang, *Trial of Democracy*, 76.

265. *CG*, 41-2, 7/4/1870, 5176-77.

respect."[266] The answer was yes, and Sumner's amendment was once again defeated, 12-26.[267] Not to be undone, and wishing to put the membership *explicitly* on the record regarding Chinese naturalization, Trumbull then offered an amendment to Warner's earlier amendment, adding the words "or persons born in the Chinese empire." The full amendment, as proposed, would now read, "That the naturalization laws are hereby extended to aliens of African nativity, and to persons of African descent, and to persons born in the Chinese empire."[268]

The Senate roundly rejected Trumbull's amendment to Warner's amendment, 9-31.[269] Only nine of thirty-three Republicans were willing to vote for Chinese naturalization.[270]

The Senate now moved to consider the amended H.R. 2201. At this point the bill included all of Davis's original proposal, Conkling's two enforcement sections, and Warner's naturalization language. It passed 33-8, with all but one Republican voting yea.[271] Rather than ask for a conference, the House proceeded to suspend the rules and concur in the Senate amendments 132-53, with only two Republicans defecting.[272] Three days later President Grant affixed his signature and the bill became law.

The Second Enforcement Act had the interesting effect of linking suffrage, race, citizenship, and naturalization. While GOP support for black interests remained strong, other splits had emerged. Nonetheless, party leaders had achieved what they set out to do in the short run. Conkling's sections of the new law made the Republicans able to rein in various fraudulent behaviors in Northern cities before the 1870 elections. How much this would matter was an open question, but it would be answered soon enough.

266. *CG*, 41-2, 7/4/1870, 5177.

267. *CG*, 41-2, 7/4/1870, 5177. Republicans voted 12-19.

268. *CG*, 41-2, 7/4/1870, 5177.

269. *CG*, 41-2, 7/4/1870, 5177.

270. Anti-Chinese sentiment would ramp up a dozen years later when Congress passed the Chinese Exclusion Act (1882), which banned Chinese immigration for ten years. It was renewed ten years later in the Geary Act (1892) and then again in 1902 (with no terminal date). See Gyory, *Closing the Gate*, and Erika Lee, *At America's Gates: Chinese Immigration during the Exclusion Era, 1882–1943* (Chapel Hill: University of North Carolina Press, 2003).

271. Republicans voted 33-1. The single defector was Arthur Boreman (WV), who was also the lone Republican to vote against Conkling's earlier amendment to H.R. 2201.

272. *CG*, 41-2, 7/11/1870, 5441. The Republicans voted 131-2. The defectors were John Hay (IL) and David Bennett (NY).

THE THIRD ENFORCEMENT ACT

New York was the Northern focus of the First and Second Enforcement Acts as Republicans worked to guarantee that voting in New York City was "fair." As well as can be determined, this was largely achieved. Voter registration dropped by nearly 30,000, and dozens were arrested. But the result for the GOP was the same: the Democratic Party's candidates for governor and for mayor of New York were reelected (with fewer votes), and the partisan distribution of House seats from New York City elections was unchanged.[273]

More generally, though, in 1870 the Democrats did well throughout the country and increased their numbers significantly in the upcoming Forty-Second Congress (1871–73). In the South, Klan violence led to significant GOP losses in Alabama, Georgia, North Carolina, and Texas.[274] In short, the Republicans saw their numbers dwindling both North and South, and party leaders called for additional enforcement legislation to stem the tide. The GOP would endeavor to make these changes in the lame-duck session of the Forty-First Congress before the larger Democratic minority was seated in the Forty-Second. Their attempts to pass Third and Fourth Enforcement Acts would be only partially successful, however. Only the Third would be enacted before the end of the session, while the Fourth would be postponed until the early months of the Forty-Second Congress. On the plus side, there were few theatrics in this round, as the party held together well.

On February 13, 1870, John Bingham (R-NY), representing the Judiciary Committee, reported yet another enforcement bill (H.R. 2634), designed to clearly establish how federal officials would provide for legitimate elections.[275] He set out the duties all enforcement officials were to perform and stipulated new crimes related to various aspects of electoral fraud in the registration and voting processes. The crimes were also designated as federal in nature, making federal courts the venue for subsequent cases. In addition, the second section of the bill incorporated language from the second enforcement bill regarding enforcement protocols in cities with more than 20,000 inhabitants. Finally, H.R. 2634 sought to modernize voting procedures in congressional elections by requiring written or printed ballots.

In reporting his bill, Bingham moved that the rules be suspended and the bill be made a special order in two days (with strict debate limits and no dila-

273. Wang, *Trial of Democracy*, 79.

274. Trelease, *White Terror*, 241–42; Foner, *Reconstruction*, 441–44.

275. The nineteen sections (as subsequently amended) are listed in *CG*, 41-3, 2/15/1871, 1281–83.

tory motions allowed). Bingham's motion was approved, and H.R. 2634 was taken up for a final vote in the late afternoon on February 15.[276] After some debate and cursory modifications, the House passed it 144-64, with all but three Republicans voting yea.[277] On February 23 the Senate took up H.R. 2634 and debated it over the course of two days. At the end of the second day, after a series of failed amendments that Democrats offered to scuttle portions of the bill, it passed 39-10 on a near party-line vote.[278] Five days later President Grant signed the bill, and it became law (the Third Enforcement Act).

As the Forty-First Congress came to a close, Republicans were in an increasingly desperate position. They retained control of the federal government, but more tenuously than in the past and with reason to believe the worst was yet to come. Ku Klux Klan violence in the South was significant, and federal enforcement power to deal with it was still lacking. Meanwhile Northern constituencies were growing restless and more willing to accept the Democrats as a solution. Although things would get better in the short run as the Klan was convincingly dealt with (thanks to the passage of the Fourth Enforcement Act in the early months of the Forty-Second Congress), the lingering electoral issues in the North and the lack of a strong biracial coalition in the South were problems that were not going away. And the onset of a financial panic and subsequent economic downturn would be a blow that the Republicans — as an interregional coalition — could not survive.

Conclusion

The first three Congresses after the Civil War — the Thirty-Ninth, Fortieth, and Forty-First — were deeply consequential for both the country and the governing Republican Party. Southern Reconstruction, and the elevation of a race of people who had been slaves, constituted a truly revolutionary experience. But it did not come easily. Lincoln's assassination empowered Andrew Johnson, who quickly became an intransigent opponent, forcing congressional Republicans to write legislation that could win veto-proof majorities. This was a problem because Republicans went into the war with-

276. *CG*, 41-3, 2/13/1871, 1190–91. The vote on Bingham's motion would be 141-52, with Republicans voting 138-1. The lone Republican defector was Isaac Hawkins (TN).

277. *CG*, 41-3, 2/15/1871, 1285. Republicans voted 143-3. The defectors were Isaac Hawkins (TN), John Hay (IL), and Oliver Dickey (PA).

278. *CG*, 41-3, 2/24/1871, 1655. Republicans voted 39-1. The lone defector was Joseph Fowler (TN).

out an agreed-on plan for handling Reconstruction. They controlled Congress but were divided internally over the consequences of Union victory. Radicals sought a dramatic redistribution of power from the states to the federal government and pushed this agenda through a variety of policy proposals. Yet they always lacked the numbers to see these plans enacted. The internal compromises required to muster legislative majorities led Republicans to settle on policies that offered some federal protection to black citizens but that they knew *at the time* would not conclusively end discrimination or disenfranchisement.

Even with these compromises, the GOP achieved a lot. As we document, the Civil Rights Act of 1866, the Reconstruction Acts, the Fourteenth and Fifteenth Amendments, and the Enforcement Acts were landmark legislative accomplishments. These enactments created (for a time) the basis of a society that fulfilled the promises advanced in our earliest declarations as a free nation. Amid these legislative successes, the seeds of the GOP's struggles in the final three Congresses of the Reconstruction era—the Forty-Second, Forty-Third, and Forty-Fourth—were planted. How much to do for the freedmen and how much to use the federal government in such endeavors would increasingly divide the party. As the Northern public tired of the political situation in the South and demanded more attention to national issues—especially those directly affecting *their* lives—Republican lawmakers would increasingly resist additional federal interventions in the South, especially those that required further expansions of federal power. And this Northern fatigue was met with resolute Southern resistance as white Democrats sought to "redeem" Southern state governments from GOP control. As quickly as civil rights for African Americans were established and protected, they would just as quickly be eroded.

CHAPTER FOUR

The Demise of Reconstruction, 1871–1877

The guiding policies of Reconstruction established new political and social arrangements in the South. Thanks to a series of landmark laws and constitutional amendments pushed through by Republican majorities, African Americans were formally granted citizenship and guaranteed rights. These legal changes also allowed the GOP to establish a reliable base of political support in the former Confederacy, thereby building a durable interregional political organization. These partisan goals were an important motivating factor in the GOP's pursuit of civil rights policy.

Landmark civil rights policies were adopted during the first six years following the Civil War, when the Republican Party held supermajorities in both chambers of Congress. The GOP put this numerical strength to work by successfully wresting control of Reconstruction policy from President Andrew Johnson. Civil rights laws are thus attributable to the institutional and electoral weakness of the Democratic Party. Republicans were able to work their will in a way unseen throughout American political history except during the Democratic ascendancy in the early New Deal years.

The underlying dynamics of Republican Party success, however, were more complex than a simple "supermajority works its will" story might imply. The GOP faced significant internal conflict over how quickly and ambitiously to pursue Reconstruction. Radicals argued for change that would truly upend Southern society by elevating blacks to equality with whites in all respects while severely punishing white traitors. They also called for new federal powers that would dissolve traditional notions of constitutional federalism. Moderates supported efforts to give freedmen formal political equality without meaningful disqualification of white voters. They also sought the prompt reconstitution of Southern state governments and an expeditious national reunion. They opposed plans for federal intrusion into state-level politics. Moderates eventually won out, and a true "Radical Reconstruction" never occurred. Nevertheless, the gains achieved still amounted to a revolution in civil and voting rights for African Americans.

Yet the Democratic Party would not remain weak forever. Democrats increasingly called for an end to federal debates over the status of African Americans. This proved persuasive for a Northern public weary of the costs of Reconstruction. The Democrats were also able to exploit various advantages, like growing immigrant populations in Northern cities and general white animosity against Republican governments in the South (which relied almost exclusively on the newly enfranchised black voting population). They were also the political beneficiaries of the catastrophic economic depression that began in late 1873.

With the Democratic Party reasserting itself electorally, Republicans found themselves debating how much further to push Reconstruction and when to declare an end. The conservative wing of the party preferred to declare victory and move on. The radicals, on the other hand, had not finished pushing new initiatives to advance black civil rights. By the early 1870s, radicals and conservatives alike worried about declining GOP seat share in Congress. The midterm elections of 1870, for example, left the party with less than a supermajority in the upcoming House of Representatives.

Waning public support exacerbated tensions over Reconstruction policy, and disagreements within the party grew louder and more frequent. In this chapter we explore how the Republican Party dealt with these conflicting pressures and how the political lives of blacks in the South were subsequently affected. Our analysis focuses on the three Congresses from 1871 to 1877: the Forty-Second (1871–73), Forty-Third (1873–75), and Forty-Fourth (1875–77). These would turn out to be the final three Reconstruction Congresses, as intraparty divisions and external pressures brought the GOP's "noble experiment" to an end. And with that end came considerable uncertainty about the durability of its hard-won legislative achievements.

To guide the analysis, we divide this chapter into three main sections, each focused on a particular policy or piece of legislation: the completion of the Enforcement Acts, which were first initiated in 1870; the passage of the Civil Rights Act of 1875, along with the removal of officeholding disqualifications for former Confederates; and the failure of a new enforcement bill in 1875.

Enforcement Legislation, 1871–72

While the Republicans pushed through a Third Enforcement Act to reduce electoral fraud in urban areas principally in the North, the lame-duck session of the Forty-First Congress expired before they could effectively address similar fraud in the South. Thus, when the Forty-Second Congress convened on March 4, 1871, the chamber's first order of business was adopting a new Enforcement Act.[1]

Such an act was necessary, many Republicans believed, because of significant Democratic gains in the 1870 midterm elections. At the national level, these Democratic victories gave them an additional thirty House seats and two Senate seats in the Forty-Second Congress, and the House result meant the Republicans would no longer have a supermajority for the first time since the start of Reconstruction. The GOP would have to pursue new enforcement legislation with a smaller majority than in the past and without the party unity they had largely enjoyed on previous enforcement bills.

THE FOURTH ENFORCEMENT ACT

The legislation that would become the Fourth Enforcement Act (or Ku Klux Klan Act of 1871) divided the GOP. All party members were concerned about the violence and intimidation black voters faced in the South, but a serious division emerged over how best to respond. Radicals argued that the president should be given significant new power — such as suspending habeas corpus, if necessary — to counter Klan activity. Only deploying power like this, radicals believed, would make free and fair elections possible in the South. In short, the radicals once again advocated expanding federal power to protect black voters and the GOP's position in the South.

Moderates were considerably more reluctant to proceed in this way. They believed the radicals' proposed solution threatened federal/state balance and accepted constitutional practice. It would also leave the GOP open to claims of "federal overreach" by the Democrats before the 1872 elections. Some moderate voices within the GOP — those who would eventually be

---

1. This would be the final Congress that officially convened an "extra" session following its election and immediately after the adjournment of the preceding Congress, as mandated by the act of January 22, 1867. The act was adopted to prevent President Johnson from dictating when Congress would convene outside its regular ("long" and "short") sessions, and thus to prevent him from having a direct hand in determining Reconstruction policy.

part of the Liberal Republican movement—also believed Congress had done enough to provide blacks with civil and political protections and given the president all the enforcement power he required to intervene in Southern elections. These Republicans believed the burden was now squarely on the "enlightened" men of the postwar South—moderate white business and political leaders—to step up, denounce vigilantism, and ensure that laws were faithfully executed. If Congress were to produce any new legislation, they felt it should be to remove the officeholding disabilities in section 3 of the Fourteenth Amendment; this would, in their minds, empower white leaders who respected the law.[2]

On March 15, 1871, GOP divisions became public. During House debate, Benjamin Butler (R-MA) sought to introduce new enforcement legislation that would greatly expand federal power to protect black voting rights. As Allen Trelease notes, "[Butler's] measure would empower the President to suspend habeas corpus and to remove state officials when there was reason to doubt the validity of their election; United States marshals were also given the power to purge disloyal members from federal juries."[3] Such legislation had been discussed in a GOP caucus the previous night, during which Butler had attempted to win commitments of support.[4] Moderates refused to go along and, led by John Peters (R-ME), sought to postpone a decision on voting enforcement in the South by appointing a new select committee to investigate the execution of laws and the condition of the citizenry. This committee would report back at the start of the next session. The floor vote on Peters's resolution would be an initial test case on the moderate/radical power struggle, which the moderates won.[5]

Butler was incensed. On March 16 he railed against the "trick" that had been sprung on him and castigated those Republicans who rejected the caucus bond and voted with the Democrats. Peters and Henry Dawes (R-MA)

2. The *Chicago Tribune*, an organ for Liberal Republicanism, voiced this argument succinctly: "Congress, by its legislation, keeps the best-informed, the most experienced and influential class of rebels, politically disenfranchised, and, thereby, excludes the very men who are most deeply interested in the re-establishment of peace and order." See *CT*, March 17, 1871, 2.

3. Allen W. Trelease, *White Terror: The Ku Klux Klan Conspiracy and Southern Reconstruction* (Baton Rouge: Louisiana State University Press, 1971), 387.

4. See *CT*, March 16, 1871, 1.

5. For these proceedings, see *CG*, 42-1, 3/15/1871, 115–17. A roll-call analysis (logistic regression) of Republican votes finds that the first (negative) NOMINATE dimension is statistically significant, with Republican members closest to the Democrats (conservatives and leftmost moderates) being more likely to support Peters's resolution to create a select committee.

challenged Butler on the limitation of the caucus bond (which they viewed as pertaining merely to organizational matters) and whether honest policy opposition constituted a "trick." Eventually Speaker James Blaine (R-ME) took to the floor to counter Butler's many accusations and "denounce his insolence."[6]

Amid this GOP squabbling it appeared that the moderate strategy would hold and the House would adjourn the extra session in short order. At that point President Grant got involved.[7] On March 23 he met with Republican leaders from both chambers and requested a new enforcement law along the lines Butler had designed. Grant noted that he had long wanted new power to combat terrorism in the South but was concerned that an explicit request would make him appear despotic. Citing the existing moderate opposition, Republican leaders told Grant they could not rally support for a new enforcement law without an explicit request from him, and that now was the time for him to act. Klan terror would only increase as the 1872 election approached, they claimed, and adopting such a measure would become harder as it appeared more politically motivated. The worst-case scenario, according to Rep. George Frisbie Hoar (R-MA), would occur if no new power was granted and Grant was forced to put down Klan activity by constitutionally questionable means.

Grant sought to avoid Hoar's scenario and immediately wrote to Congress. His communication, which was read in both chambers that same day, stated:

> A condition of affairs now exists in some States of the Union rendering life and property insecure and the carrying of the mails and the collection of the revenue dangerous. The proof that such a condition of affairs exists in some localities is now before the Senate. That the power to correct these evils is beyond the control of State authorities I do not doubt; that the power of the Executive of the United States, acting within the limits of existing laws, is sufficient for present emergencies is not clear. Therefore,

6. For these proceedings, see *CG*, 42-1, 3/16/1871, 123–26.

7. The details of Grant's involvement and meeting with GOP leaders are discussed in Trelease, *White Terror*, 387–88. Trelease bases his account in part on the recollections of George F. Hoar, *Autobiography of Seventy Years*, vol. 1 (New York: Charles Scribner's Sons, 1906), 204–6. Note that Grant had written to Speaker Blaine on March 9, asking him to make the deteriorating condition in the South the top priority in the special session. See *The Papers of Ulysses S. Grant*, vol. 21, ed. John Y. Simon (Carbondale: Southern Illinois University Press, 1918), 218–19.

FIGURE 6. Rep. Samuel Shellabarger (R-OH). Library of Congress, Prints & Photographs Division, LC-DIG-cwpbh-05067.

I urgently recommend such legislation as in the judgment of Congress shall effectively secure life, liberty, and property, and the enforcement of law in all parts of the United States. It may be expedient to provide that such law as shall be passed in pursuance of this recommendation shall expire at the end of the next session of Congress. There is no other subject upon which I would recommend legislation during the present session.[8]

8. *CG*, 42-1, 3/23/1871, 236, 244.

Grant's communication had the desired effect of jump-starting GOP congressional efforts. Rep. Samuel Shellabarger (R-OH) immediately moved that a nine-member House select committee be appointed to recommend appropriate legislation, and after some debate and vocal Democratic opposition, his motion passed.[9]

Five days later Shellabarger, representing the select committee, reported a bill (H.R. 320) to the House.[10] Designed to enforce the provisions of the Fourteenth Amendment, H.R. 320 provided a right of action in federal court for infringement of constitutional rights that occurred at the state level (section 1); punished intrastate conspiracies (involving two or more persons) that resulted in felonious violations (murder, manslaughter, robbery, and assault and battery) of constitutional rights (section 2); gave the president the authority to intervene with federal military force in cases where (a) citizens' constitutional rights were violated within a state, (b) state authorities were unable or unwilling to protect those rights, and (c) such authorities did not seek assistance from the federal government to enforce the equal protection of the laws (section 3); and allowed the president to declare martial law and suspend habeas corpus when conspiracies overwhelmed a state's ability to protect its citizens, or if state authorities were complicit in the conspiracy, such that a rebellion against the federal government was deemed to have commenced (section 4). These enforcement provisions were also temporary, and would expire in just over a year (on June 1, 1872). As Alfred Avins notes, "The bill was designed to remedy state denials of equal protection by direct federal intervention against *individuals*" (emphasis added).[11] Shellabarger and his supporters understood that criminal violations of civil rights were often committed by private individuals — most recently and disturbingly by

9. *CG*, 42-1, 3/23/1871, 244-49. The committee comprised Shellabarger, Benjamin Butler (R-MA), Glenni Scofield (R-PA), Henry Dawes (R-MA), Austin Blair (R-MI), Charles Thomas (R-NC), George Morgan (D-OH), Michael Kerr (D-IN), and Washington Whitthorne (D-TN).

10. *CG*, 42-1, 3/28/1871, 317. Excellent legislative histories of the Fourth Enforcement Act can be found in Everette Swinney, "Suppressing the Ku Klux Klan: The Enforcement of the Reconstruction Amendments, 1870–1877" (PhD diss., University of Texas at Austin, 1966), 154–79; Alfred Avins, "The Ku Klux Klan Act of 1871: Some Reflected Light on State Action and the Fourteenth Amendment," *Saint Louis University Law Journal* 11 (1967): 331–81; Robert John Kaczorowski, "The Nationalization of Civil Rights: Constitutional Theory and Practice in a Racist Society, 1866–1883" (PhD diss., University of Minnesota, 1971), 161–209; Marilyn R. Walter, "The Ku Klux Klan Act and the State Action Requirement of the Fourteenth Amendment," *Temple Law Quarterly* 58 (1985): 3–64.

11. Avins, "Ku Klux Klan Act of 1871," 333.

members of the Klan—not by state authorities. He aimed to bring federal power to bear on rights violations of this kind.

H.R. 320 was controversial and led to a debate that spanned nine days with remarks by more than eighty representatives.[12] Michael Kerr (D-MD) voiced the Democratic critique by arguing that the bill—especially section 2—was an unconstitutional attempt to federalize police power, and that the states had exclusive jurisdiction to make criminal code. Other Democrats followed Kerr, leveling charges against the GOP's "despotic" attempts to usurp state power. Many Republicans, including George Frisbie Hoar (MA), Aaron Perry (OH), David Lowe (KS), and Henry Dawes (MA), spoke at length in support of the bill's constitutionality.

A number of moderate Republicans also raised concerns. John Farnsworth (R-IL) opposed "centralization" and held that the federal government had the power to step in only when states took unjust actions to infringe on rights, not when state officials failed to act. John Hawley (R-IL) argued that Congress did not have the authority to establish a general criminal code, and he called for the second section of the bill to be revised to focus on punishment for those who would limit the exercise of constitutional rights (like the right to vote or hold federal office). James Garfield (R-OH) echoed Hawley, arguing that section 2 of the bill needed to be rewritten to indicate that the national government was not assuming original jurisdiction over the rights of persons and property—which he believed was the domain of the states. Instead he called for limiting congressional power to instances when a state denied equal protection to its citizens by failing to protect their individual rights.

Given these concerns, Shellabarger replaced sections 2, 3, and 4 of his original bill.[13] The principal change was to reword section 2 to eliminate any language that suggested a federal criminal code and to "confine the authority of [the] law to the prevention of deprivations which shall attack the equality of rights of American citizens."[14] In addition, he broadened sections 3 and 4 to include references to the "United States" instead of merely to "a State," which raised the stakes for "obstructions of the laws" or "defiance of authority." Finally, the provision in section 4 that authorized declaring martial law was eliminated, leaving only the grant of power to the president to suspend habeas corpus.

12. Swinney, *Suppressing the Ku Klux Klan*, 156.

13. *CG*, 42-1, 4/5/1871, 477–78.

14. *CG*, 42-1, 4/5/1871, 478. Shellabarger's rewording of section 2 was based on a proposed amendment Burton Cooke (R-IL) had offered the previous day.

On April 6 the House took up Shellabarger's revised H.R. 320. Jacob Ambler (R-OH) offered an amendment to strike out that portion of section 4 that would grant the president power to suspend habeas corpus to protect the public safety and overthrow a rebellion. While eight other Republicans voted with Ambler in support of his amendment, it ultimately failed 100-105 as the bulk of the GOP held firm behind the provision.[15] Eugene Hale (R-ME) followed with an amendment to add a new section that sought to prevent the Klan from dominating juries and thwarting justice. Hale's amendment would require all grand and petit jurors to take an oath in open court that they had never been involved, directly or indirectly, in a combination or conspiracy to deprive their fellow citizens of their rights, with those found to have sworn falsely to be charged with perjury. Hale's amendment, which would also eliminate the earlier "ironclad" test oath during the Civil War, was agreed to 103-74 on a division vote.[16] William Holman (D-IN) then moved an amendment that would have gutted H.R. 320 by striking out section 3, eliminating the president's ability to use military force to put down insurrection and guarantee equal protection of the laws. It failed 91-115, with all but one Republican voting nay.[17] At that point the amended Shellabarger bill was put to a vote and passed 118-91, on a pure party-line vote.[18] It was then sent on to the Senate.

On April 11 George Edmonds (R-VT), chair of the Senate Judiciary Committee, reported out H.R. 320.[19] Debate on the bill stretched over the next several days and echoed many of the concerns raised in the House. Lyman Trumbull (R-IL) appreciated Shellabarger's rewriting of section 2 so that it no longer looked like an attempt to create a federal criminal code, but he cautioned that Congress did not (in his view) have the power to intervene against conspiracies to obstruct justice in state courts. In essence, Trumbull was willing to support federalization of authority only up to a point.[20] Allen Thurman (D-OH) shared Trumbull's reservations, arguing that Congress had no authority to punish conspiracies by individuals, which he asserted

15. *CG*, 42-1, 4/6/1871, 519-20. Republicans voted 9-104.

16. *CG*, 42-1, 4/6/1871, 521. John Shanks (R-IN) called for the yeas and nays, but only one member voted yea—well short of the one-fifth needed.

17. *CG*, 42-1, 4/6/1871, 521-22. Republicans voted 1-113, with John Farnsworth (IL) the only yea vote.

18. *CG*, 42-1, 4/6/1871, 521-22. Republicans voted 115-0.

19. *CG*, 42-1, 4/11/1871, 566.

20. Indeed, Trumbull would later move an amendment to strike out section 4 (the habeas corpus section) entirely, a measure that was defeated 21-43. *CG*, 42-1, 4/14/1871, 705.

was wholly the domain of the states. Carl Schurz (LR-MO) then enunciated a position that would characterize Liberal Republicanism, arguing that federal enforcement was not the remedy for Southern problems. Although reports out of the South were clearly distressing, Schurz held that Southerners themselves, not Congress, were responsible for determining solutions.

On April 14, voting in the Senate commenced. A number of minor GOP clarifying amendments were adopted, and several Democratic amendments meant to weaken the bill were defeated. But three major complications emerged. The first was agreeing on a termination date for the grant of authority to the president to suspend habeas corpus. The Shellabarger bill established an end date of June 1, 1872, roughly the end of the next regular session. Oliver Morton (R-IN) offered an amendment that would have extended the termination date to March 4, 1873, the end of the Forty-Second Congress — which Allen Thurman wryly observed would not be "until after the next presidential election."[21] And while Morton's measure had considerable Republican support, a majority of the GOP took a more cautious approach and joined with all Democrats to defeat the amendment.[22] A follow-up vote on the Judiciary Committee's proposed amendment, to replace "June 1, 1872" with "the end of the next regular session of Congress," was successful; this mild rewording allowed for the possibility that the next regular session might extend beyond June 1.[23]

John Sherman (R-OH) then proposed an amendment to add a new section allowing citizens who incurred property damage when their civil rights were violated during a riot to hold the relevant county, city, or parish liable and to recover compensation in federal court. Sherman's amendment was based on a provision in the earlier Butler bill, and it sought "to force local government to provide adequate policy protection."[24] It passed 39-25, but

21. *CG*, 42-1, 4/14/1871, 703-4.

22. *CG*, 42-1, 4/14/1871, 704. Republicans voted 23-27. A roll-call analysis (logistic regression) of Republican votes finds that neither NOMINATE dimension is statistically significant at conventional levels, although there is weak evidence ($p < .10$) that Republican members furthest from the Democrats (the rightmost moderates and radicals) were more likely to support Morton's amendment.

23. The regular (long) session of the previous (Forty-First) Congress, for example, did not end until July 15.

24. Swinney, *Suppressing the Ku Klux Klan*, 159. Sherman also held that his provision was "copied from the law of England that has been in force for six hundred years," an assertion Allen Thurman (D-OH) disputed. *CG*, 42-1, 4/14/1871, 705.

ten of forty-eight Republicans—those with growing concerns about federal overreach—joined with all Democrats in voting nay.[25]

Finally, an amendment initially raised by Thomas Osborne (R-FL) in the Committee of the Whole, and renewed on the floor by Oliver Morton, to strike out the provision in Representative Hale's juror section (repealing an 1862 act that required a loyalty oath for persons serving on federal juries) was considered. As Everette Swinney notes, "Many Republicans as well as Democrats felt that the repeal [of the Civil War era ironclad oath] was needed as a means of expediting judicial proceedings and improving the caliber of southern juries."[26] In effect, the repeal provision in Hale's section would allow a much greater proportion of white Southerners—those who were in some manner "Confederates"—to serve on Reconstruction era juries. Osborne, Morton, and others sought instead to maintain a more punitive approach toward the former Confederates. This radical position won out, and the Osborne amendment passed 34-25.[27] As with the Sherman amendment, ten Republicans—of the more moderate persuasion—defected.[28]

The amending completed, the Senate turned to a final vote on the bill, and H.R. 320 (as amended) passed 45-19, with all but four Republicans voting in support.[29] The amended bill was then sent back to the House.

The next day, April 15, Shellabarger moved to take up the Senate-amended bill. But the House refused to concur in three of the Senate amendments: (1) the Judiciary Committee amendment to extend the habeas corpus provision to the end of the next regular session (maintaining June 1, 1872 as the termination date); (2) the Sherman amendment (limiting court damages against cities, counties, and parishes); and (3) the Osborne amendment (keeping the provision that would repeal the ironclad oath law from 1862). In the first case a large majority of Republicans (eighty-four of ninety-eight) supported concurrence, but they were outvoted by the combination of GOP

---

25. *CG*, 42-1, 4/14/1871, 705.

26. Swinney, *Suppressing the Ku Klux Klan*, 159.

27. *CG*, 42-1, 4/14/1871, 708.

28. Republicans voted 34-10. A roll-call analysis (logistic regression) of Republican votes finds that the first (positive) NOMINATE dimension is statistically significant, with Republican members furthest from the Democrats (the rightmost moderates and radicals) being more likely to support Osborne's amendment.

29. *CG*, 42-1, 4/14/1871, 709. Republicans voted 45-4. The four GOP defectors were Lyman Trumbull (IL), Thomas Tipton (NE), Joshua Hill (GA), and Thomas Robertson (SC).

dissenters and Democrats; in the second case, a division vote of 12-114 suggested that the Republicans were unified behind nonconcurrence; and in the third case the Republicans were divided, but a small majority (fifty-one of ninety-five) joined with all Democrats to vote against concurrence.[30] Shellabarger then moved to create a conference committee to sort out the chamber differences, which was agreed to.[31]

On April 18 George Edmunds presented the conference committee's bill to the Senate. It was a compromise between the positions of the two chambers: the "end of the next regular session" termination date for the habeas corpus provision was maintained (favoring the Senate bill); preemptory juror challenges on grounds of disloyalty were eliminated (a compromise between the two chamber bills); and stipulating that suits for property damages must first be brought against the individuals responsible (i.e., the rioters) — and that two months must elapse — before the municipality in question could be targeted (a compromise between the two chambers).[32] A lively debate followed over the constitutionality of the new Sherman provision and whether the federal government could impose liability on local levels of government. Finally a vote was taken on the conference report, and it passed 32-16, with thirty-two of thirty-four Republicans voting in favor.[33]

On April 18 Shellabarger presented the conference committee's bill to the House. He noted the three compromise features of the bill, paying special attention to the revised Sherman amendment.[34] In doing so he realized the amendment might be the sticking point in navigating the chamber. Shellabarger was correct: the chief complaint against the amendment in the Senate — that the federal government could not impose liability on local levels of government (which were agents of the states) — was raised not just by Democrats like Michael Kerr (IN) but by Republicans Charles Willard (VT), Luke Poland (VT), Austin Blair (MI), John Bingham (OH), and John Farnsworth (IL) as well. A vote was taken the next day, and while a significant

30. *CG*, 42-1, 4/15/1871, 724–25. Note that Shellabarger, when presenting the Senate-amended bill, advocated for not concurring in the Sherman and Osborne amendments. See *CG*, 42-1, 4/15/1871, 723.

31. The conference committee would consist of Shellabarger, Glenni Scofield (R-PA), and Michael Kerr (D-IN) from the House and Edmunds, Sherman, and John Stevenson (D-NY) from the Senate. See *CG*, 42-1, 4/15/171, 725; 4/17/1871, 728.

32. *CG*, 42-1, 4/18/1871, 751–55.

33. *CG*, 42-1, 4/18/1871, 779. The two Republican dissenters were William Sprague (RI) and Reuben Fenton (NY).

34. *CG*, 42-1, 4/18/1871, 750–52.

majority of Republicans were persuaded to support the revised Sherman amendment, a minority joined with all Democrats to vote down the conference bill 74-106.[35]

Divided and exhausted, the Republicans rallied one more time. The House called for a new conference committee, and the Senate, after insisting on its amendments, agreed.[36] A new conference bill was proposed later that day, with a revised Sherman amendment that reduced the scope of liability. As Luke Poland noted when discussing the proposal, "The section imposing liability upon towns and counties must go out or we should fail to agree."[37] At the same time, he and fellow conferees wanted to make it clear that liability needed to be significant to be a reasonable deterrent, so culpability was expanded. As Poland stated, "The substance of [the new Sherman amendment section] is that any person who has knowledge of any of the offenses named, any of the wrongs already described, any of the conspiracies indicated in the second section [that] are about to be committed, it shall be within his duty to use all reasonable diligence within his power to prevent it; and if he fails to do so, so much damage as is occasioned to anybody in consequence of his failure, for so much he shall be responsible in an action."[38]

In effect, the conference bill was creating a "statutory tort," requiring anyone who knew about Klan activities to come forward or incur liability.[39] Thus, local citizens who were not affiliated with the Klan risked being sued for damages for Klan crimes. The onus was thus placed on individuals rather than counties and towns. This shifting of responsibility eliminated the concerns of those Republicans who believed the former Sherman amendment was an excessive (and unconstitutional) federal overreach. The second conference bill passed 93-74 on a pure party-line vote.[40]

Edmunds echoed Poland when he presented the second conference bill to the Senate. He claimed that by expanding the scope of the liability *within*

35. *CG*, 42-1, 4/19/1871, 800–801. Republicans voted 73-28. A roll-call analysis (logistic regression) of Republican votes finds that the first (positive) NOMINATE dimension is statistically significant, with Republican members furthest from the Democrats (the rightmost moderates and radicals) being more likely to support adopting the conference report.

36. *CG*, 42-1, 4/19/1871, 801, 810. Members of this second conference committee included Shellabarger, Luke Poland (R-VT), and Washington Whitthorne (D-TN) from the House and Edmunds, Matthew Carpenter (R-WI), and Allen Thurman (D-OH) from the Senate.

37. *CG*, 42-1, 4/19/1871, 804.

38. *CG*, 42-1, 4/19/1871, 804.

39. Avins, "Ku Klux Klan Act of 1871," 374.

40. *CG*, 42-1, 4/19/1871, 808.

the citizenry of the area in which the outrages take place, the bill made those with knowledge of the crimes "accessories" in the actions. In this way the new conference bill had "teeth" while avoiding the constitutional issues that had stymied a successful resolution to that point.[41] Sherman believed his earlier amendment would be more effective but recognized the politics of the situation. The Senate then passed the second conference bill 36-13, with thirty-six of thirty-eight Republicans voting yea.[42] President Grant signed the bill the next day, March 20, and the Fourth Enforcement Act was now law.[43]

As Swinney notes, the heart of the new seven-section law was the second section: "Together with section six of the First Enforcement Act, [the second section of the Fourth Enforcement Act] created a new federal crime—conspiracy to deprive of civil rights—and thereby brought the basic rights of American citizenship under the protection of the general government."[44] Sections 3 and 4 were direct enforcement provisions, which gave the president new authority to suppress domestic disturbances that deprived citizens of equal protection and allowed him (for a limited time) to suspend habeas corpus if necessary.

President Grant was not shy about using this new authority. Initially he sought the white South's voluntary compliance, issuing a proclamation that called on citizens to obey the law.[45] As Allen Trelease contends: "Doubtless [Grant] hoped . . . that the mere existence of the law would scare the Ku Klux into desisting; in which case he would let bygones be bygones."[46] Through late spring and early summer 1871, however, cabinet officials planned for the worst and began to collect evidence for future prosecutions. Through the summer months, following outbreaks of Klan violence in Mississippi and North Carolina, several arrests were made that resulted in a fair number of convictions. But it wasn't until the administration turned its collective attention to South Carolina that the controversial stipulations of the Fourth Enforcement Act came into play.

South Carolina was the hub of Klan-based terror. Recurring incidents

41. *CG*, 42-1, 4/19/1871, 820–21.
42. *CG*, 42-1, 4/19/1871, 831. The two Republican dissenters were Joshua Hill (GA) and Thomas Robertson (SC).
43. *CG*, 42-1, 4/20/1871, 838, 842.
44. Swinney, *Suppressing the Ku Klux Klan*, 162.
45. Presidential Proclamation, May 3, 1871, *Grant Papers*, 21:336–37.
46. Trelease, *White Terror*, 391.

of Klan violence were reported to the president in August, and after a full cabinet meeting Grant sent Attorney General Amos Akerman to investigate. After an extensive analysis of the situation, Akerman concluded that the normal legal process would not be an adequate remedy. The Klan's reach was too pervasive, and mass arrests would be necessary to cripple the organization and restore democratic order. Akerman recommended military action and the suspension of habeas corpus in the most troubled areas.[47] Grant obliged, and on October 12 he called for the end of "unlawful combinations and conspiracies" and demanded that Klansmen disperse and surrender their arms and disguises. Five days later, after most Klan members ignored him, Grant suspended habeas corpus in nine upland counties and sent three companies of soldiers to South Carolina to assist federal marshals in discharging their duties.[48]

Hundreds of arrests followed, and an estimated two thousand Klansmen were driven from the state. From 1871 to 1872, those arrested were prosecuted in federal courts, in trials that took on national prominence. The Great South Carolina Ku Klux Klan Trials revealed the full extent of federal power to protect the rights of black citizens.[49] Moreover, the concerted federal attack on the Klan in South Carolina was replicated in neighboring Southern states; although habeas corpus was not again suspended, the enforcement momentum was not to be denied. In sum, thanks to the Fourth Enforcement Act and the active efforts of the president, the number of criminal cases tripled between 1871 and 1872. And in 1872 the conviction rate in enforcement cases in the South approached 90 percent.[50] As Jean Edward Smith notes, "Grant's willingness to bring the full legal and military authority of the government to bear had broken the Klan's back and produced a dramatic decline in violence throughout the South."[51]

Thus, although congressional Republicans struggled to adopt the Fourth Enforcement Act, once it was in place and supported by the president, it did the job. Race-based violence fell precipitously, and the rights of black citizens in the South were protected for a time. Despite these evident successes,

47. Xi Wang, *The Trial of Democracy: Black Suffrage and Northern Republicans, 1860–1910* (Athens: University of Georgia Press, 1997), 96–97; Trelease, *White Terror*, 401–2.

48. Presidential Proclamation, October 17, 1871, *Grant Papers*, 22:176–78.

49. See Lou Falkner Williams, *The Great South Carolina Ku Klux Klan Trials, 1871–1872* (Athens: University of Georgia Press, 1996).

50. Wang, *Trial of Democracy*, 300.

51. Jean Edward Smith, *Grant* (New York: Simon and Schuster, 2001), 547.

divisions persisted within the GOP on the proper scope of federal power in pursuit of civil rights. And these divisions would be on full display once again in the second session of the Forty-Second Congress.

THE FIFTH ENFORCEMENT ACT

The fifth and final Enforcement Act passed in late spring 1872. Referred to as the Amendatory Enforcement Act, it supplemented the First Enforcement Act (of May 31, 1870) and sought to strengthen election supervision by extending the powers given to federal officers under the Second and Third Enforcement Acts. Its path to eventual success was perhaps the most difficult of the five acts.

On March 11, 1872, William Kellogg (R-LA) introduced the legislation that would ultimately become the Fifth Enforcement Act.[52] The Senate took up the bill (S. 791) on May 9, and discussion began the next day.[53] The bill stated that circuit court judges would have the power, upon the request of two citizens, to appoint election supervisors in every local precinct to watch the polls and count ballots. It also stipulated that federal marshals for each district would have the power, upon the request of two citizens, to appoint deputy marshals to assist the election supervisors, to keep the peace, and to make arrests if necessary. These provisions had been part of enforcement legislation before, but only for cities with 20,000 or more inhabitants. Kellogg sought to ensure that elections in rural areas—specifically in the South—would have the same safeguards as elections in more densely populated areas. As Oliver Morton (R-IN) stated, "The object of the bill is to simply secure a fair and honest election, to give nobody the advantage."[54]

On May 11 voting commenced on S. 791, and it spanned three days. The Democrats offered a variety of amendments to scuttle the bill, many of which included limiting army involvement and establishing procedures for keeping the peace. The Republicans adopted an amendment requiring an oath of loyalty to the US Constitution before a citizen could vote. The only obstacle emerged on March 14, when Lyman Trumbull (R-IL) attempted to attach a general amnesty amendment, which would have "removed all po-

---

52. *CG*, 42-2, 3/11/1872, 1558.
53. *CG*, 42-2, 5/9/1872, 3270; 5/10/1872, 3288.
54. *CG*, 42-2, 5/10/1872, 3289.

litical disabilities imposed by Section 3 of the Fourteenth Amendment, except for certain classes of persons specified in the act itself."[55] The desire
to reintegrate white Southerners into the body politic by allowing them to
hold political office had grown in popularity because advocates of Liberal
Republicanism saw this as a way to stabilize the Southern political system
by placing a "better class" of whites in office.

Before the vote on Trumbull's amendment, Morton gained the floor and
stated, "I hope this amendment will be voted down. If it is adopted, the effect
will be to defeat this bill, upon which we have been engaged some two or
three days, and which I think it is very important to pass." More to the point,
he noted that any amnesty bill, by the provisions of the Fourteenth Amendment, would require a two-thirds majority in each chamber to pass; thus,
adopting the amnesty amendment (by a simple majority) would in all likelihood kill the new enforcement bill.[56] Several other Republicans made similar arguments, while Trumbull stood his ground. Eventually a vote was taken
on the amendment, and it failed 22–33 as only seven Republicans supported
the amnesty provision.[57] The Senate then voted on S. 791, and it passed 36–
17, with thirty-six of forty Republicans voting yea.[58]

Republicans in the House sought to maintain the momentum behind the
new enforcement legislation. On May 28 John Bingham (R-OH) moved to
suspend the rules, take S. 791 (as amended through a substitute by the Judiciary Committee) from the Speaker's table, and pass it. A short but heated
exchange then occurred on the floor. James Beck (D-KY) objected to the
substitute being read, saying, "We do not want an army at the polls to super-
intend the holding of elections," to which Bingham replied, "We propose
that the Ku Klux army shall not go to the polls." The House then voted on
the bill, and while a majority was in favor, 115–87, it fell short of the two-
thirds majority necessary to suspend the rules.[59] Every Republican who cast

55. James A. Rawley, "The General Amnesty Act of 1872: A Note," *Mississippi Valley
Historical Review* 47 (1960): 480–84. General amnesty was adopted as a separate (stand-alone)
act on May 21. The provisions removed officeholding disabilities from all but a few hundred
white Southerners.

56. *CG*, 42-2, 5/14/1872, 3418.

57. *CG*, 42-2, 5/14/1872, 3421. Republicans voted 7–33.

58. *CG*, 42-2, 5/14/1872, 3431. The four Republican defectors were Trumbull, William
Sprague (RI), Morgan Hamilton (TX), and James Alcorn (MS). Liberal Republican Carl
Schurz (MO) also voted nay.

59. *CG*, 42-2, 5/28/1872, 3934. Republicans voted 113–0.

a vote supported the measure. The GOP tried a second time three days later and again fell short—this time 101-95 (with five Republicans defecting).[60]

Rather than accept defeat, Kellogg took a different tack. On June 7, 1872, he moved to attach his enforcement bill as an amendment to the House civil appropriations bill (H.R. 2705).[61] Democrats cried foul, but the presiding officer, Henry Anthony (R-RI), considered the amendment in order, and his fellow Republicans largely agreed.[62] The Democrats then laid down a dilatory gauntlet—with sixteen motions to adjourn and one motion to postpone indefinitely—which the Republicans defeated. Finally Kellogg's amendment was considered, and it passed 31-12 with all but two Republicans voting in favor.[63] The Senate then passed H.R. 2705, with the Kellogg amendment attached, 32-10, with thirty-two of thirty-three Republicans voting yea.[64] Cole moved that the Senate insist on its amendments and that a conference committee be requested before the bill was considered by the House, which was agreed to.

H.R. 2705 then moved to the House. On June 8 the Republicans sought to suspend the rules, not concur in the Senate amendments, and agree to the Senate's request for a conference. But they were unable to secure the two-thirds vote necessary for suspension. The Democrats meanwhile sought to force the GOP's hand with multiple motions to adjourn and recess. Eventually James Garfield (R-OH) and Speaker pro tempore Henry Dawes (R-MA) created some procedural confusion around various points of order, so that Dawes asked, "Shall the decision of the Chair stand as the judgment of the House?" Amid the confusion, Democrats were unsure how to respond, to which Dawes announced, "The question being put . . . the result of the vote by sound [was] that the judgment of the Chair was sustained." And by that ruling Dawes held that Garfield's move to suspend the rules and pass his

---

60. *CG*, 42-2, 5/31/1872, 4103. Republicans voted 101-5. The five defectors were Jacob Ambler (OH), Austin Blair (MI), Milo Goodrich (NY), John Hay (IL), and Stephen Kellogg (CT).

61. *CG*, 42-2, 6/7/1872, 4361–62.

62. An appeal from the decision of the chair was tabled, 28-22, with twenty-eight of thirty-five Republicans backing Anthony. *CG*, 42-2, 6/7/1872, 4365.

63. *CG*, 42-2, 6/7/1872, 4393. Republicans voted 31-2. The two defectors were William Sprague (RI) and Morgan Hamilton (TX). This was a vote in the Committee of the Whole. When the bill was reported back to the Senate as amended, Henry Cooper (D-TN) asked that the Kellogg amendment be concurred in, which elicited a 32-11 vote with thirty-two of thirty-four Republicans voting to concur. The two Republican dissenters were Sprague and Reuben Fenton (NY). *CG*, 42-2, 6/7/1872, 4398.

64. *CG*, 42-2, 6/7/1872, 4398. The lone Republican dissenter was Reuben Fenton (NY).

resolution (not to concur in the Senate amendments and agree to the Senate's request for a conference) was agreed to. Charles Eldredge (D-WI) immediately asked for a division vote, but several members responded, "Too late."[65]

Thus a conference committee went to work.[66] A first conference report was rejected by the House 99-79 as a minority of Republicans — led by William Kelley (R-PA) — expressed their discomfort with the enforcement legislation being moved as an amendment to an appropriations bill and "by virtue of parliamentary law and of the usages of this House."[67] This group of twenty Republicans was enough, in combination with all Democrats, to defeat the legislation.[68] The bill was then recommitted, and the committee went back to work, finally producing a second conference report.[69] And as William Niblack, the Democratic member on the committee, announced gleefully, "It was a mere skeleton of that which came to us from the Senate in the first place."[70] Election supervisors could still be appointed by circuit judges, but only upon the written request of ten citizens (not two, as in the Senate bill); election supervisors and deputy marshals needed to be qualified voters in the parish in which they were appointed and were to receive no compensation (except in cities with 20,000 or more inhabitants); no additional assistant or deputy marshals were to be appointed except as provided by law; and finally (and most important) federal marshals had no power to make arrests and election supervisors had no power to challenge certificates of election (except in cities of 20,000 or more). In short, Senator Kellogg had tried to extend the earlier enforcement provisions to rural areas; the conference committee, through its deliberations and amending activity, reestablished that those enforcement provisions were operable *only* in cities with 20,000 or more inhabitants.

James Garfield, speaking as chief House manager on the committee,

65. *CG*, 42-2, 6/8/1872, 4435.

66. The conference committee comprised Cornelius Cole (R-CA), George Edmunds (R-VT), and John Stevenson (D-KY) from the Senate and James Garfield (R-OH), Frank Palmer (R-IA), and William Niblack (D-IN) from the House. *CG*, 42-2, 6/7/1872, 4398; 6/8/1872, 4436.

67. *CG*, 42-2, 6/8/1872, 4438, 4442–43.

68. A roll-call analysis (logistic regression) of Republican votes finds that neither NOMINATE dimension is statistically significant at conventional levels, suggesting that the twenty members who voted with the Democrats did so more out of procedural concerns than from any ideological concerns.

69. *CG*, 42-2, 6/8/1872, 4453.

70. *CG*, 42-2, 6/8/1872, 4455.

sheepishly agreed that federal officers would be little more than "witnesses" at the polls, but perhaps by their mere presence could provide "a moral challenge."[71] Garfield's assertions notwithstanding, all understood that Kellogg's original bill had been gutted. Moreover, as George Edmunds suggested in the Senate debate, the elimination of supervisory power was "a means of [Republicans in the House] composing their difficulties."[72] Once House debate concluded, the elimination of those intra-GOP differences was apparent, as the conference report was agreed to 102-79 with only one of 102 Republicans voting nay.[73]

On June 10 the Senate took up the conference report. Republican senators were resigned to the ineffectual enforcement provisions. Edmunds, speaking for the conference committee, noted that they "were forced to assent with a view to getting to an end." Kellogg was silent; Thurman announced that he did not wish to debate the report further and called for the yeas and nays.[74] The Senate then concurred in the report 39-17, with five of forty-four Republicans dissenting.[75] President Grant then signed it, and the Fifth Enforcement Act was law.

Xi Wang sums up the result of the Fifth Enforcement Act, as well as the state of Republican politics regarding civil rights policy more generally: "The enforcement rider in the Civil Appropriations Act of June 10, 1872, was virtually powerless and ineffective. It was, in fact, a retreat from the previous enforcement laws. More important, it was the product of the growing divergence between the still radical Senate and the already moderate and conservative House Republicans on the issue of black suffrage. For Republicans, unity on black suffrage was becoming more and more a thing of the past."[76]

And as GOP unity on black suffrage frayed and various objections to additional congressional action grew, the Fifth Enforcement Act would in fact be the *last* statutory success for those who sought to protect the voting rights of African Americans. Moderate Republicans increasingly opposed

71. *CG*, 42-2, 6/8/1872, 4454.

72. *CG*, 42-2, 6/10/1872, 4495.

73. *CG*, 42-2, 6/8/1872, 4456. The lone Republican dissenter was John Farnsworth (IL).

74. Kellogg in fact announced that his colleague, Wilson, was absent but would have voted yea if he were present. He had nothing to say, however, about the substance of the committee report. *CG*, 42-2, 6/10/1872, 4495.

75. *CG*, 42-2, 6/10/1872, 4495. The five GOP dissenters were William Sprague (RI), Morgan Hamilton (TX), Thomas Tipton (NE), Reuben Fenton (NY), and Lyman Trumbull (IL).

76. Wang, *Trial of Democracy*, 89.

federal authority as a remedy for state-level violations, while conservatives and Liberal Republicans saw the entire enterprise of federal rights protection as both unworkable and misguided.

Still, radical Republicans would continue to seek new enforcement measures. Indeed, at the same time that Congress was deliberating on the legislation that would eventually result in the Fifth Enforcement Act, it was considering a bill that would extend section 4 of the Fourth Enforcement Act—granting the president the authority to suspend habeas corpus—for an *additional* session of Congress. And while some could point to a symbolic victory in the passage of the Fifth Enforcement Act, the divisions within the GOP would allow no victory of any kind on the section 4 extension.

THE FAILED EXTENSION OF SECTION 4 OF THE FOURTH ENFORCEMENT ACT

On February 19, 1872, debate began on an extension of section 4 of the Fourth Enforcement Act when Sen. John Scott (R-PA), representing the Joint Select Committee upon the Condition of the Late Insurrectionary States, issued a report based on testimony collected in the South.[77] Speaking for the majority on the committee, Scott felt that "parts of the southern States . . . [were still] infested with the Ku Klux troubles" and recommended that the authority of the president to suspend habeas corpus be extended until the end of the next session of Congress. This recommendation was embodied in a new bill, S. 656, which was placed on the Senate calendar.[78]

The bill was called up on May 16, and discussions began the following day.[79] Scott identified Klan activities in ninety-nine counties across six states (North Carolina, South Carolina, Georgia, Alabama, Mississippi, and Florida)—constituting 2,909 outrages and resulting in 526 homicides—and argued that granting the president the authority to suspend habeas corpus had been the only effective tool thus far in breaking up the organization. He went on to state, "I believe that if the power is kept in the hands of the President this violence will not be renewed. I believe if it is not kept there, no other power will be strong enough to repress a recurrence of the same

77. *CG*, 42-2, 2/19/1872, 1109. Scott noted that testimony was also taken from locales in Georgia, Florida, Mississippi, and Alabama, which would be compiled as the subject of a future report.

78. *CG*, 42-2, 2/19/1872, 1109–11.

79. *CG*, 42-2, 5/16/1872, 3551; 5/17/1872, 3579.

violence that has been enacted henceforth."[80] Daniel Pratt (R-IN), another member of the committee, seconded Scott's recommendation, arguing that it was "prudent" to extend section 4 so as to preserve public safety and ensure the protection of rights.[81]

But Republicans were not of one mind on the extension. On May 21 James Alcorn (R-MS) stated that in his view the condition in Mississippi "was one of repose" and he saw no need to extend the president's section 4 authority for another session. Indeed, Alcorn argued that Congress should "not attempt to do everything by legislation" and that citizens of Mississippi should be allowed to sort out any future problems that occurred in the state.[82] Morgan Hamilton (R-TX) — soon to become a Liberal Republican — noted that a successful extension would allow the president's suspension authority to continue in force until *after* the November election. He then suggested that if the extension was adopted, "the President will be placed . . . in a position of extreme delicacy and embarrassment." Local Republicans might stir up trouble in areas near election time, for example, in order to have the military brought in. This would be done as a way to "nullify the election where the majority is likely to be adverse [to the GOP]."[83] Democrats echoed his argument. William Hamilton (D-MD) was forthright in this regard, calling the measure nothing more than "a bill to provide for the reelection of President Grant."[84]

After some additional debate over the bill's constitutionality, the Senate passed S. 656 by a vote of 28-15, with twenty-eight of thirty Republicans voting in support.[85] The bill was then sent to the House where, on May 28, 1872, Luke Poland (R-VT) moved to suspend the rules so that it could be taken from the Speaker's table and passed. The yeas and nays were called, and the question failed 94-108, with a minority (22 of 116) of Republicans and all Democrats voting nay.[86] Thus the vote fell well short of the two-thirds

80. *CG*, 42-2, 5/17/1872, 3584, 3586. Scott made the same points — perhaps more forcefully — a bit earlier in his remarks: "Withdraw from the President of the United States the power to suspend habeas corpus in those States where this organization exists, and no man can answer for the scenes that will follow and the retaliation that may ensue. Keep it there, and the very existence of power will render its exercise unnecessary."

81. *CG*, 42-2, 5/17/1872, 3587.

82. *CG*, 42-2, 5/21/1872, 3704.

83. *CG*, 42-2, 5/21/1872, 3707.

84. *CG*, 42-2, 5/21/1872, 3719.

85. *CG*, 42-2, 5/21/1872, 3727. The Republican dissenters were James Alcorn (MS) and William Sprague (RI).

86. *CG*, 42-2, 5/28/1872, 3931.

majority necessary to suspend the rules. After the vote, Poland gained the floor and made the following remarks:

> I desire to say, in connection with the bill just voted upon, that the same bill was reported to the House and the Senate respectively by the joint select Committee on the Condition of the late Insurrectionary States. That bill having passed the Senate, I felt it my duty to call it to the attention of the House and have a vote upon it. Our committee having leave to report at any time, had a majority voted in favor of the bill upon the vote just taken, I should immediately have offered the bill that was reported by the committee to the House, which is identical with the Senate bill. But inasmuch as this vote has disclosed that a majority of this House are opposed to the bill, I shall not offer the House bill until I have further instructions from the committee to do so.[87]

In effect, Poland argued that the rules-suspension vote was a litmus test, and if a chamber majority (but not two-thirds) had voted in favor he would have used his committee's privileged status to report the bill directly to the floor. In other words, suspension of the rules would not have been necessary, and passage of the bill would have been by (simple) majority vote. Since the Senate bill was adopted *without amendment*, the path to a successful law would have been fairly straightforward. But a chamber majority was *not* in favor of the bill, as a number of moderate Republicans both North and South followed James Garfield (OH), Charles Willard (VT), Austin Blair (MI), and John Farnsworth (IL) in breaking with the GOP's pro-extension majority.[88]

Given that Poland's remarks followed the vote itself, the Republicans tried again on June 7. The question was again on suspending the rules and passing the bill—and it failed 56-89.[89] Once more the bill did not win even a simple majority. This time fourteen of seventy Republicans defected and joined the Democrats in opposition, and ninety-five House members did not vote at all. Although there was no debate around either House vote, the same moderate concerns within the GOP—questioning the constitutionality of the measure, opposing the increased centralization of federal power, and re-

---

87. *CG*, 42-2, 5/28/1872, 3931.

88. A roll-call analysis (logistic regression) of Republican votes finds that the first (positive) NOMINATE dimension is statistically significant, with Republican members furthest from the Democrats (the rightmost moderates and radicals) being more likely to support suspending the rules and passing S. 656. The leftmost part of the GOP distribution was thus more likely to join with the Democrats in defeating the initiative.

89. *CG*, 42-2, 6/7/1872, 4323.

jecting the efficacy of Congress engineering decisions in local areas — likely explain the pattern of defections.

By failing to extend section 4 of the Fourth Enforcement Act, pro–civil rights forces within the GOP were explicitly defeated for the first time. Previous civil rights and voting rights measures were amended (or, in the case of the Fifth Enforcement Act, largely gutted), to be sure, but statutes were always enacted. By late spring 1872 a turning point seemed to be reached: a largely symbolic victory (Fifth Enforcement Act) was followed by an outright loss (section 4 extension). This loss was a product of GOP divisions within the House. The party lacked a two-thirds majority, and a sizable group of moderates stymied any meaningful attempt to implement federal civil rights protections. True differences of opinion existed on the big questions of the day, such as how far the federal government should go to protect and preserve black rights.[90] And these differences also had electoral roots, since members had to be aware of how constituents back home felt about the ongoing political drama in the South. As the 1872 presidential election approached, many believed the Liberal Republican movement, whether ultimately successful or not, had tapped into a set of genuine feelings in the United States — that Reconstruction policy had eaten up too much of the nation's time, resources, and attention and that a path for moving beyond it had to be found.[91]

The Election of 1872, Liberal Republicanism, and the Panic of 1873

In mid-spring 1872 the political situation in the nation was confused and unsettled. Long-standing members of the GOP, disappointed by President Grant and the pervasive corruption in his administration, bolted to form a rival party organization. Dubbing themselves the Liberal Republicans, many were intellectuals and "self-styled 'best men'" committed to clean and limited government, lower tariffs, and a return to the gold standard.[92] Liberal Republicans also clamored for an end to the more radical aspects of

90. On this point see Wang, *Trial of Democracy*, 90.

91. Wang, *Trial of Democracy*, 104–5; David Herbert Donald, Jean Harvey Baker, and Michael F. Holt, *The Civil War and Reconstruction* (New York: Norton, 2001), 619.

92. Eric Foner, *Reconstruction: America's Unfinished Revolution, 1863–1877* (New York: Harper and Row, 1988), 488. For more on the Liberal Republican movement, see Earle Dudley Ross, *The Liberal Republican Movement* (New York: Henry Holt, 1919); Andrew L. Slap, *The*

Reconstruction. Having moved into the Liberal Republican camp by 1871, Sen. Carl Schurz (MO) gave voice to those seeking sectional reconciliation when he called for general amnesty for former Confederates. Such a move, he claimed, would "tend to disarm the feeling of alienation caused in the south by the results of the war."[93]

In May 1872 the Liberal Republicans met in Cincinnati to nominate *New-York Tribune* editor Horace Greeley for president. The choice of someone with spotty political credentials and questionable commitment to the reform causes central to Liberal Republicanism did not go over well with many in the new party. Writing to Sen. Lyman Trumbull — himself now a Liberal Republican — one participant at the Cincinnati convention condemned Greeley's embrace of "quacks, charlatans, ignoramuses, and sentimentalists." Carl Schurz, meanwhile, argued that Greeley's nomination had destroyed Liberal Republicanism's "higher moral character," and he begged Greeley to withdraw from the race.[94] Greeley refused. Greeley's view that it was it was time to end Reconstruction and "clasp hands across the bloody chasm" also generated support from Democrats.[95] In July 1872 the Democratic Party joined with the Liberal Republicans and endorsed Greeley's nomination.

The Liberal Republican movement highlighted tensions within the GOP but generated little political momentum of its own. In the fall, Greeley made speech after speech calling for an end to Reconstruction and for restoring local self-government to Southern states. Republicans, meanwhile, condemned Greeley for providing cover to the brutal tactics of the Klan. Despite the racially charged political atmosphere, the fall 1872 elections came off with minimal violence. When the votes were counted Grant was reelected in a landslide, capturing almost 56 percent of the popular vote and 286 of 352 electoral votes.[96] Grant also won eight of the eleven Southern states (losing only Georgia, Tennessee, and Texas). His victory increased the percentage of Republican House seats in the former Confederacy, reversing a trend and suggesting that perhaps the GOP was positioned for long-standing South-

Doom of Reconstruction: The Liberal Republicans in the Civil War Era (New York: Fordham University Press, 2006).

93. Schurz quoted in Robert W. Burg, "Amnesty, Civil Rights, and the Meaning of Liberal Republicanism, 1862–1872," *American Nineteenth Century History* 4 (2003): 43.

94. Foner, *Reconstruction*, 503.

95. Greeley quoted in Foner, *Reconstruction*, 503–4.

96. All told, Grant won thirty-one of thirty-seven states.

ern success.[97] Republicans added sixty-three House seats overall, creating a 199-88 advantage over the Democrats.[98] In the Senate they lost nine seats but retained an overwhelming 47-19 majority.[99]

The Republican victory in fall 1872 was impressive, and the political situation in the South over the preceding several years suggested that a period of "normal" two-party electoral competition might be developing. Despite continued violence toward black voters by paramilitary groups, race was not defining electoral politics as it had done immediately after Reconstruction began. Former Whigs had ascended to leadership in both the Democratic and Republican Parties in the South, and they worked to downplay race. Each side sought to appeal to voters based on economic issues, and there was real hope that the virtues of Reconstruction—civil and political rights for African Americans—would become settled policy and "the new normal."[100]

But any optimism about the future was short-lived. Only one year later—in late 1873—the nation's largest banks collapsed amid a series of railroad bankruptcies and a credit crisis. As American financial institutions seized up, panic spread across the country. Surging unemployment destroyed the livelihood of workers in the country's major urban centers, the price of agricultural products collapsed along with the value of land, and violent conflicts between workers and their bosses occurred in several cities. Viewed as a whole, Eric Foner notes, "the sixty-five months following the Panic of 1873 remains the longest period of uninterrupted economic contraction in American history."[101] As the party in power, the GOP was blamed for the economic hardships plaguing the country.[102] Making matters worse for the Republicans were widely publicized investigations into official corruption.

97. See Boris Heersink and Jeffery A. Jenkins, *Republican Party Politics and the American South, 1865–1968* (New York: Cambridge University Press, 2020), fig. 3.1.

98. Note that the size of the House increased from the Forty-Second House (243 members) to the Forty-Third House (292 members).

99. Six of those nine Republican losses came from GOP senators' rebranding themselves as Liberal Republicans. For the GOP breakdown across Congresses, see Kenneth C. Martis, *The Historical Atlas of Political Parties in the United States Congress, 1789–1989* (New York: Macmillan, 1989), 126–29.

100. This turn away from race and toward economic issues as the competitive basis of Southern party politics during these years is described by Michael Perman, *The Road to Redemption: Southern Politics, 1869–1879* (Baton Rouge: Louisiana State University Press, 1984). See also Donald, Holt, and Baker, *Civil War and Reconstruction*, 597–99.

101. Foner, *Reconstruction*, 513.

102. See Nicolas Barreyre, "The Politics of Economic Crises: The Panic of 1873, the End

The "Crédit Mobilier" scandal of 1872–73, for example, cost Vice President Schuyler Colfax his spot on the ticket in 1872 and did significant damage to Grant's allies in Congress.[103]

For the Republican Party 1874 was a politically disastrous year. With the nation sinking into a depression, the fall midterm elections brought overwhelming Democratic victories. In the Senate, Republicans lost nine seats. And though they retained a fourteen-seat advantage, the GOP's long-term political prospects did not look bright. In the House, the Republicans lost a staggering ninety-three seats and the Democrats regained majority control. Overall, the 1874 midterms produced a partisan reversal of unprecedented magnitude.[104]

These various national crises had a dramatic effect on state-level politics in the South. Railroad bankruptcies hit Southern states particularly hard because many were significantly overleveraged. As a result, GOP-led state governments had to raise taxes to cover interest payments on debts incurred since the war, which proved highly unpopular. Feeling economic pressure, GOP leaders reintroduced race into electoral politics by trumpeting their support for black civil rights and recalling the passions and hardships of the recent war (i.e., "waving the bloody shirt"). Race politics was a tool they thought would increase black turnout and help Southern members win. In the end, however, this tactic had the opposite effect. Bloody-shirt politics motivated *white voters* who, thanks to terrorist efforts by paramilitary groups like the Red Shirts and the White League, outnumbered their black counterparts.[105] And Democratic politicians happily painted the GOP as the "black party" and as a force for economic ruin in the region.[106]

Organized violence and intimidation to depress black turnout in strategic parts of the South was now possible because President Grant was less willing to intercede militarily. The Northern public — given the burgeoning depression and widespread reports of corruption within the Grant administration — had grown weary of Republican policies, especially those like Re-

---

of Reconstruction, and the Realignment of American Politics," *Journal of the Gilded Age and Progressive Era* 10 (2011): 403–23.

103. "The King of Frauds: How the Crédit Mobilier Bought Its Way through Congress," *New York Sun*, September 4, 1872, 1.

104. Foner, *Reconstruction*, 523.

105. The Red Shirts were active in Mississippi, North Carolina, and South Carolina, while the White League operated in Louisiana. See George C. Rable, *But There Was No Peace: The Role of Violence in the Politics of Reconstruction* (Athens: University of Georgia Press, 1984).

106. Donald, Baker, and Holt, *Civil War and Reconstruction*, 599–602.

construction that did not address *their* most pressing concerns. Grant and other Republicans worried that further military intervention in the South would lead voters to punish GOP politicians in the *North*.[107] With no military aid forthcoming, Republican governments in the South began to fall. By 1874 the GOP retained full control only in Mississippi and South Carolina and partial control only in Florida, Louisiana, and North Carolina, the former Confederate states with the largest black populations.[108] A year later the Republicans would lose their majorities in the Mississippi legislature when violence and intimidation forced Republican Governor Adelbert Ames from office before he was impeached.[109]

It was during this period of tumult and crisis that Republicans took up the last two civil rights measures of the Reconstruction era: a civil rights bill championed by Sen. Charles Sumner (R-MA) and yet another enforcement bill backed by House radicals. Sumner's measure sought to establish federal penalties for racial discrimination practiced in most areas of public life. The enforcement bill aimed to protect the lives, property, and voting rights of black citizens in the South. Although a significantly weakened version of Sumner's bill would become law during the lame-duck session following the 1874 election (after Sumner himself had died), the enforcement bill would fail in early 1875.

The Civil Rights Act of 1875

As we documented in chapter 2, Sen. Lyman Trumbull (R-IL) wrote the Civil Rights Act of 1866 and led the effort to see it enacted. As one of the Senate's moderates, and as chairman of the Judiciary Committee, Trumbull worked to protect the rights of freedmen without granting broad authority to the federal government. The legislation he crafted allowed freedmen to sue for their rights in federal court, but only if a plaintiff could demonstrate that state laws explicitly failed to guarantee equal protection. State legislators could prevent the law from taking effect, in other words, as long as state

107. See William Gillette, *Retreat from Reconstruction, 1869–1879* (Baton Rouge: Louisiana State University Press, 1979).

108. Heersink and Jenkins, *Republican Party Politics and the American South*, table 3.5.

109. The systematic use of intimidation and violence by the Red Shirts (and other paramilitary groups) to retake the elections for the Democrats became known as the "Mississippi Plan." See Warren A. Ellem, "The Overthrow of Reconstruction in Mississippi," *Journal of Mississippi History* 54 (1992) 175-201; Nicholas Lemann, *Redemption: The Last Battle of Reconstruction* (New York: Farrar, Straus and Giroux, 2007).

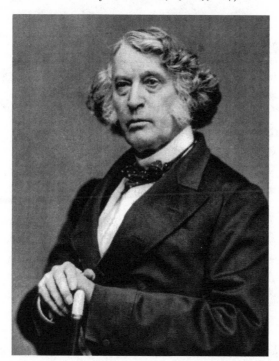

FIGURE 7. Sen. Charles Sumner (R-MA). Library of Congress, Prints & Photographs Division, LC-USZ62-66840.

laws were formally "color-blind." The explicit rights this bill set out to protect were also limited to economic and legal transactions.

To win over more radical members of the GOP, Trumbull found himself forced to include the more ambiguous language ensuring freedmen "full and equal benefit of all laws." Four years later, radical senator Charles Sumner (R-MA) took advantage of this provision to try to broaden civil rights protections for black citizens. On May 13, 1870, during the second session of the Forty-First Congress, Sumner introduced S. 916, a bill "supplementary" to the Civil Rights Act of 1866. Sumner's proposal sought to "secure equal rights in railroads, steamboats, public conveyances, hotels, licensed theaters, houses of public entertainment, common schools, and institutions of learning authorized by law, church institutions, and cemetery associations incorporated by national or State authority; also on juries in courts, national and State."[110] Sumner's bill thus aimed to counteract the move toward state and local laws that promoted racial segregation (later known as Jim Crow laws).

110. *CG*, 41-2, 5/13/1870, 3434.

As Democrats successfully "redeemed" states throughout the South and border regions, they worked to reinstall a system of white supremacy. Kentucky legally prohibited its black residents from testifying in court, while legislators in Delaware empowered those who owned "hotels, theaters, and common carriers to refuse admission to persons 'offensive' to other customers."[111] Furthermore, black officeholders throughout the South were regularly prevented from purchasing first-class tickets on trains and steamboats.[112] If they did, they were frequently prevented from taking their seats or denied basic service. The owner of a steamboat, for example, refused to serve dinner to Frederick Douglass and his companions on a government-sponsored trip to Santo Domingo.[113]

Widespread commitment to separate facilities for black and white residents also applied to the country's nascent public school system. Legislators in Tennessee incorporated a provision into the newly drafted state constitution requiring the racial separation of students. Soon thereafter, Delaware, Kentucky, and Maryland enacted laws mandating separation while simultaneously taxing newly freed residents to pay for "black only" school facilities.[114] While a handful of Northern states outlawed school segregation, a commitment to integration was not widespread.[115] Not surprisingly, schools for black children were "usually inferior to white schools in physical equipment, length of term, and quality of teaching."[116] Sumner condemned the practice in strikingly modern language. Separate facilities, he claimed, could "not fail to have a depressing effect on the mind of colored children, fostering the idea in them and others that they are not as good as other children."[117] Even in the early 1870s, legislators recognized that "separate but equal" was a rhetorical trick.

111. Foner, *Reconstruction*, 422.

112. Blair L. M. Kelley, *Right to Ride: Streetcar Boycotts and the African American Citizenship in the Era of "Plessy v. Ferguson"* (Chapel Hill: University of North Carolina Press, 2010), 34.

113. James McPherson, "Abolitionists and the Civil Rights Act of 1875," *Journal of American History* 52 (1965): 496.

114. Foner, *Reconstruction*, 422.

115. From 1867 to 1874 the state legislatures or courts in Rhode Island, Michigan, Connecticut, Minnesota, Iowa, and Kansas outlawed school segregation. McPherson, "Abolitionists and the Civil Rights Act of 1875," 498.

116. McPherson, "Abolitionists and the Civil Rights Act of 1875," 499.

117. Sumner quoted in Bertram Wyatt-Brown, "The Civil Rights Act of 1875," *Western Political Quarterly* 18 (1965): 763–64.

Although Sumner stridently opposed legal segregation, the enforcement mechanism built into his legislation was far from revolutionary. Similar to the Civil Rights Act of 1866, S. 916 made lawsuits the primary mechanism for protecting rights, thereby relying on the federal courts for enforcement. Citizens who believed their rights had been violated were encouraged to report instances of discrimination to federal officials working within the states. These officials were then expected to pursue charges against the *individuals* violating the provisions of the law. Anyone found guilty of denying these rights would pay a fine, spend up to one year in prison, or both.[118]

While Sumner's plan for enforcement mirrored the language of Trumbull's "moderate" 1866 bill, his commitment to equal access was much more radical. Sumner and his allies offered a novel constitutional justification for the bill. For them, the Fourteenth Amendment empowered the federal government to wield "police powers" within the states to protect citizens' rights.[119] In the words of John Bingham (R-OH), the Reconstruction amendments afforded Congress the power to "protect by national law the privileges and immunities of all citizens of the Republic and the inborn rights of every person within its jurisdiction."[120] GOP radicals thus believed the constitutional changes ushered in by the Fourteenth Amendment specifically made "state citizenship derivative of national citizenship" rather than the other way around.[121]

Sumner went even further. When discussing S. 916, he proclaimed a "new rule of interpretation for the Constitution, according to which, in every clause and every line and every word, it is to be interpreted uniformly for human rights."[122] In defense of those human rights, any "legal institution, anything created or regulated by law . . . must be opened equally to all without distinction of color." For radicals, laws regulating hotels, public conveyances, schools, churches, juries, and even cemeteries were to be enforced in ways that brought them into accordance with the rights guaranteed to all citizens by the civil rights acts and Reconstruction amend-

118. For more on enforcement, see John Hope Franklin, "The Enforcement of the Civil Rights Act of 1875," *Prologue Magazine* 6 (1974): 225–35.

119. S. G. F. Spackman, "American Federalism and the Civil Rights Act of 1875," *Journal of American Studies* 10 (1976): 318.

120. *CG*, 39-1, 5/9/1866, 2500.

121. Spackman, "American Federalism," 320.

122. *CG*, 42-2, 1/31/1872, 727.

ments. Discrimination perpetrated by "individuals as well as states" must be punished.[123]

Opposition to Sumner's proposal within the GOP centered on two basic ideas: doubts about congressional power to regulate state-based entities and the radical interpretation of the "rights" afforded to freedmen.[124] Lot Morrill (R-ME), who was generally sympathetic to Sumner's goals, spoke for those with constitutional qualms. He believed the Fourteenth Amendment added "nothing in the way of legislative authority or legislative power to the Congress of the United States."[125] Accordingly, he argued that it would not be constitutionally valid for Congress to assert new police powers over institutions traditionally regulated by state governments. Echoing Morrill, Orris Ferry (R-CT) warned that by accepting Sumner's argument, Congress would be "giving to the federal government complete legislative authority over every interest affecting the life, liberty, and property of every citizen." Radical proposals would leave "to the state legislatures absolutely nothing."[126] In this way, moderate Republicans who had not abandoned the party's traditional commitment to a strict separation between federal and state authority sought to thwart Sumner's "grandiose and far-reaching claims in favour of national power."[127]

Lyman Trumbull, meanwhile, spoke for those who opposed the new "rights" identified by Sumner and his allies. Trumbell believed S. 916 addressed itself to "social" rather than to "civil" rights. Civil rights included "the right to go and come; the right to enforce contracts; the right to convey property—those general rights that belong to mankind everywhere; and not a privilege that is conferred by a corporation, as a college for example."[128] S. 916 instead aimed to "force the colored people and white people into mutual contact."[129] There existed no reason to believe that citizens retained the "right" to travel in integrated train cars or attend inte-

---

123. For a detailed discussion of Sumner's attitude toward the Constitution, see Ronald B. Jager, "Charles Sumner, the Constitution, and the Civil Rights Act of 1875," *New England Quarterly* 42 (1969): 350–72.

124. For more on this point, see James M. McPherson, *The Abolitionist Legacy: From Reconstruction to the NAACP* (Princeton, NJ: Princeton University Press, 1975), 17–18.

125. *CG*, 42-2, 1/25/1872, appendix 2.

126. *CG*, 42-2, 2/8/1872, 893.

127. Spackman, "American Federalism," 316.

128. *CG*, 42-2, 5/8/1872, 3191.

129. *CG*, 42-2, 5/8/1872, 3189.

grated schools. As long as states prescribed separate facilities for black and white citizens that were "the same," he went on, "then nobody has a right to complain."[130] Here Trumbull was giving voice to the doctrine of "separate but equal" almost a quarter of a century before the Supreme Court's infamous decision in *Plessy v. Ferguson*. Trumbull did not echo the explicit racism voiced by many Democrats—who referred to Sumner's legislation as the "social equality bill,"[131] but his argument did offer political cover to those lawmakers who refused to acknowledge that "the Negro in all this is equal of the white man."[132]

Trumbull's determined opposition to Sumner's proposal helped to keep it from coming up for debate. The Judiciary Committee failed to report the bill in 1870 and again in 1871. As a consequence, the Senate did not begin debate on Sumner's proposal until 1872, during the following (Forty-Second) Congress. That year Sumner adopted a new strategy: he moved the legislation as an amendment to a pending bill that sought to provide amnesty to former Confederates. (An amendment of this form—attached to an unrelated bill—is known as a rider.) By adopting this approach, Sumner began a new round of acrimonious substantive and procedural debate.

AMNESTY AND CIVIL RIGHTS

Section 3 of the Fourteenth Amendment—the "Disability Clause"—made the following stipulation:

> No person shall be a senator or representative in Congress, or elector of President and Vice President, or hold any office, civil or military, under the United States or any state, who, having previously taken an oath, as a member of Congress, or as an officer of the United States, or as a member of any state legislature, or as an executive or judicial officer of any state, to support the Constitution of the United States, shall have engaged in insur-

130. *CG*, 42-2, 5/8/1872, 3190.

131. The use of the term social equality was not an accident. As Pamela Brandwein notes, "Social equality was a term of opprobrium and all sides converged in opposing the legal imposition of social equality. The term connoted interracial sexual intimacy, which triggered profound identity-based anxieties among whites about the loss of racial 'purity.'" Pamela Brandwein, *Rethinking the Judicial Settlement of Reconstruction* (Cambridge: Cambridge University Press, 2011), 65.

132. *CG*, 43-1, 1/5/1874, 376.

rection or rebellion against the same, or given aid or comfort to the enemies thereof. But Congress may by a vote of two-thirds of each House,
remove such disability.

For Republicans concerned that the country was tiring of battles over
Reconstruction policy, overturning the Disability Clause became an easy
way to end sectional rivalry. For President Grant, a vote to cancel section 3
also seemed like a good defense against the political attacks launched by the
Liberal Republicans.[133]

On April 10, 1871, during the first session of the Forty-Second Congress,
House Republicans took a step toward amnesty when they passed H.R. 380,
"a bill for the removal of legal and political disabilities imposed under the
third section" of the Fourteenth Amendment. Introduced by Eugene Hale
(R-ME), it passed 134-46, thus achieving the two-thirds majority necessary
as outlined in section 3, with Democrats voting as a bloc and a majority
of Republicans (fifty-two of ninety-six) joining them.[134] The bill was then
sent to the Senate, where it languished in committee for the rest of the session. On December 20, during the lame-duck session, H.R. 380 was brought
up, at which point Sumner introduced his civil rights bill as an amendment
(rider).[135] Senate Republicans rightly understood that the amnesty proposal
would never win the necessary two-thirds majority if it included Sumner's
proposal. Yet Sumner would not relent, arguing that this was his only way to
force a vote on his measure.[136]

The Senate did not begin formal debate on H.R. 380 again until February 5, 1872. That day, Thomas Robertson (R-SC) moved to table H.R. 380 and
Sumner's pending amendment and begin debate on a different amnesty proposal (H.R. 1050, a streamlined bill drafted, again, by Eugene Hale).[137] His
motion failed 20-33, with a majority of Republicans voting nay.[138] Having
failed to prevent debate on Sumner's proposal, Matthew Carpenter (R-WI)
introduced an amendment to weaken its provisions. Carpenter's amendment

133. Slap, *Doom of Reconstruction*, 183–84. On the politicking involved in the eventual Amnesty Act, see Rawley, "General Amnesty Act of 1872," and Burg, "Amnesty, Civil Rights, and
the Meaning of Liberal Republicanism."

134. *CG*, 42-1, 4/10/1871, 562.

135. *CG*, 42-2, 12/20/1871, 237–44.

136. *CG*, 42-2, 2/5/1872, 822.

137. On January 15, 1872, Hale's second amnesty bill passed 171-31, with Republicans voting 79-31. *CG*, 42-2, 1/15/1872, 398–99.

138. *CG*, 42-2, 2/5/1872, 818. Republicans voted 9-33.

deleted the language mandating equal access to juries and churches; stipulated that equal access be guaranteed only to those institutions "supported by taxation or endowment for public use"; deleted the provision allowing victims of discrimination to pursue financial damages from the individuals responsible; and deleted the provision empowering victims of discrimination to move their cases to federal courts.[139]

Sumner immediately condemned Carpenter's proposal. "At the eleventh hour," he exclaimed, "the Senator from Wisconsin comes forward with a substitute which is . . . an emasculated synonym of the original measure . . . feeble where the original is strong, incomplete where the original is ample, and without machinery for its enforcement, while the original is well-supplied and most effective."[140] Carpenter, in turn, claimed that for Sumner "the dish of civil rights . . . is tasteless unless it be flavored with some unconstitutional ingredient." In the end a coalition of Sumner's allies — comprising a majority of GOP senators — and Democrats who opposed all civil rights legislation joined to defeat Carpenter's amendment 17-35.[141] When Carpenter later worked to remove language affording black citizens the right to serve as jurors, this amendment also failed, 12-42.[142]

John Sherman (R-OH) then introduced an amendment to narrow the range of laws affected by Sumner's bill. This also failed, 25-34, with a large majority of Republicans voting against it.[143] Frederick T. Frelinghuysen (R-NJ) then offered an amendment to excise the language regulating churches. According to Frelinghuysen, Sumner's effort to force churches to open their doors to black citizens represented a "dangerous infringement" on the first amendment. His amendment passed 29-24, with twenty-seven of forty-two Republicans voting yea.[144] The final three amendments to Sumner's proposal, offered by Cornelius Cole (R-CA) and Henry Corbett (R-OR), sought to ensure that newly naturalized immigrants from China would not be able to avail themselves of the civil rights protections written into Sumner's bill. Each of these amendments failed in lopsided votes, with a majority of Republicans voting against them.[145]

After nearly a week of voting on changes to Sumner's original amend-

139. *CG*, 42-2, 2/5/1872, 818-21.
140. *CG*, 42-2, 2/5/1872, 822.
141. *CG*, 42-2, 2/7/1872, 871. Republicans voted 17-23.
142. *CG*, 42-2, 2/8/1872, 901. Republicans voted 8-36.
143. *CG*, 42-2, 2/8/1872, 896. Republicans voted 14-33.
144. *CG*, 42-2, 2/8/1872, 899.
145. *CG*, 42-2, 2/9/1872, 909-10, 918.

ment, the Senate finally moved to consider the underlying measure. In a last-ditch effort to persuade members to oppose Sumner's approach, Thomas Robertson once again proclaimed his support for Sumner's proposal *and* his belief that it would not be right to attach civil rights language to the amnesty bill. "After this [amnesty] bill shall become a law by the two-thirds vote which it requires," he explained, "then let us set aside every other measure and pass a law giving equal rights to the humblest individuals in the community."[146] A majority of Republicans (twenty-eight) rejected Robertson's appeal and voted for Sumner's amendment. But a minority (sixteen) joined with all Democrats in opposition, leading to a 28-28 deadlock. Vice President Colfax cast his tie-breaking vote in favor of Sumner, and the amendment was added to H.R. 380.[147] When the amended amnesty bill came up for a vote on February 9, it received a majority, 33-19, but not the two-thirds necessary to pass.[148] Eight Republicans voted nay, along with eleven Democrats.[149] As a result, both amnesty and civil rights were defeated.

The Senate did not take up civil rights or amnesty again for two months. In early May 1872 the Senate tried a general amnesty bill again (H.R. 1050, Hale's second bill, which was very similar to H.R. 380). On the first day of debate, Sumner again announced his plan to introduce his civil rights amendment.[150] Moderate, pro-amnesty Republicans were incensed and intended to put up a fight. Orris Ferry (R-CT) engaged in the GOP's first line of attack by raising a point of order questioning whether the rules allowed senators to attach legislation requiring a majority vote (Sumner's bill) to legislation requiring a supermajority (amnesty).[151] Lyman Trumbull backed Ferry, arguing that the "reason why [Sumner's amendment] is out of order . . . is because by the Constitution of the United States the matter pending must be passed by a different vote from that which is proposed by the amendment." He went on to call it "absurd" to "put two things together which can be passed by different votes."[152] After a heated back-and-forth over the parliamentary validity of Sumner's bill, Vice President Colfax—exercising his

146. *CG*, 42-2, 2/9/1872, 919.

147. *CG*, 42-2, 2/9/1872, 919.

148. *CG*, 42-2, 2/9/1872, 929.

149. The eight Republicans were Arthur Boreman (WV), Joshua Hill (GA), John Logan (IL), Lot Morrill (ME), John Scott (PA), Thomas Tipton (NE), Lyman Trumbull (IL), and George Wright (IA).

150. *CG*, 42-2, 5/8/1872, 3181.

151. *CG*, 42-2, 5/8/1872, 3181.

152. *CG*, 42-2, 5/8/1872, 3182-83.

prerogative as chair—sided with Sumner. The Senate would once again be forced to confront amnesty and civil rights simultaneously.

Unable to defeat Sumner's bill through parliamentary procedures, moderate Republicans resorted to their usual strategy: they attempted to weaken the bill. On May 9 the Senate began voting on a series of amendments designed to make the bill more palatable to those who held more traditional views of constitutional federalism. The first, offered by Orris Ferry, sought to excise all language mandating that black citizens be granted equal access to local schools.[153] Urging the Senate to adopt this amendment, Ferry offered a warning that would prove relevant nearly seventy-five years later: Southern whites, he claimed, would close public schools before integrating them. To adopt Sumner's proposal therefore was to put at risk the entire public school system in the South. Ferry's amendment won support from all Democrats and a minority of Republicans, but it still failed, 25-26.[154] Next came an amendment from Francis Blair (D-MO) requiring localities to vote on whether to integrate schools. Blair's amendment won support from some GOP senators, but it also failed, 23-30.[155] Next Thomas Carpenter (R-WI) tried to remove the bill's language guaranteeing black citizens the right to serve on juries. As before, his amendment failed, 16-33, with only six of thirty-seven Republicans voting in favor.[156]

As amendment after amendment went down to defeat, Lyman Trumbull grew increasingly frustrated. Gaining the floor, he declared that the "whole country and the whole world" believed Sumner's true aim was to defeat the House-passed amnesty proposal.[157] Trumbull then moved to amend Sumner's amendment by striking out all the equal protection language and all its enforcement mechanisms. This won the support of all Democrats and seventeen Republicans, but the final tally was a 29-29 deadlock.[158] Once

153. *CG*, 42-2, 5/9/1872, 3257.

154. *CG*, 42-2, 5/9/1872, 3258. Republicans voted 13-26. A roll-call analysis (logistic regression) of Republican votes finds that the first (negative) NOMINATE dimension is statistically significant, with Republican members furthest from the Democrats (the rightmost moderates and radicals) being less likely to support the Ferry amendment. The leftmost part of the GOP distribution was thus more likely to join with the Democrats in support of excising all language mandating that black citizen be granted equal access to local schools.

155. *CG*, 42-2, 5/9/1872, 3262. Republicans voted 11-30.

156. *CG*, 42-2, 5/9/1872, 3263.

157. *CG*, 42-2, 5/9/1872, 3263.

158. Republicans voted 17-29. A roll-call analysis (logistic regression) of Republican votes finds that the first (negative) NOMINATE dimension is statistically significant, with Republican members furthest from the Democrats (the rightmost moderates and radicals) being less

again Vice President Colfax broke the tie in favor of Sumner.[159] Immediately thereafter, however, Colfax voted *against* Sumner in another deadlocked vote. In this case the Senate approved language proposed by George Vickers (D-MO) outlawing discrimination *only* in cemeteries and "benevolent institutions" that are "incorporated by national [rather than state and national] authority."[160]

To conclude voting for the day, the Senate considered two final moves by Sumner. The first substituted his civil rights language for the original amnesty proposal. Here Sumner aimed to force the House to cast a vote on civil rights alone before it could deal with amnesty. This strategy failed in a close vote (27-28), with a majority of Republicans voting in support.[161] Sumner then moved to attach the civil rights bill (as amended) to the amnesty bill. The Senate once again deadlocked, and Colfax once again provided the tie-breaking vote in Sumner's favor.[162] Replicating February's result, however, the House never had a chance to address either issue. When H.R. 1050 (with Sumner's rider attached) came up for a final vote in the Senate, it won a majority, 32-22, but not the necessary two-thirds.[163] Nine Republicans joined with thirteen Democrats to defeat the bill.[164] As long as Sumner held his seat — and his ground — amnesty appeared to be dead.

As the spring of 1872 drew to a close, Republicans faced a political dilemma: they had not passed either an amnesty bill or a civil rights bill, and Congress was scheduled to adjourn in June. Once they left Washington, members would not meet again until after the November election. Only days

---

likely to support the Trumbull amendment. The leftmost part of the GOP distribution was thus more likely to join with the Democrats in support of striking out all the equal protection language and all enforcement mechanisms in Sumner's amendment.

159. *CG*, 42-2, 5/9/1872, 3265.

160. *CG*, 42-2, 5/9/1872, 3267. The vote was 21-21, with Republicans voting 10-21.

161. *CG*, 42-2, 5/9/1872, 3268. Republicans voted 27-17.

162. *CG*, 42-2, 5/9/1872, 3268. The vote was 28-28, with Republicans voting 28-17.

163. *CG*, 42-2, 5/9/1872, 3269. Republicans voted 32-9. A roll-call analysis (logistic regression) of Republican votes finds that the first (positive) NOMINATE dimension is statistically significant, with Republican members furthest from the Democrats (the rightmost moderates and radicals) being more likely to support final passage of H.R. 1050 (with Sumner's rider attached). The leftmost part of the GOP distribution was thus more likely to join with the Democrats in opposition.

164. The nine Republicans were James Alcorn (MS), Arthur Boreman (WV), Orris Ferry (CT), Morgan Hamilton (TX), Joshua Hill (GA), John Logan (IL), Thomas Tipton (NE), Lyman Trumbull (IL), and George Wright (IA).

before the failed Senate vote on amnesty, Liberal Republicans met in Cincinnati to nominate Horace Greeley for president.[165] Intraparty discord was so widespread that even the pro-Republican *New York Times* ran an editorial asking readers, "Does the Country Need the Republican Party?"[166] The editors insisted the answer was yes, but the question itself attests to the political problems facing President Grant and his fellow partisans in Congress. In fact, moderate Republicans were so desperate to settle the amnesty question that they put poor health to use in pursuit of the cause.

Toward the end of May, Sumner became ill and was forced to take time away from the Senate. On May 21–22 the Senate debated for nearly twenty-four hours straight on matters unrelated to civil rights or amnesty. But just before 6:00 a.m. on the twenty-second, Matthew Carpenter called on the Senate to renew debate on Sumner's civil rights proposal.[167] Carpenter's aim was not to see Sumner's bill passed. Instead, he introduced an amendment striking out the provisions guaranteeing equal access to schools and juries. Carpenter's move met with some substantive opposition, as well as claims that it would be "unfair and unjust to take a vote on this bill during the absence of the Senator from Massachusetts." Yet, with barely a quorum present, Carpenter's amendment passed by two votes, 22–20, with nine of twenty-nine Republicans joining with all Democrats.[168] Carpenter then offered the weakened civil rights bill as a stand-alone measure to be granted an up-or-down vote instead of as an amendment to the House-passed amnesty bill. It passed 27–14 on a pure party-line vote.[169]

Shortly after the "Carpenter bill" passed, Sumner arrived. "I understand that in my absence and without any notice to me from any quarter the Sen-

165. "Greeley's Nomination: Press Comments on the Result of Cincinnati," *NYT*, May 6, 1872, 5.

166. "Does the Country Need the Republican Party?," *NYT*, May 8, 1872, 4.

167. *CG*, 42-2, 5/21/1872, 3734.

168. *CG*, 42-2, 5/21/1872, 3734–35. The nine Republicans who voted yea were Alexander Caldwell (KS), Matthew Carpenter (WI), Cornelius Cole (CA), Henry Corbett (OR), John Logan (IL), Lot Morrill (ME), John Pool (NC), John Scott (PA), and George Wright (IA). A roll-call analysis (logistic regression) of Republican votes finds that neither NOMINATE dimension is statistically significant at conventional levels, which indicates that ideology was not the driver on Carpenter's amendment. Other, pragmatic desires—like the desire to move on from the Sumner amendment and pass an amnesty bill before the fall elections—may have been the dominant impulse for members.

169. *CG*, 42-2, 5/21/1872, 3734–36.

ate have adopted an emasculated civil rights bill," he protested.[170] Sumner then called for a vote on adding his original proposal to the amnesty bill as an amendment. This time he lost in a lopsided vote, 13-29.[171] A majority of Republicans now voted against him, suggesting they had grown weary of delays and had chosen to sacrifice the civil rights bill to ensure that amnesty would pass before the election. Once Sumner's amendment was defeated, members immediately moved to a vote on amnesty. It passed 38-2, with only Sumner and James Nye (R-NV) voting nay.[172] Amnesty legislation would now move to the White House for Grant's approval while the Senate-passed civil rights bill — the "Carpenter bill" — would die in the House. Sumner would not live to see his bill again brought up for discussion or enactment.

THE CIVIL RIGHTS ACT OF 1875: FINAL PASSAGE

Between the middle of 1872 and early 1874, Sumner's health continued to deteriorate. He was unable to advocate his supplementary civil rights bill with the same intensity as previously.[173] By March 1874 Sumner was near death and no closer to seeing the bill enacted. He reportedly told Henry Wilson — Grant's second-term vice president — "If my works were completed and my Civil Rights bill passed, no visitor could enter that door that would be more welcome than death."[174] Death arrived first, on March 11, 1874.

The next month, the Senate once again took up debate on the bill. On April 14, Frederick Frelinghuysen (R-NJ) introduced S. 1, an amended version of Sumner's proposal (without the provisions related to churches).[175] The Senate began debating the bill two weeks later. On the defensive against those who claimed the bill tried to legislate "social equality," Frelinghuysen stipulated that such equality was "not an element of citizenship. The law

---

170. *CG*, 42-2, 5/21/1872, 3737.

171. *CG*, 42-2, 5/21/1872, 3738. Republicans voted 13-14. A roll-call analysis (logistic regression) of Republican votes finds that the first (positive) NOMINATE dimension is statistically significant, with Republican members furthest from the Democrats (the rightmost moderates and radicals) being more likely to support Sumner's amendment. The left part of the GOP distribution was thus more likely to join with the Democrats in opposition.

172. *CG*, 42-2, 5/21/1872, 3738.

173. He did reintroduce the bill in December 1873, only to see it once again referred to the Judiciary Committee and ignored. *CR*, 43-1, 12/2/1873, 2.

174. Quoted in Brown, "Civil Rights Act," 769-70.

175. *CR*, 43-1, 4/14/1872, 3053.

which regulates that is found only in the tastes and affinities of the mind."[176] Instead, S. 1 aimed to ensure black and white citizens equal access to "inns, places of amusement, and public conveyances" because such institutions "bear . . . intimate relation to the public" and therefore must be open to all; cemeteries because they are supported by general tax revenues; and schools because "we know that if we establish separate schools for colored people, those schools will be inferior to those for whites."[177]

Voting on S. 1 began one month later, and opponents once again sought to weaken it with amendments.[178] Allen Thurman (D-OH) tried to reduce to $500 the penalty for those convicted of denying equal access. Aaron Sargent (R-CA) sought to allow states to provide "separate" facilities as long as they could demonstrate that black and white schools received equal funding. George Boutwell (D-MA) sought to allow for separate school facilities as long as schools received private funds. John Gordon (D-GA) tried to eliminate the school provision entirely. James Alcorn (R-MS) sought to broaden the bill's aims — suggesting that perhaps it was intended as a "killer amendment" — by extending its provision to colleges and primary schools. William Hamilton (D-MO) tried to excise the provision affording black citizens the right to serve as jurors. All of them failed by lopsided margins and garnered little or no Republican support. When the Senate at last voted on S. 1, it passed 29-16, with only three Republicans voting nay.[179]

Bertram Wyatt-Brown attributes the passage of Sumner's bill to a widespread feeling of "contrite sentimentalism" generated by his death.[180] This feeling seems not to have moved through the House, though, since the bill died on the Speaker's desk. Three days after it passed the Senate, Benjamin Butler (R-MA) tried to suspend House rules and refer the bill to the Judiciary Committee "with the right to report it to the House at any time." He failed that day and again on June 8.[181] Just over two weeks later Congress adjourned for the summer to prepare for the 1874 midterm elections. It would

176. *CR*, 43-1, 4/29/1874, 3451. Republicans routinely rejected the notion that Sumner's bill was an attempt to legislate social equality. This included Sumner himself and close radical colleagues like Benjamin Butler (R-MA). See Brandwein, *Rethinking the Judicial Settlement of Reconstruction*, 66.

177. *CR*, 43-1, 4/29/1874, 3452.

178. *CR*, 43-1, 5/22/1874, 4167-75.

179. *CR*, 43-1, 5/22/1874, 4176. The three were Arthur Boreman (WV), Matthew Carpenter (WI), and John Lewis (VA).

180. Wyatt-Brown, "Civil Rights Act," 770.

181. *CR*, 43-1, 5/25/1874, 4242; 6/8/1874, 4691.

take a GOP electoral disaster — one that relegated them to minority status in the House when the Forty-Fourth Congress opened in December 1875 — to motivate the Republicans to pass Sumner's bill.[182]

When Congress reconvened in December 1874 for the lame-duck session of the Forty-Third Congress, the Republicans were in their last months as the majority party. They sought to use this time to pass legislation (on tariffs and currency) that they considered vital to the party's electoral prospects in 1876. Democrats, meanwhile, were using delaying tactics to stymie them.[183] Benjamin Butler (R-MA) decided to make the civil rights bill a "stalking horse" for a House rules change that would limit dilatory motions and allow the GOP to act on these other agenda items.[184] To secure the votes required to bring moderate Republicans on board, however, Butler had to replace the clause mandating equal access to schools with language permitting "separate but equal" facilities.[185] Nonetheless, this provided one last chance to pass Sumner's civil rights bill.

On February 1, 1875, after dozens of votes on the GOP's effort to amend the rules and limit dilatory motions, Butler finally got his supermajority.[186] Three days later the House began debate on the civil rights measure. Stephen Kellogg (R-CT) offered the first amendment, which sought to excise all of the bill's school-related language. It passed 128-48, but without a roll call.[187] Godlove Orth (R-IN) called for the yeas and nays, but there was no support

182. As Heather Cox Richardson notes, "The civil rights bill was rescued from oblivion only by Democratic wins in the 1874 elections." Heather Cox Richardson, *The Death of Reconstruction: Race, Labor, and Politics in the Post–Civil War North* (Cambridge, MA: Harvard University Press, 2001), 143.

183. Specifically, they were putting to effective use a rule allowing them to call for time-consuming roll-call votes to "fix a day for adjournment"; *CR*, 43-2, 1/27/1875, 786.

184. McPherson, "Abolitionists and the Civil Rights Act of 1875," 508; Alfred H. Kelly, "The Congressional Controversy over School Segregation, 1867–1875," *American Historical Review* 64 (1959): 537–63.

185. Kelly, "Congressional Controversy over School Segregation," 558. The proposed rules change on dilatory motions also could not apply to spending bills other than ordinary appropriations bills, as moderate Republicans sought to prevent Butler from moving forward on radical initiatives like railroad subsidies. See Sarah A. Binder, *Minority Rights, Majority Rule: Partisanship and the Development of Congress* (New York: Cambridge University Press, 1997), 117–18.

186. *CR*, 43-2, 2/1/1875, 901–2. For an examination of the procedural changes made in January-February 1875, see Binder, *Minority Rights, Majority Rule*, 114–19.

187. *CR*, 43-2, 2/4/1875, 1010.

for tallying them—which suggested that Republicans wished to eliminate the school provision but did not want to be on record as doing so. By this time several Republicans—led by Carlton Curtis (PA) and James Monroe (OH)—opposed the separate but equal provision, referring to it as "puerile" and "a dangerous precedent," and enough of their fellow partisans agreed to prevent its inclusion in the bill.[188] More generally, as James McPherson recounts, "The bill's managers decided to amputate the school clause to save the rest of the measure."[189] When John Cessna (R-PA) offered the full Senate bill (with the equal-access school language) as a substitute, it failed 113-148, with sixty Republicans voting nay.[190] Soon thereafter, the House passed the weakened civil rights bill 162-100, with Republicans voting 161-12 in support.[191] More than three weeks later, on February 27, the Senate considered the House-passed version of Sumner's proposal. After failed votes on three minor amendments, the Senate consented to the House bill 38-26, with only two Republicans defecting.[192] On March 1, 1875, President Grant signed the bill into law.

Sumner's civil rights bill—stripped down as it was—had finally been enacted. But unlike previous civil rights legislation, it generated little enthusiasm. *Harper's Weekly* noted, for example, that the GOP "struck at the principle of the whole Republican policy of Reconstruction" in order to ensure enactment.[193] Echoing *Harper's*, William Gillette asserts, "The law . . . represented the bankruptcy of legislative sentimentalism and reconstruction rhetoric, which demeaned noble ideals and undercut vital interests. For many disillusioned radicals the act was the expiring flash of a now obsolete philanthropy."[194]

188. McPherson, *Abolitionist Legacy*, 20.

189. McPherson, *Abolitionist Legacy*, 20.

190. *CR*, 43-2, 2/4/1875, 1011. Republicans voted 113-60. A roll-call analysis (logistic regression) of Republican votes finds that the first (positive) and second (negative) NOMINATE dimensions are statistically significant, with Republican members furthest from the Democrats (most moderates and radicals) being more likely to support Cessna's amendment. The leftmost part of the GOP distribution was thus more likely to join the Democrats in opposition.

191. *CR*, 43-2, 2/4/1875, 1011. As James McPherson notes, ninety of these GOP supporters were lame ducks. McPherson, *Abolitionist Legacy*, 21.

192. *CR*, 43-2, 2/27/1875, 1867-68, 1870. The two defectors were John Lewis (VA) and Matthew Carpenter (WI).

193. Quoted in Kelly, "Congressional Controversy over School Segregation," 562.

194. Gillette, *Retreat from Reconstruction*, 279.

The Enforcement Bill of 1875

Once House Republicans were able to secure a version of Sumner's civil rights bill, they turned to constructing new enforcement legislation.[195] Violence and intimidation of black voters had ramped up considerably throughout the South in late 1874 and early 1875, especially in Alabama, Arkansas, Louisiana, and Mississippi (the last three still under Republican control). Southern Republicans appealed to Congress and President Grant for assistance, both in maintaining GOP control and with an eye toward securing electoral majorities for the Republican presidential standard bearer in 1876.

House Republicans were split on new enforcement legislation. Efforts in 1870 and 1871, which were deemed necessary at the time to fulfill the promise of civil and political equality for blacks in the South, were long past. The most recent enforcement efforts in 1872 — the emasculated enforcement rider in the civil appropriations bill and the failure to extend the habeas corpus provision in the Ku Klux Klan Act — were the new status quo. Federal enforcement of civil rights was increasingly difficult for many Republicans to justify; some had qualms about expanding federal authority, others believed maintaining social order in Southern states through military force was an unworkable strategy, and still others thought the South was a lost cause and believed Republicans should cut their losses and protect their electoral interests in the North.

While Republican dissidents had grown in numbers, a significant portion of the party still favored supporting the GOP governments that remained in power in the South. President Grant, in particular, sought new enforcement legislation in order to have the legal cover to push back against any new disturbances. Grant made his preferences clear in his annual message to Congress in December 1874 and in subsequent speeches in January and February 1875.[196]

With time running out in the lame-duck session and knowing Democrats would shortly control the House, the radicals marshaled their forces. In early February they pushed moderates, in an almost daily party caucus, until a party measure was produced on February 13.[197] Five days later, on February 18, John Coburn (R-IN), representing the House Select Commit-

195. Short legislative histories of the enforcement bill of 1875 are found in Gillette, *Retreat from Reconstruction*, 280–99, and Wang, *Trial of Democracy*, 114–19.

196. Gillette, *Retreat from Reconstruction*, 281; Brooks D. Simpson, *The Reconstruction Presidents* (Lawrence: University Press of Kansas, 1998), 180.

197. Gillette, *Retreat from Reconstruction*, 284.

tee Investigating Affairs in Alabama, reported the bill (H.R. 4745).[198] Containing thirteen sections, H.R. 4745 sought "to provide against the invasion of States, to prevent the subversion of their authority, and to maintain the security of elections." Sections 1 and 2 established strict penalties on those crossing state lines or conspiring internally to overthrow duly elected state governments; section 3 outlawed firearms at polling places; section 4 punished election officials for refusing to accept the ballots of registered voters; section 5 made it a crime to steal or destroy ballot boxes; section 6 imposed the death penalty on those who killed someone in the course of crimes related to sections 1–5; section 7 made the district courts the jurisdictional authority on all matters related to the statute; sections 8 and 9 provided for election supervisors and deputy marshals in all voting precincts, with all the powers and authority that similar officers possessed in cities with 20,000 or more inhabitants; section 10 provided for the counting of ballots and delivery of election certificates in federal elections; sections 11 and 12 forbade officer compensation and stipulated procedures for keeping election records; and section 13 gave the president the power to suspend habeas corpus in a state in order to put down armed combinations or rebellion.

H.R. 4745 was an ambitious bill, as the radicals sought to make the most of the GOP's remaining unified-government influence. It engaged recent problems like white insurgents organizing and traveling across state boundaries to stir up racial animosities and create electoral havoc. It also attempted to implement initiatives from the past. Section 13 was a direct extension of the habeas corpus provision in the Fourth Enforcement Act (Ku Klux Klan Act), but without an explicit end date.[199] And sections 8 and 9 were a reprisal of Sen. William Kellogg's (R-LA) failed 1872 bill (S. 792), which attempted to counter electoral fraud in the South by extending the power and authority of federal election supervisors and marshals to rural areas.

As the House readied for debate, it became increasingly clear that H.R. 4745 might be too "radical" to secure a majority. Thus, various elements within the GOP sought amendments that might broaden the bill's appeal. When it was formally read on March 24, four amendments were offered.[200] Benjamin Butler (R-MA) sought to amend section 13 so as to restrict coverage to districts the president deemed "insurrectionary," while adding a

198. *CR*, 43-2, 2/18/1875, 1453.

199. Recall that a similar attempt—for a single session—had been tried (unsuccessfully) once before, in 1872.

200. *CR*, 43-2, 2/24/1875, 1751.

new fourteenth section that would provide a definitive end date two years in the future (at the end of the Forty-Fourth Congress and therefore after the presidential election of 1876). Butler's amendment was meant to allay fears that the president might use his newfound power to enter Democratic-controlled states, rather than the few GOP states left in the South, while providing an explicit expiration of the law's provisions. John Hawley (R-IL) sought to streamline section 13 and extend its provision only to the next regular session of Congress (thus creating an expiration date sometime in summer of 1876, before the presidential election). Joseph Cannon (R-IL) moved to eliminate section 13 entirely, while Ebenezer Rockwood Hoar (R-MA) sought to strike out sections 1, 2, and 4.

Democrats successfully delayed action on H.R. 4745 until February 26, when a spirited debate occurred. Coburn began and held the floor for a considerable time, drawing extensively from recent reports of investigatory committees that recounted violence toward blacks and conspiracies by whites to commit electoral fraud to benefit Democratic candidates. Charles Albright (R-PA), James Biery (R-PA), and Charles Hays (R-AL) supported Coburn at length, with Hays also reading various investigatory testimony into the record. Republican opposition also emerged. George Willard (R-MI), for example, favored "a different course" and spoke favorably about encouraging "home rule."[201] And Joseph Hawley (R-CT), who had supported federal enforcement legislation to that point, announced that he would "part company" with the radicals because he believed "the existing laws on the statute-book are strong enough for the preservation of all the rights guaranteed by the Federal government."[202]

Debate continued the next day with comments by several other members, including Butler, Cannon, and Hoar, who argued for their amendments (Hawley, at this point, having dropped his). Butler's amendment was considered, and it passed 164-99, with a large majority of Republicans voting yea.[203] Section 13 was thus revised, and a fourteenth section was added to the bill. Cannon's amendment was then considered, which if passed would

---

201. *CR*, 43-2, 2/26/1875, 1839.

202. *CR*, 43-2, 2/26/1875, 1853. Hawley went on to state, "There is a social, and educational, and moral reconstruction of the South needed that will never come from any legislative halls, State or national; it must be the growth of time, of education, and Christianity. We cannot perfect that reconstruction through statutes, if we had all the powers of the State Legislature and of Congress combined. We cannot put justice, liberty, and equality into the hearts of the people by statutes alone."

203. *CR*, 43-2, 2/27/1875, 1935. Republicans voted 163-15.

strike out section 13 (as altered by the Butler amendment). It failed 121-130, with only a small minority of Republicans voting in favor.[204] Finally, Hoar's amendment was considered, which if passed would strike out sections 1, 2, and 4. It too failed, 119-126, with only a small minority of Republicans voting yea.[205] Butler had seemingly found the right modification of H.R. 4745; at the same time, some GOP support for the Cannon and Hoar amendments (thirty-eight and forty votes, respectively) suggested a diversity of opinion on what could be acceptable. Thus the successful passage of the Butler-amended H.R. 4745 was far from certain.

But when H.R. 4745 (as amended) was considered, it passed 135-114.[206] The Republicans largely held together in support, and it was enough to secure passage against unified Democratic opposition. But there were still thirty-two GOP defections, which included prominent party leaders like James Garfield (OH), George Frisbie Hoar (MA), and Henry Dawes (MA).[207] And, significantly, of the 134 Republicans who voted yea, ninety-six were "remanded to the shades of private life" (i.e., lame ducks).[208]

Little time was left in the lame-duck session, however, so the Senate would need to act quickly to move the bill to enactment. H.R. 4745 (as amended) was brought up on March 1 and was read a first time — amid almost constant dilatory behavior on the part of the Democrats.[209] The next day, March 2, the bill was read a second time, again over constant and loud Democratic objections, and Thomas Bayard (D-DE) announced that he would object to a third reading.[210] As a result "the bill was laid over, no motion being made to refer it to any committee."[211] Other business — chiefly appropriations bills — consumed the rest of the Senate's time before the session

204. *CR*, 43-2, 2/27/1875, 1929. Republicans voted 38-128.

205. *CR*, 43-2, 2/27/1875, 1933. Republicans voted 40-124.

206. *CR*, 43-2, 2/27/1875, 1935. Republicans voted 134-32.

207. A roll-call analysis (logistic regression) of Republican votes finds that the first (positive) and second (positive) NOMINATE dimensions are statistically significant, with Republican members furthest from the Democrats (rightmost moderates and radicals) being more likely to support the passage of H.R. 4745. The leftmost part of the GOP distribution was thus more likely to join the Democrats in opposition.

208. *New-York Tribune*, March 2, 1875, 6.

209. *CR*, 43-2, 3/1/1875, 1939-40. As a reporter for the *Detroit Free Press* accurately predicted after H.R. 4745 passed in the House, "The House Force bill will without doubt be earnestly fought by the Democratic Senator, who will resort to every available means to defeat its passage" (March 2, 1875, 3).

210. *CR*, 43-2, 3/2/1875, 2035.

211. *Detroit Free Press*, March 3, 1875, 4.

came to a close. Senate Republicans thus lacked both the time and the will to push the bill forward; the Democrats clearly showcased their resistance, and thus any investment by GOP senators would have come at the cost of valuable (and dwindling) agenda time.[212] Thus, H.R. 4745 died a quiet death.

For many Republicans, seeing the new enforcement bill fail produced a sigh of relief. They thought successful enactment might have had devastating effects on the GOP's fortunes in the *North*. Speaker of the House James Blaine (R-ME), looking ahead to the 1876 elections, expressed these sentiments to his black colleague John Lynch (R-MS): "In my judgment, if that bill had become a law the defeat of the Republican party throughout the country would have been a foregone conclusion. We could not have saved the South even if the bill had passed, but its passage would have lost us the North. . . . In my opinion, it was better to lose the South and save the North, than try through legislation to save the South, and thus lose both North and South."[213]

While perhaps not the majority position among Republicans, Blaine's view was shared by a significant number of party members. Both James Garfield (R-OH) and John Kasson (R-IA) voiced similar concerns, and powerful party figures outside Congress, like Joseph Medill, editor of the *Chicago Tribune*, did so as well.[214]

Reconstruction's Coda

With the expiration of the Forty-Third Congress on March 3, 1875, Republican-led Reconstruction initiatives ended. Senate Republicans, still a chamber majority, made some appeals in 1875 and 1876 to support the continued voting rights of blacks in the South, but these efforts were wholly symbolic. With the Democrats firmly in control of the House in the Forty-

212. An editorial in the *Nashville Republican Banner* laid out the politics this way: "The force bill is dead, never to be resurrected. Ostensibly it failed for lack of time to pass it in the closing hours of Congress, but, in reality, for other reasons. In going through the House, it created such a flare-up in the party ranks, alienating some of the strongest men in the body, that, to push it further, was deemed a hazardous experiment. In addition, a count of Senatorial noses doubtless developed the fact that there were a sufficient number of Republicans in the Senate who would vote against it to insure its defeat. So its friends allowed it to sleep the sleep which knows no waking, not even making an attempt to call it up" (March 5, 1875, 2).

213. Quoted in Simpson, *Reconstruction Presidents*, 181; see also John R. Lynch, *The Facts of Reconstruction* (New York: Neale, 1913), 135.

214. Gillette, *Retreat from Reconstruction*, 288–89.

Fourth Congress, an effective veto on further policy change was squarely in place.

The Forty-Fourth Congress also played a role in the presidential election of 1876, which featured two reform-minded governors: Republican Rutherford B. Hayes of Ohio and Democrat Samuel Tilden of New York. With momentum on their side, the Democrats set their sights on capturing the White House and perhaps wresting full control of the federal government from the GOP.[215] And when all votes were cast the result appeared to favor Tilden. But the electoral votes of three yet-to-be-redeemed Southern states — Florida, Louisiana, and South Carolina — were called into question,[216] with ballot fraud at the heart of the dispute, and the winner of these states would determine the election. The Republicans still controlled the canvassing boards in all three states.

In time the GOP-controlled canvassing boards threw out enough Democratic votes (based on fraudulent ballot design) to award the electoral votes of Florida, Louisiana, and South Carolina to Hayes. With these electoral votes in hand, Hayes had a one-vote majority. Democrats cried foul, and rival political actors in the three Southern states moved to certify results that would award the disputed electoral votes to Tilden. To settle the crisis, Congress set up a fifteen-member Electoral Commission to investigate and render a decision, and the eventual outcome favored Hayes 8-7.

Underlying the process of dispute settlement was a range of backdoor politicking, which culminated in the (so-called) Compromise of 1877.[217] The negotiations underlying the compromise were secret, but ultimately the Democrats acquiesced to Hayes's election in exchange for assurances from Republicans that (among other things) they would no longer use the army

215. See Keith Ian Polakoff, *The Politics of Inertia: The Election of 1876 and the End of Reconstruction* (Baton Rouge: Louisiana State University Press, 1973); Michael F. Holt, *By One Vote: The Disputed Presidential Election of 1876* (Lawrence: University Press of Kansas, 2008).

216. One electoral vote in Oregon was also contested and eventually went to Hayes.

217. The standard account of the Compromise of 1877 is C. Vann Woodward, *Reunion and Reaction: The Compromise of 1877 and the End of Reconstruction* (Boston: Little, Brown, 1951). Whether the Hayes camp and Southern Democrats settled on a true quid pro quo arrangement (such that it could be considered a "compromise") is discussed in Polakoff, *Politics of Inertia*; Allen Peskin, "Was There a Compromise of 1877?," *Journal of American History* 60 (1973): 63–75; C. Vann Woodward, "Yes, There Was a Compromise of 1877," *Journal of American History* 60 (1973): 215–23; and Michael Les Benedict, "Southern Democrats in the Crisis of 1876–1877: A Reconsideration of *Reunion and Reaction*," *Journal of Southern History* 64 (1980): 489–524.

to prop up GOP governments in the three remaining unredeemed states and instead would allow "home rule."[218] Subsequent behavior by Grant and Hayes was consistent with Republican leaders' keeping up their end of the deal.[219]

Thus, by late April 1877 the entire former Confederate South had been "redeemed" by Southern Democrats, and the GOP's ambitious policy of Reconstruction had effectively come to an end.[220] National Republican leaders would continue to hold out (some) hope for a viable Southern wing for the better part of the next two decades, but little would be achieved to make that a reality.

Conclusion

Since 1865, Republicans in Congress — sometimes with the support of the president and sometimes over his objections — had determined how the country would reconstruct itself and deal with the large population of former slaves. Through these difficult years the GOP successfully passed the Fourteenth and Fifteenth Amendments, the Civil Rights Acts of 1866 and 1875, Military Reconstruction legislation, and five Enforcement Acts. Viewed together, these bills altered the political status of the freedmen and, for a time, bolstered the federal government's authority to guarantee civil rights to all Americans. They also reflected the political goals of a Republican Party seeking to solidify its standing in the South.

At the same time, the political conservatism of many *within* the Republi-

218. Both Grant and Hayes also demanded that blacks' rights be respected in the new Democratically controlled governments and received assurances that they would be.

219. Grant withdrew the army from Florida in January 1877 when a new Democratic governor took office. And Hayes, once inaugurated, refused to support the Republican governors in Louisiana and South Carolina, who were entrenched but under fire, and directed the army guarding the statehouses back to their barracks, thus nudging the GOP governors into relinquishing their claims to office and stepping aside.

220. After the presidential election of 1876–77, the last state-level institution that remained in Republican hands was the South Carolina Senate. When the South Carolina legislature convened in April 1877, several Republican state senators resigned or were expelled. Afterward the actual partisan division in the South Carolina Senate went from eighteen Republicans and fifteen Democrats — where the GOP had a majority — to twenty-eight Democrats and five Republicans. In addition, the South Carolina House went from having a small Democratic majority (sixty-five to fifty-nine) to a large one (eighty-seven to thirty-seven). See William J. Cooper, *The Conservative Regime: South Carolina, 1877–1890* (Baltimore: Johns Hopkins University Press, 1968), 24–25.

can Party limited the effect of what might otherwise have been revolutionary changes to the political system. Congressional Republicans repeatedly found themselves in conflict with one another over Reconstruction policy. Radicals like Sen. Charles Sumner aimed to put the federal government in charge of responsibilities traditionally maintained at the state and local level. Moderates like Sen. Lyman Trumbull, on the other hand, proved unwilling to see their more conservative notions of federalism thrown overboard in the all-out pursuit of "human rights." Most often they linked civil rights policy to the ongoing war effort as a way to justify "impermanent" expansions of federal authority. Conservatives were ready to declare an end to Reconstruction and stop legislating on civil rights altogether. The legislation Congress enacted reflected the GOP's continuing effort to put together majorities based on these three competing coalitions.

By 1875, as the country suffered through a dramatic economic depression, much of the energy driving the radical policy changes had dissipated. Republicans had experienced a significant political defeat in the 1874 elections; Democrats seemed poised for a political comeback; and the party of Lincoln increasingly came to believe that the country had tired of Civil War-era debates. Donald, Baker, and Holt argue that Reconstruction "was already finished as a political process" by the 1876 presidential election.[221] We see evidence for their claim in the outcome of the Civil Rights Act of 1875 and the enforcement bill of 1875. Although the former offered merely symbolic protections to black citizens, the latter never even became law. Support for further civil rights policy, in other words, was waning among Republicans. At the same time, Southern Democrats were committed to rolling back what protections did exist. The violence carried out against black voters forced all Republicans to repeatedly confront a question that was at the core of the intraparty disagreement: To what extent should the federal government intervene in the states to protect black citizens? At this stage all the momentum was behind those who found retrenchment more appealing than further intervention. This meant the collapse of Reconstruction.

---

221. Donald, Baker, and Holt, *Civil War and Reconstruction*, 633.

CHAPTER FIVE

The Redemption Era, 1877–1891

When the Forty-Fifth Congress (1877–79) convened in October 1877, the Republicans found themselves in a vexing political situation. Democrats controlled the House, and all eleven states of the former Confederacy had been "redeemed." The GOP maintained a tenuous grip on the Senate and the presidency. Yet governing power was now clearly divided between the party of Lincoln and a resurgent white supremacist movement working through and alongside the Democrats. At the same time, it would be wrong to assume that Republicans had given up on their goal of building a southern wing.

The traditional claim about this era suggests that one-party Democratic rule and a Jim Crow state took hold in the former Confederacy immediately after Reconstruction and (until civil and voting rights reforms were finally instituted in the 1950s and 1960s) operated largely outside the more democratic two-party system that otherwise functioned in the country.[1] This ignores a period from the late 1870s through the early 1890s when state-level disenfranchisement laws were not yet in place, blacks could still vote

1. C. Vann Woodward, renowned historian of the US South, makes this point clearly: "The impression often left by cursory histories of the subject is that Negro disenfranchisement followed quickly if not immediately upon the overthrow of Reconstruction. It is perfectly true that Negroes were often coerced, defrauded, or intimidated, but they continued to vote in large parts of the South for more than two decades after Reconstruction." C. Vann Woodward, *The Strange Career of Jim Crow* (New York: Oxford University Press, 1955), 53–54. He also notes that blacks continued to hold offices in the South during this time.

throughout the former Confederacy (though they often faced violence and intimidation), and both parties vied for control of the South. Although the Democrats clearly had the upper hand, the Republicans periodically made real efforts to prevent the South from becoming truly "solid" for them.[2] This chapter explores how the GOP accommodated itself to post-Reconstruction politics.

From the late 1870s through the early 1890s the United States was taking its first real steps toward becoming an economic superpower in a rapidly industrializing world with increasingly interdependent nations. Domestically, currency issues (soft vs. hard money), transportation and internal improvements (railroads and their by-products), and tariff levels (protectionism vs. free trade) tested the nation's political economy. Labor issues, civil service reform, and military pensions also demanded attention from — and divided — the parties. Civil rights for black Americans did not disappear from the agenda, yet many Republicans now treated the issue instrumentally. Clear violations of blacks' civil rights were often used as a tool for electoral gain when it made sense to indict the Democrats for their rear-guard efforts to effectively reverse the outcome of the Civil War through fraud and violence. At the same time, Republican presidents (Rutherford Hayes, Chester Arthur, and Benjamin Harrison) and other key party leaders all de-emphasized black civil rights at various points as they sought to build the party's Southern wing by reaching out to disaffected whites.

The result of this shift was an attenuation of the relationship between black voters and the party. As the GOP downplayed civil rights and focused on framing itself as the "party of prosperity" — building a program around the tariff, the gold standard, and the regulation of railroads and interstate commerce — leaders increasingly looked west rather than south for political support.[3] That said, the final battle over Reconstruction policy would be

2. For a general discussion of the Republican Party's strategy toward the South in the post-Reconstruction era, see Vincent De Santis, *Republicans Face the Southern Question: The New Departure Years, 1877–1897* (Baltimore: Johns Hopkins University Press, 1959); Stanley Hirshson, *Farewell to the Bloody Shirt: Northern Republicans and the Southern Negro, 1877–1893* (Bloomington: Indiana University Press, 1962); Xi Wang, *The Trial of Democracy: Black Suffrage and Northern Republicans, 1860–1910* (Athens: University of Georgia Press, 1997); Charles W. Calhoun, *Conceiving a New Republic: The Republican Party and the Southern Question, 1869–1900* (Lawrence: University Press of Kansas, 2006).

3. See Heather Cox Richardson, *West from Appomattox: The Reconstruction of America after the Civil War* (New Haven, CT: Yale University Press, 2007), and Richard White, *The*

fought in the Fifty-First Congress (1889–91), as unified Republican government with an active will to protect blacks' voting rights would once again
confront Southern Democrats' fraud and violence. In many ways this battle
for a new federal elections law would be the radical Republicans' last, failed
stand.

This chapter focuses on the seven Congresses that spanned the 1877–91
era: the Forty-Fifth (1877–79) through Fifty-First (1889–91). To guide the
analysis, we divide the chapter into four sections: the Forty-Fifth and Forty-
Sixth Congresses, when black voters in the South faced continued violence
and intimidation in elections, even as President Hayes sought to build a
new Southern GOP around Whig-leaning white voters and the Democrats
sought to repeal the Enforcement Acts; the Forty-Eighth Congress, when a
black House member, James O'Hara (R-NC), tacked an antidiscrimination
amendment onto an interstate commerce bill, causing a lengthy battle over
the concept of "equal accommodations" in interstate passenger travel; the
Forty-Eighth, Forty-Ninth, Fiftieth, and Fifty-First Congresses, when federal aid to education threatened the racial caste system and governing hierarchy in the former Confederacy; and the Fifty-First Congress, when the
Republicans, led by Rep. Henry Cabot Lodge (MA), sought to leverage their
control of the House, Senate, and presidency to enact a new federal elections
law to protect blacks' voting rights in the South.

Rutherford Hayes and the Battle to Preserve Enforcement

Rutherford Hayes entered the White House in the spring of 1877 with plans
for rebuilding the Republican Party in the South. In the months before his in-
auguration, Hayes strategized over how best to achieve this end and settled
on a strategy of "conciliation." He would remove the vestiges of military-
led Reconstruction and pursue a "New Departure" with the white South. As
Vincent De Santis contends, "[Hayes] dreamed of building a strong Republican party in the South that would no longer depend upon the Negro for its
main strength and that could command the esteem and support of southern
whites."[4] He thought the radicals' desire to forcibly remake Southern society imposed an overt racial frame on Reconstruction that forced Southern
whites into a kind of massive resistance. He believed Southern whites were

*Republic for Which It Stands: The United States during Reconstruction and the Gilded Age, 1865–
1896* (Oxford: Oxford University Press, 2017), 368–404, 589–617.

4. De Santis, *Republicans Face the Southern Question*, 66.

actually heterogeneous, and that once the racial angle was removed they could be split on economic grounds.

In effect, Hayes and his supporters imagined that the Whiggish elements in the white South—principally industrialists and businessmen, but also small farmers—were prime targets for the GOP message. Hayes believed the alliance between "moderate" whites and the former planter class was a matter of short-term convenience to oppose "Radical Reconstruction," not a durable coalition. As such, he hoped to convince Whiggish white Southerners that their economic interests were better served by Republicans than by Democrats.

Hayes believed federal support for internal improvements was the key to driving an economic wedge into the Southern white population.[5] In order to industrialize the region, better connections between farms, manufacturers, ports, and other centers of economic activity were needed. In this way Hayes sought to rekindle the GOP's economic program from the early 1870s, before railroad bankruptcies and bank panics halted it in its tracks (see chapter 4). Such economic ideas appealed to many white Southerners, and a range of plans were floated for tunnels, canals, and railroads. But bringing such plans to fruition would take time, and in the short term Hayes sought to communicate his "good faith" and monetize his New Departure strategy through executive patronage appointments.[6]

Hayes began his tenure by building a pro-Southern cabinet. He nominated David Key (a Tennessee Democrat and former Confederate general) for postmaster general; William Evarts (former attorney general under Andrew Johnson) for secretary of state; and Carl Schurz (former Liberal Republican) for secretary of the interior. All three had opposed the radicals' military-style Reconstruction plan. Key, in particular, would control a vast patronage system, which could be used to reward moderate whites in the South. Radical Republicans were shocked by this turn of events, but Hayes would not be deterred—and all three of his nominees were confirmed.[7] More generally, Southern Republicans (blacks and whites alike) would be passed over for a number of lower-level appointments as Hayes sought to

5. On Hayes's internal improvements idea, see De Santis, *Republicans Face the Southern Question.*

6. De Santis, *Republicans Face the Southern Question,* 73–78; Hirshson, *Farewell to the Bloody Shirt,* 27–28; Calhoun, *Conceiving a New Republic,* 138–39.

7. On Hayes's battles with the Republican establishment over patronage more generally, see "Office-Seeking," *CT,* March 22, 1877, 2.

broaden GOP respectability through patronage "buy-ins" among Southern white Democrats.[8]

At the same time, Hayes held strongly to the idea that black rights in the South—equal protection of the laws and voting rights—should be safeguarded. He hoped that the "better elements" in white Southern society would respond to his entreaties by ensuring the rights of the freedmen.[9] But he would be disappointed. The first inkling that Southern whites would not behave as he hoped appeared in state election returns that fall. Republican vote totals in Virginia and Mississippi dropped precipitously relative to 1876: from 40 to 4.1 percent in Virginia and from 30 to 1.2 percent in Mississippi.[10] Charges of violence and intimidation permeated these elections, and similar allegations were raised before the federal midterms in fall 1878, when the GOP's declining power became even more obvious. The number of Republican House seats in the former Confederacy dropped from ten (at the start of the Forty-Fifth Congress) to three. Worse yet, the GOP lost majority control of the Senate and thus would face a Forty-Sixth Congress (1879–81) in which the Democrats controlled both chambers.

Hayes was outraged that white elites in the South did not follow through on their promises, especially in Louisiana and South Carolina, where some of the most extreme charges of voting rights infringements were made. He still believed in his general policy—that the white South would need to be split if the GOP were to be rebuilt—but he was sobered by these new realities.

Fresh from their electoral victories, the Democrats pressed their advantage. As the Forty-Fifth Congress was winding down, House Democrats successfully added amendments to the annual appropriations bills for the army and for the executive, legislative, and judicial expenses of the government that repealed elements of the Enforcement Acts. More specifically, they aimed to eliminate any troop presence at the polls (the revised army bill) and prohibit the appointment of federal marshals and their deputies to supervise elections (the revised expenses bill). Once passed, these bills were sent to the Senate, where the Republican majority removed the

8. Stanley Hirshson notes that "one-third of the Southern appointees during the first five months of the Hayes administration were [Democrats]." Hirshson, *Farewell to the Bloody Shirt*, 36.

9. And in this regard he secured promises from the incoming governors of Louisiana and South Carolina before the troop removals. See Calhoun, *Conceiving a New Republic*, 140–42.

10. Calhoun, *Conceiving a New Republic*, 150.

amendments. Conference committees were appointed (twice regarding the expenses bill), but conferees could not reach a new agreement. Thus the lame-duck session ended without these appropriations being made for fiscal year 1880, which would begin on July 1, 1879.

The Democrats pursued a "rider" strategy — tacking substantive amendments onto unrelated bills — as a stalling technique. As Xi Wang notes, "The purpose of the delays [at the end of the Forty-Fifth] was to disable the enforcement laws in the next Congress."[11] Since the Democrats would be the majority party in both chambers in the Forty-Sixth Congress (1879–81), their only obstacle would be Hayes. Applying their rider strategy to appropriations bills was strategic: they believed Hayes was more likely to accept the legislation, since vetoes of appropriations — and a subsequent deadlock — would leave important elements of the government unfunded. Riders on appropriations bills were nothing new. Republicans under Grant had made use of them, for example, to authorize the president to establish a commission to draft rules for civil service exams (1871) and to give federal circuit court judges the power to appoint marshals to supervise elections (1872).[12] However, the Democrats had taken the strategy to a new level by actually threatening to block funding. As Leonard White states, "Now for the first time a congressional majority asserted its right to stop supplies unless 'redress of grievances' was secured by executive acceptance of an obnoxious proviso."[13]

Hayes called for a special (extra) session of the Forty-Sixth Congress to begin on March 18, 1879 — since the normal first session would not convene until December 1, 1879 — in order to enact the needed appropriations and prevent important segments of the government from going unfunded beginning on July 1. Congressional Republicans — now frequently divided on the "correct" Southern policy — were up in arms, outraged at the Democrats' overt power play. Hayes also recognized the Democrats' strategy and vowed not to be coerced into supporting it:

11. Wang, *Trial of Democracy*, 165.

12. According to Horace Davis (citing a statement by John Reagan of Texas), "Between 1862 and 1875, 387 measures of general legislation had been passed as provisos upon appropriations bills." See Horace Davis, *American Constitutions: The Relations of the Three Departments as Adjusted by a Century* (San Francisco, 1884), 34.

13. Leonard D. White, *The Republican Era: 1869–1901* (New York: Macmillan, 1958), 35. On this point see also Charles H. Stewart III, *Budget Reform Politics: The Design of the Appropriations Process in the House of Representatives, 1865–1921* (Cambridge: Cambridge University Press, 1989), 86.

The Senate and House in the Forty-sixth Congress being both Democratic will insist on the right to repeal the election laws, and, in case of
my refusal, will put the repeal [as riders] on the appropriation bills. They
will . . . block the wheels of government, if I do not yield my convictions
in favor of the election laws. It will be a severe, perhaps a long contest. I
do not fear it. I do not even dread it. The people will not allow this revolutionary course to triumph.[14]

Hayes would not have long to wait before the first challenge was upon
him. A little more than a month after the opening of the special session, a
new army appropriations bill (H.R. 1) was placed on his desk, having made
its way through the House and Senate on strict party-line votes.[15] In the bill
was language that struck out a portion of a provision in section 2002 of the
Revised Statutes. The provision in question stipulated, "No military or naval
officer, or other person engaged in the civil, military, or naval service of the
United States, shall order, bring, keep, or have under his authority or control,
any troops or armed men at the place where any general or special election
is held in any State, unless it be necessary to repel the armed enemies of the
United States, or to keep the peace at the polls."[16] If enacted, H.R. 1 would
remove the last eight words: "or to keep the peace at the polls."

Republicans contended that the Southern Democrats were trying to
undo the Northern victory by preventing honest oversight of elections.
They also believed Northern Democrats were eager to help in order to remove the army's presence above the Mason-Dixon line, where densely populated areas in states like New York were prime territory for electoral shenani-
gans and vote stealing.[17] Hayes did not intend to use the army as a police
force, but he also understood that calling in the troops was the only option
when civilian authorities needed help in elections.[18] Moreover, he believed

14. Rutherford Birchard Hayes, *Diary and Letters of Rutherford Birchard Hayes: Nineteenth
President of the United States*, 5 vols., ed. Charles Richard Williams (Columbus: Ohio State
Archaeological and Historical Society, 1922–26), 3:529.

15. *CR*, 46-1, 4/5/1879, 270; 4/25/1879, 913.

16. See *Revised Statutes of the United States*, 2nd ed., Title 26, "The Elective Franchise,"
section 2002 (Washington, DC: Government Printing Office, 1878), 352.

17. On the application of federal election laws in Northern cities in the late nineteenth
century, see Albie Burke, "Federal Regulation of Congressional Elections in Northern Cities,
1871–94," *American Journal of Legal History* 14 (1970): 17–34.

18. In June 1878, for example, Hayes had signed an army appropriations bill with a
Democratic rider attached, which sought to prevent the army from being used to enforce
the law (what Hayes considered "police power") unless authorized by act of Congress or

the Democrats' rider strategy was dangerous and unconstitutional, arguing that "the House could, by withholding appropriations, force the Senate and president to agree to any legislation that the House saw fit to attach to an appropriations bill."[19] Of course, in the current context, both chambers agreed on the course of action. Hayes responded by noting that any future president would be forced to abdicate his constitutional role in the legislative process lest portions of the government shut down because they lacked funding.[20] Thus, on April 29, 1879, Hayes vetoed the measure.[21] Two days later, House Democrats attempted to override Hayes's veto but fell short of the required two-thirds majority on a party-line vote.[22]

Less than a week later, the Democrats tried to sidestep Hayes's constitutional arguments by passing a stand-alone bill (H.R. 1382) that would serve the same purpose (barring troops from the polls).[23] Hayes vetoed this as well,[24] reiterating his position that, while he disagreed with using the military as a police force, he believed troops were a vital part of the enforcement process—especially if civilian institutions in states deemed them necessary to ensure the sanctity of elections. The House Democrats again tried an override but once more fell short of the necessary two-thirds (with perfect party-line voting on both sides).[25]

The Democrats then moved from army enforcement to civilian enforcement by adding a rider to the appropriations bill for legislative, executive, and judicial expenses (H.R. 2). In doing so they sought to neutralize the supervisory election authority of federal marshals and their deputies by limiting their powers to make arrests, investigate voting records, determine voter eligibility, and participate in the counting of ballots, as well as hamper-

---

the Constitution. As Charles Calhoun notes, "In Hayes's view, this legislation [known as the Posse Comitatus Act] meant that the military could not be used to 'interfere' with an election, which he had no intention to do, but civil authorities were still perfectly free to call in the troops whenever opposition to the law was 'too powerful for the ordinary police or other civil officers to overcome.'" Calhoun, *Conceiving a New Republic*, 161.

19. Ari Hoogenboom, *The Presidency of Rutherford B. Hayes* (Lawrence: University Press of Kansas, 1988), 74–75; Calhoun, *Conceiving a New Republic*, 162.

20. Calhoun, *Conceiving a New Republic*, 163–64.

21. Veto message can be found in *CR*, 46-1, 4/29/1879, 993–95.

22. *CR*, 46-1, 5/1/1879, 1014–15. The vote was 121-110, with Republicans voting 0-102, Democrats 111-0, Greenbackers 3-8, and Independent Democrats 7-0.

23. *CR*, 46-1, 5/6/1879, 1094–95; 5/9/1879, 1189.

24. Veto message can be found in *CR*, 46-1, 5/12/1879, 1267–68.

25. *CR*, 46-1, 5/13/1879, 1298. The vote was 128-97, with Republicans voting 0-97, Democrats 114-0, Greenbackers 10-0, and Independent Democrats 4-0.

ing their ability to register voters, get paid, and pursue enforcement in rural areas.[26] Pure party-line voting in both chambers brought the bill to Hayes's desk.[27] He promptly vetoed it on the grounds that its limitations and prohibitions effectively prevented the federal government from performing its supervisory role in elections.[28] Once again, House Democrats tried to override but failed.[29]

In the face of these three defeats, and with the GOP winning the public relations war, the Democrats sought to regroup.[30] By mid-June, just weeks from the beginning of the new fiscal year, they agreed to adopt the army and legislative, executive, and judicial expenses appropriations bills largely without political restrictions. They did stipulate in the first bill, however, that the army was not to be used to police elections (something Hayes never supported anyway), while excluding in the latter bill certain judicial expenses relating to the pay of marshals. Hayes agreed to each provision, and the immediate funding crisis was over.[31]

But additional appropriations were still needed. The Democrats continued their rider strategy in a supplemental judicial expenses bill (H.R. 2252) that provided money for salaries and fees for a range of judicial employees; it also included a stipulation denying payment to general and deputy marshals for their work on election day. Since the Democrats could not repeal the laws themselves, they now tried to prevent the key enforcement agents from getting paid. This scenario followed the expected path: party-line votes in each chamber and a Hayes veto, once again predicated on the would-be law's making the federal government unable to supervise elections.[32] House Democrats again failed (for the fourth time) to override.[33] The Democrats then produced a new judicial expenses bill (H.R. 2381) on

26. See Wang, *Trial of Democracy*, 171–72.

27. *CR*, 46-1, 4/26/1879, 960; 5/20/1879, 1484–85.

28. Veto message can be found in *CR*, 46-1, 5/29/1879, 1709–10.

29. *CR*, 46-1, 5/29/1879, 1711. The vote was 114-93, with Republicans voting 0-91, Democrats 107-0, Greenbackers 2-2, and Independent Democrats 5-0.

30. On support for Hayes from Republican newspaper editors, state legislators, and social clubs, see Frank P. Vazzano, "President Hayes, Congress and the Appropriations Riders Vetoes," *Congress and the Presidency* 20 (1993): 25–37.

31. The army appropriations bill was enacted on June 23, 1879 (21 *Stat.* 30), and the legislative, executive, and judicial expenses bill was enacted on June 21, 1879 (21 *Stat.* 23).

32. *CR*, 46-1, 6/19/1879, 2185–86; 6/21/1879, 2257. The veto message can be found in *CR*, 46-1, 6/23/1879, 2291–92.

33. *CR*, 46-1, 6/23/1879, 2292. The vote was 102-78, with Republicans voting 0-78, Democrats 98-0, and Independent Democrats 4-0.

June 30, the last day of the fiscal year, which included no stipulation for the payment of marshals but prohibited race-based discrimination on juries and eliminated test oaths for jurors.[34] Hayes saw nothing objectionable in the bill — believing the test-oath ban was a relic of Reconstruction that should be eliminated — and signed it.[35]

This left only the issue of payment for election supervision. The Democrats deleted the provision from the previous rider (in H.R. 2252) and produced a stand-alone bill for the payment of US marshals and their general deputies. The bill (H.R. 2382) provided an appropriation of $600,000 but prohibited any of this money from being used for deputies (and their prescribed activities) on election day.[36] As before, the bill passed in both chambers with all participating Democrats opposing all participating Republicans.[37] Hayes again issued a veto — along now-familiar lines, that the legislation would prevent the federal government from performing its job in overseeing elections[38] — and the House Democrats failed, yet again, to override.[39]

Thus the first session of the Forty-Sixth Congress (and the fiscal year ending June 30, 1879) ended with Hayes having preserved the enforcement laws but without funding for US marshals and their deputies. Attorney General Charles Devens instructed marshals and deputies to continue their supervisory duties until the requisite appropriation could be generated.[40] Overall, though, Hayes had done his job, vetoing five bills and watching the Democrats fail in their five attempts to override. The Democrats' erosion of the GOP's Reconstruction era institutions had been stopped for the moment, and Republican cohesion around "bloody shirt" rhetoric had been produced before the 1879 elections in the North — which went very well for the GOP — and the general election of 1880. Hayes himself would not be seeking reelection, but he was doing his best to help his party, even though his New Departure strategy had proved a failure.

34. Hoogenboom suggests that the stipulations in this new bill were constructed in consultation with Hayes, given the tight time frame. See Hoogenboom, *Presidency of Rutherford B. Hayes*, 77–78.

35. The new judicial expenses bill was enacted on June 30, 1879 (21 *Stat.* 43).

36. See *CR*, 46-1, 6/27/1879, 2392.

37. *CR*, 46-1, 6/27/1879, 2397–98; 6/28/1879, 2413.

38. Veto message can be found in *CR*, 46-1, 6/30/1879, 2442.

39. *CR*, 46-1, 6/30/1879, 2442–43. The vote was 85–63, with Republicans voting 0-62, Democrats 81-0, Greenbackers 0-1, and Independent Democrats 4-0.

40. Wang, *Trial of Democracy*, 174–75; Calhoun, *Conceiving a New Republic*, 164. Devens would make an urgent request for this appropriation when Congress reconvened for the second session on December 1, 1879.

The battle between Hayes and the Democratic majority in Congress resumed in the second (regular) session of the Forty-Sixth Congress. As Republican politicking for the presidential nomination was shifting into high
gear, and shortly after the Supreme Court upheld the constitutionality of the
Enforcement Acts (including those sections that dealt with election supervision) in *Ex parte Siebold*, the Democrats tried a different tack in their attempt
to scuttle enforcement.[41] In late March 1880, House Democrats attached a
rider to an $8 million special deficiency appropriations bill (for payment of
expenses for the fiscal year ending June 30, 1880), which would have taken
the appointment of special deputy marshals (who were added at election
time, to help marshals in their general deputies) from federal district marshals and given it to the federal circuit court (or the federal district court,
if the circuit court was not in session). Compensation ($5 a day) for special
deputy marshals was also included, as well as a stipulation to ensure that the
allocation of such special deputies would be divided equally between the
parties. "The object [of this rider]," writes Ari Hoogenboom, "was to divide
and undermine the authority, responsibility, and effectiveness of federal officers who supervised elections."[42] The special deficiency appropriations bill
(H.R. 4924), with the rider attached, was passed in both chambers by party-
line votes (with only sporadic defections in the House) and sent to Hayes for
his signature.[43] On May 4 Hayes vetoed the bill, once again citing its un-
constitutionality as well as the blatant coercion demonstrated by attaching
riders to appropriations bills.[44]

This time the Democrats did not try to override Hayes. Instead, two days
after his veto, they attempted to circumvent his constitutional argument by
passing a freestanding bill (in much the same way they tried with military
interference in the first session). This bill (S. 1726) was effectively identical
to the deficiency appropriations bill rider. Once again special deputy marshals would be appointed by courts rather that by marshals, which (from
the GOP's perspective) would hamper election supervision. The Democrats
jammed the bill through both chambers and presented it to Hayes near the
end of the second session.[45] On June 15 he vetoed it, asserting that the dis-
juncture between federal marshals and their special deputies that the bill

41. Calhoun, *Conceiving a New Republic*, 171–72.

42. Hoogenboom, *Presidency of Rutherford B. Hayes*, 196.

43. *CR*, 46-2, 3/19/1880, 1716; 4/1/1880, 2027.

44. Veto message can be found in *CR*, 46-2, 5/4/1880, 2987–88.

45. *CR*, 46-2, 5/21/1880, 3607; 6/11/1880, 4452.

would have created would adversely affect the government's ability to supervise elections.[46] Once again the Democrats chose not to pursue an override.

With these seven vetoes, Hayes had effectively stymied Democratic attempts to undermine the supervision of elections. He did have to make a concession to keep the general government going, and on June 16, 1880 (the last day of the session, with the end of the fiscal year two weeks off), he signed a special deficiency appropriations bill and a sundry civil appropriations bill.[47] The deficiency bill—shorn of the Democrats' rider and any pay for special deputies—provided back pay for marshals (for the fiscal year ending June 30, 1880) but prohibited payment for marshals' (and deputy marshals') services at any election.[48] The sundry appropriations bill provided $650,000 for marshals and their general deputies (for the fiscal year ending June 30, 1881) but prohibited payment for services at elections.[49] But from Hayes's perspective, the Enforcement Acts were preserved.

The Republicans performed well in the 1880 elections, winning the presidency and the House and gaining a measure of control of the Senate (more on this below). Perhaps because of this GOP momentum, as Burke A. Hinsdale notes, "The Democrats now abandoned the [enforcement-repeal] contest."[50] Specifically, in the third (lame-duck) session, Hayes would sign into law a new special deficiency appropriations bill (for the fiscal year ending June 30, 1881)[51] and a new sundry civil appropriations bill (for the fiscal year ending June 30, 1882),[52] neither of them including the elections restrictions that were part of previous versions.

Overall, Hayes's battle with the Democratic majority in Congress was meaningful, at least viewed contemporaneously. By keeping the Enforcement Acts on the books, Hayes gave the attorney general the capacity to pursue criminal prosecutions and thereby ensure a fair ballot and a fair count in Southern elections. And the momentum generated by Hayes's steadfast-

46. Veto message referred to in *CR*, 46-2, 6/16/1880, 4612. For the full veto message, see "Killing a Partisan Bill," *NYT*, June 16, 1880, 2.

47. For the politics behind these bills, see "Congress To-day," *WP*, June 16, 1880, 1; "The Veto," *WP*, June 16, 1880, 2; and "Crooked Ways," *WP*, June 17, 1880, 2.

48. See 21 *Stat*. 238. Key provision is on p. 250.

49. See 21 *Stat*. 259. Key provision is on p. 278.

50. James A. Garfield, *The Works of James Abram Garfield*, ed. Burke A. Hinsdale (Boston: James R. Osgood, 1883), 2:733. More generally, see 2:731–33 for a review of the spring 1880 enforcement battle politics.

51. See 21 *Stat*. 414. Key provision providing back pay for marshals is on p. 429.

52. See 21 *Stat*. 259. Key provision providing $600,000 for marshals and their deputies (with no conditional language) is on p. 278.

ness seemed to carry over into Justice Department activity.[53] The number of enforcement cases in the South in 1881 more than tripled that of 1880, and remained at a high level for the next four years (during Chester Arthur's administration).[54] Still, convictions were difficult given the Southern composition of courts, and the bite of enforcement never reached the level of the early Reconstruction era (1871–73). But in refusing to be bullied by Democrats in Congress, Hayes allowed for the possibility of criminal enforcement—something that could be a powerful tool if the GOP ever reemerged as a serious presence in the South.[55]

Discrimination in Interstate Travel

Despite having unified control of the federal government in the Forty-Seventh Congress (1881–83), the Republicans did little to protect or promote the rights of blacks in the South. Although the Justice Department was more active than in the recent past, no new legislation was pursued in Congress. There were attempts to buttress the party as a whole, however. For example, House Republicans pursued contested (disputed) election cases, mostly as a way to add seats and give themselves a bit more wiggle room to govern (they otherwise had a bare majority). In all, five Southern seats were "flipped" from Democrat to Republican by election contests.[56] And President Arthur followed up on Hayes's strategy of seeking a new vehicle for a Southern GOP not by courting Democrats with Whiggish tastes but by negotiating with Independents with economically radical leanings.[57]

A wave of populism had swept the South, with disaffected whites resist-

53. See Wang, *Trial of Democracy*, app. 7, 300–301.

54. The number of cases (convictions) was 53 (0) in 1880, 177 (95) in 1881, 154 (23) in 1882, 201 (12) in 1883, 160 (17) in 1884, and 107 (1) in 1885. Wang, *Trial of Democracy*, 300.

55. For a general history of the enforcement of voting rights in the South during the time frame of this chapter, see Robert M. Goldman, *"A Free Ballot and a Fair Count": The Department of Justice and the Enforcement of Voting Rights in the South, 1877–1893* (New York: Fordham University Press, 2001).

56. See Jeffery A. Jenkins, "Partisanship and Contested Election Cases in the U.S. House, 1789–2002," *Studies in American Political Development* 18 (2004): 112–35; Jeffery A. Jenkins, "The First 'Southern Strategy': The Republican Party and Contested Election Cases in the Late-Nineteenth Century House," in *Party, Process, and Political Change in Congress*, vol. 2, *Further New Perspectives on the History of Congress*, ed. David W. Brady and Mathew D. McCubbins (Stanford, CA: Stanford University Press, 2007).

57. On Arthur's strategy toward the Independents, and its consequences, see De Santis,

ing the reemergence of the old planter class. Arthur pinned his hopes on fusion arrangements with these disaffected whites, chief among them the Readjusters in Virginia, led by former Confederate general William Mahone. After some negotiation, Mahone agreed to caucus with the Republicans in the Senate (thereby giving the GOP marginal control of the chamber) in exchange for key committee assignments and control of executive patronage in his state.[58] Fusion paid dividends in the 1882 midterms, when the Republicans saw their share of Southern House seats nearly double. All these gains were wiped out two years later, however, as the Democrats regrouped and consolidated their power.

Although organized Republican efforts in Congress to support black rights were absent in the Arthur years — the lack of GOP measures in the Forty-Seventh Congress carried over into the Forty-Eighth, when the Republicans were once again the minority party in the House — an individual GOP initiative created significant distress for the Democrats. In December 1884, during the lame-duck session of the Forty-Eighth Congress, the House was considering a bill to regulate interstate commerce. Proposed by John Reagan (D-TX), chairman of the Commerce Committee, the bill sought to place a number of limits on railroads as a way of reducing monopolistic practices.[59] On December 16, as the proceedings were winding down and a vote on Reagan's bill neared, James O'Hara, a black freshman Republican from North Carolina, sought to add an amendment reading: "And any person or persons having purchased a ticket to be conveyed from one State to another, or paid the required fare, shall receive the same treatment and be afforded equal facilities and accommodations as are furnished all others persons holding tickets of the same class without discrimination."[60]

In proposing his amendment, O'Hara was responding, in part, to the recent Supreme Court decision in the *Civil Rights Cases* (1883), which deemed unconstitutional the Civil Rights Act of 1875 providing that "all persons

---

Republicans Face the Southern Question, 133–81, and Justus D. Doenecke, *The Presidencies of James A. Garfield and Chester A. Arthur* (Lawrence: University Press of Kansas, 1981), 105–24.

58. For more details on the GOP agreement with Mahone, see Boris Heersink and Jeffery A. Jenkins, *Republican Party Politics and the American South, 1865–1968* (New York: Cambridge University Press, 2020).

59. For a discussion of the railroad-regulation provisions and the history of actions in Congress during this era, see Lewis H. Haney, *A Congressional History of Railways in the United States*, vol. 2 (Madison, WI: Democrat Printing, 1910).

60. *CR*, 48-1, 12/16/1884, 296–97.

FIGURE 8.   Rep. James O'Hara (R-NC). Special Collections Research Center, University of Chicago Library.

within the jurisdiction of the United States shall be entitled to the full and equal enjoyment of the accommodations, advantages, facilities, and privileges of inns, public conveyances on land or water, theaters, and other places of public amusement; subject only to the conditions and limitations established by law, and applicable alike to citizens of every race and color, regardless of any previous condition of servitude."[61] The Court ruled that Congress did not have the constitutional authority under the enforcement provisions of the Fourteenth Amendment to outlaw racial discrimination by *private*

61. See 18 *Stat.* 335.

individuals and organizations — which would be necessary given the provisions and language of the 1875 act.[62]

During the first session of the Forty-Eighth Congress, O'Hara had introduced a joint resolution (H.J. Res. 92) proposing a constitutional amendment that would have legally reinstituted the 1875 act, safely insulated from Supreme Court challenge.[63] But once the joint resolution was referred to the Judiciary Committee, the House took no further action on it. Recognizing that his chief goal was beyond reach, O'Hara sought to attach his amendment to the Reagan bill. It would not reestablish the provisions of the 1875 act, but it would chart a course that would be immune to Supreme Court challenge. That is, O'Hara was using Congress's power to regulate interstate commerce, provided in article 1, section 8 of the Constitution. The language of his amendment was tailored to address discriminatory treatment in accommodations for fares purchased for travel *between* states. It was thus considerably narrower than the 1875 Civil Rights Act, since it did not apply to discrimination in accommodations for travel *within* states. Nevertheless, O'Hara sought to accomplish what was feasible with congressional legislation, and his amendment threatened the otherwise easy road ahead for the Reagan bill.[64]

Having introduced his amendment, O'Hara went on to defend it. After discussing its constitutionality, based on the Commerce Clause, he then laid out the issue as he saw it:

> Now an evil exists, and none will deny that discriminations are made unjustly, and to a great disadvantage, between persons holding the same class of tickets who are compelled to travel on business from one State to another, and perchance across several States, *en route* to their destination in another State. I therefore hold it to be not only within the power but the imperative duty of Congress to abate the evil and protect all classes of citizens from discrimination in any and every form.[65]

---

62. According to the Court's ruling, the enforcement provisions of the Fourteenth Amendment applied only to discriminatory behavior undertaken by state and local governments.

63. See *CR*, 48-1, 1/8/1884, 282.

64. For a description of the proceedings surrounding the O'Hara amendment, see Maurine Christopher, *America's Black Congressmen* (New York: Thomas W. Crowell, 1971), 153–59; Lawrence Grossman, *The Democratic Party and the Negro: Northern and National Politics, 1868–92* (Urbana: University of Illinois Press, 1976), 110–12; Eric Anderson, *Race and Politics in North Carolina, 1872–1901: The Black Second* (Baton Rouge: Louisiana State University Press, 1981), 120–23.

65. *CR*, 48-2, 12/16/1884, 297.

That said, O'Hara took pains to frame the issue broadly:

> Mr. Speaker, this is not class legislation. I do not nor would I ask such. It is not a race question, nor is it a political action. It rises far above all these. It is plain, healthy legislation, strictly in keeping with enlightened sentiment and spirit of the age in which we live; it is legislation looking to and guarding the rights of every citizen of this great Republic, however humble his station in our social scale.[66]

The Democrats, on the verge of pushing through the Reagan bill, were taken by surprise. As the *Chicago Tribune* reported: "The amendment and speech [by O'Hara] seemed to paralyze Reagan."[67] Regaining his composure, Reagan noted that his bill was designed to regulate commerce, and that "the subject of transportation of persons" was never considered by his committee.[68] He thus hoped the House would not enlarge the bill to include that subject at such a late date. His hopes were dashed when the O'Hara amendment passed 134-97.[69] Republicans voted as a bloc in support, Southern Democrats voted as a group against (with only two defections),[70] while — critically — a majority of Northern Democrats supported the amendment.[71] Confusion and panic set in. James H. Blount (D-GA) moved to reconsider the vote by which the amendment was agreed to, and O'Hara responded by moving to table Blount's motion. Reagan quickly moved for adjournment, which was granted.[72]

Reagan's adjournment motion was strategic, since he and his supporters needed time to regroup. The O'Hara amendment put the entire interstate commerce bill at risk, and Reagan sought advice from seasoned poli-

66. *CR*, 48-2, 12/16/1884, 297.

67. "The National Capital," *CT*, December 17, 1884, 6.

68. *CR*, 48-2, 12/16/1884, 297.

69. *CR*, 48-2, 12/16/1884, 297.

70. Southern Democrats voted 2-65. One defection was James H. Blount (GA), who changed his vote from nay to yea so that he could offer a motion to reconsider. The other was George Dargan (SC).

71. Northern Democrats voted 46-30. A roll-call analysis (logistic regression) of Northern Democratic votes finds that the first (positive) NOMINATE dimension is statistically significant, with Northern Democrats closest to the Republicans being more likely to vote in favor of the O'Hara amendment. This relationship would hold for the remaining seven votes analyzed in this section — that is, those Northern Democrats closest to the Republicans (the right part of the Northern Democratic distribution) were more likely to vote with the GOP.

72. *CR*, 48-2, 12/16/1884, 297-98.

ticians William Holman (D-IN) and William Morrison (D-IL) on how best to proceed when the House reconvened. In the meantime, Republicans— who opposed the interstate commerce legislation—reveled in the sectional rift that O'Hara's amendment created within the Democratic Party. When a *Washington Post* reporter asked him what the likely effect of the O'Hara amendment would be, Thomas B. Reed (R-ME) replied: "I think it will result in [the Reagan bill's] defeat. It is simply another case of 'Rum, Romanism, and Rebellion.' Except for the drawing of the color line, the bill would have passed. Now it is not likely."[73]

When the House reconvened the next day, December 17, the pending question (O'Hara's motion to table Blount's motion to reconsider) on the Reagan bill was taken, and it passed 149-121.[74] Once again Republicans and Southern Democrats voted against one another as blocs. And this time a small majority of Northern Democrats (forty-nine of ninety-three) voted with Southern Democrats in opposing the tabling motion. But a large minority aligned with the Republicans, and that was enough to table reconsideration.

Unable to reconsider the vote, the Democrats sought to sanitize the amendment's content. Charles Crisp (D-GA) proposed tacking an amendment onto the end of O'Hara's amendment: "Nothing in his act contained shall be construed as to prevent any railroad company from providing separate accommodations for white and colored persons." Crisp went on to defend his amendment, stating that the federal court in Georgia had upheld separate accommodations under a rule of equality. Moreover, he argued that his amendment would not require companies to provide separate accommodations but left that to their discretion (which they might pursue based on public sentiment). Crisp concluded by asking, "Why agitate anew this question? The law is well settled. The rights of the colored man are absolutely protected. Nobody wants to interfere with his rights. He has the same accommodations, the same kind of cars as the white man when he pays the same fare." Robert Smalls, a black Republican from South Carolina, responded directly to Crisp: "We have no objection to riding in a separate car when the car is of the same character as that provided for the white people to ride in. But I state here to the House that colored men and women do have trouble in riding through the State of Georgia." He went on to describe how

73. "Inter-state Commerce," *WP*, December 17, 1884, 5.
74. *CR*, 48-2, 12/17/1884, 315–16.

blacks traveling across states were, once in Georgia, routinely forced into second-class "Jim Crow cars."[75]

William Breckenridge (D-AR) then offered a substitute for Crisp's amendment: "But nothing in this act shall be construed to deny to railroads the right to classify passengers as they may deem best for the public comfort and safety, or to relate to transportation between points wholly within the limits of one State." As Maurine Christopher notes, "[Breckinridge's amendment] was designed to retain discrimination in a somewhat more mannerly, less blatant fashion [than Crisp's amendment]."[76] In defending his amendment, Breckenridge argued that corporations (railroads) must be free to "assort passengers" from the standpoint of "public convenience and public safety," and that O'Hara's amendment would inject a social question into a matter of commerce (and, in doing so, impose social equality in society).[77]

In response to Breckenridge, Thomas Reed gained the floor and shared with the House an example of his sardonic wit:

> Mr. Speaker, I must say that I rejoice to see this question lifted by the last suggestion from a mere question of politics or of color. I did not propose to discuss it in that light. I thought it very desirable that we should have a vote on the main question without bringing up questions of color or stirring up feelings of race or partisanship. Let wisdom be justified of her children. So I am very much pleased, indeed, to see this amendment of the gentleman from Arkansas. This at once ceases to be a question of politics or color, and has now become a question of assortment [*laughter*]; and now, this House, which is determined to pursue these "robber barons," has before it the plain question whether it will not merely leave to them the privilege of assorting us, but whether it will absolutely confer upon them the privilege of assortment by direct enactment on the part of Congress. [*Renewed laughter.*]
>
> Now I appeal to this House, engaged as it is in the pursuit of wicked monopolists, if it intends to confer upon them a privilege of assortment without rights of law? Why, surely we must have some Treasury regulations as to the method of assortment. [*Laughter.*] Are we to be assorted on the grounds of size? [*Great laughter.*] Am I to be put into one car because

75. For quotations by Crisp and Smalls, see *CR*, 48-2, 12/17/1884, 316.

76. Christopher, *America's Black Congressmen*, 154.

77. Here Breckenridge harked back to the Civil Rights Act of 1875 — repudiated by the Supreme Court — which Southerners often called the "social equality bill."

of my size and the gentleman from Arkansas into another because of his? [*Renewed laughter and applause.*] Is this to be done on account of our unfortunate difference of measurement? Or are we to be assorted on the moustache grounds? Are we to be assorted on the question of complexion, or are we to be assorted on the beard basis?

If not any of these, what basis of assortment are we to have? For my part I object to having these "robber barons" overlook and assort us on any whimsical basis they undertake to set up. [*Laughter.*]

Why, surely, Mr. Speaker, this House, engaged as it in putting down discriminations against good men, can not tolerate an amendment of this character for an instant. [*Applause.*][78]

Reagan responded by referring to Reed as "facetious" and argued that railroad conductors by "universal practice" possessed the power to sort people, so as, for example, to keep a "drunken man or a rowdy or a desperado" out of "a lady's car." Further, he asked, "Now, does the gentleman insist on his humor in getting up a laugh about assorting people, or does he wish to pile all sorts of people and all classes into the same car?" Moreover, Reagan stated that he attached "no importance to [O'Hara's amendment]," because "it simply reaffirms the common law and the law and the practice in every Southern State in this Union."[79]

A short but spirited debate ensued over the actual intent and consequences of the O'Hara amendment. Crisp suggested the amendment's purpose was "to prevent a separation of the colors" (or to desegregate accommodations in interstate travel). Barclay Henley (D-CA) remarked that he was not sure of O'Hara's intent but believed that the "the introduction of this race question, this social question, . . . was seized upon by the other side and taken up for the purpose . . . of defeating [the Reagan bill], a bill designed to relieve the people of this great Republic against the exactions and aggressions of the railroad companies." Ethelbert Barksdale (D-MS) asserted that he would vote for the Reagan bill, even encumbered with the O'Hara amendment, since he felt that the amendment's provisions "[do] not prevent railroad companies from providing separate accommodations for persons, provided they are equally comfortable." Thomas Browne (R-IN) spoke more broadly, arguing that "emancipation, citizenship, and enfran-

78. *CR*, 48-2, 12/17/1884, 317.
79. *CR*, 48-2, 12/17/1884, 317–18.

chisement have come, and the social relations between races continue, as they were, a matter of personal choice,"[80] but that the current question was *not* a social question but rather one of commerce: "It is a question between common carriers, engaged in transportation of passengers for hire and exacting particular fare in return of particular accommodations agreed to be furnished by them and the passenger. That is the contract."[81]

Finally the question of adopting the Breckenridge substitute (in lieu of the Crisp amendment) was before the House. It was defeated on an 80-111 division vote, after which Holman demanded the yeas and nays.[82] After some parliamentary back-and-forth, the yeas and nays were called, and the result flipped as the Breckenridge substitute was adopted 137-127. Most Northern Democrats joined with almost all Southern Democrats to oppose and defeat the mass of Republicans.[83] The House then moved to consider the Breckenridge substitute as an amendment to the O'Hara amendment, and it passed—first on a 148-117 division vote and then on a 137-131 roll call (after Reed demanded the yeas and nays). Again, most Northern Democrats joined with all Southern Democrats to defeat a unified bloc of Republicans.[84]

Thus the Democrats had succeeded in granting railroads the discretion "to classify passengers" as they deemed fit. This was a distinct victory, but if Democratic leaders thought they were in the clear, they were mistaken. Nathan Goff (R-WV) was recognized and sought to add the following to the end of the Breckenridge substitute: "*Provided*, That no discrimination is made on account of race or color."[85] A roll call followed, and the

---

80. Browne went on to tweak the Democrats regarding their fear of race-based social equality laws: "Gentlemen do not seem to know that this question of social life is not, never was, and never can be regulated by law. It is a question of individual tastes. I associate with gentlemen because I believe them to be my social equals. I decline to associate with other gentlemen, whether they be white or black, because I do not so regard them. If this was a statute to make a colored Republican equal to a white Democrat I should vote against it. I would not vote for it. It could not be possible either to reduce the one or to elevate the other by an act of Congress. [*Laughter.*]" See *CR*, 48-2, 12/17/1884, 320.

81. For quotations by Crisp, Henley, Barksdale, and Browne, see *CR*, 48-2, 12/17/1884, 318-20.

82. *CR*, 48-2, 12/17/1884, 320.

83. *CR*, 48-2, 12/17/1884, 320-21. Northern Democrats voted 67-22, Southern Democrats 67-4, Republicans 1-98, Greenbackers 1-1, and Independents 1-2.

84. *CR*, 48-2, 12/17/1884, 321-22. Northern Democrats voted 66-25, Southern Democrats 70-0, Republicans 0-102, Greenbackers 0-2, and Independents 1-2.

85. *CR*, 48-2, 12/17/1884, 323.

Goff amendment passed 141-102. A small majority of Northern Democrats now joined with all Republicans to defeat a near-unified group of Southern Democrats.[86] Goff then moved to reconsider the move and also to table the motion to reconsider—but Reagan pushed for adjournment, which was granted.[87] As had happened the day before, Reagan needed to regroup, since his interstate commerce bill (now with Goff's amendment attached) was once again in danger.

The following day Goff's tabling motion was considered and passed, first on an 87-77 division vote and then on a 140-108 roll call (after Reagan demanded the yeas and nays). All Republicans joined with a minority of Northern Democrats to defeat a near-unified group of Southern Democrats.[88] Thus the motion to reconsider the vote on the Goff amendment was tabled. The pro-discrimination Democrats now turned to negating the impact of the Goff amendment. Here Barksdale reentered the fray by moving an amendment to the Goff amendment, which would add the following words (as a clause) after the word "color": "And that furnishing separate accommodations, with equal facilities and equal comfort, at the same charges, shall not be considered a discrimination."[89] Barksdale's amendment passed, first 112-81 on a division vote and then 132-124 on a roll call (after Republican Roswell Horr of Michigan demanded the yeas and nays).[90] Barksdale then moved to reconsider the vote by which his amendment was adopted and to table the motion to reconsider—and it was agreed to. The antidiscrimination forces would make one last push, as Horr moved an amendment to the Barksdale amendment, which would add these words (as a clause) after the word "discrimination": "*Provided*, That such separation shall not be made on the basis of race or color."[91] Horr's amendment failed 114-121 on a roll call, with a larger proportion of Northern Democrats than on previous votes joining with all Southern Democrats to oppose all Republicans.[92]

86. *CR*, 48-2, 12/17/1884, 323. Northern Democrats voted 41-35, Southern Democrats 2-66, Republicans 94-0, Greenbackers 2-0, and Independents 2-1.

87. *CR*, 48-2, 12/17/1884, 323.

88. *CR*, 48-2, 12/18/1884, 332. Northern Democrats voted 37-41, Southern Democrats 2-66, Republicans 97-0, Greenbackers 2-0, and Independents 2-1.

89. *CR*, 48-2, 12/18/1884, 332.

90. *CR*, 48-2, 12/18/1884, 332-33. Northern Democrats voted 62-21, Southern Democrats 68-1, Republicans 0-99, Greenbackers 0-2, and Independents 2-1.

91. *CR*, 48-2, 12/18/1884, 339.

92. *CR*, 48-2, 12/18/1884, 343. Northern Democrats voted 19-56, Southern Democrats 0-63, Republicans 93-0, Greenbackers 2-0, and Independents 0-2.

With the defeat of the Horr amendment, the matter of race, discrimination, and accommodations in interstate travel was settled. On January 8, 1885, the House would pass the Reagan bill 161-75. However, the Senate would not agree — passing instead a bill endorsed by Shelby Cullom (R-IL), which called for a regulatory commission (and thus was similar to a bill Reagan had earlier pushed aside in the House). Eventually a bill was agreed to (in conference) in the Forty-Ninth Congress (1885-87) that included both a commission (a demand of Cullom's) and an antipooling provision (a demand of Reagan's), among other compromises, and it was enacted on February 4, 1887, during the lame-duck session.[93] The Interstate Commerce Act made no specific mention of race but instead included (in section 3) somewhat ambiguous language regarding what constituted discriminatory behavior by railroads:

> It shall be unlawful for any common carrier subject to the provisions of this part to make, give, or cause any undue or unreasonable preference or advantage to any particular person, company, firm, corporation, association, locality, port, port district, gateway, transit point, region, district, territory, or any particular description of traffic, in any respect whatsoever; or to subject any particular person, company, firm, corporation, association, locality, port, port district, gateway, transit point, region, district, territory, or any particular description of traffic to any undue or unreasonable prejudice or disadvantage in any respect whatsoever.

For this O'Hara no doubt deserves credit, since there was no attempt to speak to the nature of personal accommodations in interstate commerce before he offered his amendment in late 1884. And the section 3 provision would form the foundation of antidiscrimination rulings — in response to acts of racial segregation in train and bus service, in keeping with state code — by the Supreme Court decades later in *Mitchell v. United States* (1941), *Morgan v. Virginia* (1946), *Henderson v. United States* (1950), *Keys v. Carolina Coach Co.* (1955), and *Boyton v. Virginia* (1960).[94] In 1961 the Interstate Commerce Commission (ICC), at the behest of Attorney General Robert Ken-

93. 24 *Stat.* 379. For a discussion of these political dynamics, see Ben H. Proctor, *Not without Honor: The Life of John H. Reagan* (Austin: University of Texas Press, 1962), 255-60.

94. Derek Charles Catsam, *Freedom's Main Line: The Journey of Reconciliation and the Freedom Rides* (Lexington: University Press of Kentucky, 2009). The Court's rulings in the *Mitchell* and *Henderson* cases overturned initial ICC decisions that favored the interstate carriers.

nedy, would require all interstate bus companies to display the following message in all their buses: "Seating aboard this vehicle is without regard to race, color, creed, or national origin, by order of the Interstate Commerce Commission."[95]

One question that permeates the entire O'Hara amendment episode is, Why did a significant number of Northern Democrats—and sometimes a *majority*—join with Republicans in support of civil rights legislation that was anathema to their Southern fellow partisans?[96] According to David Bateman, Ira Katznelson, and John Lapinski, "Although there were probably some Democrats, North and South, who supported the amendment in order to kill the bill, contemporaries mostly understood the northern Democratic support as an extension of their recent efforts during the 1884 presidential campaign to cultivate support among northern black voters."[97] In fact, while Southern Democrats routinely used violence and intimidation against blacks in the former Confederacy, since 1873 Northern Democrats had been reaching out to black voters in their localities—often with little to show for their efforts, but with occasional successes.[98]

Finally, the question of Republicans' political intent deserves consideration. Was their support of the O'Hara amendment in 1884 sincere, or was it a strategic attempt to kill legislation (the Reagan bill) they opposed? And if such an attempt was strategic, commentators at the time—in thinly veiled racist terms—wondered whether O'Hara himself was capable of designing the antidiscrimination rider. More likely, these commentators believed, O'Hara was the willing dupe of Thomas Reed or, perhaps, the presidents or attorneys of the railroads.[99] Of course, O'Hara introduced civil rights legis-

95. Halil Kürşad Aslan, "Civil Rights Movement," in *The Sage Encyclopedia of Economics and Society*, ed. Frederick F. Wherry and Juliet B. Schor (Thousand Oaks, CA: Sage, 2015), 380–85.

96. Lawrence Grossman breaks the Northern Democrats into subregional groups on the O'Hara, Breckinridge, Goff, and Barksdale amendment votes and finds that Democrats from New England, the Middle Atlantic, and the Midwest were the most supportive of black rights. Democrats from the Far West and border states generally joined the Southern Democrats in opposing black rights. See Grossman, *Democratic Party and the Negro*, 110–12.

97. David A. Bateman, Ira Katznelson, and John S. Lapinski, *Southern Nation: Congress and White Supremacy after Reconstruction* (Princeton, NJ: Princeton University Press, 2018), 130.

98. For a detailed discussion of Northern Democrats' efforts in this regard from 1873 to 1892, see Grossman, *Democratic Party and the Negro*, 60–106.

99. See Anderson, *Race and Politics in North Carolina*, 123.

lation in the Forty-Eighth Congress both *before and after* offering his amendment in December 1884.[100] And on the general matter of sincere vs. strategic behavior on the part of the GOP the evidence is unclear, since explaining Republicans' votes is confounded by "observational equivalence." That is, sincere and strategic behavior are both consistent with—or predict—the same thing: opposition to discrimination.

Federal Aid to Education

As Congress dealt with discrimination in interstate travel, members also fought over providing federal funds for education. The best-known and most protracted example was legislation offered by Senator Henry Blair (R-NH) to provide federal aid for public elementary schools in a race-blind way so that both white and black children would be better educated. His efforts spanned five Congresses—the Forty-Seventh through the Fifty-First—in total. Less well known was the bill offered by Senator Justin Morrill (R-VT), during the Fifty-First Congress, which sought to expand the program he started in 1862 to fund public land-grant colleges for the study of agriculture and mechanical arts. Morrill's expansion initiative also sought to be race-blind in its disbursement of funds. Of the two legislative measures, only Morrill's bill would pass, and only after language was added via amendment that satisfied Southern senators.

THE BLAIR EDUCATION BILL(S)

As white redeemers worked to erode the gains black Southerners made during Reconstruction, W. E. B. Du Bois wrote that the "dream of political power" was replaced with "the ideal of 'book learning.'" "Here at last," he argued, "seemed to have been discovered the mountain path to Canaan; longer than the highway of Emancipation and law, steep and rugged, but straight, leading to heights high enough to overlook life."[101] Education proved no substitute for political power. But by skillfully describing the emergence of education as a Redemption era political project, Du Bois con-

100. Bateman, Katznelson, and Lapinski make a similar argument in characterizing O'Hara's amendment as a "sincere effort by its author to reestablish some measure of protection for African Americans in the wake of the recent Supreme Court ruling." See Bateman, Katznelson, and Lapinski, *Southern Nation*, 130.

101. W. E. B Du Bois, *The Souls of Black Folk*, ed. Henry Louis Gates Jr. and Terry Hume Oliver (New York: Norton, 1999), 13.

FIGURE 9.   Sen. Henry Blair (R-NH). Library of Congress, Prints & Photographs Division, LC-DIG-cwpbh-04463.

textualizes the effort mounted by Senator Henry Blair (R-NH) to pass legis-lation providing federal aid to public ("common") schools.

First elected to the House in 1875, Henry Blair immediately demon-strated an interest in the American educational system. He saw education as a policy area that could help the GOP in the South by appealing to the inter-ests of both white and black voters. Educational opportunities were central to the aspirations of freedmen in particular. From 1865 to 1870, the Freedmen's Bureau spent more than $5 million on schools throughout the South. By July 1870 there were 4,239 schools, employing 9,307 teachers and educating 247,333 students.[102] Blair recognized the value of these schools, and in 1876 he argued, "We are rapidly nearing the time when the American people will vote directly upon the question, 'Shall the common-school system, which is under God the source and defense of American liberty, continue to exist?'"[103] For Blair and many of his supporters, education was central to the survival of republican government.

After serving two House terms, Blair was elected to the Senate in 1879. In his first Senate term he was made chairman of the Committee on Education and Labor. In December 1881 he introduced S. 151 "to aid in the establishment and temporary support of common schools."[104] As written, the bill called for $105 million in federal appropriations distributed to each state over ten years based on the number of "illiterates"—those unable to write—living within its borders. This provision guaranteed that approximately 75 percent of all money appropriated would go to Southern states, because illiteracy rates there were dramatically higher than in the North or West.[105] S. 151 also mandated that recipient states appropriate funds equal to those provided by the federal government. In its first year the federal government would spend $15 million; for each subsequent year the total appropriation would decrease by $1 million. Blair structured the bill in this way to preempt arguments that he was proposing a federal takeover of the nation's schools. He claimed that the allocation formula would allow states to use federal funding to jump-start self-sustaining public education systems. Permanent federal intervention would therefore not be necessary.[106] To ensure that the funds were distributed fairly, the bill created a federal supervisor for each state who was empowered to recommend rescinding funds as punishment for fraud or misuse.

102. W. E. B. Du Bois, *Black Reconstruction in America, 1860–1880* (New York: Harcourt, Brace, 1935), 648.

103. Blair quoted in Daniel W. Crofts, "The Black Response to the Blair Education Bill," *Journal of Southern History* 37 (1971): 47.

104. *CR*, 47-1, 12/6/1881, 21.

105. Crofts, "Black Response to the Blair Education Bill," 42. According to data included in the 1880 census, eight of the eleven states of the Confederacy had illiteracy rates over 40 percent. Among freedmen specifically, the illiteracy rate topped 75 percent. For more, see "Support of Common Schools," H.R. Rep. No. 495, 48th Cong., 1st Sess., 1–5.

106. *CR*, 47-1, 12/20/1881, 226–28.

In an important concession to the South, S. 151 "demanded literal adherence to the idea of 'separate but equal.'"[107] In particular it stipulated, "Nothing herein shall deprive children of different races, living in the same community but attending separate schools, from receiving the benefits of this act, the same as though the attendance therein were without distinction of race."[108] This provision sought to guarantee that the only way white children would benefit from federal money would be for states to ensure that schools for white and black children received an equal portion of total funds spent. If states did not provide an equal allocation to black schools, they would forgo federal support. As we discuss below, Blair's defense of "separate but equal" did not prevent black political organizations from rallying around the bill.

In advocating for his bill, Blair marshaled mountains of census data designed to reveal the condition of public education in the country. He illustrated just how little Southern states in particular were doing to educate their children. From Blair's perspective, republican government would survive only if the public could read and write. Commenting on the South, Blair characterized universal education as "part of the [Civil] War" insofar as North and South were now combating the "forces of ignorance" that put the nation's survival in jeopardy.[109] Federal funding for elementary and secondary schools was an important way the government worked to preserve itself.[110] Accordingly, Blair argued, the opportunity for learning must "be provided at the public charge."[111] Many Southern Democrats endorsed this view. Senator Lucius Lamar (D-MS), for example, declared his support for S. 151 because "no state could stand secure but on the ground of right, virtue, knowledge, and truth."[112]

Congress took no action on Blair's proposal before adjournment in August 1882. Between August and December, when Congress reconvened in a lame-duck session, President Arthur, the American Social Science Association, and the National Education Assembly endorsed S. 151.[113] The Interstate Education Alliance—a coalition of white Southern educators, associations

107. Crofts, "Black Response to the Blair Education Bill," 43.

108. *CR*, 47-1, 6/13/1882, 4833.

109. *CR*, 47-1, 6/13/1882, 4831.

110. *CR*, 47-1, 6/13/1882, 4820-33.

111. *CR*, 47-1, 6/13/1882, 4824.

112. "Education in the South," *WP*, March 29, 1884, 1.

113. Gordon B. McKinney, *Henry W. Blair's Campaign to Reform America: From the Civil War to the U.S. Senate* (Lexington: University Press of Kentucky, 2013), 91.

of state superintendents, and other local civic organizations in Southern states — also mobilized behind the bill. From 1881 to 1883 Congress also received 272 petitions — 225 from the South — in support of S. 151.[114]

Responding to these demonstrations of support, Blair moved quickly to procure a special order that would bring his bill up for debate. Here he was opposed by John Logan (R-IL), who had drafted his own education proposal and did not want to set it aside. Where Blair's bill sought to fund education through general revenue, Logan's aimed to raise funds through a new tax on whiskey.[115] Logan also opposed appropriating money in proportion to state illiteracy rates, arguing "that the proposition to distribute this money according to illiteracy is a proposition to ask a certain number of states to pay taxes to educate others. I do not think the country is in favor of any such proposition."[116] The sectional rivalry motivating Logan's opposition would consistently handicap Blair's efforts. In early 1883, however, Republican infighting simply led the Senate to table both education bills until the next Congress.[117]

When the Forty-Eighth Congress (1883–85) convened in December 1883, Blair immediately reintroduced his bill (now S. 398).[118] By this time the political environment had shifted considerably, and the Democrats now controlled the House. But with a Republican president and a two-vote GOP majority in the Senate, the Republicans retained significant political influence. Yet the new political context convinced Blair that enactment would be impossible without the support of Southern members. As a result, there were key substantive differences between S. 151 and S. 398. Highly suspicious of federal intervention into state functions, Southern Democrats opposed the supervisor position written into S. 151. Blair proved willing to drop that section and instead allow for state administration of funds.[119]

Blair also worked to maintain Southern support by protecting funding for states with segregated schools. Despite being a concession to Southern whites, this provision did not disqualify the bill in the eyes of many black

114. Gordon Canfield Lee, *The Struggle for Federal Aid, First Phase: A History of the Attempts to Obtain Federal Aid for the Common Schools, 1870–1890* (New York: Bureau of Publications, Teachers College, Columbia University, 1949), 95.

115. Daniel W. Crofts, "The Blair Bill and the Elections Bill: The Congressional Aftermath to Reconstruction" (PhD diss., Yale University, 1968), 55.

116. *CR*, 47-2, 1/9/1883, 1015.

117. Crofts, "Blair Bill and the Elections Bill," 55.

118. *CR*, 48-1, 12/5/1883, 36.

119. McKinney, *Henry Blair's Campaign to Reform America*, 92.

citizens. An April 1884 story in the *Washington Post*, for example, recounts a "largely attended mass meeting" organized by the Union Bethel Historical and Literary Association to support Blair's bill.[120] Frederick Douglass and other notable black public intellectuals were among those at the meeting.[121] Black teachers' associations in some Southern states also lobbied elected officials to support the bill.[122] While Daniel Crofts makes it clear that not all black civic organizations and leaders were supportive, he notes that many considered federal education funding a "ray of hope."[123] Thus Blair's bill proved an effective vehicle for Republicans motivated to continue reaching out to black voters.

Debate on Blair's new proposal began in March 1884. S. 398 proposed to distribute $105 million over ten years. It called for allocating funds to states based on the illiteracy rate, required states to match one-third of federal funds appropriated over the first five years after enactment and to match dollar-for-dollar during the last five years, and allowed states — rather than a federal authority — to oversee the expenditures.[124] Recognizing that an endorsement of "separate but equal" was politically questionable, Blair spent significant time defending the provision. "The distribution shall be made in such a way as to equalize the money that goes to each child per capita throughout the state . . . to produce an equalization of school privileges throughout the state. I do not think that anything could be more just," he proclaimed.[125] Blair would trust Southern states to distribute the money equally, and if they did not, Congress would punish them accordingly.

Senate consideration of S. 398 ran through April. Over the course of four weeks, Blair again confronted sectional opposition from fellow Republicans. For example, John Ingalls (R-KS) doubted that "we are under any obligation to educate the blacks of the south."[126] Similarly, Joseph Dolph (R-OR) argued that the states outside the South had no obligation to give former

---

120. "The Blair Educational Bill: A Mass Meeting Held by Colored Citizens to Urge Its Passage," *WP*, April 16, 1884, 1.

121. Douglass would continue speaking on behalf of the bill until it failed for the final time in 1890. See "Douglass to His Race: A Notable Address Delivered by the Colored Statesman," *WP*, October 22, 1890, 7.

122. Willard B. Gatewood Jr., "North Carolina and Federal Aid to Education: Public Reaction to the Blair Bill, 1881–1890," *North Carolina Historical Review* 40 (1963): 474.

123. Crofts, "Black Response to the Blair Education Bill," 51.

124. McKinney, *Henry Blair's Campaign to Reform America*, 93.

125. *CR*, 48-1, 4/7/1884, 2715.

126. Ingalls quoted in Crofts, "Blair Bill and the Elections Bill," 64.

Confederate states funds to educate their poor white citizens or poor black citizens.[127] Further testifying to the strength of GOP opposition, a March 1884 article in the *Washington Post* argued that, should the bill fail, Republican "sectional conspirators" would be to blame.[128] Democrats, on the other hand, tended to object for "constitutional" reasons. The 1884 Democratic Party platform, for example, declared the party "opposed to all propositions which, upon any pretext, would convert the general government into a machine for collecting taxes to be distributed among the states or the citizens thereof."[129] Contemporaneous news accounts attribute this provision to those who opposed Blair's bill.[130]

In order to agree on a compromise measure, Senate Republicans met in caucus and appointed a nine-member committee to develop a consensus approach to federal funding.[131] The revised measure called for an appropriation of $77 million distributed over eight years, stipulated that states would not receive more money from the federal government than they spent on education at the state/local level, required that black schools and white schools receive equal funding, and mandated that states submit annual reports to the federal government detailing how they spent the money they received.[132]

On April 7, 1884, the Senate passed Blair's bill 33-11. Republicans and Southern Democrats supported the bill by wide margins, while Northern Democrats largely opposed it.[133] GOP support, however, was weaker than the numbers suggest. Eleven Republicans—including many of the bill's most outspoken opponents—chose to absent themselves instead of voting nay.[134] And as sectional tensions increased during the latter half of the decade, Blair would find it harder to keep Southern Democrats in tow. But one thing evident from this roll call, along with all subsequent ones, was the dis-

127. *CR*, 48-1, 3/26/1884, 2285.

128. "Why the Blair Bill Is Opposed," *WP*, March 26, 1884, 2.

129. The platform can be read at http://www.presidency.ucsb.edu/ws/index.php?pid=29583.

130. "The National Campaign: Effect of the Failure of the Blair School Bill on the Democrats," *CT*, August 24, 1884, 3.

131. Crofts, "Blair Bill and the Elections Bill," 67; "Republican Senatorial Caucus," *WP*, April 1, 1884, 1.

132. Crofts, "Blair Bill and the Elections Bill," 95.

133. *CR*, 48-1, 4/7/1884, 2724. Republicans voted 20-2, Southern Democrats 12-5, and Northern Democrats 1-4.

134. Crofts, "Blair Bill and the Elections Bill," 71.

tributive nature of the voting. Senators from states that would benefit more from the policy — because they had a high number of illiterates — were more supportive (after accounting for ideology, party, and region) than senators from states that would benefit less. All else equal, there was a positive relation between a state's illiteracy rate and a senator's vote. Regression results on all the Blair bill votes appear in appendixes 5.1 and 5.2.[135]

Senate passage was just the first step for Blair and his supporters; they would need to get a similar bill through the House, where Democrats were in control. House Speaker John Carlisle (D-KY) was an outspoken opponent of the bill and used his institutional power to prevent the House from considering it before adjourning in early fall 1884.[136] This delay would prove particularly important because Democrat Grover Cleveland defeated Republican James Blaine in the November 1884 presidential election. As a consequence, as Gordon McKinney notes, "many Republicans who felt comfortable with a Republican president overseeing the Southern Democrats administration of the program were much less enthusiastic about having a Democratic administration in charge."[137]

Because the Forty-Eighth Congress took no additional action on his bill, Blair reintroduced it in January 1886, near the start of the Forty-Ninth Congress (1885–87). Public support for the proposal (now S. 194) was still high as measured by the number of supportive petitions received, a threefold increase over the previous Congress.[138] Before congressional debate on S. 194 began, Blair wrote to President Cleveland trying to win his support.[139] He also worked hard to convince skeptical Republicans that the Democratic

135. We tap distributive politics using the percentage of individuals in a state at least ten years of age who could not write (and thus were considered "illiterate"). Data on illiteracy were drawn from the 1880 US Census. The expectation is that senators from states with a greater (lesser) proportion of illiterates would benefit more (less) from the provisions of the Blair bill, and thus all else being equal would have a greater (lesser) likelihood of supporting the legislation. We also include NOMINATE scores (appendix 5.1) and party and region (appendix 5.2) as covariates in the models.

136. James Barnes, *John G. Carlisle: Financial Statesman* (New York: Dodd, Mead, 1931), 110–12, 152–53. Carlisle — a tariff reformer — tied education funding to the tariff in that he opposed any policy that would spend down the federal surplus generated from high tariff rates.

137. McKinney, *Henry W. Blair's Campaign to Reform America*, 97.

138. Lee, *Struggle for Federal Aid, First* Phase, 95. The Forty-Eighth Congress received 151 petitions; the Forty-Ninth Congress received 465. Beginning in the Forty-Eighth Congress, the Northeast became the predominant region originating petitions.

139. Crofts, "Blair Bill and the Elections Bill," 106.

president could be trusted to administer the program. Although Cleveland chose not to take a position on the bill, Blair won over his GOP colleagues. The bill passed 36-11, with twenty of twenty-five Republicans voting yea.[140]

Here again, however, the vote tally obscures Republican opposition. Echoing many of the objections made in 1884, John Ingalls (R-KS) inveighed against the bill because of its lopsided distribution of funds to Southern states. He then introduced an amendment mandating that the federal government distribute aid based on the number of school-age children living in a given state instead of the number of illiterates. If adopted, this amendment would have significantly reduced the money committed to the South and put at risk the support of Southern Democrats.[141] The amendment lost 18-22, but a majority of Republicans (twelve of twenty-one) voted for it.[142] Eugene Hale (R-ME) then sought to base funding on the "proportion that the illiteracy of white and colored persons . . . had to each other."[143] If passed, Hale's amendment would have required Southern states to devote significantly more money to black schools than to white schools. Hale's amendment also lost, 14-37, but a large minority of Republicans (fourteen of thirty-one) voted for it.[144] Despite the failure of both amendments, the GOP support they received suggested that a significant number of Republican senators were looking for a politically palatable way to undermine Blair's proposal.

Having passed the Senate, the bill moved to the Democratic-controlled House, where Speaker Carlisle was still in charge. To kill the bill, Carlisle packed the House Education Committee with members who opposed it. Recognizing the strength of the committee's opposition, House Republicans managed to move the bill to the Labor Committee.[145] The change in venues, however, created a different problem: the Labor Committee replaced the provisions allocating funding based on the number of illiterates living in a state with language guaranteeing all states an equal amount of federal aid.[146] This change was unpalatable to Blair's supporters, but House leadership would not allow a vote on legislation with language identical to

140. *CR*, 49-1, 3/5/1886, 2105. Northern Democrats voted 3-3 and Southern Democrats voted 13-3.

141. Crofts, "Blair Bill and the Elections Bill," 113.

142. *CR*, 49-1, 2/17/1886, 1561.

143. Crofts, "Blair Bill and the Elections Bill," 113.

144. *CR*, 49-2, 3/5/1886, 2102.

145. McKinney, *Henry Blair's Campaign to Reform America*, 119.

146. Crofts, "Blair Bill and the Elections Bill," 126.

S. 194. In the end, the House did not consider any federal aid proposals, so Blair was once again stymied.

In January 1888, at the beginning of the Fiftieth Congress (1887–89), Blair once again introduced his bill (now S. 371). Public support (as measured by petitions) was at its highest level ever.[147] During the debate, Blair's adversaries took their usual positions. Some Democrats opposed the measure because they did not believe in educating black citizens. John Morgan (D-AL), for example, claimed that state-sponsored schooling for black children would keep them "out of the cotton fields, where their labor was needed."[148] More important than these racist arguments, however, was the growing amount of cross-party opposition from those who believed federal aid would do more harm than good. Summing up the position of these members, a *New York Times* editorial in February 1888 stated that "one of the most precious rights of a State is that character for stability and self-control which comes of the necessity of taking care of its own interests."[149]

As he had in the past, Blair overcame his opponents, and S. 371 passed 39-29.[150] The number of Republicans voting against the bill, however, grew significantly (from five to twelve) in just two years—signaling increasing skepticism among Blair's fellow partisans. In the House, the Democrats were still in the majority, and Speaker Carlisle once again killed the bill by sending it to the Education Committee.[151] Some Republicans attempted to discharge the committee, but they failed.

The GOP won a landslide victory in the election of 1888 and would enjoy unified control of government in the Fifty-First Congress (1889–91). Blair took this victory as a sign that the time had finally come for his bill to be enacted. Yet because Blair's bill relied so much on the Southern Democratic support, the Republican landslide generated a new political problem: sectional tensions were on the rise, and Democrats in the South "awaited

147. Lee, *Struggle for Federal Aid, First* Phase, 95. The Fiftieth Congress received 515 petitions.

148. Crofts, "Blair Bill and the Elections Bill," 159.

149. "Education and State Rights," *NYT*, February 15, 1888, 4.

150. *CR*, 50-1, 2/15/1888, 1223. Republicans voted 23-12, Southern Democrats 14-8, and Northern Democrats 2-9.

151. As a reporter for the *St. Louis Post-Dispatch* noted: "The House Education Committee had a sharp fight this morning on the Blair Education Bill, and finally, as predicted in these dispatches, voted to table it. This practically kills the bill." See "Washington," *St. Louis News-Dispatch*, March 12, 1886, 2.

the Republican rule with growing suspicion." Racial violence was on the upswing and, according to Albion Tourgee, a longtime advocate for black rights in the South, the year 1890 represented "the most dangerous epoch [for blacks] since 1860."[152] As a result, Southern Democrats proved more skeptical of all GOP-initiated federal programs.[153] Republicans, too, did not interpret their victory as a mandate to implement Blair's education proposal. Instead, they now believed conciliation was unnecessary. Moreover, according to Stanley Hirshson, the 1888 election had produced a rift between those Republicans who wanted to "play down the Negro question and emphasize the tariff issue" and those who were unwilling to sacrifice the party's long-standing commitment to blacks in the South.[154]

Debate on Blair's bill (now S. 185) began for the final time on February 5, 1890. By this point the arguments for and against the bill were so well known that few members lingered in the chamber to hear Blair make his case. According to one contemporaneous account, "When Mr. Blair began his speech there was a general exodus of senators on both sides of the chamber, and of the eighty-two senators, only five remained while Blair was talking. The press gallery also vacated."[155] Giving voice to the opinion of many senators, an editorial in the *New York Times* characterized Blair as a "bore" and argued that he continued to advocate for the bill simply to "relieve his own mind."[156]

What distinguished this stage of the debate from those preceding it, according to Blair, was that "several leading Republicans who had always supported the bill . . . would do so no longer."[157] This pattern started with President Benjamin Harrison, who, in his first annual message as president, chose not to provide an endorsement. Only three years earlier, Harrison had implored the Senate to pass the Blair bill so that "an increasing body of Southern men" would be taught to show a more "kindly disposition toward the elevation of the colored man." In early 1889, however, Harrison expressed dissatisfaction with the bill's plan to appropriate money over eight years. "One Congress cannot bind a succeeding one," he now argued.[158] Furthermore, when Republicans called for a final vote on the measure in March

---

152. Tourgee quoted in Crofts, "Blair Bill and the Elections Bill," 235.

153. Crofts, "Blair Bill and the Elections Bill," 181.

154. Hirshson, *Farewell to the Bloody Shirt*, 143–67.

155. McKinney, *Henry W. Blair's Campaign to Reform America*, 127.

156. "Senator Blair's Speech," *NYT*, February 21, 1890, 4.

157. McKinney, *Henry W. Blair's Campaign to Reform America*, 129.

158. Crofts, "Blair Bill and the Elections Bill," 198.

1890, President Harrison did not explicitly call on Senate Republicans to vote yea.[159]

In an interview published in the *New York Mail and Press*, Blair recounted his dawning awareness that a significant number of Republicans had turned against the measure. "If an early vote was taken," Blair recalled, "the bill would be defeated by about a ten or twelve [vote] majority." In response, he "adopted the tactics of getting time." From February 17 to 20, Blair mounted a one-man "reverse filibuster" on behalf of his bill. Over these four days he begged Republicans to honor their obligations to the freedmen. "You can reconstruct the South," Blair argued, "in no other way than by beginning with the children."[160]

Despite Blair's pleas and his delaying tactics, the bill could not overcome the sectional animosities plaguing the Fifty-First Congress. Outraged by the murder of a deputy US marshal in Florida, Republicans condemned South-erners for failing to protect those responsible for enforcing federal law. Act-ing on their anger, some previous supporters of the bill now argued that it conceded too much to the South. Meanwhile, Southerners threatened once again to withhold their support if the bill placed any conditions on how the money could be spent or if it included any mechanism for federal oversight. Blair's bill, argued Wilkinson Call (D-FL), provided black citizens with "no claim to social or political equality."[161]

After nearly two months of debate on the measure, Blair agreed to bring S. 185 to a vote. Newspaper accounts published on March 20, 1890, predicted a close result, but, according to Daniel Crofts and Gordon McKinney, Blair was confident he had the necessary support to ensure its enactment.[162] He had miscalculated, and the bill failed 31-37.[163] "Sometime during the night," Blair recalled in an interview, Henry Payne (D-OH) and John Sherman (R-OH) both decided to reverse positions and oppose the measure. Sher-man's reversal in particular surprised Blair.[164] Yet Sherman was not alone; the final vote tally reveals that slightly more than 42 percent of Republicans (seventeen of forty) now opposed federal education aid. And a majority of Southern Democrats (nine of sixteen) also voted against the bill.

159. McKinney, *Henry W. Blair's Campaign to Reform America*, 129.

160. Blair interview quoted in Crofts, "Blair Bill and the Elections Bill," 199–201.

161. Quoted in Crofts, "Blair Bill and the Elections Bill," 203.

162. Crofts, "Blair Bill and the Elections Bill," 203; McKinney, *Henry W. Blair's Campaign to Reform America*, 128–29.

163. *CR*, 51-1, 3/20/1890, 2436.

164. Crofts, "Blair Bill and the Elections Bill," 208–10.

Exactly how did Blair's coalition fall apart? We can examine this by look-ing at individual voting decisions—including "pairing"—by party across the four Senate roll-call votes.[165] Republicans appear in table 5.1. First, there were very few explicit vote switchers. Only four Republicans switched their votes from yea to nay across the series of votes: William Frey of Maine (Forty-Eighth to Forty-Ninth), John Spooner of Wisconsin (Forty-Ninth to Fiftieth), Philetus Sawyer of Wisconsin (Fiftieth to Fifty-First), and Henry Blair (Fiftieth to Fifty-First).[166] Some change occurred from replacement, as a senator who voted yea was replaced by one who voted nay. Examples in-cluded John Logan to Charles Farwell (Forty-Ninth to Fiftieth) in Illinois, Warner Miller to Frank Hiscock (Forty-Ninth to Fiftieth) in New York, and Thomas Bowen to Edward Wolcott (Fiftieth to Fifty-First) in Colorado. But a range of others moved from not voting to nay—like John Sherman (OH) and Nelson Aldrich (RI)—or abstained on a key vote—like Matthew Quay (PA) and J. David Cameron (PA). Ultimately, the erosion of Republican sup-port occurred in multiple ways.[167]

Democrats appear in table 5.2. Some significant vote switches occurred between the Forty-Ninth and Fiftieth Congresses as Daniel Voorhees (IN), Joseph Blackburn (KY), and John Kenna (WV) all changed from yea to nay, while William Bate (TN) voted nay after replacing Howell Jackson (TN), who had voted yea in the previous Congress. Between the Fiftieth and Fifty-First Congresses, three Southern Democrats switched from yea to nay— James Berry (AR), James Jones (AR), and Edward Walthall (MS)—while

165. "Pairing" occurs when two members on opposite sides of an issue agree to be absent when it comes to a vote so that their absence has no effect on its outcome. Pairing allows an absent member to have recorded (in the *Congressional Record*) how he would have voted had he been present.

166. Blair switched from yea to nay before the clerk finalized his count. Blair did this be-cause he saw that his proposal was about to lose, and by switching before the final tabula-tion was announced he put himself in a position (by Senate rules) to call for reconsideration. Without his switch, the final tally would have been 32–36.

167. Blair lost on the roll call in the Fifty-First Congress despite benefiting from the sig-nificant support (four yea votes against only one nay vote) of Republicans from three new states: North Dakota, South Dakota, and Washington. These states were brought into the Union by an ambitious Republican Party, which saw the unified party control of govern-ment as a unique (and strategic) opportunity. See Charles Stewart III and Barry R. Wein-gast, "Stacking the Senate, Changing the Nation: Republican Rotten Boroughs, Statehood Politics, and American Political Development," *Studies in American Political Development* 6 (1992): 223–71.

four others who voted yea in the Fiftieth Congress chose to pair off or not vote at all—Wilkinson Call (FL), James Eustis (LA), Matt Ransom (NC), and Zebulon Vance (NC). Henry Payne (OH) also switched from yea to nay.

In explaining the loss of Southern Democratic support on the final Blair bill vote, scholars have typically focused on race as the motivating factor; that is, Southern Democrats feared that Republicans, now in control of the presidency and both chambers of Congress, might go back on some of their states' rights promises regarding the administration of the new education program.[168] On why Republicans turned against the Blair bill, scholars have not reached a consensus. Gordon McKinney suggests that Republicans from the Midwest believed economic issues were a higher priority than the education bill, while Daniel Crofts suggests that sectional tensions made Republicans believe Blair's bill was too conciliatory.[169] Regardless of the reason, enthusiasm for the Blair bill—marked by the number of petitions sent to Congress on behalf of the legislation—declined significantly between the Fiftieth and Fifty-First Congresses.[170] Perhaps reflecting this decline in support, increased GOP opposition emerged that led to the bill's defeat. Of course it had passed the Senate on three previous occasions, so there was no guarantee that Senate passage in the Fifty-First Congress portended enactment. Yet with a Republican president and a GOP majority in the House, this appeared to be Blair's best chance for success. By 1890, however, Senate Republicans looked askance at Blair's bill.

THE SECOND MORRILL ACT

Before completely moving on from federal aid to education, however, the Fifty-First Congress considered a separate bill "to apply a portion of the proceeds of the public lands to the more complete endowment and support of the colleges for the benefit of agriculture and the mechanical arts estab-

168. See, for example, Grossman, *Democratic Party and the Negro*, 119.

169. McKinney, *Henry W. Blair's Campaign to Reform America*, 126; Crofts, "Blair Bill and the Elections Bill," 209.

170. Petitions went from 515 in the Fiftieth Congress to 95 in the Fifty-First. Gordon Canfield Lee attributes this reduction to "those who, in the late 1880s, were arguing that Southern self-help had begun to solve the educational problem and therefore federal funds were no longer needed. There is evidence here to indicate that the desire on the part of Southerners for federal assistance had noticeably decreased by 1890." See Lee, *Struggle for Federal Aid, First Phase*, 96.

TABLE 5.1 Republican Votes in the Senate on the Blair Bill, 48th–51st Congresses

State	Name	48	49	50	51	State	Name	48	49	50	51
California	Miller, J. F.	N	NV	.	.	Nevada	Jones, J. P.	NV	N	N	N
California	Stanford, L.	.	pY	Y	Y	Nevada	Stewart, W.	.	.	Y	Y
Colorado	Bowen, T. M.	NV	Y	Y	.	New Hampshire	Blair, H. W.	Y	Y	Y	N
Colorado	Hill, N. P.	NV	.	.	.	New Hampshire	Pike, A. F.	Y	pY	.	.
Colorado	Teller, H.	.	Y	Y	Y	New Hampshire	Chandler, W.	.	.	Y	Y
Colorado	Wolcott, E.	.	.	.	N	New Jersey	Sewell, W. J.	NV	pN	.	.
Connecticut	Hawley, J. R.	N	pN	N	N	New York	Lapham, E. G.	pY	.	.	.
Connecticut	Platt, O. H.	Y	NV	Y	Y	New York	Miller, W.	Y	Y	.	Y
Delaware	Higgins, A.	.	.	.	Y	New York	Evarts, W.	.	Y	Y	N
Illinois	Cullom, S. M.	Y	Y	Y	Y	New York	Hiscock, F.	.	.	N	N
Illinois	Logan, J. A.	Y	Y	.	.	North Dakota	Casey, L. R.	.	.	.	NV
Illinois	Farwell, C.	.	.	N	N	North Dakota	Pierce, G. A	.	.	.	N
Indiana	Harrison, B.	Y	pY	.	.	Ohio	Sherman, J.	NV	NV	NV	N
Iowa	Allison, W. B	pY	NV	Y	Y	Oregon	Dolph, J. N.	Y	Y	Y	Y
Iowa	Wilson, J. F.	Y	Y	Y	Y	Oregon	Mitchell,	.	Y	Y	Y
Kansas	Ingalls, J. J.	pN	N	N	N	Pennsylvania	Cameron, J. D	NV	NV	Y	NV
Kansas	Plumb, P. B.	pN	N	N	N	Pennsylvania	Mitchell, J.	pY	pY	.	.

State	Senator				
Maine	Frye, W. P.	Y	N	N	N
Maine	Hale, E.	pN	N	N	N
Massachusetts	Dawes, H. L.	Y	pY	Y	Y
Massachusetts	Hoar, G. F.	Y	Y	Y	Y
Michigan	Conger, O. D.	Y	Y	.	.
Michigan	Palmer, T. W.	pY	Y	Y	.
Michigan	Stockbridge, F.	.	.	Y	Y
Michigan	McMillan, J.	.	.	.	Y
Minnesota	McMillan, S.	Y	pY	.	.
Minnesota	Sabin, D. M.	pN	NV	N	.
Minnesota	Davis, C. K.	.	.	N	N
Minnesota	Washburn, W	.	.	.	pN
Nebraska	Manderson, C	Y	Y	Y	Y
Nebraska	Van Wyck, C.	NV	Y	.	.
Nebraska	Paddock, A.	.	.	pY	pY
Pennsylvania	Quay, M. S.	.	.	Y	NV
Rhode Island	Aldrich, N. W	NV	NV	N	N
Rhode Island	Anthony, H. B	NV	.	.	.
Rhode Island	Chace, J.	.	pN	pN	.
Rhode Island	Dixon, N. F.	.	.	.	N
South Dakota	Moody, G. C.	.	.	.	Y
South Dakota	Pettigrew, R.	.	.	Y	Y
Vermont	Edmunds, G. F.	Y	pY	pY	Y
Vermont	Morrill, J. S	Y	Y	Y	Y
Virginia	Mahone, W.	NV	Y	.	.
Virginia	Riddleberger	Y	Y	Y	.
Washington	Allen, J. B.	.	.	.	Y
Washington	Squire, W. C	.	.	.	Y
Wisconsin	Cameron, A.	Y	.	.	.
Wisconsin	Sawyer, P.	Y	Y	Y	N
Wisconsin	Spooner, J.	.	Y	N	N

Note: Codes for votes are as follows: Y = yea; N = nay; pY = paired yea; pN = paired nay; NV = not voting; and . = not a member.

Light gray indicates a shift in support for the Blair bill by the same person. Dark gray indicates a shift in support for the Blair bill due to replacement (of one senator for another).

TABLE 5.2. Democratic Votes in the Senate on the Blair Bill, 48th–51st Congresses

State	Name	48	49	50	51
Alabama	Morgan, J. T.	N	pN	N	N
Alabama	Pugh, J. L.	Y	Y	Y	Y
Arkansas	Garland, A. H	Y	.	.	.
Arkansas	Walker, J. D.	pY	.	.	.
Arkansas	Berry, J. H.	.	Y	Y	N
Arkansas	Jones, J. K.	.	Y	Y	N
California	Farley, J. T.	pN	.	.	.
California	Hearst, G.	.	.	Y	Y
Delaware	Bayard, T. F.	N	.	.	.
Delaware	Saulsbury, E	N	pN	N	.
Delaware	Gray, G.	.	N	N	N
Florida	Call, W.	Y	Y	Y	pY
Florida	Jones, C. W.	Y	NV	.	.
Florida	Pasco, S.	.	.	Y	Y

State	Name	48	49	50	51
Mississippi	George, J. Z.	Y	Y	Y	Y
Mississippi	Lamar, L. Q. C	pY	.	.	.
Mississippi	Walthall, E.	.	Y	Y	N
Missouri	Cockrell, F.	NV	N	pN	N
Missouri	Vest, G. G.	pN	pN	N	N
Nevada	Fair, J. G.	NV	NV	.	.
New Jersey	McPherson, J	pN	NV	pN	pN
New Jersey	Blodgett, R.	.	.	N	N
North Carolina	Ransom, M. W.	Y	Y	Y	NV
North Carolina	Vance, Z. B.	pY	Y	Y	pY
Ohio	Pendleton, G	N	.	.	.
Ohio	Payne, H. B.	.	Y	Y	N
Oregon	Slater, J. H.	pN	.	.	.
South Carolina	Butler, M. C.	N	pN	N	NV

State	Senator					
Georgia	Brown, J. E.	Y	pY	Y	Y	NV
Georgia	Colquitt, A.	Y	Y	Y	Y	Y
Indiana	Voorhees, D.	pY	Y	N	N	N
Indiana	Turpie, D.	.	.	N	N	N
Kentucky	Beck, J. B.	pN	NV	N	N	pN
Kentucky	Williams, J.	Y	.	.	.	.
Kentucky	Blackburn, J.	.	Y	Y	N	N
Louisiana	Gibson, R. L.	pY	Y	pY	pY	pY
Louisiana	Jonas, B. F.	Y	.	.	.	.
Louisiana	Eustis, J.	.	Y	Y	Y	pN
Maryland	Gorman, A. P.	NV	pN	pN	N	N
Maryland	Groome, J. B.	N	.	.	.	.
Maryland	Wilson, E.	.	N	N	N	N

State	Senator					
South Carolina	Hampton, W.	Y	Y	pY	Y	Y
Tennessee	Harris, I. G.	N	N	N	N	N
Tennessee	Jackson, H. E	Y	Y	.	N	.
Tennessee	Bate, W. B.	.	.	N	N	N
Texas	Coke, R.	N	N	N	N	N
Texas	Maxey, S. B.	N	N	.	N	.
Texas	Reagan, J.	.	.	.	.	.
Virginia	Daniel, J.	.	N	Y	Y	Y
Virginia	Barbour, J.	.	.	Y	Y	Y
West Virginia	Camden, J. N.	pY	NV	.	N	.
West Virginia	Kenna, J. E.	Y	Y	N	N	N
West Virginia	Faulkner, C. J.	.	.	.	N	N

Note: Codes for votes are as follows: Y = yea; N = nay; pY = paired yea; pN = paired nay; NV = not voting; and . = not a member.

Light gray indicates a shift in support for the Blair bill by the same person. Dark gray indicates a shift in support for the Blair bill due to replacement (of one senator for another).

lished under the provisions of an act of Congress approved July 2. 1862."[171]
This bill, introduced on April 30, 1890, by Senator Justin Morrill (R-VT),
sought to increase the annual appropriation to the public land-grant colleges established in the Morrill Act of 1862.[172] Morrill's plan proposed giving
an extra $15,000 to each state in each year, increasing by $1,000 a year up
to $25,000. Morrill had been introducing such federal-aid bills since 1872,
and previous attempts included both common schools and colleges. After
the Blair bill's (presumed) final defeat, Morrill stripped the common-school
provision and focused exclusively on land-grant colleges.[173]

Morrill's bill (S. 3714) was referred to the Committee on Education and
Labor, where on May 17 it was reported out with amendments. Debate began
in June. After a lengthy introduction by Morrill expounding on the value
of the land-grant colleges and the need for additional funds, the Senate
began consideration of the committee's amendments. The second amendment read, "*Provided*, That no money shall be paid out under this act to any
State or Territory for the support or maintenance of a college where a distinction of race or color is made in the admission of students, but the establishment and maintenance of such colleges separately for white and colored
students shall be held to be in compliance with the provision of this act."[174]
This amendment was agreed to without a roll call.

While this seemed to be a victory for the pro–civil rights forces, even if a
race-blind admission criterion was paired with a "separate but equal" provision, the fight was far from over. John Reagan (D-TX) raised concerns about
language in the bill that—in his mind—would give the federal government
control over the curriculum in a state's land-grant colleges. After some additional remarks, the Senate postponed further debate.

One week later, on June 21, debate on S. 3714 resumed. John Morgan
(D-AL) voiced the same concerns Reagan had raised earlier: "It seems to
me the purpose of this bill is to fix upon our legislation the principle that

171. This section incorporates legislative histories of the Second Morrill Act found in
John W. Davis, "The Negro Land-Grant College," *Journal of Negro Education* 2 (1933): 312–
28; Chester Wilbert Wright, "A History of the Black Land-Grant Colleges, 1890–1916" (PhD
diss., American University, 1981); and Roger Lea Williams, "George W. Atherton and the Beginnings of Federal Support for Higher Education" (PhD diss., Penn State University, 1988).

172. *CR*, 51-1, 4/30/1890, 4003.

173. Williams, "George W. Atherton and the Beginnings of Federal Support for Higher
Education," 265–66.

174. *CR*, 51-1, 6/14/1890, 6085.

Congress is to go into the States, take charge of educational institutions, and regulate what is to be done with them."[175] Morrill responded that he sought no such thing and did not believe the bill's language could be construed to support Morgan's argument. Nevertheless, seeking to secure passage, Morrill and his allies agreed to rewrite the bill.

Race reemerged as a point of contention when James Pugh (D-AL) offered the following amendment:

> *Provided further*, That the Legislature of any State in which institutions of like character have been or may be established for the education of colored students in agricultural or the mechanical arts, whether styled colleges or not, and whether they have or [have] not received money heretofore under the act to which this is an amendment, may appropriate any portion of the fund received under this bill to such institutions so established and aided by such State as a compliance with the provision in reference to separate colleges for white and colored students.[176]

"The necessity for my amendment," he argued "grows out of the proviso in the original bill reported from the committee that there shall be no distinction in the admission of students to the college on account of race or color, but that provision might be complied with by the establishment of separate colleges."[177] The creation of a more explicit "separate but equal" provision made the bill more palatable for Southerners, since they could accept the funds without having to agree to integrate their existing land-grant colleges.

Concerns were raised regarding various ambiguities in the language of Pugh's amendment, which spurred Randall Gibson (D-LA) to offer a more succinct substitute: "That no money shall be paid out under this act to any State or Territory for the support and maintenance of a college where a distinction of race or color is made in the admission of students, but the establishment and maintenance of colleges, universities, and institutes for agricultural and mechanical education separate for whites and colored students shall be held to be a compliance with the provisions of this act."[178]

Pugh agreed to Gibson's modification, leaving two issues to be resolved: Could multiple colleges in each state get a portion of the funds, or were they

175. *CR*, 51-1, 6/21/1890, 6333.
176. *CR*, 51-1, 6/21/1890, 6347.
177. *CR*, 51-1, 6/21/1890, 6347.
178. *CR*, 51-1, 6/21/1890, 6347.

reserved for at most two (one black college and one white college)?[179] and How would the funds be divided?

The second issue was the bigger sticking point because Republicans were skeptical that Southern legislatures, given disbursement power under the bill, would divide the funds fairly. According to S. 3714, a legislature "may appropriate any portion of the fund received under this bill to such institution." This was unacceptable, argued John Ingalls (R-KS), because "the appropriation of $1 out of this fund will be a technical compliance with the terms of that provision." Instead, he suggested, "It should read that there shall be an equal or proportionate share of the fund distributed for the education of the colored people in the several States."[180]

Ingalls's comments elicited a number of suggestions about how it might be acceptable to describe the division of funds. William Chandler (R-NH) suggested dividing "the amount received among such colleges according to the relative numbers of the white and colored population within said State or Territory."[181] Pugh and James George (D-MS) opposed this language. Gibson then countered that the division ought to be "in proportion to the number of students in attendance in each college," to which Ingalls said, "That will not do."[182] After additional remarks, the Senate postponed further debate on Morrill's bill.

Debate resumed two days later when Morrill immediately offered an amendment that he believed would satisfy lingering concerns.[183] It read:

Provided further, That in any State in which there has been one college established in pursuance of the act of July 2, 1862, and also in which an educational institution of like character has been established and is now aided by such State from its own revenue for the education of colored students in agriculture and the mechanic arts, however named or styled, or whether or not it has received money heretofore under the act to which

179. Eugene Hale (R-ME), in particular, was concerned about the number of institutions that could demand a share of the funds and sought to narrow the number explicitly in the bill. See *CR*, 51-1, 6/21/1890, 6347.

180. *CR*, 51-1, 6/21/1890, 6349.

181. *CR*, 51-1, 6/21/1890, 6349.

182. *CR*, 51-1, 6/21/1890, 6350.

183. Morrill said he had conferred with senators from both parties before completing work on his amendment: "I have shown this amendment to members on both sides of the Chamber who took at interest in the question on Saturday, and I believe all are content with the amendment as now proposed." *CR*, 51-1, 6/23/1890, 6369.

this act is an amendment, the Legislature of such State may propose and report to the Secretary of the Interior a just and equitable division of the fund to be received under this act between one college for white students and one institution for colored students established as aforesaid, which shall be divided into two parts and paid accordingly. And thereupon such institution for colored students shall be entitled to the benefits of this act and subject to its provisions as much as it would have been if it had been included under the act of 1862; and the fulfillment of the foregoing provisions shall be taken as a compliance with the provision in reference to separate colleges for white and colored students.[184]

Morrill then confirmed in an exchange with Hale that the funds would be distributed only to one white and one black college. As to the concern regarding the division of funds between the two colleges, the amendment simply stated that a state legislature would propose a "just and equitable division." In response to a question from Edward Walthall (D-MS) about how the division would be made, Morrill replied that proportions would be determined by state legislatures. Gibson and Pugh quickly agreed to the amendment.

Several other amendments were then adopted. The most important was proposed by William Chandler, who sought to add the words "or that may be hereafter established" after the word "established" in the following clause: "in which an educational institution of like character has been established and is now aided by such State from its own revenue for the education of colored students in agriculture and the mechanic arts." The bill was then read a third time and passed.[185] On August 19 the House passed it on a division vote, 135-59.[186] The next day the Senate concurred in the House amendment, and the bill was signed into law shortly thereafter.[187]

In examining the last two changes Morrill made to the bill before the Senate reconvened on June 21, it appears that he made a wholesale concession to Southern Democrats. As Chester Wright notes, "The state legisla-

184. *CR*, 51-1, 6/23/1890, 6369.

185. *CR*, 51-1, 6/23/1890, 6369-72. There was no roll call.

186. *CR*, 51-1, 8/19/1890, 8828-40. The amendment, which was made to section 1, stated that the funds ($25,000) were "to be applied to instruction in agriculture, the mechanical arts, the English language, and the various branches of mathematical, physical, natural, and economic science, with special reference to their applications in the industries of life, and to the facilities for such instruction."

187. *CR*, 51-1, 8/20/1890, 8874; 8/30/1890, 9388.

TABLE 5.3. The 1890 Institutions

	State	Founded	Initiated Four-Year Program	Achieved Regional Accreditation
Alabama A&M University	AL	1875	1939	1963
Alcorn State University	MS	1871	1871	1961
University of Arkansas, Pine Bluff	AR	1873	1929	1933
Delaware State University	DE	1891	1947	1957
Florida A&M University	FL	1887	1909	1949
Fort Valley State University	GA	1895	1945	1957
Kentucky State University	KY	1886	1929	1939
Langston University	OK	1897	1897	1939
Lincoln University	MO	1866	1935	1935
University of Maryland, Eastern Shore	MD	1886	1936	1953
North Carolina A&T University	NC	1891	1925	1936
Prairie View A&M University	TX	1876	1901	1958
South Carolina State University	SC	1872	1924	1960
Southern University	LA	1880	1922	1958
Tennessee State University	TN	1909	1922	1946
West Virginia State University	WV	1892	1915	1927
Virginia State University	VA	1882	1943	1933

tures were given the authority to divide the funds anyway [*sic*] they saw fit as long as the money was divided into two parts. The consequence of this was that southern legislatures devised diverse formulas for apportioning the fund between the white and black schools, but no matter what formula was used, black schools did not receive enough money to develop adequately."[188] On the other hand, if Southern states did not want to integrate their public land-grant colleges, S. 3714 (thanks to the Chandler amendment) required them to have a separate "A&M" college for black students in order to gain access to the annual supplementary Morrill funds. Some states already had such colleges, while others—Georgia, Delaware, North Carolina, West Virginia, and Oklahoma—quickly established new land-grant colleges under state control. In all, seventeen states in which slavery was legal before the Civil War sought funds for segregated colleges. Table 5.3 lists the original seventeen black land-grant public colleges (under their current names).[189]

188. Wright, "History of the Black Land-Grant Colleges," 79.

189. The list was based on information in Davis, "Negro Land-Grant College"; Wright, "History of the Black Land-Grant Colleges"; and Thomas T. Williams and Handy William-

These seventeen black colleges would become known as the "1890 Institutions" and would serve a vital role in helping to create a black middle class in America.[190]

This, then, was the deal Morrill struck with the Southern Democrats: money would be provided to public land-grant colleges, and segregation would be respected. In return, black students would be provided with educational resources and, in some cases, colleges that did not previously exist. Clearly there was an understanding that the "just and equitable division" in the South would not be fifty-fifty between black and white colleges.[191] But that was the cost of creating this opportunity. In the end this was purely a distributive program, since all states in the Union would be provided with resources resulting from the sale of public lands. The racial element — and Republicans' desire to provide some aid for blacks in the South — meant that deals had to be made behind closed doors, away from the eyes of the public. As a result, there were no roll calls on any of the amendment or final-passage votes.[192]

The Second Morrill Act would be meaningful in subsequent policy decisions toward the South. For the mechanism that allowed the act to pass

son Jr., "Teaching, Research, and Extension Programs at Historically Black (1890) Land-Grant Institutions," *Agricultural History* 62 (1988): 244–57.

190. Juan Williams and Dwayne Ashley, *I'll Find a Way or Make One: A Tribute to Historically Black Colleges and Universities* (New York: Amistad, 2004).

191. For example, years later John Davis found that in the 1930–31 academic year, only three of the seventeen "1890 Institutions" received 50 percent or more of the funds from the 1890 act. South Carolina and Florida received exactly 50 percent, while Mississippi received 53.4 percent. The lowest recipient was Missouri, which received only 6.2 percent. See Davis, "Negro Land-Grant College," 317.

192. The issue of public cover and roll-call voting would come up indirectly on the first day of the debate. After Morrill introduced his amendment and secured the no-discrimination amendment, he sought to move the measure forward immediately. At that point Arthur Pue Gorman (D-MD) offered these remarks: "It is perfectly well known that a great many Senators look to other public business on Saturday, when they know that the rule has been that we would proceed only with unobjected cases on the Calendar. I think it is manifestly unfair to them to take up a bill of this kind. . . . I shall therefore be compelled to call for the yeas and nays on this vote, and I shall not regard it as a test vote upon the merits of the bill, but a vote in the negative being simply to adhere to the rule which has prevailed for the past six weeks or two months of this body. I trust the Senator from Vermont will not insist upon his motion and compel us to resort to the yeas and nays." And Morrill did not, agreeing instead to postpone further consideration of his bill, since Gorman's remarks implied that a roll-call majority did not exist. Only by operating outside the yeas and nays could the bill secure passage. See *CR*, 51-1, 6/14/1890, 6087.

was the GOP's acquiescence to its "separate but equal" provision. Southern Democrats would support distributive policy benefits for all members (and their constituents) only if they could segregate by race. Republicans' general acceptance of the "separate but equal" provision would effectively "mainstream" this approach, presaging the Supreme Court's decision in *Plessy v. Ferguson* later in the decade.[193] That Court decision would help to solidify and expand Jim Crow throughout the South.

The Federal Elections Bill

The 1888 Republican Party platform stipulated the GOP's commitment to "support free institutions of learning sufficient to afford every child growing up in the land the opportunity of a good common school education" as well as "the supreme and sovereign right of every lawful citizen . . . to cast one free ballot in public elections, and to have that ballot duly counted."[194] As we have documented, Republicans who were ostensibly committed to universal common schooling helped to defeat Henry Blair's education funding bill. During the Fifty-First Congress (1889–91), intraparty fighting would also bring down legislation that would have given the federal government new powers to oversee elections.

The federal elections bill—dubbed the "force bill" by its opponents—addressed the obvious fraud in Southern elections. It was also an acknowledgment by Republicans that they had failed to win Southern votes through conciliation. More specifically, GOP support for this bill suggests that many in the party had turned their backs on the "southern strategies" implemented by Presidents Hayes and Arthur.[195] The battle over the federal elections bill thus not only stands as the GOP's final political confrontation during the first civil rights era, it also demonstrates the power of a pivotal bloc of Republicans who thought the party should give economic issues priority over civil rights. These Republicans would actively coordinate with Democrats to prevent new voting-rights protections.

Accepting the Republican nomination in 1888, Benjamin Harrison wrote that he believed in the "right of every qualified elector to cast one free ballot

---

193. See Williamjames Hull Hoffer, *"Plessy v. Ferguson": Race and Inequality in Jim Crow America* (Lawrence: University Press of Kansas, 2012).

194. The 1888 platform can be read at http://www.presidency.ucsb.edu/ws/index.php?pid=29627.

195. Vincent P. De Santis, "Benjamin Harrison and the Republican Party in the South, 1889–1893," *Indiana Magazine of History* 51 (1955): 279–302.

and to have it honestly counted."[196] Harrison thus echoed an argument commonly invoked by Republicans that "the Democratic majority in Congress owe their existence to the suppression of the ballot by a criminal nullification of the Constitution and the laws of the United States."[197] Indeed, by the late 1880s the GOP's inability to generate support in the South persuaded many that the losses were due to fraud instead of simple unpopularity. Republican leaders had some justification for this position. One-third of Southern congressional districts at the time housed a majority of African Americans, and black voters had long-standing ties to the GOP. Republicans believed they were being "cheated" out of approximately fifteen to nineteen seats in each Congress.[198] This view led William Chandler—then advising Harrison—to write that "there is no southern question except the question whether the Fifteenth Amendment of the Constitution shall be obeyed."[199] With Republicans now in control of all three branches of government, many in the GOP saw the Fifty-First Congress as an opportunity for passing new legislation to root out election fraud in the South.

As late as 1889, however, many Republican elites were not yet ready to give up on converting Southern whites to the Republican Party. The Republicans had swept the 1888 election with a high-tariff platform,[200] and while Harrison did not capture any states in the South, he came reasonably close to winning Virginia and North Carolina. The GOP responded by downplaying sectionalism and emphasizing protectionism before the fall 1889 elections. They focused on two Southern elections in particular—a House race in Louisiana (Third District) and the gubernatorial race in Virginia—and marshaled their men and resources to win them.[201] Yet in both races the Re-

---

196. Quoted in De Santis, "Benjamin Harrison and the Republican Party," 283.

197. The 1888 Republican Party platform.

198. Richard M. Valelly, "Partisan Entrepreneurship and Policy Windows: George Frisbie Hoar and the 1890 Federal Elections Bill," in *Formative Acts: American Politics in the Making*, ed. Stephen Skowronek and Matthew Glassman (Philadelphia: University of Pennsylvania Press, 2007), 139, 142.

199. Chandler quoted in Wang, *Trial of Democracy*, 230.

200. The 1888 presidential election would come down to party positions on tariff policy, with President Cleveland in favor of tariff reform (reduction). Joanne R. Reitano, *The Tariff Question in the Gilded Age: The Great Debate of 1888* (University Park: Pennsylvania State University Press, 1994); Charles W. Calhoun, *Minority Victory: Gilded Age Politics and the Front Porch Campaign of 1888* (Lawrence: University Press of Kansas, 2008).

201. In Virginia, the Republican gubernatorial candidate was former Readjuster (and US senator) William Mahone. A number of high-profile Republicans actively stumped for him, including House Speaker Thomas Reed (ME), Sen. J. Donald Cameron (PA), Rep. William

publican candidate was soundly defeated in the face of violence, fraud, and intimidation.[202] As Stanley Hirshson contends, "The defeats in Louisiana and Virginia finally convinced [the Republicans] that the [Democrats] were not to be trusted and that only federal regulation of elections could solve the sectional problem."[203] Thus Republicans made ensuring a free and fair vote their first priority.

As chairman of the Senate Committee on Privileges and Elections, George Frisbie Hoar (R-MA) had long been interested in electoral reform. In an 1884 speech to the Commonwealth Club of Boston, for example, Hoar declared his commitment to a system of "laws, institutions, and administration under which . . . millions of men will represent the black race in the mankind and citizenship of the republic."[204] Additionally, in an 1889 article for the *North American Review*, Hoar listed the "absolute freedom and purity of elections" as one of six "essential propositions" that underlay the GOP's governing philosophy.[205] During the Fiftieth Congress (1887–89), Hoar led an investigation into the lynching of three black men in Texas during the 1886 election campaign and called for a revision of "the existing laws relating to elections of members of Congress, with a view of providing for the more complete protection of the exercise of the elective franchise."[206] Accordingly, on April 24, 1890, Hoar introduced S. 3652, a bill to "amend and supplement the elections laws . . . and to provide for the more efficient enforcement of such laws." Hoar's bill initiated the debate about new federal authority over elections.[207]

McKinley (OH), Sen. John Sherman (OH), Sen. Matthew Quay (PA, chairman of the Republican National Committee), Rep. Julius Caesar Burrows (MI), and James Clarkson (NC member). In addition, the Republican National Committee provided him with $25,000 in support. See Heersink and Jenkins, *Republican Party Politics and the American South*.

202. Hirshson, *Farewell to the Bloody Shirt*, 182–89.

203. Hirshson, *Farewell to the Bloody Shirt*, 205.

204. Hoar quoted in Valelly, "Partisan Entrepreneurship and Policy Windows," 136.

205. George F. Hoar, "Are the Republicans in to Stay?" *North American Review* 149 (1889): 623.

206. Quoted in Valelly, "Partisan Entrepreneurship," 136–37.

207. *CR*, 51-1, 4/24/1890, 3760. For lengthy discussions of the politics surrounding the Lodge bill, see Valelly, "Partisan Entrepreneurship and Policy Windows," 126–52; Calhoun, *Conceiving a New Republic*, 226–59; Rayford W. Logan, *The Betrayal of the Negro: From Rutherford B. Hayes to Woodrow Wilson* (New York: Da Capo Press, 1997), 61–73; and Richard E. Welch Jr., "The Federal Elections Bill of 1890: Postscripts and Preludes," *Journal of American History* 52 (1965): 511–26.

S. 3652 authorized the appointment of "federal supervisors and canvass-ers" to any congressional district if at least one hundred voters signed a peti-tion requesting their presence. Additionally, two supervisors — one from each party — would be assigned to every voting precinct to observe regis-tration, balloting, and vote counting. Once voting had finished, three fed-eral canvassers, appointed by federal circuit court judges, would certify the winner in those districts needing supervision.[208] By raising once again the specter of federal intervention into the South, Hoar provoked an immediate and strident response from James L. Pugh (D-AL). "The minority regard this bill as revolutionary in its character," Pugh argued. "If the bill becomes a law," he went on, "its execution will insure the shedding of blood and the destruction of the peace and good order of this country."[209]

Hoar was not the only Republican committed to electoral reform. At the outset of the Fifty-First Congress, House Republicans organized a special committee — led by Henry Cabot Lodge (MA) — to draft a federal elections bill. Believing that "the country does not want a force bill or anything resem-bling it," Lodge aimed to write a "nonpartisan" reform bill.[210] He proposed to "nationalize the Australian [or secret] ballot" in any congressional district with five hundred or more voters willing to sign a petition requesting its introduction, and he also argued that federal judges should be empowered to appoint "registrars and inspectors" and to certify election results.[211] Ac-cording to Xi Wang, Lodge's approach shows that "Republicans had to treat [election reform law] as a long-term national policy to perpetuate an orderly practice of political democracy rather than as a temporary, expedient mea-sure for obtaining immediate gains."[212] Hoar's bill — introduced without the consent or knowledge of House Republicans — departed from this "non-partisan" approach. Lodge argued that because any electoral reform bill would directly affect House members only — since the Seventeenth Amend-ment would not be ratified until 1913 — the House should take the lead in writing it. Thus the two Massachusetts lawmakers worked out a compro-mise: Lodge would incorporate aspects of Hoar's proposal in his bill, and Hoar would report the House bill in the Senate.[213]

208. Crofts, "Blair Bill and the Elections Bill," 251.
209. *CR*, 51-1, 4/24/1890, 3760.
210. Wang, *Trial of Democracy*, 235.
211. Crofts, "Blair Bill and the Elections Bill," 253.
212. Wang, *Trial of Democracy*, 235.
213. Welch, "Federal Elections Bill of 1890," 513.

Lodge introduced the first version of his reform bill in March 1890. It faced immediate opposition from Republicans who believed it did not go far enough.[214] For example, Jonathan Rowell (IL)—chairman of the House Committee on Elections—argued that any reform measure should make federal supervision of registration, counting, and certification a top priority. He backed a slightly modified version of the Hoar bill.[215] Additionally, Harrison Kelley (KS) offered a proposal that "instructed the federal government to 'take entire control'" of elections. If enacted, Kelley's bill would have mandated voting districts with approximately equal populations and empowered Congress—rather than state legislatures—to construct them. It also would have granted federal supervisors the authority to run every aspect of the election process "from registration through certification."[216] Thus, before confronting Democrats who were threatening violence in response to any new federal oversight of elections, Lodge had to persuade Republicans to adopt his approach.

Speaker Thomas Reed—"one of the most anxious of all the Republicans to have a 'force' bill of some sort put on the books"—requested that Lodge and Rowell develop a compromise.[217] The bill they crafted called for appointing a "chief" electoral supervisor to each judicial circuit. In addition, three federal supervisors—no more than two from a single party—would be posted to each registration office and polling station to "observe and report on registration, to watch the reception of the votes, to participate in the count, and to make their own returns." Such supervision would be activated by a petition signed by one hundred legal voters in a given congressional district or a city of 20,000 or more inhabitants. It could also go into effect through a petition signed by "fifty citizens in any section forming only part of a congressional district." Finally, the bill created a board of canvassers charged with making judgments about the legitimacy of the votes transmitted by state officials and federal supervisors. If the canvassing board and state officials agreed on a victor, that candidate would be declared the winner. If the board and state officials disagreed, however, the board would determine the winner. These judgments were, in turn, subject to appeal to fed-

214. *CR*, 51-1, 3/15/1890, 2285.

215. Crofts, "Blair Bill and the Elections Bill," 253.

216. Crofts, "Blair Bill and the Elections Bill," 254.

217. "Party Rule above Right: The South to Suffer for Republican Party Needs," *NYT*, June 12, 1890, 5. See also Thomas B. Reed, "The Federal Control of Elections," *North American Review* 50 (1890): 671–80.

eral circuit courts.[218] Taken as a whole, the Lodge bill (H.R. 11045) sought to "deter the intimidation and corruption of voters" by creating a layered system of federal supervision.[219]

On June 25, 1890, the House Rules Committee reported H.R. 11045 under the stipulation that it receive a vote within one week.[220] "The first principle in this bill," Lodge argued, "is to secure the absolute publicity in regard to everything connected with the election of a member of Congress. The second is to make sure that every man who is entitled to vote has an opportunity to cast his vote freely and have it counted."[221] He then went on to detail the extent and severity of electoral fraud in congressional districts around the country, before concluding with a direct message to Southern members and citizens. "The first step . . . toward the settlement of the negro problem . . . is to take it out of national party politics," he claimed (without irony), and "this can be done in but one way. The United States must extend to every citizen equal rights. . . . If all is fair and honest and free in southern elections this law will interfere with no one, but will demonstrate the fact to the people of the United States."[222]

House Democrats immediately condemned H.R. 11045. John Hemphill (SC) argued that the bill "rob[s] the people of the states of the dearest rights of American citizenship, and it aims to put the colored man . . . again in control of the government of the southern states."[223] Democrats would repeat these charges over the course of the weeklong debate, but they were not the only ones with objections. Southern Republicans, in particular, inveighed against the bill for being too weak.[224] One GOP official from North Carolina published a formal condemnation of the bill on these grounds in the *North American Review*:

Suppose for illustration that the president, teller, cashier, and other officers of a great national bank in New York should enter into a conspiracy to rob the vaults, falsify the books, destroy the records, and perpetuate

218. All quotations above were taken from De Santis, "Benjamin Harrison and the Republican Party," 286.

219. Welch, "Federal Elections Bill," 514.

220. *CR*, 51-1, 6/25/1890, 6505–11.

221. *CR*, 51-1, 6/26/1890, 6538.

222. *CR*, 51-1, 6/26/1890, 6544.

223. *CR*, 51-1, 6/26/1890, 6549–53.

224. For a summary of Southern Republican opposition, see Crofts, "Blair Bill and the Elections Bill," 265.

themselves in office and power: what would the directors do when they detected the crime? Would they create a duplicate set of officers, under duplicate salaries, and set them in supervision over the rogues, to reduce subsequent crimes to a minimum?[225]

More extreme was the argument of Harrison Kelley (R-KS), whose call for a stronger bill came with a jarring prediction. Any effort by Southern officials to "nullify" a strong electoral reform measure "will surely bring on a conflict in this country. . . . [B]lood would flow and flow freely, but better rivers of it should flow and liberty survive than that the conditions that have existed in many places in the south for a quarter of a century should remain."[226]

Despite the condemnation from both Democrats and Republicans, Speaker Reed made H.R. 11045 a caucus measure and threw his full support and parliamentary authority behind it.[227] On July 2, 1890, the Lodge bill passed 155-149, with no Democrats supporting the bill and only two Republicans opposing it.[228] This outcome signaled to Senate reformers that they would need uniform GOP support if they hoped to see the bill enacted.

Despite the Lodge bill's importance, Senate Republicans did not view it as their top priority during the summer of 1890. Instead, they were embroiled in a debate over the tariff and the coinage of silver. As Fred Wellborn writes, by 1889 the "'silver question' . . . was forcing a considerable and growing amount of attention, and had found advocates in most of the senators west of the Mississippi."[229] Specifically, Republican senators from Colorado, Nevada, California, Idaho, Minnesota, and Kansas worked together to push the free coinage of both gold and silver. Known as the "Silver Republicans," this group constituted a pivotal bloc of senators during the Fifty-First Congress.[230]

---

225. A. W. Schaffer, "A Southern Republican on the Lodge Bill," *North American Review* 151 (1890): 602.

226. *CR*, 51-1, 6/26/1890, 6883.

227. William A. Robinson, *Thomas B. Reed: Parliamentarian* (New York: Dodd, Mead, 1930), 235-39.

228. *CR*, 51-1, 7/2/1890, 6940-41. The two Republican nay voters were H. Dudley Coleman (LA) and Herman Lehlbach (NJ).

229. Fred Wellborn, "The Influence of the Silver-Republican Senators, 1889-1891," *Mississippi Valley Historical Review* 14 (1928): 462.

230. Wellborn, "Influence of the Silver-Republican Senators," 463.

At the same time that the Silver Republicans were pushing their agenda, eastern Republicans were seeking enactment of a significant tariff hike — what would become known as the McKinley Tariff.[231] According to Robert Welch, the most "ardent Republican protectionists" considered a tariff bill to be of the utmost importance and worried that opening debate on Lodge's measure would jeopardize it.[232] Accordingly, on August 18, 1890, Matthew Quay (R-PA) — one such protectionist — introduced a resolution declaring that the Senate's top priority for the rest of the first session would be the tariff.[233] To get the McKinley Tariff through the Senate, the protectionists needed the support of the Silver Republicans. To that end, they traded votes on the tariff measure for votes on the Sherman Silver Purchase Act, at the expense of any discussion of the elections bill.[234] This was not a problem, since neither group was particularly invested in the elections bill. Western Republicans opposed it because they were "not concerned with the old issue of inequality of representation between North and South," just as they were not concerned with the significant number of illiterate citizens living in former Confederate states.[235] Eastern Republicans, meanwhile, worried that any election reform proposal threatened to "disturb the community of commercial interests" that was developing between North and South.[236]

Senator Hoar was displeased by the move to forgo action on the Lodge bill. On August 20, 1890, he asked rhetorically what was motivating Quay and his supporters, and answered himself this way: "It is this and only this: that the national election bill . . . shall be slain."[237] Hoar's appeal led to an evening meeting among Republicans at the home of Senator James McMillan (R-MI). According to Welch, this meeting led to a unanimous agreement to postpone action on the Lodge bill until Congress reconvened in December so that the Senate could act on the tariff bill without delay. In return for agreeing to the delay, Hoar was assured that when Congress reconvened, the Lodge bill would be granted "undisputed and continuous priority." Hoar

231. William McKinley (R-OH), the chair of the Ways and Means Committee, helped design the bill and introduced it in the House.

232. Welch, "Federal Elections Bill," 515.

233. *CR*, 51-1, 8/18/1890, 8724.

234. Welch, "Federal Elections Bill," 516–18.

235. Wellborn, "Influence of the Silver-Republican Senators," 472.

236. This quotation comes from Sen. J. Donald Cameron (PA) and appears in De Santis, "Benjamin Harrison and the Republican Party," 289.

237. *CR*, 51-1, 8/20/1890, 8847.

went so far as to persuade all GOP senators but one to agree to this deal. Every Silver Republican was on board.[238]

Congress reconvened in December, after the GOP was routed in the midterm elections and lost control of the House in the upcoming Fifty-Second Congress (1891–93). Yet Republicans held to their promise. For the first full month of the lame-duck session, the Senate focused only on the Lodge bill. The debate echoed many of the same themes raised in the House, with Democrats raising the specter of armed confrontation and Republicans appealing to the "nonpartisan" nature of their proposal. As December gave way to January, however, Silver Republicans started to grow weary. They were dissatisfied with the Sherman Silver Purchase Act and thought more silver policy was needed. The time spent debating the Lodge bill, they argued, came at the expense of new currency legislation.[239] By the end of December they were giving speeches declaring their intent to oppose the Lodge bill.[240]

Finally, on January 5, 1891, the Silver Republicans reneged on their agreement with Hoar. Working in conjunction with Senate Democrats, they pushed through a procedural motion—introduced by Sen. William Stewart (R-NV)—that set aside the elections bill in order to begin debate on a free-coinage bill (S. 4675). Stewart, who had long championed black voting rights, argued that the Lodge bill was unworkable in its current form, since it would take the active use of the military to enforce it, which was no longer supported by national public opinion.[241] The Senate adopted Stewart's motion 34–29, with eight Republicans joining all Democrats against the majority of Republicans.[242] Of the eight Republican dissidents, seven were from silver states.[243]

238. Welch, "Federal Elections Bill," 517–18. The one Republican senator who refused to go along was the maverick Richard F. Pettigrew (SD).

239. Welch, "Federal Elections Bill," 519–20.

240. Wellborn, "Influence of the Silver-Republican Senators," 472.

241. Recall that Stewart was a major contributor to the passage of the Fifteenth Amendment and the Enforcement Acts.

242. See *CR*, 51-2, 1/5/1891, 912–13. A roll-call analysis (logistic regression) of Republican votes finds that the second (positive) NOMINATE dimension is statistically significant, with Republican members toward the top of the second dimension being more likely to join with the Democrats and adopt Stewart's motion. In terms of the substantive content of the second NOMINATE dimension during this time, Keith Poole and Howard Rosenthal argue, "From the Civil War until the realignment of the 1890s, the predominant second-dimension issue is bimetallism (U.S. currency; banking and finance)." See Keith T. Poole and Howard Rosenthal, *Ideology and Congress* (New Brunswick, NJ: Transaction, 2007), 57.

243. The eight Republicans were John P. Jones (NV), William J. McConnell (ID),

Working together, Senators Hoar, John Coit Spooner (R-WI), and Nelson Aldrich (R-RI) made one more effort to save the Lodge bill. On January 14, 1891, they successfully pushed through a procedural motion that again made H.R. 11045 the order of business in the Senate. They had no room to spare. The vote was 33-33 — as six of the eight Republicans who supported Stewart's motion voted with all the Democrats — and Vice President Levi Morton cast the tie-breaking vote in favor.[244] With debate on the Lodge bill now reopened, Hoar announced that the Senate would remain in session until it received a vote. Democrats were determined to filibuster. Republicans responded by "leaving all the talking to [them]" during the thirty-six-hour marathon session, in hopes that they would exhaust themselves and relent.[245]

On January 17 Aldrich announced that the Senate would adjourn, but that when it reconvened he would "ask the Senate to consider the gag rule."[246] For a while Republican senators had considered pursuing a cloture (or "gag") rule to bring debate to a close. Now they seemed intent on doing so. The Democrats, however, skillfully blocked Aldrich's motion to amend Senate rules until January 22. That day, Edward Wolcott (R-CO) surprised his fellow partisans by requesting that the Senate begin debate on a pending apportionment bill (and thus drop consideration of the Lodge bill). Joseph Dolph (R-OR) then moved to table Wolcott's motion, triggering a roll-call vote. Despite their best efforts, Lodge and his allies lost the tabling vote 34-35.[247] Six Republicans voted with all Democrats in support of Wolcott's motion against the rest of the GOP. Five of these six Republicans were part of Stewart's previous coalition, and they were joined by J. David Cameron (R-PA), "who was speculating in silver at the time."[248] The Senate then voted 35-34 to take up the apportionment bill, as the voting coalition flipped.[249] The Lodge bill was dead.

George L. Shoup (NV), Leland Stanford (CA), William Stewart (NV), Henry M. Teller (CO), William D. Washburn (MN), and Edward O. Wolcott (CO).

244. *CR*, 51-2, 1/14/1891, 1323-24. The six Republicans were Jones, Stanford, Stewart, Teller, Washburn, and Wolcott.

245. "Thirty Hours in Session: Senator Hoar's Force Bill Is Not Passed Yet," *NYT*, January 17, 1891, 1.

246. "Nothing to Brag About: Little Cause for Hoar and the Radicals to Rejoice," *NYT*, January 19, 1891, 1.

247. *CR*, 51-2, 1/22/1891, 1739-40.

248. Hirshson, *Farewell to the Bloody Shirt*, 233. Joining Wolcott and Cameron were Jones, Teller, Stewart, and Washburn.

249. *CR*, 51-2, 1/22/1891, 1740.

FIGURE 10. Lodge bill cartoon. Artist: Charles J. Taylor. *Puck* Magazine, August 20, 1890. US Senate Collection, Catalogue No. 38.00746.001.

According to Stanley Hirshson: "The Lodge bill had been buried by a bargain between the Democrats and the free silverites." He notes that before moving his coinage legislation on January 5, Stewart conferred with Albert Pue Gorman (MD), the Democratic leader, and together they pushed the Lodge bill off the agenda in favor of Stewart's bill. Then, on January 20, "six Silver Republicans [repaid] their debt to Gorman . . . and joined with the Democrats . . . to sidetrack the election bill and consider an apportionment act."[250] The Silver Republicans and the Democrats had successfully orchestrated a "logroll" (or vote trade). Mainstream Republicans were furious but had no recourse. They were beaten.

Although the "silver alliance" between the South and the West was easy to blame for the death of the Lodge bill, other forces were also at work. Northern businessmen, wanting to maintain a stable economic environment in the South, also sought the bill's demise. And the behavior of their advocates in Congress—Quay and Cameron—provides some evidence of this.[251] In addition, as Vincent De Santis notes, "During the summer and fall

250. All quotations are from Hirshson, *Farewell to the Bloody Shirt*, 233.
251. De Santis, *Republicans Face the Southern Question*, 214.

of 1890, public opinion in the country turned against the Force Bill. While a large number of petitions favoring it descended upon Congress, an even greater number opposing the measure poured in."[252] Special interests (the Farmers' Alliance, Manufacturers' Clubs, and Republican clubs at the state level) came out against the bill, negative editorials appeared in leading party papers (like the *Philadelphia Inquirer*), and informal polls of party members indicated considerable opposition to the bill and its (perceived) federal encroachment.[253] Which of these forces was most important is unclear, but the effect of the bill's failure was apparent. "Defeat of the Lodge bill," Charles Calhoun asserts, "dealt a devastating blow to Republican efforts to fulfill their republican aims in the South."[254]

Conclusion

The Lodge bill's defeat in 1891 was a pivotal moment in American political development. A new coalition emerged inside and outside Congress to ensure that much of what had been accomplished during Reconstruction would be eroded or reversed. For example, at the same time the Lodge bill was being debated, white supremacists in the South were looking for a different way to fend off current and future GOP attacks. Their solution was to employ legal mechanisms to disenfranchise black voters, as they increasingly saw their contemporaneous techniques (fraud, intimidation, and violence) as inefficient for the goal at hand. State-level legal remedies — ostensibly race neutral — offered more security and limited what could be done to help blacks at the federal level. Thus, beginning in Mississippi in 1890, Southern states adopted a wide variety of legal means aimed at restricting black suffrage. And within two decades every Southern state had such institutions in place. These state-level disenfranchisement efforts, along with state-level segregation laws, would form the basis of Jim Crow society for the next three generations.

Thus the fifteen-year period of intra- and interparty contestation over the status of black civil rights examined in this chapter explains the rise of Jim Crow. While Republicans did not sever their ties to black Southerners without a fight — as demonstrated by the battles they waged to defend the Enforcement Acts and to end discrimination in interstate travel — later in

252. De Santis, *Republicans Face the Southern Question*, 210.

253. De Santis, *Republicans Face the Southern Question*, 210–14; Hirshson, *Farewell to the Bloody Shirt*, 234–35; Calhoun, *Conceiving a New Republic*, 258–59.

254. Calhoun, *Conceiving a New Republic*, 260.

the Redemption era an increasing number of them were willing to sacrifice the party's long-standing support for civil rights in exchange for economic issues. Specifically, a pivotal bloc of congressional Republicans made common cause with Democrats at critical moments to defeat Blair's education bill and Lodge's federal elections bill.

The congressional debates we explore thus help reveal how the "Solid South" came into existence. Democratic party strength in the former Confederacy did not go uncontested immediately after Reconstruction ended. Instead, Republicans attempted to win support in Southern states, and their efforts often (but not always) included advocating civil rights. As it became clear to GOP leaders that the party lacked the political strength to compete in the South, however, Republican lawmakers were increasingly willing to abandon black citizens. As a result, former slaves and their children would be subjected to new forms of rights subjugation.

APPENDIX 5.1. Logit Analyses of Blair Bill Votes, Using Ideology and Illiteracy

	48th Congress (S. 398)		49th Congress (S. 194)		50th Congress (S. 371)		51st Congress (S. 185)	
NOMINATE 1	1.89*	3.97**	0.65	2.80**	0.70	2.71**	1.08*	3.30**
	(0.77)	(1.26)	(0.59)	(1.04)	(0.41)	(0.83)	(0.43)	(1.01)
NOMINATE 2	0.56	−0.17	−0.72	−0.25	1.17	1.90	1.30	2.30
	(2.35)	(2.50)	(1.78)	(1.83)	(1.39)	(1.56)	(1.16)	(1.33)
Percentage illiterate		0.086*		0.102*		0.088**		0.100**
		(0.039)		(0.042)		(0.029)		(0.036)
Constant	1.59**	−0.31	1.26**	−0.40	0.41	−1.18*	−0.18	−1.95*
	(0.58)	(1.00)	(0.37)	(0.72)	(0.27)	(0.60)	(0.27)	(0.74)
N	44	44	47	47	68	68	68	68
LR χ^2	8.24*	14.85**	1.35	9.91**	3.41	15.92**	7.64*	18.09**
Percentage correctly predicted	79.6	86.4	76.6	74.5	63.2	73.5	58.8	69.1
PRE (naive model)	0.182	0.455	0	−0.091	0.138	0.379	0.097	0.323

Note: Standard errors in parentheses. Baseline model for PRE calculation is a naive (minority-vote) model.
*$p < .05$; **$p < .01$.

APPENDIX 5.2. Logit Analyses of Blair Bill Votes, Using Party, Section, and Illiteracy

	48th Congress (S. 398)		49th Congress (S. 194)		50th Congress (S. 371)		51st Congress (S. 185)	
Southern Democrat	−1.51 (0.92)	−6.23* (2.80)	−0.00 (0.82)	−5.93* (2.96)	0.20 (0.60)	−1.06 (1.78)	−0.44 (0.61)	−3.31 (2.32)
Northern Democrat	−3.00** (1.14)	−4.63** (1.55)	−1.10 (0.93)	−2.71* (1.30)	−2.36** (0.85)	−2.68** (0.98)	−2.79** (1.09)	−3.57** (1.31)
Percentage illiterate		0.125 (0.070)		0.169* (0.083)		0.033 (0.044)		0.077 (0.060)
Constant	2.30** (0.74)	1.54 (0.84)	1.39** (0.50)	0.40 (0.67)	0.65 (0.36)	0.44 (0.45)	0.30 (0.32)	−0.16 (0.48)
N	44	44	47	47	68	68	68	68
LR χ^2	8.57*	12.54**	1.55	7.76	12.19**	12.79**	11.41**	13.20**
Percentage correctly predicted	79.6	86.4	76.6	78.7	70.6	70.6	63.2	66.2
PRE (naive model)	0.182	0.455	0	0.091	0.310	0.310	0.097	0.323

Note: Standard errors in parentheses. Baseline model for PRE calculation is a naïve (minority-vote) model. "Republican" is the excluded partisan category.

*$p < .05$; **$p < .01$.

CHAPTER SIX

The Wilderness Years, 1891–1918

Once the Lodge bill failed, Republicans used the only resources they could muster—executive patronage and contested election cases—to maintain a slight foothold in the South.[1] On the whole, however, party leaders no longer believed their electoral fortunes hinged on black voters. African Americans' civil rights declined in importance among GOP members.[2] Democrats, meanwhile, continued their attack on Reconstruction. After gaining unified control of the national government for the first time since the late 1850s, in the Fifty-Third Congress (1893–95) they acted quickly to repeal the Enforcement Acts. Although laws ensuring federal supervision of state elections had not been followed for some time, many Democrats viewed their repeal as a necessary step toward erasing the policy legacy of Reconstruction from both the statute books and popular memory.[3]

As Southern Democrats were pursuing repeal at the national level, state officials pursued legal strategies to systematically disenfranchise black

1. Given the electoral balance between the Republicans and Democrats during the late nineteenth century, the Republicans could not afford to disregard the South entirely, even as the center of gravity in the party clearly shifted to the political-economic needs of the Northeast and West.

2. Stanley P. Hirshson, *Farewell to the Bloody Shirt: Northern Republicans and the Southern Negro, 1877–1893* (Bloomington: Indiana University Press, 1962), 246–50.

3. Indeed, the Lodge bill was pushed in 1890–91 in part because the previous Enforcement Acts, as written, were no longer suitable for federal supervision in the post-Reconstruction environment. For example, the Lodge bill placed much greater supervisory power with the federal circuit courts.

voters.[4] Before the 1890s, Democrats had used violence and intimidation to discourage black voter participation. The GOP's efforts to push a new federal elections bill, however, convinced Democrats they should pursue more durable solutions. They thus adopted legal measures like poll taxes, literacy tests, residency requirements, and grandfather clauses — that would disenfranchise but not involve race directly, thereby evading federal constitutional challenges. By 1908, every state in the former Confederacy had adopted either constitutional or statutory provisions to disenfranchise African Americans and solidify the Democrats' hold on political power throughout the region.[5]

Laws designed to keep black voters from the polls were also just one part of a more expansive congressional effort to undermine black civil rights. Democrats tried to pass legislation banning interracial marriage and permitting formal segregation on public transportation. These efforts failed. Republicans, meanwhile, were divided on reducing Southern representation in Congress based on section 2 of the Fourteenth Amendment. The GOP fought internally over Theodore Roosevelt's decision to "discharge without honor" more than 150 black troops after a violent episode in Brownsville, Texas. Republicans also sought to enforce a "separate but equal" policy in federal education policy (they failed), and to ensure federal supervision of Senate elections (they succeeded). On the whole, however, the GOP lacked support to advance civil rights in any meaningful way.

In short, for the nearly three decades we cover in this chapter — which we refer to as the "wilderness years"[6] — civil rights policy largely disappeared from the congressional agenda. As Stanley Hirshson notes: "A student of the period between the Force Bill struggle and the First World War will search in vain if he looks for election acts, education bills, and other

4. These efforts are discussed in detail in J. Morgan Kousser, *The Shaping of Southern Politics: Suffrage Restriction and the Establishment of the One-Party South* (New Haven, CT: Yale University Press, 1974), and Michael Perman, *Struggle for Mastery: Disfranchisement in the South, 1888–1908* (Chapel Hill: University of North Carolina Press, 2001).

5. Black political leaders and activists in the South would challenge these disenfranchisement laws in the courts, albeit unsuccessfully. See R. Volney Riser, *Defying Disfranchisement: Black Voting Rights Activism in the Jim Crow South, 1890–1908* (Baton Rouge: Louisiana State University Press, 2010).

6. An alternative description for this era is the "civil rights nadir." See Rayford W. Logan, *The Betrayal of the Negro: From Rutherford B. Hayes to Woodrow Wilson* (New York: Da Capo Press, 1997), 79–96. In particular, Logan notes, "At the beginning of the twentieth century both major parties had decided that American principles of justice, liberty and democracy did not have to be applied alike to white men and to Negroes" (96).

political measures designed to aid the Negro."[7] Although Republicans in Congress lacked the political will to advance a civil rights agenda, they were able to prevent Democrats from further turning the federal government against African Americans. Stalemate was of course terrible for black citizens. As Congress dithered, the country endured a lynching epidemic that went largely unchallenged.[8] Despite the GOP's inaction, conditions were not yet in place for the irrevocable split between black voters and the party of Lincoln that would culminate in the "Second Reconstruction." The events we cover here laid the early groundwork for this significant political realignment.

Repeal of the Enforcement Acts

The Democratic Party's effort to repeal the Enforcement Acts began slowly. In July 1892 a new House committee tasked with investigating the application of federal election laws recommended that the Enforcement Acts be abolished, arguing that they were applied too broadly, interfered with the rights of qualified voters, and produced too few convictions.[9] Without control of the Senate and the White House, however, the Democrats' recommendations were purely symbolic. The results of the 1892 elections turned symbol to substance.

When the Fifty-Third Congress (1893–95) convened, Democrats held unified control of government for the first time since before the Civil War. The House immediately considered black voting rights when, on September 11, 1893, Henry St. George Tucker (D-VA) introduced H.R. 2331, legislation "to repeal all statutes relating to supervisors of elections and special deputy marshals, and for other purposes." Tucker questioned the entire premise of the Reconstruction project. "I hold that the power of the citizen and the right of the citizen to vote is a right given to him not by the Constitution of the United States or by the Federal Government," Tucker argued, "but is a right reserved to the State and recognized in the Constitution."[10] Only states had the legitimate authority to determine the "conditions of suffrage." Leaving it to the states to determine voter eligibility was, of course, just a

---

7. Hirshson, *Farewell to the Bloody Shirt*, 252–53.

8. Horace Samuel Merrill and Marion Galbraith Merrill, *The Republican Command, 1897–1913* (Lexington: University Press of Kentucky, 1971), 113–15.

9. Xi Wang, *The Trial of Democracy: Black Suffrage and Northern Republicans, 1860–1910* (Athens: University of Georgia Press, 1997), 254.

10. *CR*, 53-1, 9/26/1893, 1804.

stratagem for disenfranchising black voters. As Xi Wang argues, Tucker's bill "was so comprehensive and thorough that it intended to eliminate all of the five enforcement laws enacted by the Republican Congress between 1870 and 1872."[11]

Republicans characterized the Enforcement Acts as absolutely essential to fair elections everywhere in the country.[12] According to George Washington Ray (R-NY), they guarded against corruption in *both* Northern and Southern elections; they were not "aimed at the South." Democrats pushing a states' rights argument, Ray claimed, were using it as a smokescreen to justify the elimination of black suffrage.[13] The Fourteenth and Fifteenth Amendments, Republicans like Ray argued, had specifically given Congress the power to adopt legislation to enforce the new rights they created and guaranteed to all citizens.[14]

H.R. 2331 was referred to the Committee on the Election of the President, Vice President, and Representatives in Congress, which Tucker himself chaired.[15] It was taken up less than a week later under a special order that provided for debate until October 10. On that day, all pending amendments and the underlying bill would be voted on.[16] In the interim, Julius Burrows (R-MI) and John F. Lacey (R-IA) introduced two amendments aimed at preserving those aspects of the Enforcement Acts that guaranteed suffrage for qualified voters and punished those who conspired to restrict voting rights. These amendments were defeated on pure party-line votes.[17] The House then voted on H.R. 2331 and passed it 201-102, with all Democrats supporting the bill and all Republicans opposing it.[18]

The Senate began consideration of the House-passed measure in mid-

11. Wang, *Trial of Democracy*, 255.

12. On the distribution of voting rights enforcement by region from 1872 to 1892, see Scott C. James and Brian L. Lawson, "The Political Economy of Voting Rights Enforcement in America's Gilded Age: Electoral College Competition, Partisan Commitment, and the Federal Election Law," *American Political Science Review* 93 (1999): 115–31.

13. *CR*, 53-1, 10/6/1893, 2227.

14. When Republicans referenced the text of the Fourteenth and Fifteenth Amendments as a counter to anticonstitutional critiques, Democrats generally responded with arguments similar to that made by Thomas English (D-NJ): "While [a law for the regulation or supervision of voters engaged in electing members to Congress] may stand within the letter, it is in direct conflict with the spirit of the Constitution." *CR*, 53-1, 10/6/1893, 2236.

15. *CR*, 53-1, 9/11/1893, 1395.

16. *CR*, 53-1, 9/26/1893, 1803.

17. *CR*, 53-1, 10/10/1893, 2375–76, 2377.

18. *CR*, 53-1, 10/10/1893, 2378.

December 1893, when Zebulon Vance (D-NC), chair of the Committee on Privileges and Elections, referred H.R. 2331 (without amendment) to the floor and recommended its passage.[19] In response, William E. Chandler (R-NH), speaking for a group of four GOP dissenters on the committee, pledged to fight the Democrats' repeal attempt.[20] Manipulating parliamentary procedure, Chandler and his allies were able to extend the debate on the repeal legislation into January 1894. Their opposition called attention to Mississippi's newly ratified constitution, specifically the provisions disenfranchising African Americans through the biased administration of literacy tests. They claimed it would be even easier to disenfranchise voters without federal election supervisors present.

In February, despite the GOP's efforts to delay, the Senate was finally moving to a conclusion on H.R. 2331. Chandler and his allies had tried to postpone further consideration of the bill until December (in the lame-duck session after the 1894 midterms), but their motion was defeated in yet another party-line vote.[21] Chandler also offered several amendments to strip out provisions of the underlying bill that defunded election supervisors, abolished "crimes against the elective franchise," and punished anyone found guilty of denying voting rights.[22] All were defeated on party-line votes.[23] On February 7, 1894, the Senate finally voted on H.R. 2331 and passed it 39-28.[24] All Democrats voted against all Republicans. The next day, President Cleveland signed H.R. 2331 into law.[25]

By enacting H.R. 2331, the Democrats had achieved in the Fifty-Third Congress what the Republicans could not in the Fifty-First: a significant statutory change to voting-rights enforcement. The Republicans in the Fifty-First Congress had tried to enact a new law—embodied in the Lodge bill—to bolster federal oversight of Southern elections. They lacked the political will in the Senate to do so. The Democrats in the Fifty-Third Con-

19. *CR*, 53-2, 12/14/1893, 224.

20. The other three were George F. Hoar (R-MA), Anthony Higgins (R-DE), and John Hipple Mitchell (R-OR). For a description of Chandler's efforts in opposing the repeal of the Enforcement Acts, see Leon Burr Richardson, *William Chandler: Republican* (New York: Dodd, Mead, 1940), 461–64.

21. *CR*, 53-2, 1/27/1894, 1583.

22. *CR*, 53-2, 2/7/1894, 1994–95.

23. *CR*, 53-2, 2/7/1894, 1995–98.

24. *CR*, 53-2, 2/7/1894, 1999.

25. 28 *Stat.* 36-37. As to why Cleveland, a president historians often extol for his "courage," did not veto the bill, see Logan, *Betrayal of the Negro*, 81–83.

gress sought to scuttle the existing Enforcement Acts, to ensure that control of Southern politics would remain firmly in white hands. They succeeded. Whereas the Republicans were stymied by internal division, the Democrats were unified around the idea of white supremacy.

Reduction in Congressional Representation

As Southern states began systematically disenfranchising black voters in the 1890s, not all Republicans were willing to watch the party's postwar policy legacy wither away. And they would get their opportunities to stop it as the GOP retook the House and Senate in the 1894 midterms and elected William McKinley (OH) president (thus securing unified Republican government) in 1896. The Republicans maintained this unified control of government for the next decade and a half.

Beginning in 1899, a small contingent of lawmakers confronted black disenfranchisement. If white Southerners wanted to deny voting rights to black citizens, these Republicans argued, they should face the punishment set out in section 2 of the Fourteenth Amendment:

> Representatives shall be apportioned among the several States according to their respective numbers, counting the whole number of persons in each State, excluding Indians not taxed. But when the right to vote at any election for the choice of electors for President and Vice President of the United States, Representatives in Congress, the Executive and Judicial officers of a State, or the members of the Legislature thereof, is denied to any of the male inhabitants of such State, being twenty-one years of age, and citizens of the United States, or in any way abridged, except for participation in rebellion, or other crime, the basis of representation therein shall be reduced in the proportion which the number of such male citizens shall bear to the whole number of male citizens twenty-one years of age in such State.

Simply stated, the systematic disenfranchisement campaign against black citizens by Southern state governments should have reduced the share of House seats held by Democrats. Yet section 2 was not self-enforcing, and Republicans were left to pursue an implementation campaign.

In late 1899 Senators Marion Butler (P-NC) and Jeter C. Pritchard (R-NC) led the first formal effort to enforce section 2. That year, North Carolina was preparing to follow Mississippi (1890), South Carolina (1895), and Louisiana (1898) in amending its constitution to limit African Americans' voting rights.[26] Both Butler and Pritchard had been elected on Populist-Republican fusion tickets, relying heavily on the votes of the state's black residents. Thus voting rights enforcement was a matter of political survival for both. Butler laid the groundwork for a Fourteenth Amendment challenge in October 1899, arguing that North Carolina's move toward Jim Crow was unconstitutional.[27] Pritchard followed up in December 1899, stating that North Carolina's decision to disenfranchise its black citizens was proof that the state did not possess a "republican form of government."[28]

Pritchard's accusation precipitated an angry back-and-forth with Southern Democrats. John T. Morgan (D-AL), for example, condemned his reading of the US Constitution. Butler and Pritchard relied on the text of the Fourteenth Amendment to make their case, whereas Morgan and his colleagues clung to the notion that states had the authority to determine suffrage requirements (based on the text of the original Constitution). Morgan argued that neither the Fourteenth nor the Fifteenth Amendment guaranteed suffrage rights to all citizens. As long as the condition for voting was not explicitly race-based, he argued, states were free to regulate access to the polls.

After almost four months of debate, Pritchard's resolution was referred to the Committee on Privileges and Elections. In early June 1900 William Chandler (R-NH), chairman of the committee, reported that a majority favored a weaker form of Pritchard's resolution. This new version, Chandler argued, would not empower congressional investigators to "send for persons and papers." Instead, it would direct the committee to do a "general" inquiry into voter disenfranchisement.[29] On two occasions he sought to bring the committee resolution to the Senate floor, only to have his unanimous con-

---

26. Earlier that year (January 1899), Rep. George White (R-NC), the last black member of Congress from the South during this era, alluded to a reduction in representation for Southern states but did not offer legislation to that end. During an extended floor speech, White stated, "If we are unworthy of suffrage, if it is necessary to maintain white supremacy, if it is necessary for the Anglo-Saxon to sway scepter in those States, then you ought to have the benefit only of those who are allowed to vote, and the poor men, whether they be black or white, who are disfranchised ought not to go into the representation of the district or the State. It is a question that this House must deal with some time, sooner or later." See *CR*, 55-3, 1/26/1899, 1125.

27. Richard B. Sherman, *The Republican Party and Black America: From McKinley to Hoover, 1896–1933* (Charlottesville: University of Virginia Press, 1973), 16.

28. *CR*, 56-1, 12/12/1899, 233.

29. *CR*, 56-1, 6/7/1900, 6866.

sent request blocked by Southern Democrats. The committee resolution was thus buried on the Senate calendar.[30]

During the debate over Southern disenfranchisement, Chandler was the only Republican to formally support Pritchard. Every other Republican in the Senate sat silent. A decade after the defeat of the Lodge bill, the party of Lincoln no longer appeared to view protecting blacks' civil rights as important. Indeed, President McKinley had made North-South reconciliation a top priority during his first administration, and he conducted a grand Southern tour in 1898 in an attempt "to bury the lines of sectional division once and for all."[31] Richard Sherman provides a useful summary of the political environment going into the November 1900 presidential election:

> A determined attempt by the Republicans to protect the Negro's vote would have wrecked [President] McKinley's efforts at reconciliation, and the immediate political gains for such a move would not have compensated for the losses. Republicans could not control the South by Negro votes alone, and congressional interference would have destroyed the prospects of building up GOP strength among southern whites.[32]

Although GOP leaders' dreams of building a "lily white" party in the South would prove to be a chimera,[33] their decision to forgo active opposition to disenfranchisement would be maintained into the future.

After McKinley's reelection, another small group of Republicans tried to ensure that voting-rights violations would be punished. During the lame-duck session of the Fifty-Sixth Congress (1899–1901), House Republicans initiated a debate over Southern representation that revolved around new apportionment legislation based on the recently completed Twelfth Census. They would make two attempts to stem the tide of disenfranchisement: an investigatory measure offered by Marlin Olmsted (R-PA) and a punitive measure offered by Edgar Crumpacker (R-IN). Both sought to establish a foundation for limiting Southern representation in the House based on violations of the Fourteenth Amendment.

Olmsted offered his resolution on January 3, 1901, as the House began consideration of the apportionment bill. It instructed the Committee on the

---

30. *CR*, 56-1, 7/1/1900, 6370; 7/7/1900, 6866, 6875.

31. Edward O. Frantz, *The Door of Hope: Republican Presidents and the First Southern Strategy, 1877–1933* (Gainesville: University Press of Florida, 2011), 112.

32. Sherman, *Republican Party and Black America*, 16.

33. See Boris Heersink and Jeffery A. Jenkins, *Republican Party Politics and the American South, 1865–1968* (New York: Cambridge University Press, 2020).

Census to investigate suffrage violations in the South and present the results in a report to Congress — which could justify a reduction in Southern House seats. Olmsted's resolution took the Republican leadership by surprise and, according to one contemporaneous report, led to "confusion" on the House floor.[34] Once order was restored, the House refused 80-83 to consider Olmsted's resolution, with all but one Republican voting yea and all Democrats voting nay.[35] Oscar Underwood (D-AL) then moved to adjourn, which passed 78-74 on a near party-line vote.[36] However, twice as many Republicans as Democrats (thirty-two to sixteen) abstained on the vote. This suggests that a significant number of Republicans, including party leaders, did not view representational reduction as a serious goal, especially if it got in the way of a GOP-crafted apportionment plan.[37]

The next day, Albert Hopkins (R-IL), chairman of the Committee on the Census, predicted that Olmsted's resolution would be reintroduced and agreed to. At the same time, Hopkins conceded that "he did not think the idea of reducing the representation of the Southern States was practicable."[38] The Republicans had decided that it made for good politics to signal publicly that the party was solidly opposed to Southern disenfranchisement efforts.[39] Olmsted reintroduced his resolution, and the House agreed 104-91 to consider it.[40] The Republicans then passed a previous question motion 103-98, ending debate. On each of these votes, approximately thirty additional Republicans participated and supported the pro-civil rights side.[41] Finally, the motion to refer Olmsted's resolution to the Committee on the Census was agreed to without a recorded vote.[42]

The actual benefits associated with the resolution were negligible. As the *Washington Post* noted, "It was well understood nothing definite will ever

34. *Dallas Morning News*, January 4, 1901, 2.

35. *CR*, 56-2, 1/3/1901, 521. The one Republican nay vote was Joseph Graff (IL).

36. *CR*, 56-2, 1/3/1901, 521. Two Democrats — Joseph Sibley (PA) and Charles Snodgrass (TN) — voted nay while one Republican — Malcolm Moody (OR) — voted yea.

37. *NYT*, January 4, 1901, 5; *WP*, January 4, 1901, 3.

38. *Baltimore Sun*, January 4, 1901, 2.

39. As a reporter for the *Baltimore Sun* noted, "The Republicans were placed in a bad hole because they did not want to adopt the resolution and feared they would be accused of cowardice if it were defeated" (January 5, 1901, 2).

40. *CR*, 56-2, 1/4/1901, 545-55.

41. Both were essentially pure party-line votes. Only one Democrat — James Ryan (NY) — voted yea on the first vote, and only one Republican — Theodore Burton (OH) — voted nay on the second vote.

42. *CR*, 56-2, 1/4/1901, 559.

come of it. . . . [While Olmsted] tried to persuade Chairman Hopkins to promise that a special meeting would be called within a week to consider the resolution . . . it is certain that the new apportionment of Representatives will be made before any such data as the resolution calls for can be collected."[43] In short, Republican leaders supported making a symbolic gesture to the nation's black citizens but offered no action that would risk their other policy goals—notably passage of new pro-GOP apportionment legislation.[44] Four days later, on January 8, the apportionment issue was considered on the House floor. The Olmsted resolution had no bearing on the debate because Hopkins personally ensured that it was safely buried in committee. After some wrangling, a GOP-supported apportionment bill passed without any reduction in Southern representation.[45]

Yet debate over section 2 enforcement was not dead. Edgar Crumpacker (R-IN) moved to recommit the just-passed apportionment bill to committee with instructions to ascertain which states had unconstitutionally abridged the right to vote and determine how much their congressional representation should be reduced.[46] A contentious debate followed, with a number of Southern Democrats denouncing the motion but only two Republicans— George White (NC) and Charles Grosvenor (MA)—supporting Crumpacker.[47] Finally debate ceased, and Crumpacker's motion to recommit was considered by a division vote. It failed 94-136. James Stewart (R-NJ) demanded the yeas and nays, but only fourteen members seconded, thus falling short of the required minimum.[48]

Although individual-level data do not exist on division votes, news reports suggested that "several Republicans, including Messrs. [Richmond] Pearson (NC), [Charles] Littlefield (ME), [Amos] Allen (ME), [Ebenezer] Hill (CT), [John] Jenkins (WI), and [Charles] Joy (MO) voted with the

---

43. *WP*, January 5, 1901, 3.

44. The strategic thinking of the GOP leadership is nicely summarized by a reporter for the *Birmingham Age Herald*: "The fact remains that if the Republicans had insisted on debating the Olmsted resolution at length and had finally passed it, the Democrats in retaliation would have seriously delayed the business of the House, and probably forced an extra session . . . by insisting on roll calls on every proposition advanced and every amendment to each bill considered" (January 7, 1901, 2).

45. In fact, the Hopkins bill (i.e., the bill reported out of the Census Committee) was rejected, and a substitute bill, proposed by Edwin Burleigh (R-ME), was passed instead.

46. Crumpacker's motion was thus one step beyond Olmsted's, which (as written) had been mainly informational.

47. *CR*, 56-2, 1/8/1901, 731-48.

48. *CR*, 56-2, 1/8/1901, 748; "House Will Be Larger," *WP*, January 9, 1901, 1.

FIGURE 11. Cartoon of the Fourteenth Amendment, section 2. Artist: Edward Windsor Kemble. 1902. Library of Congress, Prints & Photographs Division, LC-DIG-ppmsca-07161.

Democrats against the motion."[49] Just as in the Olmsted case, the Republicans were unwilling to jeopardize their legislative agenda by supporting a measure that would penalize disenfranchisement efforts and thus promote black voting rights.

Thus, like Senate Republicans earlier in the Fifty-Sixth Congress, House Republicans had largely abandoned substantive civil rights policy.[50] GOP

49. "House Increases Its Membership to 386," *NYT*, January 9, 1901, 7.

50. One such initiative was H.R. 3597, a bill "to incorporate a memorial to the late Frederick Douglass, for the purpose of collecting and preserving a historical record of the antislavery movement in the United States and to assemble all said exhibits in the village of Anacostia in the District of Columbia, as a monument to the anti-slavery movement." H.R. 3597 was introduced by Joseph Babcock (R-WI) on March 5, 1900, and the Republicans voted as a bloc — against nearly unanimous Democratic opposition — to table a Democratic motion to shift the debate, to call the previous question, and to order the engrossment and a third reading of the bill. The House then passed the bill (with a minor amendment) two weeks later without a roll call. For debate and roll-call votes, see *CR*, 56-1, 3/5/1900, 2550–55; 3/19/1900, 3061. On May 26 the Senate passed the bill (with minor amendments) without a roll call. A conference committee was eventually assigned, as the House nonconcurred in the Senate

leaders saw few benefits in being responsive to black voters. Given the rise of Jim Crow, the South was considered beyond the party's reach, and too few blacks lived in the North to be electorally pivotal. Sporadic attempts to investigate suffrage restrictions and reduce Southern representation in Congress would be made in the next few years, but none gained any headway. Sen. Thomas Platt (R-NY), for example, introduced one such measure, which would have cost the Southern states nineteen seats. It was referred to the Committee on the Census, and no further action was taken.[51] This lack of traction was due in part to President Theodore Roosevelt, who opposed an activist approach in dealing with Southern disenfranchisement and representational reduction.[52]

Undeterred, Crumpacker would continue to pursue section 2 enforcement.[53] His closest brush with success came in May 1908, during the Sixtieth Congress. While the House was considering a campaign-contribution reform bill (H.R. 20112),[54] Crumpacker moved to suspend the rules and pass the bill with committee and other amendments. One of these "other" amendments was the following:

That for the purpose of enabling Congress to apportion Representatives among the several States in accordance with the plan provided in the second section of the fourteenth amendment to the Constitution, the Director of the Census, as soon as practicable after each decennial census of population, shall submit to Congress a report of the population by States as shown by such census, which report shall also show the number of male citizens, white and colored, respectively, in each State, 21 years of

amendments and the Senate insisted on them. Both chambers agreed to the conference report without a roll call, and it was signed into law by President McKinley. See *CR*, 56-1, 5/26/1900, 6095; 5/28/1900, 6177; 5/29/1900, 6221; 6/5/1900, 6686; 6/6/1900, 6819, 6858.

51. See Sherman, *Republican Party and Black America*, 76; Perman, *Struggle for Mastery*, 242–44.

52. Sherman, *Republican Party and Black America*, 76–77. Later attempts at representational reduction in the early and late 1920s, led by Rep. George H. Tinkham (R-MA), met with similar opposition from Republican presidents Harding and Coolidge. See Sherman, *Republican Party and Black America*, 169–71, 221–22.

53. For an overview of the proceedings on the Crumpacker amendment and the amended campaign-contribution reform bill, see *CR*, 60-1, 5/22/1908, 6763–68.

54. H.R. 20112, sponsored by Samuel McCall (R-MA), was "a bill providing for publicity of contributions made for the purpose of influencing elections at which Representatives in Congress are elected, prohibiting fraud in registrations and elections, and providing data for the apportionment of Representatives among the States."

age and over, the number of such male citizens in each State found to be illiterate, the number of votes cast by male citizens In each Congressional district at the last preceding general election, the number of such male citizens in each State that had not complied with the registration and election laws therein requiring the payment of a poll or property tax as a condition precedent to the right to register or vote, and the number of such male citizens in each State to whom the right to vote at any election for the choice of electors for President and Vice-President of the United States, Representatives in Congress, the executive and judicial offices of the State or members of the legislature thereof, has been denied or in any way abridged except for participation in crime.[55]

In addition to this new attempt to pursue representational reduction, Crumpacker also added amendments similar to the Enforcement Acts that the Democrats had stripped in the early 1890s. Crumpacker stated that these amendments were

reenactments of sections that were contained in the Federal election law that was repealed under the last Cleveland Administration. They have been upheld by the courts; they are salutary provisions, and make it a crime for any person or association of persons to bribe or corrupt or intimidate electors. They make it a crime in the election for registration officers to commit any kind of fraud against the ballot. They surround the ballot in the selection of Members of this body with sufficient safeguards to warrant its purity, and I undertake to say that no man, no Member of this body, should object to a law the only purpose of which is to secure honest elections.[56]

Democrats immediately cried foul. William Rucker (D-MO) charged the Republicans with "hypocrisy" and "deceit" and noted that whereas "[Democrats] earnestly favor publicity of campaign contributions, we are unalterably opposed to force bills and Federal supervision of elections." Thomas Hardwick (D-GA) described the representational reduction amendment as a "sop thrown to the negro voters in the doubtful States, in the hope that their flagging zeal may be revived and renewed." "Everybody knows that the bill can not possibly pass the Senate," he went on, "or even receive con-

55. *CR*, 60-1, 5/22/1908, 6764.
56. *CR*, 60-1, 5/22/1908, 6764.

sideration in that body . . . when even a half-dead Senate from the South could easily speak it to death." John Sharp Williams (D-MS) then railed at length against Crumpacker's amendments before asking, "Is there any one of you [on the GOP side] that is fool enough to imagine the South is ever again going to submit to policies to which she submitted when she was weak and helpless, during reconstruction days?"[57]

Despite this demonization, the House voted 161-126 to suspend the rules and pass the bill with Crumpacker's amendments attached.[58] All Republicans voted against all but one Democrat.[59] And while the Crumpacker-amended bill received considerable attention in the press — with vivid headlines in Southern newspapers — it had no more momentum.[60] H.R. 20112 died in the Senate Committee on Privileges and Elections.

Were the Republicans serious in their support of representational reduction (and a new "force bill")? Crumpacker, given his efforts over time, probably was. Other Republicans likely supported him for more instrumental reasons: to kill the campaign-contribution reform bill, which was largely an initiative of a few progressive Republicans and Democrats,[61] or to score some easy "position taking" points back home before the November elections.[62] Yet few Republicans in Congress by this time sought to actively use federal power to pursue civil rights. As David Bateman, Ira Katznelson, and John Lapinski note, "The emerging national consensus was that the South should no longer be threatened with federal intervention to pursue a hope-

57. Comments by Rucker, Hardwick, and Williams appear in *CR*, 60-1, 5/22/1908, 6765–67.

58. *CR*, 60-1, 5/22/1908, 6767-68. A simple majority vote was needed to suspend the rules in this case. As Bateman, Katznelson, and Lapinski note, "Republicans had recently supported a temporary change in the rules of the House to allow a bare majority to suspend the rules, a move that was needed to expedite passage of legislation at the end of the session and avoid Democratic filibusters." See David A. Bateman, Ira Katznelson, and John S. Lapinski, *Southern Nation: Congress and White Supremacy after Reconstruction* (Princeton, NJ: Princeton University Press, 2018), 227.

59. The only Democrat to vote yea was Thomas Nicholls (PA).

60. See, e.g., "House Upholds Stroke at South by Crumpacker," *Atlanta Constitution*, May 23, 1908, 1; "Cowardly Trick of Republicans," *Louisville Courier-Journal*, May 23, 1908, 1; "Democrats Are Tricked," *Baltimore Sun*, May 23, 1908, 2; "Republicans of House Stir Up Sectional Fire," *Nashville American*, May 23, 1908, 1.

61. "Pass Publicity Bill That Angers South," *NYT*, May 23, 1908, 3.

62. On position taking as a congressional activity, see David R. Mayhew, *Congress: The Electoral Connection* (1974; repr., New Haven, CT: Yale University Press, 2004), 61–77.

less and fatally flawed idea. Black Americans were now peculiar citizens, with their rights and privileges to be determined by southern whites rather than by the terms of the national constitution and legislature."[63]

The "Brownsville Affray"

In his 1905 inaugural address, Theodore Roosevelt did not make explicit reference to race or to the status of black citizens. His silence was not an indication of racial peace. African Americans continued to live under "lynch law" throughout the South; race riots exploded in Wilmington, North Carolina, in 1898, New York City in 1900, and Atlanta in 1906; and widespread voter suppression gave the lie to the Fourteenth and Fifteenth Amendments. Speaking in 1909, one participant in the National Negro Conference described the quickly deteriorating conditions in stark terms: "[Black citizens are] standing on the very threshold of a physical slavery almost as bad and hopeless as that from which [they were] emancipated."[64] Three divisions of black soldiers making up part of the Twenty-Fifth Infantry, stationed in Brownsville, Texas, would soon learn that their service to the country did not guarantee them equality. Their treatment at the hands of President Roosevelt and congressional Republicans further demonstrates how far the GOP had departed from its historical commitment to black civil rights.

In May 1906 the War Department announced that the 167 black soldiers who made up the First Battalion, Twenty-Fifth Infantry, would replace a white division housed at Fort Brown in Brownsville, Texas. The white residents of Brownsville were not pleased by the news. The fort's white surgeon, Benjamin J. Edgar Jr., told Congress that every resident he spoke to said the black soldiers would not be welcome.[65] The soldiers, of course, did nothing to justify such hostility: the battalion had won acclaim for its efforts against the Sioux Indians on the Plains, as well as in Cuba and the Philippines. In response to citizen outrage, Secretary of War William Howard Taft explained that "while a certain amount of race prejudice between white and black seems to have become almost universal throughout the country . . . colored troops are quite as well disciplined and behaved as the average of other troops."[66]

63. Bateman, Katznelson, and Lapinski, *Southern Nation*, 229.

64. Quoted in Ann J. Lane, *The Brownsville Affair: National Crisis and Black Reaction* (Port Washington, NY: National University Publications/Kennikat Press, 1971), 7.

65. Edgar, quoted in John D. Weaver, *The Brownsville Raid* (New York: Norton, 1970), 21.

66. Quoted in Weaver, *Brownsville Raid*, 22.

Despite Taft's admonition, residents proved hostile from the moment the black soldiers arrived in late July 1906. Major Charles Penrose, the commanding officer at the fort, recalled that when the troops made their way into town "people were standing along the streets but there were no smiling faces or anything of that kind, as you might imagine when you are coming to a new post." More ominously, one of the departing soldiers testified that a white resident threatened that "the first crooked move [black soldiers] would make, [the townspeople] would annihilate" the entire battalion.[67] Sensing widespread hostility, Israel Harris—one of the black soldiers stationed at Fort Brown—told Congress he wanted to leave Texas as soon as he was discharged. Townspeople "were unfriendly toward the soldiers," he explained, "and that is why I did not want to stay there."[68] Neither Harris nor any of his fellow battalion members would have this choice.

About midnight on August 13, 1906, from nine to twenty armed men ran through Brownsville shooting indiscriminately into the city's homes and businesses. The marauders killed a bartender and wounded a police officer who had responded to the sound of gunfire. A nighttime attack in a poorly lighted city, witnesses claimed, made it impossible to identify the guilty parties. Yet suspicion immediately fell on black soldiers. Empty shell casings found along the attack route appeared to match those issued to the soldiers. No townspeople claimed to have seen any of the raiders, but multiple witnesses told investigators they had heard "negro voices."[69] Investigators, however, were not trying to objectively identify the guilty parties. Most witness interviews started like this: "We are inquiring into the matter of last night with a view to ascertaining who the guilty parties are. We know they were negro soldiers. If there is anything that would throw any light on the subject we would like to have it."[70]

The soldiers maintained their innocence. After publication of the government's initial inquiry into the shooting, the *New York Times* noted, "No evidence had been gathered to prove a conspiracy on the part of members of the battalion."[71] Advocates for the soldiers, who were part of the interracial "Constitution League," issued their own report defending the troops.

67. Quotes in Weaver, *Brownsville Raid*, 23–24.

68. "Affray at Brownsville, Tex.," Hearings before the Committee on Military Affairs, United States Senate, 1907, 42.

69. "Report on the Brownsville Affray," *U.S. Senate Docs.*, 60-1, doc. 402, pt. 1, 1908, 440–53.

70. "Report on the Brownsville Affray," 446.

71. "Roosevelt Is Firm and Taft Gives Way," *NYT*, November 22, 1906, 1.

The shell casings found at the scene, they claimed, could have been collected from rifle ranges and dropped along the shooters' path to incriminate the black troops.[72] The witness statements were also called into question, because old uniforms were discarded in a trash pile that was accessible to the public. Any town resident could easily have disguised himself as a member of the black battalion. There was "'fair reason' to believe that the commotion was created by civilians, partly to gratify a long harbored hatred against black soldiers."[73]

President Roosevelt did not take seriously the many inconsistencies raised during the government's investigation. Instead he followed the recommendation of General E. A. Garlington, the government's inspector general, who demanded that all 167 soldiers be "discharged without honor." Despite Garlington's repeated and harsh interrogations, not a single member of the battalion provided any reason to suspect their involvement. Garlington portrayed the soldiers' failure to incriminate one another as a conspiracy to "stand together in a determination to resist the detection of the guilty."[74] As a consequence, he argued, all 167 soldiers "should stand together when the penalty falls."[75]

Roosevelt accepted this explanation, claiming in a statement to the Senate that the black soldiers "banded together in a conspiracy to protect the assassins and would-be assassins."[76] On November 5, 1906, he carried out Garlington's recommendation. Roosevelt's invocation of "discharge without honor" was notable, as this was a "new and little-known administrative device" that was distinguishable from a "dishonorable discharge." To be dishonorably discharged, a soldier had to be provided with counsel and court-martialed. The status "discharge without honor" carried with it no such requirement, allowing Roosevelt to disband the black battalion without formally charging anyone. None of the 167 black troops had an opportunity to defend themselves in a court of law or through a formal court-martial.[77]

Roosevelt understood that discharging the black troops in this way

72. James A. Tinsley, "Roosevelt, Foraker, and the Brownsville Affray," *Journal of Negro History* 41 (1956): 57.

73. Constitution League report quoted in Lane, *Brownsville Affair*, 29–31.

74. Quoted in Weaver, *Brownsville Raid*, 95.

75. "Report on the Brownsville Affray," 182.

76. "Report on the Brownsville Affray," 5–6.

77. Weaver, *Brownsville Raid*, 133.

threatened to generate anger among African American voters, especially since some Republicans were relying on black turnout in the 1906 midterm elections. He worked to limit fallout by waiting to announce his decision until November 9, 1906, three days after the elections. Recognizing the political opportunism behind the delayed announcement, the *Washington Post* noted that the election of Nicholas Longworth, Roosevelt's son-in-law, who was running for an Ohio House seat, "would not have been possible if the colored voters in his district had been arrayed against him."[78] Black defections might also have tipped the New York governor's race against Charles Evans Hughes, with significant political consequences for the 1908 presidential election.[79] In short, Roosevelt expected black voters to be outraged by his decision. He was right.

Black civic, political, and religious leaders from around the country vilified Roosevelt. T. Thomas Fortune's *New York Age*, one of the most widely read black newspapers, condemned the administration for "carrying into the federal government the demand of the Southern white devils that innocent and law-abiding black men shall help the legal authorities spy out and deliver practically to the mob black men alleged to have committed some sort of crime."[80] The Niagara Movement, forerunner to the National Association for the Advancement of Colored People (NAACP), followed suit. At its 1908 conference in Oberlin, Ohio, participants endorsed a platform calling on black citizens to "remember that the conduct of the Republican party toward Negroes has been a disgraceful failure to keep just promises."[81] Booker T. Washington, founder of the National Negro Business League, remained loyal to Roosevelt and Taft, but he could do little to calm the outrage among the black elite.[82]

Senator Joseph Foraker (R-OH), a Civil War veteran, former governor, and sometime political ally of black citizens, saw the potential black defections from the GOP as a political opportunity. Specifically, he saw the Brownsville incident as a vehicle for peeling enough GOP voters away from

78. "Sharp Comment in New York," *WP*, November 22, 1906, 2.

79. Tinsley, "Roosevelt, Foraker, and the Brownsville Affray," 47.

80. Quoted in Emma Lou Thornbrough, "The Brownsville Episode and the Negro Vote," *Mississippi Valley Historical Review* 44 (1957): 471.

81. Quoted in Lane, *Brownsville Affair*, 79.

82. Harry Lembeck, *Taking on Theodore Roosevelt: How One Senator Defied the President on Brownsville and Shook American Politics* (Amherst, NY: Prometheus Books, 2015), 313-15, 320-22, 340-41.

FIGURE 12. Cartoon of President Theodore Roosevelt. 1906. Library of Congress, Rare Book and Special Collections Division, Printed Ephemera Collection, Portfolio 240, Folder 10a.

William Howard Taft to deny him the Republican presidential nomination in 1908.[83] Should Taft fail, Foraker considered himself a likely candidate. Once the Constitution League published its report raising doubts about the guilt of the black troops, Foraker called for a Senate investigation.

83. For more on Foraker, see Everett Walters, *Joseph Benson Foraker: An Uncompromising Republican* (Columbus: Ohio History Press, 1948).

The conflict between Roosevelt and Foraker over Brownsville began on December 3, 1906, the first day of the Fifty-Ninth Congress. Aware that Foraker planned to pursue a Senate investigation, Boies Penrose (R-PA) — a Roosevelt ally — called on the president to provide "to the Senate, if not incompatible with public interests, full information bearing upon the recent order" dismissing the black troops.[84] Foraker immediately responded with his own resolution directing Secretary of War Taft to provide all "official letters, telegrams, reports, orders, etc." connected to Roosevelt's order. Foraker's resolution also directed the War Department to explain how Roosevelt's order materially harmed the discharged troops by denying them pensions, the right to enroll in a "national soldiers home," and the opportunity to be buried in a national cemetery.[85] Whereas Penrose's resolution would have granted Roosevelt the discretion to decide what information he gave the Senate, Foraker's obligated Secretary Taft to turn over everything relevant. Foraker's inquiry into the status of pay, burial, and accessibility of soldiers' homes also threatened to reveal how the black troops were denied benefits without a trial or due process. Such harm could justify calls for official court proceedings against the accused. By this point it was clear that the administration was unlikely to win in court. Without a suspect, court proceedings could not even begin.

Senate debate over these dueling resolutions continued through the first week of the session. Roosevelt's allies, led by Henry Cabot Lodge (R-MA), insisted on the importance of presidential discretion concerning military information provided to Congress.[86] In response, Foraker declared, "We want all of [the information held by the War Department], and and we want it without regard to whether somebody might think it was incompatible with the public interest or not."[87] Confronted with a difficult choice, Senate Republicans hedged their bets. On December 6, 1906, the Senate passed both resolutions by voice vote.[88]

Roosevelt used his December 19 message to the Senate to respond. Citing the investigations already undertaken by the government, he condemned the "murderous conduct" of the black troops and the "conspiracy by which many of the other members of these companies saved the criminals from

84. *CR*, 59-2, 12/3/1906, 2.
85. *CR*, 59-2, 12/3/1906, 2.
86. *CR*, 59-2, 12/5/1906, 55.
87. *CR*, 59-2, 12/5/1906, 55.
88. *CR*, 59-2, 12/6/1906, 106.

justice."[89] He also directly addressed Foraker's argument that the troops were punished without due process. "I deny emphatically that such is the case," Roosevelt proclaimed, "because as punishment [discharge without honor] is utterly inadequate. The punishment for mutineers and murderers such as those guilty of the Brownsville assault is death. . . . I would that it were possible for me to have punished the guilty men."[90] Roosevelt's aggressive response—described by the *Washington Post* as "defiance as an explanation"—reflects the administration's defensiveness over race issues.[91] According to the *New York Times*, the "Negro vote cast in a Republican National Convention is the greatest asset a politician can have."[92] Foraker was making a play for those votes.

Immediately after the official reading of Roosevelt's message, Foraker introduced a new resolution calling on the Committee on Military Affairs to "take further testimony to establish all facts connected with the discharge" of the troops.[93] Foraker wanted an official congressional investigation, and he wanted his committee to lead it. The next day he made a prolonged floor speech casting doubt on Roosevelt's assertions as well as on the evidence behind them. Lodge again stepped in to defend Roosevelt. "It is not conceivable," Lodge asserted, "that either of them [Roosevelt or Taft] would be influenced in this matter by any local or race prejudice."[94] Roosevelt also made it known to the *New York Times* that "not even to avoid impeachment" would he rescind the discharge order. Describing himself as "fighting mad," the president went on to refer to Foraker's call for an official investigation as the "most contemptible playing of politics," motivated by his desire to "damage Secretary Taft so as to make it impossible for him to obtain the support of the Ohio delegation" at the 1908 Republican National Convention.[95]

Despite the president's vehement opposition to a congressional investigation, the politics around the Brownsville incident made it impossible for Senate Republicans to formally oppose Foraker's efforts. Debate over the precise wording of the resolution continued into late January 1907. Over the course of the month Lodge introduced, then withdrew, a resolution re-

89. "Report on the Brownsville Affray," 1–7.
90. "Report on the Brownsville Affray," 6.
91. "The Brownsville Affair," *WP*, December 20, 1906, 6.
92. "Mingo Sanders Centre of Fight on Roosevelt," *NYT*, December 25, 1906, 1.
93. *CR*, 59-2, 12/19/1906, 552.
94. *CR*, 59-2, 12/20/1906, 579.
95. "Mr. Roosevelt Defies Negro Troops' Friends," *NYT*, December 23, 1906, 1.

affirming the validity of Roosevelt's decision.[96] On January 22 Foraker also forced roll-call votes to table two substitute resolutions. The first, offered by Stephen Mallory (D-FL), endorsed a full investigation. Mallory introduced this resolution not to get to the truth, but to embarrass Roosevelt. The Senate voted 43-22 to table Mallory's substitute, with all but three Republicans voting yea.[97] Next, Charles Culberson (D-TX) introduced a resolution stipulating that it was "the judgment of the Senate" that President Roosevelt "was authorized by law and justified by the facts" when he issued his discharge order. The Senate voted 46-19 to set aside Culberson's substitute, with all Republicans voting yea.[98] The Senate then adopted Foraker's resolution by voice vote.[99] Hearings would begin one month later.

The Senate investigation of Brownsville ran from February to June 1907, then resumed for additional hearings from November 1907 to March 1908. Over these many months, the Committee on Military Affairs took testimony from 160 witnesses.[100] The committee's final judgment was not clearcut. The majority report—signed by all the committee's Democrats and four of eight Republicans—endorsed Roosevelt's position. According to these senators, the weight of the evidence demonstrated that the attack was carried out by black troops stationed at Fort Brown. The majority also found with "reasonable certainty" that soldiers who did not personally aid in the attack helped protect the identities of those who did.

The four Republicans who signed on to the majority report—Francis Warren (R-WY), William Warner (R-MO), Henry Cabot Lodge (R-MA), and Henry du Pont (R-DE)—also issued their own statement calling on Congress to write legislation that would allow reenlistment for any of the discharged troops who, within one year, could demonstrate their innocence to the satisfaction of the president. The four remaining Republicans—Nathan B. Scott (R-WV), Joseph Foraker (R-OH), Morgan Bulkeley (R-CT), and James Hemenway (R-IN)—issued two different minority reports. The first, signed by all four, argued that all 167 soldiers should be immediately reinstated pending any formal charges brought against specific

96. *CR*, 59-2, 1/1/1907, 626.

97. *CR*, 59-2, 1/22/1907, 1508. The three Republicans voting nay were Robert La Follette (WI), Porter McCumber (ND), and William Warner (MO).

98. *CR*, 59-2, 1/22/1907, 1510–12.

99. *CR*, 59-2, 1/22/1907, 1512.

100. For a summary of the hearings see Lane, *Brownsville Affair*, 34–52.

individuals. The second, signed by Foraker and Bulkeley, declared that all the soldiers were innocent.

Not long after the committee released its reports, Foraker took to the floor to discuss new legislation motivated by the committee's findings. After denying that he aimed to use the Brownsville incident as an opportunity to "attack the President or Secretary Taft in connection with this matter," Foraker gave an impassioned defense of the troops, poking holes in the evidence against them, defending their military records, and calling into question the motives of the government investigators. He then went on to discuss S. 6206, legislation introduced by William Warner, which reflected the position of the Republicans who signed the majority report. It gave soldiers the opportunity for full enlistment "if at any time within one year after the approval of this act the president shall be satisfied that any former enlisted man . . . had no participation in the affray or guilty knowledge" of those who did.[101] Foraker attacked S. 6206 on the grounds that "practically every man of this battalion would have to provide his innocence before one who has over and over again formally and publicly adjudged him guilty."[102] Foraker's substitute proposal (S. 5729) allowed immediate reenlistment, cleared service records, and provided full back pay for all soldiers willing to take an oath attesting their innocence.[103]

The Senate took no further action on Brownsville-related legislation in 1908. Indeed, it looked as though both bills were dead. Warner's bill lacked majority support, and Roosevelt characterized Foraker's proposal as "a purely academic measure." Should the bill pass, Roosevelt intended to veto it. Should it pass over his veto, Roosevelt argued, "it would be clearly unconstitutional and I should pay not the slightest heed to it."[104] Meanwhile, Taft wrapped up the GOP presidential nomination, and Foraker's relentless attacks on the administration earned him Roosevelt's "virulent hostility."[105]

Enter newspaperman William Randolph Hearst. On September 17, 1908, Hearst traveled to Ohio intending to prove that "the Republican Party has been for a long time the beneficiary of trust corruption." To make this point, Hearst publicized a number of letters between Foraker and Standard Oil making it seem that the senator was paid $50,000 to oppose antitrust legis-

---

101. *CR*, 60-1, 4/14/1908, 4721.
102. *CR*, 60-1, 4/14/1908, 4723.
103. *CR*, 60-1, 4/14/1908, 4721.
104. Quoted in Lembeck, *Taking on Theodore Roosevelt*, 497.
105. Foraker's wife quoted in Weaver, *Brownsville Raid*, 207.

lation. Roosevelt gleefully broadcast Hearst's accusation. Writing to one friend, he described the letters as showing "what everyone on the inside knew, that Foraker was not really influenced in the least by any feeling for the Negro, but that he acted as the agent of corporations."[106] On January 2, 1909, as a result of Hearst's revelations, Ohio Republicans chose Theodore Burton to succeed Foraker. His career in the Senate was over.

Surprisingly, Foraker's political fate did not kill the discussion around the Brownsville legislation. Instead, with his time in office winding down, Foraker pushed the Senate to debate two amended versions of S. 5729. The first empowered Foraker himself to name five military officers to a Court of Military Inquiry to review the case materials under the assumption that some or all of the soldiers were innocent. It would then certify those soldiers as available for reenlistment, and the president would be bound by any decisions.[107] Lacking the votes to pass this version of the bill, Foraker agreed to a substitute offered by Nelson Aldrich (R-NH), which empowered the secretary of war to convene a similar court of inquiry composed of five military officers.[108] This court would then determine if any of the discharged soldiers qualified for reenlistment.[109] Aldrich's proposal, in other words, assumed the soldiers were guilty and simply gave them an opportunity to exonerate themselves for crimes they were assumed to have committed.

On February 23 the Senate passed S. 5729 (as amended by Aldrich), 56-26, with all Republicans opposing all but one Democrat.[110] Four days later the House passed the bill 212-102.[111] President Roosevelt signed it into law on March 2. Despite the measure's enactment, however, the soldiers Roosevelt discharged would not be cleared of all crimes for more than sixty years. In 1972 the army finally acted. As the *New York Times* described it, "Declaring the action a gross injustice, Secretary of the Army Robert F. Froehlke

106. The Hearst incident and Roosevelt's reaction are described in Weaver, *Brownsville Raid*, 209–12.

107. *CR*, 60-2, 2/23/1909, 2932–33.

108. Aldrich was the Republican majority leader in the Senate, and his goal in seeking a compromise was strategic. As Harry Lembeck states, "[Aldrich] would have to protect President Taft and shepherd his legislation through, and he did not want Brownsville, which had tied the Senate up in knots for more than two years, snarling things up." Lembeck, *Taking on Theodore Roosevelt*, 381.

109. *CR*, 60-2, 1/29/1909, 1579.

110. *CR*, 60-2, 2/23/1909, 2948. The one Democrat was Henry Teller (CO).

111. *CR*, 60-2, 2/27/1909, 3400. Republicans voted 179-1, Northern Democrats 30-15, and Southern Democrats 1-86.

ordered the discharges changed to honorable for the 167 members of the First Battalion, 25th Infantry."[112]

Overall, the conflict Foraker instigated with Roosevelt and his GOP allies backfired and cost him his political career. More significantly, however, the GOP's defense of Roosevelt's decision, and the anger directed at Foraker's efforts, reveals how completely the GOP had abandoned the political interests of black citizens by the early twentieth century.

Further Congressional Dueling on Race, 1908–18

From 1908 to 1918, the Democrats once again made a concerted effort to enact policy that would undermine the rights of black citizens. Before winning back unified control of government in 1912, they focused on mandating segregated streetcars in Washington, DC. This effort failed. After 1912 they fought to strip the federal government of its authority to supervise Senate elections under the Seventeenth Amendment and attempted to legally prohibit interracial marriage.[113] These efforts also failed. Democrats were successful, however, in beating back GOP efforts to ensure an equal distribution of federal funds to black and white land-grant colleges in the South. These cases indicate that when Congress considered civil rights during the Wilson administration, the outcome would never favor black citizens.

SEGREGATION ON STREETCARS IN
THE DISTRICT OF COLUMBIA

The Democratic Party's initial attempt to bring Jim Crow to the District of Columbia came in the form of an amendment to a bill appropriating money to buy streetcar track. During House debate on the appropriations bill, James Thomas "Cotton Tom" Heflin (D-AL) sought to formally segregate seating areas in coaches. The "truthful white man will tell you," Heflin argued, "that he prefers to ride in a car with his own race, separate and dis-

---

112. "Army Clears 167 Black Soldiers Disciplined in a Shooting in 1906," *NYT*, September 29, 1972, 1. The story also reports, "The Army said the disciplinary action was the only documented case of mass punishment in its history." For events leading up to and including the army decision, see John D. Weaver, *The Senator and the Sharecropper's Son: Exoneration of the Brownsville Soldiers* (College Station: Texas A&M University Press, 1998), 198–213.

113. See Desmond King, *Separate and Unequal: Black Americans and the U.S. Federal Government* (Oxford: Oxford University Press, 1995), 20–27.

tinct from the negro race."[114] Heflin's proposed amendment drew immediate protest from House Republicans. David Foster (R-VT), for example, characterized the proposal as "un-American" and "unworthy of our twentieth-century civilization."[115] With Republicans in the majority, such a blatant endorsement of Jim Crow had little chance of success. And when the House took a division vote on Heflin's amendment, it failed 104-57.[116] Heflin and other Southern Democrats would have to accept integrated streetcars in the District of Columbia if they chose to ride them.[117]

SEVENTEENTH AMENDMENT

Four years after Heflin's failed streetcar proposal, Congress passed the Seventeenth Amendment.[118] In keeping with a broader effort to democratize American politics, progressives sought the direct election of senators as a way to bolster the political standing of the individual in a world increasingly dominated by concentrated power.[119] During the Sixty-Second Con-

114. *CR*, 60-1, 2/22/1908, 2340.

115. *CR*, 60-1, 2/22/1908, 2340.

116. *CR*, 60-1, 2/22/1908, 2350.

117. Heflin and Washington streetcars would continue to be in the news. A month after introducing his segregation amendment, Heflin — who often carried an unlicensed weapon — was riding a DC streetcar with Rep. Edwin J. Ellerbe (D-SC) on the way to deliver a temperance lecture at the Metropolitan Methodist Episcopal Church. As Blair Kelley recounts it, "Heflin ordered a black man, Lewis Lundy, off [the] streetcar for drinking in the presence of white women. When Lundy argued and fought back, Heflin threw him to the ground as the other passengers ran away. When Lundy tried to run, Heflin fired two shots from the window of the car: the first hit a white bystander, and the second struck Lundy in the head. Even though both Lundy and the bystander were severely injured, Heflin faced no consequences in criminal court and remained proud of his actions: 'Under the circumstances, there was nothing else for me to do. I am glad to say I have not yet reached the point where I will see a negro . . . take a drink in the presence of a lady without saying something.' He was indicted but never convicted and continued to hold his seat in the U.S. House for another twenty-four years, bragging that the shooting was the highlight of his career." Blair L. M. Kelley, *Right to Ride: Streetcar Boycotts and the African American Citizenship in the Era of "Plessy v. Ferguson"* (Chapel Hill: University of North Carolina Press, 2010), 160.

118. The conference report that became the Seventeenth Amendment passed in the Senate on April 12, 1912. It passed the House one month later, on May 13, 1912.

119. For details on the Progressive Era roots of the Seventeenth Amendment, see Terry Smith, "Rediscovering the Sovereignty of the People: The Case for Senate Districts," *North Carolina Law Review* 75 (1996): 1–75. For more on the Seventeenth Amendment generally, see

gress (1911–13), with Democrats controlling the House and Republicans the Senate, a debate over federal supervision of direct Senate elections nearly prevented Congress from adopting the proposal. Race proved to be the central factor driving this conflict.

The House moved first. In April 1911, H.J. Res. 39 passed by an overwhelming vote, 296-16.[120] The only opposition came from a small subset of Republicans who objected to a provision in the legislation stipulating that "the times, places, and manner of holding elections of Senators shall be as prescribed in each state by the legislature thereof."[121] Republican opponents rightly saw this provision—characterized as the "race rider"—as a way to erase the federal power delineated in the Elections Clause of article 1.[122] Without federal authority to supervise Senate elections, they worried, Southern Democrats would be further empowered to disenfranchise black voters. Indeed, some saw it as a concession to those Southerners who sought to "nullify" the Fourteenth and Fifteenth Amendments.[123] Immediately before voting on the underlying language of H.J. Res. 39, H. Olin Young (R-MI) forced the House to vote on an amendment stripping this provision from the bill. Young's amendment failed 123-190, on a pure party-line vote.[124]

Senate Republicans now faced a decision: pass H.J. Res. 39 with the "race rider" attached, or work to strip it out and risk undermining the amendment itself. Joseph Bristow (R-KS) chose the latter option when he introduced an amendment identical to the one just voted down in the House. On June 12, 1911, Bristow's amendment came up for a vote and resulted in a tie, 44-44. Republican vice president James Sherman then cast the tie-breaking vote

John S. Lapinski, "Representation and Reform: A Congress Centered Approach to American Political Development" (PhD diss., Columbia University, 2000), 160–200; Ralph A. Rossum, *Federalism, the Supreme Court, and the Seventeenth Amendment: The Irony of Constitutional Democracy* (Lanham, MD: Lexington Books, 2001), 208–14; Wendy J. Schiller and Charles Stewart III, *Electing the Senate: Indirect Democracy before the Seventeenth Amendment* (Princeton, NJ: Princeton University Press, 2015).

120. *CR*, 62-1, 4/13/1911, 242–43.

121. The entire amendment is printed in *CR*, 62-1, 4/13/1911, 203.

122. Article 1, section 4, clause 1 stipulates the following: "The Times, Places, and Manner of holding Elections for Senators and Representatives, shall be prescribed in each State by the Legislature thereof; *but the Congress may at any time by Law make or alter such Regulations, except as to the Places of chusing [sic] Senators*" (emphasis added).

123. Howard W. Allen, Aage R. Clausen, and Jerome M. Clubb, "Political Reform and Negro Rights in the Senate, 1909–1915," *Journal of Southern History* 37 (1971): 194.

124. *CR*, 62-1, 4/13/1911, 241.

in favor.[125] Five Republicans from the party's western progressive faction voted against Bristow: William E. Borah (ID), Asle J. Gronna (ND), Robert La Follette (WI), Miles Poindexter (WA), and John D. Works (CA). Thus the yea vote of Democrat James Clarke (AR) saved the amendment from defeat. The Senate then passed H.J. Res. 39 (as amended), 64-24.[126]

The now-amended proposal moved back to the House for concurrence. On two occasions — in 1911 and 1912 — the House refused.[127] As the *New York Times* reported, "Southern members, mindful of the malodorous Force bill and reconstruction days, have been bitter and determined in their opposition to the Bristow amendment."[128] Yet Senate Republicans refused to concede. In late April 1912 they staged a floor vote to insist on their amendment (as a way of demonstrating their resolve). They reaffirmed their support for the measure 42-36, with only one GOP defection.[129] Approximately three weeks later, the House gave in and voted 237-39 to concur with the Senate and pass what would become the Seventeenth Amendment.[130] The only dissenting votes came from Southern Democrats.

Why did the House give in? According to the *New York Times*,

> The surrender of the House to the Senate on the Bristow proposal for the maintenance of the status quo of Federal supervision over Congressional elections followed a conference last week between Speaker [Champ] Clark [D-MO], Chairman [Robert Lee] Henry [D-TX] of the Rules Committee, Chairman [William] Rucker [D-MO] of the committee in charge of the bill, and William Jennings Bryan, in which it was agreed that while the joint resolution as amended by the Senate is not all that the Democrats desired it would be better to accept what they could get than sacrifice the whole movement.[131]

Before agreeing to concur with the Senate, however, the House was locked in a bitter fight, led by Charles Lafayette Bartlett (D-GA). Bartlett

---

125. *CR*, 62-1, 6/12/1911, 1923. Republicans voted 43-5.

126. *CR*, 62-1, 6/12/1911, 1924. Republicans voted 33-16, and Democrats voted 31-8.

127. *CR*, 62-1, 6/27/1911, 2548; 62-2, 4/17/1912, 4905.

128. "Senators by Direct Vote Passes House," *NYT*, May 14, 1912, 1.

129. *CR*, 62-2, 4/23/1912, 5172. Republicans voted 41-1. The GOP defector was William Borah (ID).

130. *CR*, 62-2, 5/13/1912, 6367-68. Republicans voted 104-0, Northern Democrats 92-0, and Southern Democrats 41-39.

131. "Senators by Direct Vote Passes House," *NYT*, May 14, 1912, 1.

led a group of Southern Democrats against the deal that Democrat leaders were trying to arrange.[132] He moved to concur in the Senate amendment but with an amendment attached:

> *Provided*, That Congress shall not have power or authority to provide for the qualifications of electors of United States Senators within the various States of the United States, nor to authorize the appointment of supervisors of election, Judges of election, or returning boards to certify the results of any such election, nor to authorize the use of United States marshals or the military forces of the United States or troops of the United States at the polls during said election.[133]

Two hours of contentious debate followed, in which "[Southern Democrats] based their opposition almost entirely on the danger of negro domination."[134] Amid the debate, Bartlett exchanged heated remarks with William Rucker (D-MO) and others. Majority Leader Oscar Underwood (D-AL) sought to underscore the importance of not tacking on the Bartlett amendment, lest direct election of senators be lost entirely. Finally Bartlett's motion came to a vote, and it failed 89-189.[135] All but four Southern Democrats voted for the Bartlett amendment, against all but nine Northern Democrats and all but three Republicans. In defeating the Bartlett amendment and pushing back against Southern fears of federal intrusion in Southern elections, the coalition for the direct election of senators prevailed.

ANTIMISCEGENATION LEGISLATION

Later that year Democrats tried to reassert themselves during the lame-duck session of the Sixty-Second Congress. In the House, Seaborn Roddenbery (D-GA) proposed a constitutional amendment to prohibit interracial marriage.[136] Roddenbery's proposal came at a moment of significant racial unrest. Race riots had broken out throughout the country in 1912, due in part to the athletic success of Jack Johnson, the black boxing champion who had recently retained his title against Jim Jeffries, the white former world

132. For the full debate, see *CR*, 62-2, 5/13/1912, 6345–67.

133. *CR*, 62-2, 5/13/1912, 6346.

134. "Direct Election Wins," *WP*, May 14, 1912, 1.

135. *CR*, 62-2, 5/13/1912, 6366–67. The three Republicans were Everis Hayes (CA), Julius Kahn (CA), and Joseph Knowland (CA).

136. Roddenbery's amendment was H.J. Res. 368. See *CR*, 62-3, 12/11/1912, 507.

champion. Even on its own Johnson's athletic triumph might have been too much for white Southerners to accept. Combined with Johnson's marriage to two white women, it spurred Southern Democrats to action. Roddenbery mentioned Johnson by name in his floor diatribe, condemning Northerners for allowing intermarriage and thereby making possible Johnson's racially subversive behavior.[137]

Roddenbery hoped to goad Congress into forcing Southern views of interracial relationships onto the rest of the nation. He noted that legislatures in twenty-nine of the forty-eight states had already passed laws against miscegenation, while eleven other states were considering them.[138] With this in mind, Roddenbery claimed that the proposal would simply codify a practice that was already accepted by much of the country.[139] In the end his proposal went nowhere — it was referred to the Judiciary Committee, where it died.[140] Moreover, only one additional state — Wyoming in 1913 — would adopt legislation against miscegenation.

The issue of miscegenation would emerge again in the lame-duck session. On February 10, 1913, Thomas Hardwick (D-GA) introduced H.R. 598, which sought to "prohibit in the District of Columbia the intermarriage of whites with negroes or Mongolians" and make it a felony.[141] Democratic opponents of interracial marriage had thus narrowed the scope of their at-

---

137. For the full text of Roddenbery's floor speech, see *CR*, 62-3, 12/11/1912, 502-4. For more on the connection between Jack Johnson and antimiscegenation laws, see Peggy Pascoe, *What Comes Naturally: Miscegenation Law and the Making of Race in America* (Oxford: Oxford University Press, 2009), 163-73. Johnson was also later prosecuted under the Mann Act. This law, enacted in 1913, sought to punish the transport of women across state lines "for the purpose of prostitution or debauchery, or for any other immoral purpose." It became a tool for enforcing the spirit of antimiscegenation legislation even though Congress failed to enact a formal prohibition on interracial marriage. On May 24, 2018, President Donald Trump issued a posthumous pardon for Johnson. See https://www.nytimes.com/2018/05/24/sports/jack-johnson-pardon-trump.html. For more on the Mann Act see David J. Langum, *Crossing over the Line: Legislating Morality and the Mann Act* (Chicago: University of Chicago Press, 1994).

138. See Pascoe, *What Comes Naturally*, 167-68.

139. *CR*, 62-3, 12/11/1912, 504.

140. Roddenbery would strike again in January 1913, raising the subject of miscegenation and pushing for the passage of his constitutional amendment. While earning applause for his forceful appeal, he made no further progress on his proposal. See *CR*, 62-3, 1/30/1913, 2312.

141. H.R. 5948 set a penalty of up to $500, two years in prison, or both. See *CR*, 62-3, 2/10/1913, 2929.

tack. Rather than pushing a constitutional amendment, they simply sought to ban interracial marriage within the District of Columbia.[142] Somewhat surprisingly, Hardwick's antimiscegenation bill was passed in "less than five minutes," with absolutely no debate.[143] A simple voice vote would have decided the matter before James Mann (R-IL) asked for a division, and it was reported that there were ninety-two votes in favor and twelve votes opposed.[144]

In explaining the outcome and the lack of debate on the bill, a correspondent for the *New York Times* reported, "Almost every State has a law prohibiting such marriages, and the feeling generally among House members is that the Nation's capital should be in line with the general sentiment of the States on this subject."[145] Thus House Republicans, perhaps intimidated by the Democrats' bluster and worried about shifting public opinion and further legislative activism by states in the North, quietly acquiesced and allowed the bill to pass. In the end nothing would come of the legislation: it was referred to the Senate Judiciary Committee — controlled by Republicans — and not reported out before the session expired less than a month later.[146]

Just two years later, during the Sixty-Third Congress (1913–15), House Democrats — now with majorities in both chambers — again pushed legislation against miscegenation in the District of Columbia. H.R. 1710, offered by Frank Clark (D-FL), was even more draconian than the 1913 version. It proposed to ban the practice and impose a penalty of up to $5,000, five years

142. Article 1, section 8, clause 17 of the Constitution gives Congress explicit jurisdiction to govern on matters involving the District of Columbia.

143. "Upholds Race Purity," *WP*, February 11, 1913, 1.

144. *CR*, 62-3, 2/10/1913, 2929. Individual-level vote data for division roll calls were not recorded. However, a reporter for the *Chicago Tribune* (who mistakenly counted eight nay votes instead of twelve) identified the following members voting in opposition: Martin Madden (R-IL), James Mann (R-IL), H. Robert Fowler (D-IL), Franklin Wheeler Mondell (R-WY), Edward Hamilton (R-MI), Richard Bartholdt (R-MO), William Leroy La Follette (R-WA), and Nathan Kendall (R-IA). See "Bars Diverse Race Union in District of Columbia," *CT*, February 11, 1913, 21.

145. "To Forbid Race Intermarriage," *NYT*, February 11, 1913, 7. In addition, the continued influence of boxer Jack Johnson on the Southern mind was apparent in an editorial in the *Charlotte Daily Observer*: "Passage through the National House of Representatives of a bill prohibiting intermarriage of whites with negroes, Chinese, Japanese or Malays in the District of Columbia is the latest evidence of the good which the abominable Jack Johnson case brought forth" (February 13, 1913, 4).

146. *CR*, 62-3, 2/11/1913, 2972.

in prison, or both.[147] Clark's antimiscegenation bill was considered on January 11, 1915, and unlike the Hardwick bill two years earlier it elicited a short discussion.[148] Clark argued that enactment of his bill "was in the interest of both of the races." Maintaining racial purity was paramount, he believed, because "the future of the world is dependent upon the preservation of [the white race's] integrity."[149]

James Mann (R-IL) spoke for the Republican side, stating that while he opposed interracial marriage, he also opposed making such marriages a crime. Moreover, Mann articulated what he believed was the more basic intent of the legislation against miscegenation: "The purpose of this law is to further degrade the negro, to make him feel the iron hand of tyranny so long practiced against his race."[150] After a few more brief remarks, the previous question was ordered, and it was carried 175-119; Mann quickly moved to recommit the legislation to committee, which failed 90-201; and Clark's antimiscegenation bill was then passed 238-60.[151]

Whereas the Hardwick bill was adopted without debate and by a simple division vote, the Clark bill elicited some sharp debate and necessitated three roll calls before an outcome was generated. What explains these differences? There is considerable evidence that pressure from black citizens — newspaper editorials along with individual and group initiatives — increased after the passage of the Hardwick bill and ramped up considerably after Clark reintroduced the miscegenation issue. For example, a number of public meetings were scheduled post-Hardwick, to ensure that additional segregationist legislation would meet active resistance.[152] And groups like the Independent Equal Rights League, led by civil rights luminaries like Ida B. Wells, lobbied individual House members during Clark's antimiscegenation mission.[153] Thus black voices had raised the visibility of the issue and the stakes in Washington, forcing members of both parties to reveal their preferences to their constituents through public statements and recorded roll-call votes.

147. H.R. 1710 was "an act to prohibit the intermarriage of persons of the white and negro races within the District of Columbia; to declare such contracts of marriage null and void; to prescribe punishments for violations and attempts to violate its provisions."

148. For the full debate on H.R. 1710, see *CR*, 63-3, 1/11/1915, 1362–68.

149. *CR*, 63-3, 1/11/1915, 1362.

150. *CR*, 63-3, 1/11/1915, 1363.

151. *CR*, 63-3, 1/11/1915, 1366–68.

152. *Chicago Defender*, February 15, 1913, 1.

153. *Chicago Defender*, January 16, 1913, 1, 8.

All three votes were cross-regional party votes: a majority of Northern Democrats joined with all Southern Democrats against a majority of Republicans.[154] However, some interesting variation appears within the two parties. Roughly a quarter of Northern Democrats opposed shutting off debate on H.R. 1710; this opposition largely melted away across the remaining two votes.[155] Although Republicans were nearly unanimous in opposing the initial motion on the previous question, the party's solidarity crumbled thereafter. On the final-passage roll call, nearly half (forty of ninety) of the Republicans defected and voted in favor of the antimiscegenation legislation.

Republican voting can be broken down further based on type of state represented.[156] More than half of GOP votes in favor of the federal legislation against miscegenation (twenty-one of forty) came from members who represented states with an antimiscegenation law on the books. In total, a majority of House Republicans from states with laws against miscegenation (twenty-one of twenty-seven, or 77.8 percent) voted for the legislation, while only a minority of House Republicans from states without such laws (nineteen of sixty-three, or 30.2 percent) supported it. Thus, when push came to shove many Republicans eschewed the party's historical connection to black voters and focused on representing the (antimiscegenation) interests of the whites who elected them.

This electoral connection story can be seen in more detail by examining Republican vote choices statistically. As we show in appendix 6.1, the typical variables we associate with explaining individual vote choices—members' ideological preferences—are not significant on the roll call for final passage. Stated differently, a strictly ideological model—with the two NOMINATE scores as the sole independent variables—provides no leverage in explaining Republican vote choice on H.R. 1710. Only when a variable is

154. On the previous question vote, Northern Democrats voted 77-26, Southern Democrats 96-0, and Republicans 2-89. On recommittal, Northern Democrats voted 11-88, Southern Democrats 0-99, and Republicans 76-13. On final passage, Northern Democrats voted 95-7, Southern Democrats 102-0, and Republicans 40-50. (Remaining votes were cast by four Progressives.)

155. Why this small group of Northern Democrats opposed shutting off debate is unclear. One possibility is that they wanted more time to debate the issue and "position take" (or grandstand). That is, they wanted to be able to go on the record with public statements, for their constituents' benefit and consumption, and this could not happen if debate was shut off (in their minds) prematurely.

156. Data on state laws are drawn from Pascoe, *What Comes Naturally*, 168.

added to account for whether a state had an antimiscegenation law in place does the model begin to explain individual vote choices. Finally, whether a state's legislature was considering an antimiscegenation law did not matter in terms of explaining vote choice; a variable capturing this situation provides no additional explanatory leverage (and even results in a model that performs less well).[157]

On January 12, 1915, the Senate received H.R. 1710 and referred it to the Committee on the District of Columbia. It was never reported out of committee before the session ended. Thus the House Democrats' actions were for naught. While Democrats achieved a symbolic victory—and no doubt scored electoral "points" in the South and some parts of the North—federal antimiscegenation policy was not produced. The District of Columbia would continue to be a haven for interracial couples in the South who wished to marry. Indeed, Richard and Mildred Loving, the interracial (white-black) couple who would be at the center of *Loving v. Virginia* (1967), the Supreme Court case that struck down state-level laws against miscegenation, were married in the District of Columbia in 1958.

RACE AND EDUCATION

Between the two efforts against miscegenation, in 1913 and 1915, Congress once again dealt with the issue of race and education. In early 1914 two Southern Democrats—Sen. Hoke Smith (GA) and Rep. Asbury Lever (SC)—introduced legislation to allocate funds to land-grant colleges in the states to "administer and disseminate cooperative agricultural and home economics information."[158] Smith-Lever, as the bill became known, directed money from the federal government to the state governments, which were then responsible for distributing it to agricultural colleges.

157. As appendix 6.1 indicates, the first- and second-dimension NOMINATE scores are not statistically significant in any of the three vote models. When a state law variable is added (model 2), the percentage of votes correctly predicted increases from 55.6 percent to 72.2 percent. Finally, when a variable is added to indicate whether an antimiscegenation law was introduced in a state's legislature, the percentage of votes correctly predicted decreases from 72.2 percent to 70 percent. The latter result is perhaps not surprising, since the momentum for antimiscegenation laws stalled by 1913. Wyoming adopted a new law that year, but none of the other states did then or in later years. Thus, while legislation may have been introduced in those states, there was not a significant push for change. As a result, Republican House members from those states were not influenced.

158. Samuel H. Shannon, "Land-Grant College Legislation and Black Tennesseans: A Case Study in the Politics of Education," *History of Education Quarterly* 22 (1982): 150.

Smith and Lever wrote the bill to give an advantage to their home region. One study finds that even though Southern states in 1914 "produced only a quarter of the nation's agricultural produce, they would get fully half of the Smith-Lever appropriation."[159] Congressional debate over federal appropriations to Southern universities inevitably led to questions about how black colleges — validated in principle by the Second Morrill Act — would be treated.

In February 1914 Sen. Wesley Jones (R-WA) offered an amendment to Smith-Lever based on his belief that the bill's underlying proposal would "result in causing a very large class of our citizens to feel that they have been untreated by the bill." "In fact," Jones went on, "I believe that under the operation of the measure they will be very seriously discriminated against." Here Jones is referring to the bill's stipulation that "in any state in which two or more [agricultural] colleges have been or hereafter may be established the appropriations hereafter made to such State shall be administered by such college or colleges as the legislature of such State may direct."[160]

As Jones pointed out, this provision ensured that "in certain of our States, the legislatures will provide that all the funds going to the State shall be used by the white college in the state." Jones cited a raft of statistics demonstrating how, and to what extent, Southern states actively discriminated against black colleges. He then proposed an amendment stipulating that state legislatures would be required to come up with a "just and equitable distribution of funds" and to submit their proposed allocation to the secretary of agriculture for approval. The Jones amendment also stipulated that administrators of black colleges — and not state legislatures — would be responsible for administering the "just and equitable" division of funds. This was, in short, federal supervision of the "separate but equal" policy to ensure that it was actually implemented.[161]

The politics of the moment were such that even federal supervision of "separate but equal" elicited rabid opposition. James Vardaman (D-MS) offered an immediate condemnation of the Jones amendment. "No man who has given any thought to this subject," he claimed, "would any more think of turning the money over to the Negro race to be disbursed than would the

159. R. Grant Seals, "The Formation of Agricultural and Rural Development Policy with Emphasis on African-Americans: The Hatch-George and Smith-Lever Acts," *Agricultural History* 65 (1991): 24.

160. Smith-Lever Act, 38 *Stat.* 372 (1914).

161. *CR*, 63-2, 2/5/1914, 2929.

FIGURE 13. White supremacist Democrats: Sen. James K. Vardaman (MS), Rep. James Thomas "Cotton Tom" Heflin (AL), and Rep. Ollie James (KY). 1912. Library of Congress, Prints & Photographs Division, LC-DIG-ggbain-13322.

Senator from Washington think of turning it over to the Japanese in the state of Washington."[162] According to Vardaman, black Southerners were not to be thought of as citizens. Hoke Smith, the bill's lead sponsor in the Senate, suggested that the Jones amendment would "waste half of this fund" because "there is nobody competent [among black college officials]" to administer it.[163] Smith also claimed that the distribution of funds was inequitable because black Southerners were not interested in education. "It is difficult to move them to work beyond what is absolutely necessary and what they are almost forced to do in order to live," Smith claimed.[164] Racist stereotypes of this kind emerged frequently during the debate on Jones's proposal.[165]

Debate on the Jones amendment continued for two full days, during which John Works (R-CA) and Jacob Gallinger (R-NH) read letters they re-

162. *CR*, 63-2, 2/5/1914, 2931.

163. *CR*, 63-2, 2/5/1914, 2934.

164. *CR*, 63-2, 2/5/1914, 2933.

165. For more see Seals, "Formation of Agricultural and Rural Development Policy," 25–31.

ceived from the NAACP urging them to support the Jones amendment.[166] Finally, on February 7, 1914, Jones took the floor one more time to defend his proposal against a barrage of racist invective. "We think it is a matter of justice," he argued, "that it will lead to no waste of the public money; that it will guarantee . . . that this part of our population will have their share" of federal appropriations.[167] Jones's appeal to "separate but equal" notwithstanding, the amendment failed 23-32.[168] All Southern Democrats and all but two Northern Democrats opposed the amendment.[169] Four of twenty-four Republican senators also opposed it.[170] The Smith-Lever bill—without the Jones amendment—ultimately went on to pass and was signed into law by President Wilson.

W. E. B. Du Bois, writing in the *Crisis*, referred to the Smith-Lever bill as "a triumph in prejudice."[171] A number of social activists of the time, like Jane Addams, Moorfield Storey, and Oswald Garrison Villard, expressed their outrage to President Wilson—to no avail.[172] Looking for any kind of silver lining in the tragic events, R. Grant Seals notes, "While the pro-Negro forces in the 1914 Congress were not successful, the debate brought out in the open for the first time the virulent racism which infected the nation and reflected the supreme confidence of the South getting its way."[173]

Conclusion

After winning unified control of government in the 1892 election, Democrats quickly pushed through a repeal of the Enforcement Acts. After the repeal, civil rights policy was no longer a primary subject of congressional debate. As we have described in this chapter, issues bearing on black civil rights emerged as Congress was considering other topics: apportionment, marriage, federal funds to land-grant universities, the direct election of

166. See Seals, "Formation of Agricultural and Rural Development Policy," 25, 30–31.

167. *CR*, 63-2, 2/7/1914, 3116.

168. *CR*, 63-2, 2/7/1914, 3124.

169. The two Democrats were Gilbert Hitchcock (NE) and Altee Pomerene (OH).

170. The four Republicans were James Brady (ID), Albert Cummins (IA), Albert Fall (NM), and William Kenyon (IA).

171. W. E. B. Du Bois, "The Smith Lever Bill," *Crisis* 8 (1914): 124.

172. See Carmen V. Harris, " 'The Extension Service Is Not an Integration Agency': The Idea of Race in the Cooperative Extension Service," *Agricultural History* 82 (2008): 193–219.

173. Seals, "Formation of Agricultural and Rural Development Policy," 22.

senators, segregation on streetcars, and violence in Texas. On the one hand, this shows how deeply race permeated American political life. On the other hand, members seeking to suppress the discussion of race came to signal the declining electoral influence of black citizens.

In his 1909 inaugural address, William Howard Taft announced where the Republican Party now stood: "There was a time when Northerners who sympathized with the negro in his necessary struggle for better conditions sought to give him the suffrage as a protection to enforce its exercise against the prevailing sentiment of the South. The movement proved to be a failure."[174] The GOP would work to prevent the repeal of the Fourteenth and Fifteenth Amendments, Taft proclaimed, but would do little else. As Richard Sherman states, Taft's "message [was] clear. [He] intended to accept the white South's handling of the Negro question."[175] In Congress, accordingly, Republicans voted against white-supremacist policy but failed to advance civil rights protections in any meaningful way.

The Democrats, meanwhile, remained overtly hostile to black voters. Woodrow Wilson—a self-proclaimed "progressive"—made this clear on becoming president in 1913, when he segregated the federal workforce and drastically limited advancement opportunities for African Americans.[176] In Congress, Southern Democrats on several occasions worked to adopt similar Jim Crow policies. Yet their efforts to outlaw interracial marriage, to segregate streetcars in the District of Columbia, and to prohibit federal supervision of direct Senate elections failed. Through the first two decades of the twentieth century, there was a stalemate on civil rights policy in Congress. Southern legislatures were implicitly permitted to disenfranchise black voters, but Congress would not be brought in as an official advocate for Jim Crow.

Black Americans' political fortunes would begin to improve at the outset of the 1920s. As many Southern blacks settled in the North after World War I, their status as an "unimportant electoral coalition" would begin to change. Republicans in Congress would take notice of these new demographic patterns, and later Northern Democrats would as well. For the succeeding two decades—from the end of World War I to 1940—civil rights

174. William Howard Taft, Inaugural Address (1909), accessed at http://avalon.law.yale.edu/20th_century/taft.asp.

175. Sherman, *Republican Party and Black America*, 88.

176. See Eric S. Yellin, *Racism in the Nation's Service: Government Works and the Color Line in Woodrow Wilson's America* (Chapel Hill: University of North Carolina Press, 2013).

would reemerge on the congressional agenda and would follow the same basic form. The goal of black leaders, and their supporters in Congress, would be to pass a federal antilynching bill. This would be the litmus test for civil rights success before World War II, would help define the second civil rights era, and would serve as the early foundation for the construction of a civil rights coalition.[177]

APPENDIX 6.1. Logit Analyses of Republican Votes on Antimiscegenation Legislation, 63rd Congress

	(1)	(2)	(3)
NOMINATE 1	0.46	2.60	2.09
	(2.70)	(3.02)	(3.14)
NOMINATE 2	0.14	−0.26	−0.05
	(0.54)	(0.63)	(0.67)
State law		2.32***	1.71*
		(0.57)	(0.84)
Law introduced			−0.67
			(0.74)
Constant	−0.43	−1.91	−1.19
	(1.14)	(1.28)	(1.50)
N	90	90	90
LR χ^2	0.07	16.81***	17.28**
Percentage correctly predicted	55.6	72.2	70.0
PRE (naive model)	0	0.375	0.325

Note: Standard errors in parentheses. Baseline model for PRE calculation is a naive (minority-vote) model.
*p < .05; **p < .01; ***p < .001.

177. See Jeffery A. Jenkins, Justin Peck, and Vesla M. Weaver, "Between Reconstructions: Congressional Action on Civil Rights, 1891–1940," *Studies in American Political Development* 24 (2010): 57–89.

CHAPTER SEVEN

Conclusion

The United States entered World War I in April 1917, fifty-six years to the month after secessionists in South Carolina fired on Fort Sumter. Just as they had done during the Civil War, African American soldiers contributed to the war effort in segregated units, largely denied combat roles. American soldiers — both black and white — fought, in President Wilson's words, to make the world "safe for democracy." Yet neither the army nor the laws of the country guaranteed enlisted black soldiers, or their families back home, the rights that democracies ostensibly guaranteed to all citizens. Indeed, the years directly preceding 1917 proved to be the nadir in post–Civil War race relations, during which black Americans were systematically and intentionally forced "back toward slavery."[1]

In the preceding chapters we described the period between the Civil War and World War I as the United States' "first civil rights era." We explored how Republicans in Congress, aided by the political activism of black citizens in the states, established an inclusive, multiracial democracy in the United States. More specifically, we illustrated how and why the GOP created and enforced legal reforms extending freedom, citizenship, and voting rights to former slaves — and how freedmen, in turn, acted on those rights by voting, running for office, and demanding their fair share of government aid. Beginning in the 1870s, however, the GOP's political weakness throughout the South, as well as the shifting political preferences of North-

---

1. W. E. B. Du Bois, *Black Reconstruction in America, 1860–1880* (New York: Harcourt, Brace, 1935), 707.

ern voters, allowed the white majority in the former Confederacy to degrade and ignore these reforms in ways specifically designed to deprive African Americans of their rights.

Our analysis provides an explicitly Congress-centered perspective on this transformation by exploring the Republican Party's role in undermining the multiracial democracy it had helped to build. We have set out alternative paths that might have been taken to demonstrate that the legal regime segregation, disenfranchisement, and systematic racial violence were based on was not inevitable. Legislators chose to enact policies that made it possible. They could have chosen differently, and sometimes they nearly did.

Members of Congress in the immediate postwar years faced a challenge similar to the one faced by the first generation of lawmakers after the ratification of the Constitution. According to Jonathan Gienapp, through the 1790s those in Congress had "only a faint, contested grasp of . . . what the Constitution did or did not license." For this reason, "proving that a particular position was constitutional was vital, yet exactly what defined 'constitutional' was an open question."[2] A similar dynamic permeated Congress after Robert E. Lee's surrender at Appomattox, with legislators struggling to decide how the Constitution would be adapted to accommodate the Union victory. Setting out the contours of those debates, explaining how they were resolved, and making it clear how these decisions drove politics into the twentieth century are the subjects prompting each of the preceding chapters.

In particular, we have shown that the GOP's numerical advantage at the national level did not guarantee the seamless enactment of a set policy agenda. The "party of Lincoln" was never really a unitary actor because Republican members never agreed on what freedom meant, how it would be protected, how it would be advanced (if at all), who was responsible for enforcing violations, or what tools the enforcers would have. These are explicitly constitutional subjects, and writing policy to address them led to heated intraparty arguments over doctrine. Conflict erupted almost immediately between the radicals—who supported a more durable and muscular exercise of federal power—and their moderate and conservative fellow partisans—who were reluctant to exercise power in this way. With neither side able to win outright, the policies Republicans enacted reflected the compromises necessary to produce congressional majorities. By 1917 the policies they crafted were either reversed or ignored by the white majority.

2. Jonathan Gienapp, *The Second Constitution: Fixing the Constitution in the Founding Era* (Cambridge, MA: Harvard University Press, 2018), 8–9.

The protracted effort to degrade and reverse postwar civil rights gains began only a few years after the war ended. Indeed, by the mid-1870s those Republicans advocating black civil rights faced insurmountable bipartisan opposition. The Civil Rights Act of 1875 marked the end of the period when the GOP could put together majorities supporting laws designed specifically to advance black equality. Up to that point, Republican majorities had pushed through three constitutional amendments (the Thirteenth, Fourteenth, and Fifteenth) and a series of supporting bills intended to bolster black civil and political rights. Yet the Civil Rights Act of 1875 achieved majority support only after Republicans removed those provisions that made it more than purely symbolic. Every subsequent civil rights proposal taken up by Congress failed to win a roll-call majority. Republican Party defections from the civil rights agenda help to explain why, beginning in the Forty-Fourth Congress, bills intended to support black lives went down to defeat. Most notoriously, in 1891 a pivotal faction *within* the GOP worked with the Democrats to bring down Henry Cabot Lodge's federal elections bill.

Although the conflict within the GOP contributed to the rise and fall of the first civil rights era in Congress, we also attribute this pattern to political forces attenuating the relationship between black voters and the Republican Party. In particular, we demonstrate a growing belief among Republican elites that the party's fortunes no longer hinged on black political activism in the South. During the period of military occupation, majorities could be found to support laws bolstering black rights as a way of mobilizing black voters, who were disproportionately concentrated in Southern states.[3] Yet the Democratic Party's campaign of terror, fraud, and eventually legal disenfranchisement against Southern blacks convinced many Republicans that protecting the party's Southern wing would require prolonged federal intervention into state politics. Moderate and conservative elements within the party resisted this, and a growing number of Republicans adopted the "moderate" approach.

One consequence of Redemption, then, was to leave black citizens hoping that the party's Northern wing could be persuaded to defend postwar legal reforms. African Americans proved to be loyal members of a nonregional party whose members, over time, faced diminishing electoral pressure to defend or advance civil rights. Making matters worse, popular support for the

---

3. For more on the GOP in the South see Richard M. Valelly, *The Two Reconstructions: The Struggle for Black Enfranchisement* (Chicago: University of Chicago Press, 2004); Boris Heersink and Jeffery A. Jenkins, *Republican Party Politics and the American South, 1865–1968* (New York: Cambridge University Press, 2020).

GOP outside the South withered in the wake of the 1873 financial panic and subsequent depression. As the economy sagged, Northern white opinion shifted against Reconstruction.[4] By the turn of the twentieth century, the uncertainty about how the postwar Constitution would operate gave way to the reliability of Jim Crow. A general consensus emerged among legislators in Washington, DC, that Southern state governments would be allowed to exist as "authoritarian enclaves" within the United States.[5] As we show, Republicans in Congress would not, and could not, muster the political will required to intervene on behalf of black citizens.

In the words of modern social science, civil rights policies enacted in the immediate postwar years failed to "generate self-reinforcing dynamics of social adaptation."[6] Laws to protect black rights collapsed because the bills that could win Republican majorities relied on state-level enforcement, the continuing political activism of blacks in the South, and public support from white voters in the North and West. These sources of reinforcement quickly evaporated, and the white backlash that powered Southern redemption led to the construction of a new Jim Crow regime with a more durable political support system. The revolutionary consequences of the war, the aims of the white counterrevolutionaries, and the contours of the equilibrium decided on at the turn of the twentieth century can be seen in the congressional behavior we discuss here.

For black citizens, this new equilibrium was politically and physically deadly. A 1919 report published by the NAACP states that from 1889 to 1918 more than three thousand African Americans were lynched.[7] Monroe Work illustrates that lynching peaked in frequency in 1901 and remained a significant social problem until the late 1920s.[8] Yet lynching was not a federal crime and, despite its pervasiveness, the federal government did little to prevent it. Congress also stood by as Southern state governments

4. David Herbert Donald, Jean Harvey Baker, and Michael F. Holt, *The Civil War and Reconstruction* (New York: Norton, 2001), 626–28.

5. Robert Mickey, *Paths Out of Dixie: The Democratization of Authoritarian Enclaves in America's Deep South, 1944–1972* (Princeton, NJ: Princeton University Press, 2014), 15.

6. Paul Pierson, "The Study of Policy Development," *Journal of Policy History* 17 (2005): 37.

7. National Association for the Advancement of Colored People, *Thirty Years of Lynching in the United States* (New York: National Association for the Advancement of Colored People, National Office, 1909), 8.

8. Monroe N. Work, ed., *Negro Year Book* (Tuskegee Institute, AL: Negro Year Book, 1947).

created new forms of involuntary servitude for African Americans. Owing to "sharecropping, tenantry, the crop-lien system, and peonage," William Cohen writes, as well as the convict lease program, state governments in the South made it possible to "hold black labor virtually at will."[9] Leon Litwack finds that during the Jim Crow era the majority of black laborers were paid, at most, $1.50 a week.[10] Making matters worse, Kent Redding and David James estimate that whereas 61 percent of eligible black voters in the South went to the polls in 1880, in 1912 only 2 percent voted.[11] This precipitous decline in political participation was the result of the campaign of terror waged against black citizens through the 1870s, combined with subsequent "legal" disenfranchisement schemes. Black citizens were effectively barred from the political activity required to escape Jim Crow. Through the first two decades of the twentieth century, black lives were under siege on all fronts, but for members of Congress the electorally "safe" decision was to do nothing.

The Political Significance of First Civil Rights Era

By the end of the first civil rights era, African Americans were once again denied citizenship rights by the white majority. Their former Republican allies had mostly abandoned them in the face of Democrats' explicit efforts to erode those few legal protections they could still invoke. Yet an exclusive focus on the decline of the first civil rights era need not entirely overshadow the significant legal advances implemented after the Civil War. The GOP's drive to eliminate slavery and then to guarantee African Americans citizenship and voting rights had real, though nondurable, consequences in a variety of domains. These effects gave the lie to contemporary analysts who portrayed African Americans as incapable of citizenship. They also served as a foundation later civil rights advocates could build on. We explore two such consequences here: successful political organizing by black citizens throughout the South, and the Republican Party's failed effort to build a viable Southern wing.

9. William Cohen, "Negro Involuntary Servitude in the South, 1865–1940: A Preliminary Analysis," *Journal of Southern History* 42 (1976): 31.

10. Leon Litwack, *Trouble in Mind: Black Southerners in the Age of Jim Crow* (New York: Knopf, 1998), 115.

11. Kent Redding and David R. James, "Estimating Levels of and Modeling Determinants of Black and White Voter Turnout in the South, 1880–1912," *Historical Methods* 34 (2001): 141–58.

AFRICAN AMERICAN POLITICS
AFTER THE CIVIL WAR

From the beginning of the Civil War through the middle of Reconstruction, the status of black Americans changed in unprecedented ways. They went from being classified as legal property — the human chattels of white land-owners — to full-fledged citizens of the United States with constitutionally protected civil rights and voting rights. These were radical steps forward in a very short time.

Despite some national Republican leaders' working to limit black office-holding — in order to attract enough Southern whites to build a true and lasting biracial coalition in the South — black candidates won elections all over the South.[12] Black participation in state constitutional conventions was in fact central to the creation of "loyal" governments in the former Confederacy. Beginning in 1868, black candidates also won a sizable number of seats in Southern state legislatures — especially in the lower chambers. African Americans would constitute a third of the state House in Florida and Louisiana through 1870 and a majority in South Carolina through 1876. Blacks would also be a vital part of the Mississippi state House in the early 1870s and compose a near-majority in the chamber after the 1873 elections. African American Speakers of the House would also be elected in both Mississippi and South Carolina.[13]

Overall, more than 630 African Americans would serve as state legislators in the former Confederate states during Reconstruction.[14] Blacks would also be elected to prominent statewide positions, including superintendent of education (Arkansas, Florida, Louisiana, and Mississippi), treasurer (Louisiana and South Carolina), secretary of state (Florida, Mississippi, and South Carolina), and lieutenant governor (Louisiana, Mississippi, and South Carolina),[15] along with a range of lower offices like mayor, alderman, justice

12. For more details on black electoral success during Reconstruction, see Heersink and Jenkins, *Republican Party Politics and the American South*.

13. These individuals would be John R. Lynch (1872–73) and I. D. Shad (1874–76) in Mississippi and Samuel J. Lee (1872–74) and Robert B. Elliott (1874–76) in South Carolina. See Eric Foner, *Reconstruction: America's Unfinished Revolution, 1863–1877* (New York: Harper and Row, 1988), 354n5.

14. Foner, *Reconstruction*, 354–55n15, complemented by Tennessee data. The high-water mark for several states, in terms of raw numbers, was 1873–74, coinciding with the GOP's desperate push to maintain a foothold in the South by actively courting blacks for office.

15. P. B. S. Pinchback would also hold the governorship in Louisiana for a short time

TABLE 7.1. Black Members of the US Congress, Reconstruction through the Wilderness Years

Name (State)	Congress	Chamber	Former Slave
Joseph Rainey (SC)	41st–45th	House	Yes
Jefferson F. Long (GA)	41st	House	Yes
Hiram R. Revels (MS)	41st	Senate	No
Robert C. De Large (SC)	42nd	House	No
Robert B. Elliott (SC)	42nd–43rd	House	No
Benjamin S. Turner (AL)	42nd	House	Yes
Josiah T. Walls (FL)	42nd–44th	House	Yes
Richard H. Cain (SC)	43rd, 45th	House	No
John R. Lynch (MS)	43rd–44th, 47th	House	Yes
Alonso J. Ransier (SC)	43rd	House	No
James T. Rapier (AL)	43rd	House	No
Blanche K. Bruce (MS)	44th–46th	Senate	Yes
Jeremiah Haralson (AL)	44th	House	Yes
John Adams Hyman (NC)	44th	House	Yes
Charles E. Nash (LA)	44th	House	No
Robert Smalls (SC)	44th–45th, 47th–49th	House	Yes
James E. O'Hara (NC)	48th–49th	House	No
Henry P. Cheatham (NC)	51st–52nd	House	Yes
John Mercer Langston (VA)	51st	House	No
Thomas E. Miller (SC)	51st	House	No
George W. Murray (SC)	53rd–54th	House	Yes
George H. White (NC)	55th–56th	House	Yes

Source: Matthew A. Wasniewski, ed., *Black Americans in Congress, 1870–2007* (Washington, DC: Government Printing Office, 2008); *Biographical Directory of the United States Congress*, accessed at http://bioguide.congress.gov/biosearch/biosearch.asp.

of the peace, county commissioner, and sheriff.[16] In addition, African Americans made up a sizable portion of Southern state delegates to the Republican National Convention. In the 1870s, about one-third of GOP Southern delegates. From 1880 through 1896, over 40 percent of GOP Southern delegates were black.[17]

African American candidates also won election to the United States Congress. As table 7.1 details, twenty-two were elected during the period covered in this book. Most of them (twelve of twenty-two) had once been

(December 1872 to January 1873), having been elevated to the office owing to the suspension of the sitting (white) governor (Henry C. Warmoth).

16. Foner, *Reconstruction*, 352–56.

17. See Heersink and Jenkins, *Republican Party Politics and the American South*.

slaves. Not surprisingly, sixteen — more than 70 percent — were first elected during Reconstruction.[18] Of these, fourteen were elected to the House and two served in the Senate. And although the terrorism carried out against black voters immediately after Reconstruction drove down participation, many brave citizens continued to vote. African Americans in fact still voted in large numbers in some states (or parts of some states) through the 1890s. As a result, six African Americans were elected to Congress — along with three who had served previously — in the post-Reconstruction era.

Thus, while Democrats regained control of Southern state governments in the late 1870s and worked to consolidate their hold on them through the 1880s, black political rights and black officeholding were not eliminated immediately. The white Redeemer governments decided to mostly tread lightly to avoid federal intervention (especially with a Republican in the White House through early 1885). To keep black voting power in check and retain power, they initially used state registration and canvassing boards strategically, to redraw legislative district boundaries for their benefit. Thus, even as black voters continued to participate in large numbers in parts of the South and some blacks continued to hold elective office, Democratic leaders carefully calibrated these political "successes" and orchestrated the electoral process more generally. Moreover, as white Democratic sheriffs, judges, and other authorities reclaimed their subnational offices in the South during Redemption, African Americans' civil rights suffered greatly, since their Fourteenth Amendment protections were typically ignored. By the 1890s, as Democratic leaders throughout the South began to legally disenfranchise blacks, any remaining rights and electoral successes that African Americans enjoyed would be further eroded.

The last black member of Congress during this era was Rep. George White (R-NC).[19] As the only African American in the Fifty-Fifth and Fifty-Sixth Congresses (1897-1901), White fought to advance black civil rights. He pushed back against blatantly racist remarks made on the House floor by John Sharp Williams (D-MS) and other Southern Democrats, introduced

18. Here, "elected during Reconstruction" includes elections through 1876, and thus Congresses through the Forty-Fifth.

19. For background on George Henry White and his activities as a member of Congress, see Matthew A. Wasniewski, ed., *Black Americans in Congress, 1870–2007* (Washington, DC: Government Printing Office, 2008), 228–33; Louis-Alejandro Dinnella-Borrego, *The Risen Phoenix: Black Politics in the Post–Civil War South* (Charlottesville: University of Virginia Press, 2016), 199–207.

Testimonial To

Hon. George H. White,

At Metropolitan A. M. E. Church,

Friday Evening March 22, 1901.

DAILY RECORD PRINT

FIGURE 14. Testimonial to Rep. George H. White (R-NC). Metropolitan A.M.E. Church, Washington, DC Friday, March 22, 1901. Library of Congress, Control Number 91898217.

evidence of electoral fraud in Mississippi and South Carolina, actively supported Edgar Crumpacker's bill to reduce Southern representation, and
oversaw the appointment of several African American constituents as post-
masters in North Carolina. White also introduced the first bill in Congress to
make lynching a federal crime. His legislation was blocked, but it presaged
the beginning of the next civil rights era.

By 1900, White knew his days in Congress were numbered. Democrats
in North Carolina—following Mississippi, Louisiana, and South Carolina—
had taken steps to amend the state constitution to disenfranchise black
voters. Thus he did not seek reelection. In his last floor speech in the House,
White characterized his departure as "perhaps the negroes' temporary farewell to the American Congress; but let me say, Phoenix-like he will rise up
some day and come again. These parting words are in behalf of an outraged,
heart-broken, bruised, and bleeding, but God-fearing people, faithful, in-
dustrious, loyal people—rising people, full of potential force."[20]

White was correct. African Americans would be back to Congress,
though not for some time. The next black member was Rep. Oscar De Priest
(R-IL), from a district encompassing the South Side of Chicago, who was
first elected in 1928. The next African American members of Congress from
the South would be Barbara Jordan (D-TX) and Andrew Young Jr. (D-GA),
who were elected in 1972.

THE REPUBLICAN PARTY IN THE SOUTH

Coming out of the Civil War, the desire to create a Republican Party in the
South, built (initially) around the votes of former slaves, was a radical dream.
Early in Reconstruction there was no support for such an enterprise in the
North and little in the GOP Congress (apart from radical members). Moderate Republicans saw providing voting rights to the freedmen as too extreme,
given Northern public opinion. In time, however, the moderate position
shifted. Many came to believe that voting rights were the only legitimate
self-defense against draconian Black Codes designed to keep former slaves
tethered to the pre–Civil War economic system. President Johnson's opposition to even minimal rights protections reinforced this perspective. The
landslide election of 1866 afforded GOP lawmakers an opportunity to provide freedmen with the political power—through voting rights—to help
them control their own fate. That moral/ethical consideration matched

20. *CR*, 56-2, 1/29/1901, 1638.

nicely with a more instrumental consideration — that of creating a Republican wing in the former Confederacy.

By the Reconstruction Act of 1867, congressional Republicans set the tone for the constitutional conventions throughout the South that were convened to "recharter" the former Confederate states before they were admitted back into the Union. The Reconstruction Act allowed African Americans in the Southern states to vote for convention delegates and limited the participation of some white former Confederates. The new constitutions provided black men with voting rights more generally and maintained former Confederate disenfranchisement (for a time). The result was that the Republican Party was quickly established in every Southern state and came to power immediately in all but one (Virginia). In the 1868 elections to choose members for the Fortieth Congress, the GOP captured almost 88 percent of the available House seats in the South. And in November 1868 Republican Ulysses S. Grant won six of the eight former Confederate states that were back in the Union, while the GOP captured over 75 percent of available Southern House seats. The radical dream had become a reality: a Republican South now existed. And the GOP increasingly looked like a durable, nationally viable political coalition.

Yet the Republican Party's political success was built on rules keeping large numbers of likely Democratic voters out of competitive politics. Its durability therefore depended on continuing voting restrictions on the white majority, high levels of participation from black voters, and the willingness of loyal whites to work with newly enfranchised freedmen. These conditions proved sustainable. But Democrats worked to rebuild their party in the South and used fraud, intimidation, and violence to reclaim power. By the 1870 midterms the GOP won only 50 percent of the available House seats in the South. Thanks to the passage of the Fourth Enforcement Act in the spring of 1871, providing President Grant with the power and authority to break the Ku Klux Klan, the GOP was able to reverse the negative momentum. The 1872 election saw Grant win eight of eleven former Confederate states and the Republicans increase their share of House seats in the South to over 56 percent.

This political "second wind" for the GOP did not survive the Panic of 1873 and the subsequent depression that spanned the rest of the decade. The economic hardship led the Northern public to steer their elected representatives away from further entanglements in the South. Republican politicians, like President Grant, became more reluctant to use federal power in and around Southern elections. Emboldened white Southern Democrats and their terrorist allies ramped up their fraud, intimidation, and violence. As a result, the Republicans lost majority control of the House in the 1874 midterms (to the Forty-Fourth Congress), and the GOP was decimated in Southern elections — winning just over 19 percent of available House seats. By 1876 the GOP's share of available Southern House seats fell to 11 percent, and the Republicans lost control of every Southern state except Florida, Louisiana, and South Carolina. And while those states were crucial in helping Republican Rutherford B. Hayes win the presidential election of 1876–77, they would be "redeemed" by the Democrats shortly thereafter.

Even after the entire South had fallen to the Democrats, the Republicans continued to work to maintain some kind of Southern presence. These efforts would take different forms: Republican presidents (Hayes, Chester Arthur, and Benjamin Harrison) sought support from various groups of whites in the South, trying to persuade them to join with the GOP against the Democrats; Republicans in Congress, when there were a majority, used the power in article 1, section 5 of the Constitution to "flip" seats in the South (away from Democrats and toward Republicans) when fraud and other irregularities were present; and during a brief period of unified control of government Republicans attempted to pass a new federal elections bill to protect the voting rights of African Americans in the South.[21] None of these efforts did much to reinvigorate or rebuild the party in the South.

The emergence of disenfranchisement laws in the South in the 1890s, along with President William McKinley's active pursuit of "reconciliation" with the white South, appeared to be the final nail in the coffin of a viable Republican Party in the former Confederacy. After McKinley's reelection in 1900, with congressional Republicans secure as the nation's new majority party,[22] any real efforts to interfere in the electoral process in the South had ended. As table 7.2 indicates, even after the 1894, 1896, and 1898 elections the Republican Congress still spent some time and energy flipping House

21. On the GOP's use of contested elections during this era, see Jeffery A. Jenkins, "Partisanship and Contested Election Cases in the House of Representatives, 1789–2002," *Studies in American Political Development* 18 (1): 113–35; Jeffery A. Jenkins, "The First 'Southern Strategy': The Republican Party and Contested-Election Cases in the Late-19th Century House," in *Party, Process, and Political Change in Congress*, vol. 2, *Further New Perspectives on the History of Congress*, ed. David W. Brady and Mathew D. McCubbins (Stanford, CA: Stanford University Press, 2007), 78–90.

22. After the realignment of 1894–96, the American public had moved away from the Democrats and would essentially stay away for more than three decades.

seats in the GOP's direction. After the 1900 elections this behavior ended completely. As a consequence, all real efforts to protect black voters in the South disappeared.

To best see the decline of the Republican Party in the South, the data in table 7.2 should be divided into three parts. During the Reconstruction era (Fortieth through Forty-Fifth Congresses), the Republicans controlled over 54 percent of the Southern House seats. By the Forty-Fourth Congress their support had dwindled to less than 20 percent. During the Redemption era (Forty-Fifth to Fifty-First Congresses), the Republicans controlled just over 11 percent of Southern House seats. And twelve of the GOP's sixty-three Southern House seats during this time — 19 percent — were acquired through contested elections rather than outright election victories. Finally, during the "wilderness years" (Fifty-Second to Sixty-Fifth Congresses), the Republicans controlled just over 5.5 percent of Southern House seats. And, again, seven of the GOP's seventy-three Southern House seats during these years — 13.7 percent — were acquired through contested elections rather than outright election victories. By the twentieth century, the Republicans were electorally active in a serious way in only three parts of the South: southwest Virginia, eastern Tennessee, and western North Carolina. All their House seats from the Fifty-Seventh through Sixty-Fifth Congresses — thirty-four in all — came from districts in these three regions.[23]

As scholars, we always find "what ifs?" intriguing. In our minds the key "what if" about Reconstruction is the post-1873 erosion and eventual demise of the GOP in the South. In the preceding few years, as Michael Perman describes it, partisan politics in the South had moved in a more traditional two-party direction as former Whigs in both the Democratic Party and the Republican Party had gained leadership positions and guided popular discussions away from race and white supremacy and toward economic issues.[24] Thus, despite continued activity by terror groups in the South, a fragile "normalcy" had begun to trickle into the political process. Democratic leaders had begun to accept Reconstruction and black suffrage as settled policy, and a battle for the electoral middle in society had begun.

23. V. O. Key Jr., *Southern Politics in State and Nation* (1949; repr., Knoxville: University of Tennessee Press, 1984); Heersink and Jenkins, *Republican Party Politics and the American South.*

24. Michael Perman, *The Road to Redemption: Southern Politics, 1869–1979* (Chapel Hill: University of North Carolina Press, 1984), 1–131. See also Donald, Baker, and Holt, *Civil War and Reconstruction,* 597–99.

TABLE 7.2. Republican Southern Seat Share in the US House, 40th–65th Congresses

Congress	Years	Majority Party	Total GOP Seats	GOP Seats Due to Contested Elections	Total Seats	Percentage of Seats That Were GOP
40	1867–69	Republicans	36	0	41	87.8
41	1869–71	Republicans	44	5	58	75.9
42	1871–73	Republicans	29	1	58	50.0
43	1873–75	Republicans	41	1	73	56.2
44	1875–79	Democrats	14	0	73	19.2
45	1877–79	Democrats	8	0	73	11.0
46	1879–81	Democrats	3	1	73	4.1
47	1881–83	Republicans	12	5	73	16.4
48	1883–85	Democrats	9	1	85	10.6
49	1885–87	Democrats	8	0	85	9.4
50	1887–89	Democrats	9	0	85	10.6
51	1889–91	Republicans	14	5	85	16.5
52	1891–93	Democrats	3	0	85	3.5
53	1893–95	Democrats	4	0	90	4.4
54	1895–97	Republicans	13	4	90	14.4
55	1897–99	Republicans	11	3	90	12.2
56	1899–1901	Republicans	8	3	90	8.9
57	1901–3	Republicans	4	0	90	4.4
58	1903–5	Republicans	3	0	98	3.1
59	1905–7	Republicans	4	0	98	4.1
60	1907–9	Republicans	3	0	98	3.1
61	1909–11	Republicans	6	0	98	6.1
62	1911–13	Democrats	3	0	98	3.1
63	1913–15	Democrats	3	0	104	2.9
64	1915–17	Democrats	4	0	104	3.8
65	1917–19	Democrats	4	0	104	3.8

Source: Jeffery A. Jenkins, "Partisanship and Contested Election Cases in the House of Representatives, 1789–2002," Studies in American Political Development 18 (2004): 113–35; Kenneth C. Martis, The Historical Atlas of Political Parties in the United States Congress, 1789–1989 (New York: Macmillan, 1989).

As David Donald, Jean Harvey Baker, and Michael Holt state, "Moderates at the center of the political spectrum, not ideologues at the extremes, thus dictated the terms of debate and competition."[25] The Panic of 1873 and subsequent economic depression ended all that. Mainstream Southern leaders in each party were swept out, and more extreme leaders moved in. White carpetbaggers and African Americans grew more prominent in the GOP — thus rejecting the Whig-leaning scalawags — and white supremacists took control of the Democratic Party. Race became the key issue in electoral politics once again, as the color line was effectively drawn by both sides.

Had a panic and resulting economic collapse not occurred in 1873, could the moderate-led two-party system in the South, which (fragile though it was) had operated since 1869, have continued and perhaps succeeded? And, if so, could a more moderate South have developed — one that would have treated African Americans as first-class citizens and would not have adopted Jim Crow? And could the Republican Party have maintained itself as a true interregional party? These are interesting questions, but like many hypotheticals, they are beyond our ability to answer definitively. But considering them does showcase the influence of some "critical junctures" in shaping the contours of American political development.

Previewing the Second Civil Rights Era

By the second decade of the twentieth century both political parties had abandoned black civil rights in the name of national reconciliation and in favor of political opportunism. The first civil rights era is thus a coherent epoch in the larger story of American political development. With civil rights on the national agenda in the early years covered by our study, the lives and fortunes of black Americans improved. But as the two parties converged on an uneasy truce, mostly by agreeing to allow Southern whites to govern their region unimpeded, black Americans found themselves subjected to new forms of rights restrictions and arbitrary state power. Only after the effects of the First Great Migration were felt did members of Congress — first Republicans and then, shortly thereafter, Democrats — once again feel pressure to advance black civil rights. Thus we argue that the post–World War I years mark the beginning of yet another civil rights era, culminating in the landmark civil rights laws of the 1960s.

25. Donald, Baker, and Holt, *Civil War and Reconstruction*, 598.

Central to the politics of the twentieth century is the "second reconstruction" brought on by the New Deal's "racial realignment." Through the 1930s and 1940s, continued black migration into Northern cities and an emerging coalition of civil rights activists and labor activists turned the Democratic Party into a vehicle for civil rights reform.[26] This new liberal coalition then—decades later—pushed through landmark civil rights legislation.[27] Legislative success came at a political cost, however. As Northern Democrats embraced civil rights, Southern support for the party cratered. The backlash against civil rights reforms drove conservatives into the GOP, helping to generate today's racially polarized political environment.[28] The consequences of America's second civil rights era are very much with us still.

Obscured from this discussion is a clear explanation of why the second civil rights era and the racial realignment preceding it were necessary. The politics around civil rights that we described in the prior chapters precipitated the civil rights movement of the mid-twentieth century. During the first civil rights era, the Republicans were the party of civil rights. Yet by the early twentieth century the GOP was no longer an advocate for black civil rights and political equality. Some Republicans even helped defeat the few civil rights initiatives that made it onto the agenda between 1890 and 1918. African Americans needed a new political home because their loyalty to the GOP no longer ensured that the party would support policies backed by black pressure groups and their allies. The Republican Party's decisions through the first civil rights era, in particular the party's transformation from active advocate for civil rights to passive opponent, set the stage for the civil rights movement of the mid-twentieth century. This sequence of events is vital to a full understanding of the contemporary politics around black civil rights.

Although the GOP continued to do more for civil rights than the Democrats did until the racial realignment of New Deal era, we show here that

---

26. Eric Schickler, *Racial Realignment: The Transformation of American Liberalism, 1932–1965* (Princeton, NJ: Princeton University Press, 2016), 45–81.

27. Valelly, *Two Reconstructions*, 173–224.

28. Michael Tesler, *Post-racial or Most Racial?: Race and Politics in the Obama Era* (Chicago: University of Chicago Press, 2016); Alan Abramowitz, "The New American Electorate: Partisan, Sorted, and Polarized," in *American Gridlock: The Sources, Character, and Impact of Political Polarization*, ed. James A. Thurber and Antoine Yoshinaka (New York: Cambridge University Press, 2015), 19–44.

the Republicans abandoned the cause of civil rights well before the election of Franklin Roosevelt. For example, despite hosting Booker T. Washington for dinner at the White House when he was president, Theodore Roosevelt did not see the GOP as a vehicle for promoting black civil rights. Indeed, Roosevelt's "Progressive" Party explicitly refrained from advocating black civil and political equality.[29] And in his first inaugural address, Republican William Howard Taft endorsed Southern efforts to restrict black voting and made it clear that "[it is] not the disposition or within the province of the Federal Government to interfere with the regulation by Southern States of their domestic affairs."[30]

Aside from brief periods during the presidencies of Warren Harding and Herbert Hoover,[31] the Republican Party would not again seriously entertain a Southern wing until after World War II. Dwight D. Eisenhower was successful in the presidential elections of 1952 and 1956 — winning four and five Southern states, respectively — which gave GOP leaders a sense that the South could be ripe for Republican causes more generally. Significant congressional successes would first occur in the 1960s and would become increasingly prominent in the 1970s. By the 1980s, thanks to the success of Ronald Reagan, the South seemed open to the GOP in ways not seen in more than a century. After the 1994 midterms, the Republicans captured a majority of House and Senate seats in the South for the first time since Reconstruction, and they have maintained that majority ever since. In many ways the Republican leaders in the 1870s and 1880s who believed conservative elements in the white South would be viable building blocks for a successful Southern wing of the party were correct. They were just off by about a century. In addition, they were wrong about the type of conservatism that would lend itself to a Republican South — it was not the economic conservatism that was pushed in the late nineteenth century, but the racial conservatism of the late twentieth century.

Right-wing populism has a long history in the United States. In this book we have described how the white majority succeeds in its organized efforts to transform American democracy into a vehicle for exclusion. Indeed, a central theme of American political development is the way political elites in this country have served the political preferences of the white majority by

29. George E. Mowery, "The South and the Progressive Lily White Party of 1912," *Journal of Southern History* 6 (1940): 237–47.

30. Taft's speech can be read at http://avalon.law.yale.edu/20th_century/taft.asp.

31. See Heersink and Jenkins, *Republican Party Politics and the American South*.

depriving African Americans of civil and political rights. Majoritarian institutions in the United States have been used to advance the rights of long-oppressed minorities, *and* they have been used by the powerful against the most vulnerable. Congressional decision making during the first civil rights era shows us both, providing an important lesson and illustrating the complexity of American political development.

Index